Urban Sprawl
and Public Health

ABOUT ISLAND PRESS

Island Press is the only nonprofit organization in the United States whose principal purpose is the publication of books on environmental issues and natural resource management. We provide solutions-oriented information to professionals, public officials, business and community leaders, and concerned citizens who are shaping responses to environmental problems.

In 2004, Island Press celebrates its twentieth anniversary as the leading provider of timely and practical books that take a multidisciplinary approach to critical environmental concerns. Our growing list of titles reflects our commitment to bringing the best of an expanding body of literature to the environmental community throughout North America and the world.

Support for Island Press is provided by the Agua Fund, Brainerd Foundation, Geraldine R. Dodge Foundation, Doris Duke Charitable Foundation, Educational Foundation of America, The Ford Foundation, The George Gund Foundation, The William and Flora Hewlett Foundation, Henry Luce Foundation, The John D. and Catherine T. MacArthur Foundation, The Andrew W. Mellon Foundation, The Curtis and Edith Munson Foundation, National Environmental Trust, The New-Land Foundation, Oak Foundation, The Overbrook Foundation, The David and Lucile Packard Foundation, The Pew Charitable Trusts, The Rockefeller Foundation, The Winslow Foundation, and other generous donors.

The opinions expressed in this book are those of the author(s) and do not necessarily reflect the views of these foundations.

Urban Sprawl and Public Health

■━━━━━━■

Designing, Planning, and Building
for Healthy Communities

HOWARD FRUMKIN
LAWRENCE FRANK
RICHARD JACKSON

ISLAND PRESS
WASHINGTON • COVELO • LONDON

ISLAND PRESS is a trademark of The Center for Resource Economics.

Library of Congress Cataloging-in-Publication data.
Frumkin, Howard.
    Urban sprawl and public health: designing, planning, and building for healthy
communities / Howard Frumkin, Lawrence Frank, Richard Jackson.
        p.   cm.
    Includes bibliographical references and index.
    ISBN 1-55963-912-1 (cloth: alk. paper) — ISBN 1-55963-305-0 (pbk.: alk.
paper)
    1. Cities and towns—Growth. 2. Public health. 3. City planning—
Environmental aspects. I. Frank, Lawrence D. II. Jackson, Richard, 1945–
III. Title. HT371.F78 2004
    307.76—dc22
                2004002136

British Cataloguing-in-Publication data available.

Printed on recycled, acid-free paper ♻

Design by PreMediaONE, a Black Dot Group Company

Manufactured in the United States of America
10 9 8 7 6 5 4

CONTENTS

■═══■

PREFACE

■ ═══════════ ■

Read the health care pages, and you will find plenty of good news. Compared to a generation ago or even a decade ago, we have better treatment for hypertension, better treatment for heart attacks, better treatment for depression. Surgical techniques have improved, in some cases dramatically. The Human Genome Project promises wonders in understanding the genetic basis of disease and in treating accordingly. We can prevent many diseases; there are immunizations against measles, hepatitis, pneumonia, and others, and many people receive them. Even some root causes of disease are on the wane; in many groups, smoking rates have declined.

But all is not well. The proportion of Americans who are overweight has been rising alarmingly, from 24 percent of adults in 1960, to 47 percent in 1980 (including 15 percent who were obese), and to no less than 64 percent in 2000 (including 31 percent who were obese).[1] If this continues, the last remaining slim American will cross over into corpulence sometime before 2040. One of the fastest-growing surgical procedures in the United States is bariatric surgery, shrinking the stomachs of so-called morbidly obese people. Overweight and obesity increase the risks of cancer, heart disease, stroke, high blood pressure, arthritis, and many other afflictions.[2] Obese people are as much as 40 times more likely to develop diabetes.[3] It is not surprising that the prevalence of diabetes has doubled since 1980,[4] and one in three Americans born today will eventually be diagnosed with the disease. Those who develop diabetes before age forty will forfeit an average of fourteen years of life, or twenty-two years if quality of life is taken into account.[5] Overweight is rapidly overtaking tobacco as the major cause of death in the Unites States.[6]

Asthma has increased to the point that nearly 10 percent of Americans are affected,[7] with much higher rates in some groups. As the population ages, there is more arthritis, more osteoporosis, more disability. On an average day, 120 Americans are killed by motor vehicles; one such death will occur in the time it takes to read this preface.[8] Millions of Americans suffer from depression and anxiety, and rates seem to be rising. Antidepressant prescribing more than tripled during the 1990s, and for many health plans they represent the second largest medication expense.[9] Children are increasingly medicated for inattentiveness or hyperactivity,[10] even as many are losing their opportunities for exercise at school or in their neighborhood. There are third-grade classes in which as many as a third of the boys are on Ritalin or similar medications.

More subjective indicators of health and well-being are also worrisome. In less than ten years, the number of days that the average American reports feeling unwell or outright sick has increased by one full day per month, from five to six days, an increase of twelve unwell days per year—more than the total paid vacation time of most newly hired employees.[11]

The costs of all this boggle the mind. In 1960 we spent 5.1 percent of our gross domestic product on health care. By 2001 the proportion had nearly tripled to 14.1 percent, representing annual expenditures of $1.4 trillion.[12] The cost of medical care for a single American adult doubles about every twenty years of life, and for people who have reached the age of seventy-five, the average cost of health care now exceeds $6,000 a year, not counting nursing home costs.[13]

If a patient reported such problems—gaining weight, feeling unwell, fighting depression, constantly getting injured, spending far too much on medicines—we would take a careful history. What changed in the patient's life? What circumstances might be contributing? Can we get at the root causes? Can we do something to help? On a national scale, the very same questions are inescapable.

In some ways we are better off than we were a generation ago. We have more money; per capita income (adjusted for inflation) rose by 79 percent between 1974 and 2000. But the Genuine Progress Indicator—a measure of overall quality of life that includes financial, social, and environmental factors—has barely budged, increasing by only 2 percent over twenty-six years.[14]

Our built environment has changed profoundly. In just the last fifteen years, the United States has developed 25 percent of all the land developed in the entire 225 years of the life of our republic.[15] ("Developing," in this context, means replacing farms and forests with buildings, roadways, and parking lots.) Cities have sprawled over vast expanses, and metropolitan areas have become "doughnuts" with areas of concentrated poverty in the center surrounded by suburban tracts for long-distance commuters. Consider this irony: New York City has

47,500 vacant land parcels totaling more than 17,000 acres,[16] New York City faces an acute housing shortage, and the fastest growing part of the New York area is in the Pocono Mountains of northeastern Pennsylvania. There, far from the city core, forests are being cleared for big-box stores, high-speed roadways, and low-density subdivisions for long-distance commuters.

What is life like in the expanding metropolitan areas? It is automobile oriented; many young families live in neighborhoods with neither sidewalks nor walkable destinations. It is transient; most Americans cannot live in the same community throughout their lives and grow old with friends from school or child-raising years. It lacks diversity; in homogeneous subdivisions, many children grow up never befriending or even meeting anybody from a lower social class or, for that matter, from a wealthier social class. It is restrictive; many young people without driving licenses or cars, living in subdivisions without shops, community centers, and public transportation, are bored and alienated. As we age and reach the point where we no longer should be driving, there are few options such as walkable town centers with nearby services and user-friendly transit, a matter of growing concern to the baby boomer generation.

In just over one generation, from 1960 to 2000, the average American's yearly driving has more than doubled, from 4,000 to nearly 10,000 miles per year.[17] In just twenty years, the "rush hour" in major cities has swollen from four-and-a-half hours of the day to seven, and the average driver's time spent stuck in traffic each year has skyrocketed—from six hours to thirty-six hours in Dallas, from one hour to twenty-eight hours in Minneapolis, and from six hours to thirty-four hours in Atlanta.[18] The average American mother spends more than an hour per day in her car, half of that time chauffeuring children or doing errands, again way up from a generation ago.[19]

As we look over the horizon, it is clear that many of these trends will continue. Our nation will have twice the population at the end of this century that we have today, nearly 600 million people, on precisely the same amount of land. We are aging rapidly. In the year 2000 just 9 percent of Americans were older than sixty-five years of age; in 2020 nearly 20 percent will be. Future health costs will be staggering.

These doleful statistics feel overwhelming, but they are not surprising to the average American. For many of us, *things don't feel right.* We can afford homes, but they are far from work and we spend more time working and commuting than our parents did. The average American works 1,821 hours per year, more than in any other developed country except Korea and Australia, and we sit in our cars for stupefying amounts of time.[20] Home-prepared meals have become infrequent, and we have much less time for community work, whether it is church, scouting, or the PTA, and less time for quiet reading or unhurried talk with neighbors and family.[21] Despite faster, cheaper, electronic toys, cell phones, and the Internet, many of our children are lonelier and more disconnected than the children of the "Leave It to Beaver" generation; more than three million American children today have significant depression symptoms.[22] The "goofing around" time walking or biking from school has evaporated, and children's friendships require parents' cars and scheduling. Despite plenty of evidence that children need quality fantasy play as part of their development, spontaneous "make-believe" play with friends has become a rarity. Learning to handle yourself in the school yard or sandlot is also an important part of growing up, yet pickup ball games with kids you don't yet know are nonexistent for many, perhaps most, American children.

The modern America of obesity, inactivity, depression, and loss of community has not "happened" to us. We legislated, subsidized, and planned it this way. Through zoning, we separated different land uses—a sensible idea when tanneries and foundries were close to homes, but an idea that has left us, nearly a century later, unable to walk from homes to offices or shops. Our taxes subsidized the highways that turned the downtowns of most American cities into no-man's-lands (and certainly no-child's-lands). In the historical riverside city of Hartford, Connecticut, birthplace of the father of American landscape architecture, Frederick Law Olmsted, highways built over the last half century have separated the city from its beautiful river and lacerated the city's neighborhoods. The Hartford home of Mark Twain, author of landmark American novels, was located in an artists' colony and enclave of lovely old homes, which is now surrounded by neglected and even dangerous neighborhoods. Tax subsidies for mortgages on new, distant homes, reached by driving on subsidized highways, as well as declining public schools and the abolition of subsidy for public transit, pulled the tax base away from the city.

Two of us, Richard Jackson and Howard Frumkin, are physicians who have specialized in health and environment for more than twenty years. Our careers have been challenging. We have studied the health effects of air and water pollution, of hazardous waste sites, and of pesticides and other toxic substances. We have responded to clusters of cancer, birth defects, asthma, and many other diseases. For years, we focused heavily on "toxic hazards"—what environmental engineers recognize as "end of the pipe" problems. We looked at the health effects of air pollution, but didn't pay enough attention to the upstream issue that much of the air pollution comes from cars and trucks driving more and more miles. We looked at birth defects and other disease clusters related to water, but didn't analyze how rapidly surface and groundwater was being depleted by removing forests and paving over the landscape, and how water was being polluted by the toxic materials that run off parking lots into creeks, rivers, and eventually drinking water every time it rains. We looked at automobile-related injury and death rates among passengers, bicyclists, and pedestrians, but didn't examine how the design of cities, suburbs, and country roads contributed. When a pedestrian is sideswiped and killed by a passing truck on Buford Highway, Atlanta, a seven-lane road lined with apartment buildings, big-box stores, and no sidewalks (see Fig. 10.1), the health department lists the cause of death "motor vehicle trauma." Should not the actual cause of death be listed as "negligent road design and city governance"?

When Richard Jackson was a young pediatrician, he never saw a child with type 2 diabetes; in fact, the disease was called "adult onset diabetes." Now about one in three diabetic children has this condition. Some of this is due to a "toxic" nutrition environment: abundant, cheap, high-calorie junk food and drinks (even at school) and a saturation of junk-food advertising. But the condition is exacerbated because our children cannot walk to where they need to do their life work: schools, sports fields, friends' homes, libraries, shops, or places of worship. One of the best approaches to preventing and treating diabetes is weight loss and exercise. And the most common, popular, and safe kind of exercise is walking. For people with diabetes, walking for exercise just two hours per week reduces their death rate by nearly 40 percent.[23] Clearly, reducing opportunities for walking is a national health threat.

One of us, Larry Frank, is a landscape architect, transportation planner, and land use planner who has studied how urban design influences travel behavior, physical activity, obesity, air pollution, and climate change. As a young landscape architect, he often found himself "shrubbing up" automobile-oriented business parks and residential developments; engineers and planners had made major design decisions early in the development process without regard for environmental quality or opportunities for walking. He began to recognize that he was creating places for cars as opposed to places for people. These experiences led him back to graduate school in civil engineering and urban design and planning. His research has shown that in sprawling areas, people drive more, pollute more, and weigh more. Where destinations like workplaces, shops, and restaurants are closer to home, people walk and ride transit more frequently. He and his colleagues have shown that there is a considerable unmet demand for walkable environments.[24]

This book is the work of three men who care deeply about our nation, our communities, and the health of our people. Despite enormous investments in medical research and treatment, the trajectory of health and the costs of health care in the United States are fearsome. This book is a call for rebuilding American communities so that every child can walk or bicycle safely to school, so that every older person who surrenders her driver's license does not feel she has been sentenced to solitary confinement, and so that all parents have enough time to spend with their children, every day.

Our critics will say that we are arguing for an old idea, that we are trying to return to the trolley car era of dense, walkable central cities with generous parks and lively commercial districts, surrounded by countryside, farmland, and smaller towns. Our critics argue that Americans have voted with their pocketbooks and their feet (or more correctly, tires), and have abandoned the cities for the big house on the half-acre lot on the cul-de-sac, and the long commute. They argue: Americans do not want density, and rightly demand safe neighborhoods and good schools. Finally, our critics argue that we seek to reexamine longstanding public policies and funding priorities, from tax structures to building and zoning codes.

And our critics are in many ways correct.

We do not argue for removing choices; rather, we argue for more choices. It would be foolish to tell anybody where to live. And nobody would wish to live in a place without privacy, tranquility, safety, or community. But, we argue, good density can be created—density that is aesthetically appealing, environmentally sustainable, and safe, healthy, and uplifting to inhabit. The old American cities and neighborhoods we enjoy so much—Boston and San Francisco, Annapolis and Georgetown, Charleston and Savannah—combine density and quality of life. Smart building and zoning codes can give us housing choices, nearby parks, and other destinations, sightlines that assure visibility and "eyes on the street," daylit stairways and walkways. The more that people with jobs, families, and responsibilities are on the sidewalks and riding public transit, the better off we are. Safe and abundant sidewalks and bicycle routes for children, adults, and police on patrol make neighborhoods cleaner and safer. Neighborhood schools that are also community centers not only build social capital, but help with bond issues to improve schools. When a school is located at a community's heart, as it should be, well-patrolled, well-lit, clean basketball courts and running tracks become resources for the community, not just the school.

Yes, it is true, we do have a vision for a world in which people can walk to shops, school, friends' homes, or transit stations; in which they can mingle with their neighbors and admire trees, plants, and waterways; in which the air and water are clean; and in which there are parks and play areas for children, gathering spots for teens and the elderly, and convenient work and recreation places for the rest of us. We do have a vision of an America in which people can "age in place." We do have a vision that every lake, stream, and river be swimable and fishable, and every shoreline walkable. We do have a vision of places designed and built with health and equity in mind, based on the best data. This book is our effort to lay out how the built environment affects us all, and how by building smarter, we can promote the health and well-being, and protect the environment, of Americans now and in coming generations.

ACKNOWLEDGMENTS

W hen we began writing this book in the middle of 2000, there were few links between the worlds of planning and public health. The change since then has been dramatic. We have ridden a tidal wave of interest among planners, architects, developers, health professionals, elected officials, and many others; what began as an academic study has come to feel like part of a movement. This issue has attracted interest and traction beyond anything we could have predicted. We owe a debt of gratitude to many people.

First, we want to thank those who directly contributed to the book: our colleague Steve Gaffield, previously with the U.S. Environmental Protection Agency and now with Montgomery Associates Resource Solutions in Madison, Wisconsin, for his key contributions to Chapter 7; Peter Engelke at Georgia Tech for his work on Chapter 5; students Heather Strosnider at Emory for reference checking, Stephanie Macari at Georgia Tech for background research, and Gerrit McGowan at the University of British Columbia for his work on graphics; and graphic artist Charles Dobson for his talented work.

The U.S. Centers for Disease Control and Prevention in Atlanta is a phenomenal nucleus of public health thinking and doing, and a source of inspiration, collaboration, and support for all of us. At the CDC we especially thank Andy Dannenberg, Chris Kochtitzky, Catherine Staunton, Bobby Milstein, Bob Delany, Lori Adams, Rich Scheiber, Jessica Shisler, Martha Katz (now at the Georgia Healthcare Foundation), Jeff Koplan (now at Emory), Julie Gerberding, Jim Marks, Bill Dietz, Tom Schmid, David Buchner, Michael Pratt, Sue Binder, and Christine Branche, and students Todd Cramer and Chris Gibson for their dedication to public health and their insights about the role of the built environment.

But there is much, much more to Atlanta than the CDC. If the city has been a poster child for sprawl, it is also blessed with an incompara-ble wealth of thoughtful, dedicated, and visionary leaders. Among the wonderful colleagues and friends we have shared are: Cheryl Contant, Steve French, Tom Galloway, Ellen Dunham-Jones, and Jim Chapman at Georgia Tech; Peggy Barlett, Bill Buzbee, Karen Mumford, and John Wegner at Emory; Catherine Ross at GRTA (and now at Georgia Tech); Dennis Creech at the Southface Energy Institute; Sally Flocks at PEDS; Tom Weyandt at the Atlanta Regional Commission; Jim Durrett at the Urban Land Institute; Ray Anderson at Interface; Laura Turner Seydel at the Turner Foundation; Robert Bullard at Clark Atlanta University; the Reverend Joseph Lowery, formerly at the Southern Christian Leadership Conference; Steve Nygren at the Chattahoochee Hill Country Alliance; Charles Brewer and Walter Brown at Green Street Properties; John Sibley, Julie Mayfield, and Susan Kidd at the Georgia Conservancy; Jack White at Southeast Waters AmeriCorps; Jeff Rader at the Greater Atlanta Home Builders Association; Sam Williams at the Metro Atlanta Chamber of Commerce; Eric Meyer at the Regional Business Coalition (now at the South Carolina Coastal Conservation League); Bryan Hager at the Sierra Club; Michael Kilgallon at the Pacific Group; Doug Spohn at Spohntown Corporation; Janet Frankston and Charles Seabrook at the Atlanta Journal-Constitution; Davis Fox and Stuart Meddin at the Alliance to Improve Emory Village; Peter Drey at Peter Drey and Company; Gordon Kenna at Cool Communities; and Ellen Macht and Michael Halicki at the Clean Air Campaign. Howie also thanks his classmates at the Institute for Georgia Environmental Leadership, and his colleagues and fellow board members at the Clean Air Campaign, who form some of his most important bonds in Atlanta and in Georgia, and from whom he has learned more than he can say.

At the Institute of Medicine, Dick and Howie have benefited from their membership on the Roundtable on Environmental Health Sciences, Research, and Medicine, under the leadership of the Honorable Paul Rogers and Dr. Lynn Goldman. Among its many activities, the Roundtable sponsored a forum in Atlanta in November, 2002, that brought together a large number of participants from the region to discuss links between health and the environment, and helped identify the built environment as a crucial issue for health.

The Robert Wood Johnson Foundation has provided outstanding leadership in calling attention to the role of the built environment in promoting active living. We acknowledge Risa Lavizzo-Mourey, J. Michael McGinnis, Kate Kraft, Rich Killingsworth (at the University of North Carolina), and Jim Sallis (at San Diego State University) for their vision and good work.

And the many other people who have inspired us, taught us, and supported us are too numerous to name. Among them are Glen Andersen, Geoff Anderson, John Balbus, Jerry Barondess, Kaid Benfield, Georges Benjamin, Phyllis Bleiweis, Ross Brownson, Dan Burden, Tom Burke, Anne Canby, Tony Capon, Robert Cervero, Don Chen, Judy Corbett, Robert Davis, Allen Dearry, Cushing Dolbeare, Andres Duany, Len Duhl, Reid Ewing, Chris Forinash, Mindy Fullilove, Sandro Galea, Robert Glandon, David Goldberg, Susan Handy, James Hill, Joel Hirschhorn, Allan Jacobs, Rachel Kaplan, Steve Kaplan, Ichiro Kawachi, Doug Kelbaugh, Fred Kent, Jim Kunstler, Frances Kuo, Patrick Lenihan, Donald Leslie, Patrick Libbey, Anne Lusk, Clare Cooper Marcus, Joyce Martin, Barbara McCann, Carol McClendon, Tracy McMillan, Rebecca Miles, Paul Morris, Anne Verdez Moudon, Jon Nordquist, Mary Northridge, Ken Olden, David Orr, Thom Penney, Elizabeth Plater-Zyberk, Karen Roof, Brian Saelens, David Satterthwaite, Elliot Sclar, Daniel Stokols, Bill Sullivan, Tim Torma, Harriet Tregoning, David Vlahov, Rand Wentworth, Walt Willett, and Sam Wilson.

We couldn't have done any of this without the assistance of Terrie Slaton at CDC and Robin Thompson at Emory. Thank you both!

We owe enormous gratitude to Island Press, not only for publishing this book (that would be enough!) but for being the best environmental publisher anywhere. Our editor, Heather Boyer, has been a delight to work with—thoughtful, professional, supportive, and dedicated.

Bringing it closer to home, each of us wants to thank the other. Collaborating on a book, especially when new ideas are constantly emerging, is exhilarating, exciting, challenging, and exhausting. The joy of discovery and the creative process was matched by the joy of our friendships. Each of us is quite sure that the others contributed more than he did. All of us are sure that this was a true team effort.

Finally, we thank our families: Beryl, Gabe, and Amara; Joan, Brendan, Devin, and Galen; and Eric. *Omnia vincit amor, et nos cedamus amori.*

CHAPTER 1

■ ══════════ ■

WHAT IS SPRAWL?
WHAT DOES IT HAVE
TO DO WITH HEALTH?

In 1956, the Federal Highway Act set out to "disperse our factories, our stores, our people, in short, to create a revolution in living habits." Within a year, writer and social critic William H. Whyte was already deeply disturbed by what he saw. Highways were allowing cities to expand rapidly into surrounding rural areas. In a short article published in *Fortune* magazine in January 1958, entitled simply "Urban Sprawl," Whyte observed that "huge patches of once green countryside have been turned into vast, smog-filled deserts that are neither city, suburb, nor country." "It is not merely that the countryside is ever receding," he warned, but "in the great expansion of the metropolitan areas the subdivisions of one city are beginning to meet up with the subdivisions of another."[1]

Nearly a half century later, the term "sprawl" has entered the American vernacular. Originally a reference to a bodily position—"to lie or sit with arms and legs spread out"—the word has more recently assumed a broader meaning: "to spread or develop irregularly." The Vermont Forum on Sprawl (www.vtsprawl.org) offers a succinct definition of sprawl as "dispersed, auto-dependent development outside of compact urban and village centers, along highways, and in rural countryside."

In common use, sprawl has become a pejorative term. It seems to take on a variety of meanings: cheaply and quickly built neighborhoods at the edge of metropolitan areas, architecturally monotonous residential subdivisions, ugly feeder roads lined with strip malls, lifestyles that center around car trips. Critics of sprawl have unleashed a torrent of pungent prose. William H. Whyte, in his original *Fortune* magazine article, wrote:

> Sprawl is bad aesthetics; it is bad economics. Five acres is being made to do the work of one, and do it very poorly. This is bad for the farmers, it is bad for communities, it is bad for industry, it is bad for utilities, it is bad for the railroads, it is bad for the recreation groups, it is bad even for the developers.[2]

Forty years later, a less measured James Kunstler derided sprawl in *The Geography of Nowhere* as "depressing, brutal, ugly, unhealthy, and spiritually degrading."[3]

In this book, we do not use sprawl as a pejorative term. Instead, we use it as a neutral descriptive term, as convenient shorthand for a complex set of characteristics of towns and cities. Sprawl refers to the way land is used, the way people travel from place to place, and even the way a place "feels." In sprawling metropolitan areas, the city expands outward over large geographic areas, sometimes in a "leapfrog" pattern (see Figure 1-1). Different land uses—residential, commercial, office, recreational, and so on—tend to be separated from each other. Busy arterial roads are lined with commercial strips, accessible only by car, and there is a relative scarcity of both walkable "town center" neighborhoods and public open space. Distances between things are large, which makes walking and biking impractical, and the low density makes mass transit uneconomical. There is a heavy reliance on the automobile, and the road system may provide few direct connections (see Figure 1-2). Oliver Gillham, in *The Limitless City*, provides a thorough review of various definitions of sprawl, and offers one of his own: "a form of urbanization distinguished by leapfrog patterns of development, commercial strips, low density, separated land uses, automobile dominance, and a minimum of public open space."[4]

Land use and transportation interact to affect many aspects of human activity, well-being, and health. Heavy reliance on the automobile for transportation results in more air pollution, which contributes to respiratory and cardiovascular disease. More driving also means less physical activity, contributing to a national epidemic of overweight and associated diseases. More time on the roads means a greater risk of collisions with other cars and with pedestrians, with associated injuries and deaths. Sprawling cities threaten the quality of drinking

■ **FIGURE 1-1**   Sprawl on a regional scale. A subdivision near Columbus, Ohio, encroaching on farmland.

SOURCE: Photo by Alex MacLean, courtesy of Landslides.com.

water sources and the availability of green spaces. Even mental health and the network of social interactions and trust known as "social capital" may be affected. To come to grips with the health implications of sprawl and to develop better public policy requires, therefore, an understanding of the physical attributes of sprawl and how they affect people.

DEFINING AND MEASURING SPRAWL

"Urban form" refers to the amalgamation of individual elements of the towns and cities in which we live, work, play, and travel: the schools, houses, parking lots, shopping malls, gas stations, post offices, houses of worship, streets, parks, and stadiums, with which we are all familiar. Urban form is partly determined by natural features—the coastlines of Boston and San Francisco, the riverfronts of Pittsburgh and St. Louis, the mountains outside Denver and Salt Lake City. And urban form is

■ **FIGURE 1-2**   Sprawl on a neighborhood scale. This configuration is
sometimes called "loop and lollipop" development. Note
the monotonous architecture, the exclusively residential
land use, poor connectivity, and automobile dependence.

SOURCE: Photo by Jim Wark, courtesy of Photostogo.com.

partly the result of public and private decisions made over many years,
some explicit, others unintended and even unrecognized. Some aspects
of urban form, such as regional commuter train systems, exist on a very
large scale, whereas others, such as courtyards and sidewalks, are very
small and localized. Architects and urban planners have used many
concepts to classify this seemingly infinite variety, to allow urban form
to be ordered, studied, and understood. Terms such as density, concentration, centrality, diversity, mixed uses, connectivity, and proximity are
all used to define and conceptualize urban form.[5]

Sprawl is one kind of urban form (see Figure 1-3). In this book, as
we explore the impact of sprawl on human health and well-being, we
look to many sources of empirical evidence. To study the relationship
between sprawl and health, a general definition of sprawl is not
enough. Scientists need a definition that can be operationalized and
measured. This allows them to test specific hypotheses about the
impact of sprawl on people.

The literature on sprawl offers a wide variety of definitions. A recent review of many of these[6] found "no common definition of sprawl, and relatively few attempts to operationally define it in a manner that would lead to useful comparisons" of metropolitan areas. Some definitions were narrowly oriented to a single metropolitan area such as Los Angeles. Some definitions were historical, based on the planning process that gave rise to a place; some were subjective, based on notions of ugliness; and some were incomplete, measuring only one or a few dimensions of sprawl such as density[7] or land area.

A widely accepted approach to measuring sprawl was proposed by Ewing, Pendall, and Chen.[8] These researchers aimed to incorporate both land use and transportation in their definition and, accordingly, identified four categories for measurement: the strength or vibrancy of activity centers and downtown areas; accessibility of the street network; residential density; and the mix of homes, jobs, and services at the neighborhood level. Each, they maintained, measures a different and important component of urban form; these might be defined as compactness (density), diversity (the mixture of uses over an area), sense of place (strength or vibrancy of activity centers in a region), and connectivity (street network accessibility, meaning how easy it is to get from point to point on the street system). They created a Sprawl Index with data on twenty-two specific measures grouped under the four categories. This showed the most sprawling areas to be in the South and Southeast, with a few in California. The least sprawling areas are in the Northeast, California (San Francisco), and Hawaii (Honolulu).

CORE CONCEPTS: LAND USE AND TRANSPORTATION

In this book, we also take the approach that both land use and transportation are intrinsic to sprawl. We emphasize two core land use concepts, *density* and *land use mix*, and two core transportation concepts, *automobile dependence* and *connectivity*. (We acknowledge many other important features of urban form, such as whether development is contiguous or leapfrog, the level of architectural variety, and the supply of bicycle paths and sidewalks.) We recognize that sprawl has different meanings on different spatial scales; the most important features of a sprawling metropolitan area are different than the most important features of a residential subdivision (although they are closely related to each other). And we recognize that sprawl is not a single pattern; different places sprawl in different ways.

Land Use: Density and Land Use Mix

Land use patterns determine the degree of proximity between different places. A higher level of proximity means that destinations are close together, and a lower level of proximity means that they are farther apart. The density and variety of uses in a neighborhood, community, or city district largely determine the functional distances that separate the places in which we live, work, and play. Low-proximity levels typify sprawl; there are both fewer destinations and less variety of destinations in sprawling development patterns compared to other types of urban form. This book shows how land use patterns have direct implications for travel behavior.

The density of a place refers to the quantity of people, households, or employment distributed over a unit of area such as an acre, a square kilometer, or a square mile.[9] The relationship of density to travel behavior has been the subject of considerable study in the discipline of urban and regional planning. Higher density is associated with shorter trips, an increased number of trips taken from home, an increase in transportation options ("mode choices"), and reduced vehicle ownership, compared to lower density.[10] Because of its conceptual simplicity and the ease with which it is measured, density is one of the most commonly used measures in planning.

The land use mix is a necessary and important complement to density. Land use mix is a measure of how many types of uses—offices, housing, retail, entertainment, services, and so on—are located in a given area. A high level of land use mix should in theory reduce the need to travel outside of that area to meet one's needs.

Land use mix is relevant over both vertical and horizontal spaces. In older parts of American cities and towns, the vertical mixing of uses was quite common, and it remains the norm in many parts of Europe. Different types of uses, usually retail and housing, are arranged in a single building, typically with retail on the ground floor and housing stacked above it. With the advent of zoning in the first quarter of the twentieth century, however, the vertical mixing of uses was effectively outlawed in most parts of the United States. Horizontal mixing of uses refers to the location of different types of land uses on adjacent or near-adjacent parcels of land. Empirical research has shown that households located in less mixed environments generate longer automobile trips and fewer trips on foot, bicycle, and transit[11] than do similar households located in more mixed use environments.

Transportation: Connectivity and Automobile Dependence

Connectivity refers to how destinations are linked through transportation systems. While the proximity of destinations is central to shaping how people travel, connectivity also has tremendous importance. A poorly connected transportation system can make even nearby destinations functionally far apart. Conversely, a well-connected system can ease travel between destinations by shortening on-the-ground distances. Connectivity is almost always discussed in the context of the street network. Because streets are the primary arteries upon which travel by most modes occurs, they have a central importance in determining travel patterns.

A well-connected street network features many street linkages between trip origins and trip destinations. A poorly connected network has fewer linkages. One way to think of connectivity is to think of how easy it is to "go around the block." Simply put, going around the block becomes much more difficult where streets do not connect. Block size is the area bounded by streets that form its perimeter. The larger the block size, the more difficult it becomes to get to a destination in a reasonably direct path. Connectivity can also be viewed as the number of street intersections scattered across a neighborhood or district. More intersections mean that there are more possible routes between point A and point B. Conversely, poorly connected systems have fewer intersections, offering fewer travel routes, generally implying a less direct and more circuitous route between points A and B.

The street arrangement with the greatest connectivity is the grid pattern, a simple network consisting of regularly intersecting horizontal and vertical streets framing small blocks (see Figure 1-3). Such networks reduce the distances between trip origins and destinations by providing many intersections and, therefore, many possible routes. In contrast, the dendritic street network (the upper part of Figure 1-3) is characterized by fewer streets organized into a hierarchy based upon the amount of traffic each is intended to carry. Like the lifelines in the leaf on a tree, this dendritic form of transportation is highly specialized. At the core of the dendritic system are major arterial roadways, designed to carry cross-regional traffic. Residential streets form the edges of the dendritic network and are designed exclusively for local traffic; to exclude high-speed vehicles, there are very few connections between these streets and arterials. These form the "loop and lollipop" neighborhoods seen in Figure 1-2. As a result, trips to destinations, especially those out of the neighborhood, become more circuitous, and trip lengths increase. Trips to destinations that are nearby in terms of straight-line distance can become long journeys.[12]

Low proximity (reflecting low density and low land use mix) and low connectivity together predict the fourth cardinal feature of sprawl: automobile dependence. In theory, when proximity and connectivity are high, people would be expected to depend less on automobiles,

■ **FIGURE 1-3** Schematic comparison of street networks and land use in sprawl (upper part of diagram) and traditional neighborhood (lower part of diagram)

Suburban Sprawl

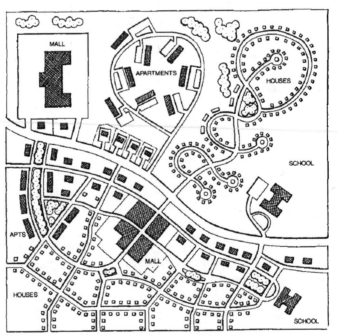

Traditional Neighborhood

SOURCE: Drawing by Duany Plater Zyberk as shown in F. Spielberg, "The Traditional Neighborhood Development: How will Traffic Engineers Respond?" *ITE Journal* 1989;59:17–18.

because other modes of travel such as transit and walking are more competitive with automobile travel. In addition, when proximity and connectivity are high, the average automobile trip would be expected to be shorter. Sprawling areas, accordingly, would be expected to feature enormous amounts of driving.

An overview of recent urban development in the United States lends support to this view. During the past few decades, the fastest growing regions have also featured the most extensive road construction, the greatest geographic expansion into exurban areas, and the steepest increases in automobile travel. These trends seem to emerge in tandem; sprawl toward the edges of a metropolitan area is associated with more driving. For instance, from 1982 to 1997, Atlanta added 571,000 acres to its urbanized area, and added approximately 1.3 million people, meaning that the region urbanized approximately 1 acre of land for every two new residents.[13] During the same interval, the number of miles driven per person in the region more than doubled.[14] Figure 1-4 shows the distribution of average vehicle miles traveled (VMT) per day across the Atlanta region, and illustrates that travel distances are greatest on the region's periphery and shortest nearer its center. By 2001, the average Atlantan (including nondrivers) was driving 34 miles each day—a citywide total of 102,000,000 miles, enough to reach from Peachtree Street to the sun and partway back. The city's rush hour had grown to 7.8 hours each day, and the average Atlantan was spending 34 hours per year stuck in congested traffic.[15]

Atlanta is not alone in this regard; across the country, sprawling development patterns tend to be associated with similar travel patterns at the regional level. Keith Lawton, noted transportation planner in Portland, Oregon, writes:

> When looking at the amount of travel in U.S. cities, it is clear that those cities with lower densities and a larger road supply consume significantly more vehicle miles of travel. The three cities that have been mainly formed in the last fifty years, under a policy of plentiful supply of roads and freeways, Houston, Atlanta, and Dallas–Ft. Worth, clearly have the best road supply, the lowest densities *and the most vehicle use*—Houston and Atlanta in the order of 50 percent more vehicle miles of travel per capita than comparable sized cities.[16]

Observations such as these have given rise to dozens of studies in recent years, examining the association between urban form and travel behavior. The studies measure urban form and travel behavior in a variety of ways, use a variety of study designs, and consider a variety of

■ **FIGURE 1-4** Daily per capita home-based vehicle miles traveled in Greater Atlanta, 1998

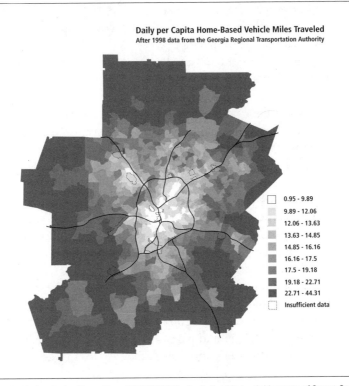

Daily per Capita Home-Based Vehicle Miles Traveled
After 1998 data from the Georgia Regional Transportation Authority

0.95 - 9.89
9.89 - 12.06
12.06 - 13.63
13.63 - 14.85
14.85 - 16.16
16.16 - 17.5
17.5 - 19.18
19.18 - 22.71
22.71 - 44.31
Insufficient data

SOURCE: "Daily Per Capita Home-Based VMT 1998" in *Analysis of Potential Impacts of Smart Growth Land-Use Planning.* Prepared by Criterion Planning Engineers for the Georgia Regional Transportation Authority. April 4, 2000.

spatial scales, from the neighborhood to the census tract to the entire metropolitan region. The results reveal that sprawl leads to more driving. Lower density levels, low land use mix, and poorly connected "loop and lollipop" street networks are associated with more VMTs, more vehicle hours of travel (VHT), fewer transit trips, and greater vehicle ownership. These findings are intuitive.[17]

Some of these studies have used nationwide data sets. For instance, Cervero[18] used a national database, the American Housing Survey, which covers forty-four metropolitan areas with populations over 1 million. In reviewing data from approximately 10,000 households, he found that both higher density and higher land use mix decreased the probability of automobile commuting as opposed to transit use or walking.

Other studies have focused on smaller geographic scales such as neighborhoods. These studies are useful when large-area data are too coarse to be informative. Researchers typically select nearby neighborhoods that differ in density, land use mix, and connectivity, but share similar levels of income, household size, and other factors that might affect travel. These studies almost always find that neighborhood features significantly affect travel behavior.

For example, a well-known study by Holtzclaw[19] assessed the travel patterns of residents in twenty-eight neighborhoods across northern California, and found that greater household density was associated with lower automobile ownership and lower VMTs. Greater access to transit was also associated with lower VMTs. In this study, a doubling of density yielded up to 30 percent fewer VMTs when higher density levels were accompanied by high transit service, a mixture of land uses, and pedestrian amenities. In another such study, Cervero and Gorham[20] identified thirteen pairs of neighborhoods in the Los Angeles and San Francisco regions. In each pair, the two neighborhoods were located within 4 miles of each other and had similar income levels, but one was "transit-oriented" and one was "auto-oriented." Transit-oriented neighborhoods, built along streetcar lines before World War II, were relatively dense and had gridlike street networks. In contrast, auto-oriented neighborhoods were built after 1945, were not built around streetcar lines, had disconnected street networks, and had lower residential density. The researchers found consistently lower rates of automobile commuting by residents of the transit-oriented neighborhoods as compared to those in auto-oriented neighborhoods, particularly in the San Francisco region, a finding attributable, they hypothesized, to the more compact and transit-friendly nature of the Bay Area compared with Los Angeles. When the authors repeated their analysis on a larger scale, the census tracts in which their study neighborhoods were located, they found consistent results: commuting by transit rather than automobile increased with residential density, especially in the transit-oriented neighborhoods. Many studies have reported similar results.[21]

The relationship between land use and travel behavior is not simple and linear. It seems to be characterized by thresholds. In sparse rural areas, doubling the residential density has very little effect on VMTs. However, as density increases toward that of older suburbs, VMTs begin to decline significantly.[22] In one study, in the Seattle area, automobile commuting began to decrease when the employment density reached about thirty employees per acre, and dropped sharply at

BOX 1-1
Sprawl and Travel Behavior: An Example

Tom and Marsha Goodman are in their late forties. When they moved to the Atlanta area almost ten years ago, they wanted to find the best school system for their three boys. After careful research, they bought a home on a cul-de-sac in a suburban subdivision of large but look-alike homes, surrounded by similar subdivisions. The school system is excellent, but the area has no sidewalks, bicycle routes, or local parks. The nearest place to shop is a gas station convenience store on a main road just over a mile from their subdivision. For any real shopping, a large mall is nearly 3 miles away. Even simple trips to church, the library, or the post office must be made by car.

Marsha works as an import/export buyer in another suburb about 15 miles from home when she drives directly. Tom is an executive of a real estate firm located in an office park on Atlanta's northern perimeter, 27 miles from home. Both commute by car. Each afternoon, they negotiate the "arsenic hours"—the late afternoon, dinner, and homework time. With the boys' schools each at least 4 miles from

home, along roads that do not allow safe walking or bicycling, and with no public transportation, Tom and Marsha negotiate who will pick up which child, how they will juggle sports and guitar lessons and after-school activities, who will do the shopping and who will make dinner. Both help with homework. If dinner is anything more than a frozen pizza or fast-food takeout, it won't be on the table until 7:30, when the boys are ravenous. A late meeting at work, out-of-town travel, a doctor's visit, or car trouble means more negotiations about whose work is more important that day. And as congestion worsens on the nearby roads, it becomes more and more difficult to squeeze in any errands before dinner. Frustration, pressure, and tension are a routine part of every day.

The boys, too, are affected by the family's travel patterns. If traffic problems delay school pickups, the boys wait on the school steps, sometimes being shooed off by school staff. They often ask to go to a friend's house, but the only way to get there is for a parent to drive them. This makes them feel dependent, precisely the

---

levels above seventy-five. A similar pattern was evident for shopping trips. Shopping trips by transit and walking increased, and automobile use for shopping fell off, at densities above thirteen people per acre, a level well above that found in most sprawling communities.[23] This nonlinear pattern is shown in Figure 1-5.

Not every aspect of automobile travel is equally affected by sprawl. Ewing and Cervero[24] reviewed over fifty studies and examined several dimensions of automobile use: trip frequency, trip length, mode

feeling they are trying to outgrow. A party or a date means begging and then resenting their parents. Some of the boys' 16-year-old friends have cars, but Tom and Marsha are keenly aware of the high rate of car crashes among teen drivers in their community and do not trust their driving. The boys describe their community with the inevitable teen epithet: BORING!

Suppose that the Goodmans maintain a travel diary on a typical weekday. Marsha leaves home at 7:20 a.m., drives the 4 miles to the junior high school to drop off their youngest son at 7:30, and continues on to work, arriving at 8:05 a.m. The actual commute portion of the trip takes 35 minutes, a 17-mile distance at an average of 30 miles per hour. Marsha's office is in an old town center with a mixture of uses. This allows her to walk to a restaurant or do her banking and other errands during her lunch hour. On the way home, she stops at the high school at 5:15 for the two older sons. The younger son got a ride home from junior high school.

On this same day, Tom also leaves home at 7:15 a.m., drops their two older sons at the high school 5 miles from home, and arrives at his job at 8:40 a.m. Tom's travel diary shows a chain of trips at midday, beginning at 12:15 p.m. and ending at 1:30 p.m., presumably in association with eating lunch and other errands. While these trips were too short to estimate distance or speed, we assume the first one to be a cold-start trip. Tom leaves work at 6:00 p.m. and arrives home at approximately 6:45 p.m. At 7:00 p.m., the family goes out for dinner to a restaurant located 6 miles from their home, returning at 8:30 p.m. This trip is registered in Tom's diary as a driver with passengers.

On this Tuesday, the Goodman family generates ten vehicle trips, of which seven are cold starts, and they log 106 "vehicle miles traveled." They generate 110 grams of NOx, exceeding Atlanta's regional household average of 83 grams. Aside from a couple of very short walks during their lunch periods, none of Marsha or Tom's are on foot, and no walking trips originated from home.

The Goodmans and their neighbors are largely automobile dependent for travel both to work and for other purposes. The results are clearly seen in a quantitative tally of their miles traveled and emissions. They are just as clearly felt every day by the Goodmans, as they struggle to balance the demands of their jobs, schools, other activities, and travel, constrained by both time and community design.

choice, vehicle miles traveled (VMT), and vehicle hours traveled (VHT). They concluded that the frequency of trips is influenced much more by people's socioeconomic status than by features of the built environment. In contrast, the built environment is the most important determinant of trip length, VMTs, and VHTs. Mode choice (the decision of whether to travel by car or by another means such as transit or walking) is influenced by both socioeconomic status and the built environment.

■ FIGURE 1-5 Average number of vehicle trips by household density, Seattle area, 1994–1996

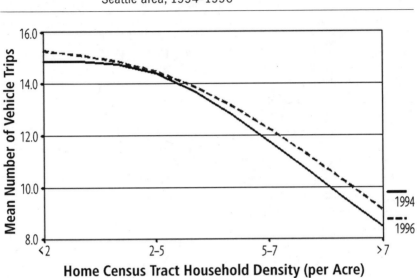

SOURCE: L. Frank, B. Stone, Jr, and W. Bachman, "Linking Land Use with Household Vehicle Emissions in the Central Puget Sound: Methodological Framework and Findings," *Transportation Research Part D* 2000;5(3):173-96.

Some transportation planners challenge the conclusion that density and land use mix predict automobile use. Indeed, not all empirical studies have supported this association.[25] Other factors, such as income and household size, may play an important role in determining travel behavior, and many studies have failed to take these into account.[26] Some investigators point out that travel and activity choices are made every day, while decisions about neighborhood, vehicle ownership, and employment location are made on a time frame of years, and values and circumstances change over an entire lifetime, challenging any simple conclusions about the role of the built environment in travel behavior.[27] Other investigators argue that travel behavior is motivated by personal preferences—that some people drive because they just like to drive, irrespective of the kinds of neighborhoods in which they reside.[28] This implies that even if the built environment is associated with travel behavior, the association may not be causal. Instead, people who like to walk may selectively move to walkable neighborhoods, and people who like to drive may selectively move to sprawling subdivisions. A person's neighborhood would therefore be a *result* of preferences instead of a *determinant* of behavior.[29]

There is likely to be some truth to this view. It would not be surprising if people who like to walk choose walkable neighborhoods, and if couch potatoes choose automobile-oriented neighborhoods. However, people are not always free to choose their preferred neighborhood type. In many cities, housing in sprawling subdivisions is more plentiful and affordable than in-town housing. Recent research suggests that many people who live in sprawling suburbs would prefer more walkable communities. Surveys in Boston and Atlanta confirm that there is indeed a latent demand for communities that permit less driving and more walking,[30] and national polling data, while revealing some mixed views, generally confirm that Americans value walkable neighborhoods with mixed uses and connectivity.[31]

For advocates and critics alike, the question is not limited to whether urban form has an impact on travel behavior. What is the magnitude of this impact? Which study methodologies are most valid in characterizing the impact? What policy responses should follow? Overall, available evidence supports the view that sprawl is associated with more driving, less walking, and less transit use.

VARIETIES OF SPRAWL

There is no single arrangement called sprawl. Sprawl has different meanings on different spatial scales. In Figure 1-1, the aerial view emphasizes the geographic spread of the metropolitan area, the low density of land use, and the long distances between things. In Figure 1-2, a closer view of a residential development, the absence of mixed land use, and the automobile-oriented street design stand out. At the larger scale, our health concerns might focus on air pollution from heavy reliance on motor vehicles, and on threats to waterways. At the smaller scale, we might worry about the absence of walkable environments and the risks of pedestrian fatalities. Similarly, if we were to swing our lens from the neighborhood in Figure 1-2 to an inner-city neighborhood, one suffering from abandonment and neglect, we would confront the health consequences of poverty.

Sprawl is not a single pattern; different places sprawl in different ways. In fact, communities cannot be easily divided into those that sprawl and those that do not (although at the extremes, it is easy to recognize a sprawling area or a traditional town center). Communities vary along the spectrum of density, land use mix, and connectivity. The continuum formed by these factors has been called a transect by architect and planner Andres Duany (see Figure 1-6). The left end of the transect is rural. The outer edge of the city (T3), where density, land use mix, and connectivity are all low, would fit anyone's definition of sprawl. Most new suburban development in the United States fits this model. Residential densities are kept low through regulatory devices such as zoning and subdivision codes and through the operation of market forces. Similarly, regulations and private mechanisms keep distinct uses separated in newer developments. People reside in self-contained neighborhoods, work in office parks and complexes, and shop in shopping districts, usually "big-box" stores and large malls surrounded by vast parking lots. Finally, road networks are built to funnel all traffic onto major arterials and to keep it away from neighborhoods. High connectivity, therefore, is engineered out of the equation.

However, there is considerable variability in this pattern. In the suburban zone of the continuum are communities that score higher on one or more of the three variables. Three identifiable patterns are exemplary: areas near suburban strip malls, old town centers, and regional downtowns.

■ **FIGURE 1-6**   The "transect": A continuum from sprawl to compact neighborhoods.

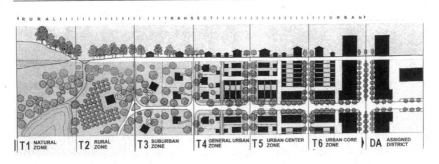

SOURCE: Image courtesy of Duany Plater-Zyberk and Company (2003) *Transect 03-03-03.*
http://www.dpz.com/pdf/02-a-TRANSECT_03-03-03.pdf, accessed 01/20/2004.

Locations with strip malls frequently differ from the "low density/ low land use mix/low connectivity" profile of typical suburban environments, due to nearby or even adjacent apartment housing. (Often, such housing is for lower income groups.) This arrangement features moderate density and a nominal mixture of uses, but connectivity is typically very poor. Walls are constructed between apartment buildings and the rear of the malls, requiring long and circuitous journeys to travel what would otherwise be a very short distance. Additionally, other factors make such places unappetizing for the pedestrian: strip malls are always built on major arterial roads that contain few, if any, pedestrian amenities such as sidewalks and well-designed crosswalks.

Similarly, because of the separation of multifamily from single-family housing in the United States, in some cases residential enclaves within a sea of sprawl can have relatively high residential densities. One study in the Seattle area showed that 20 percent of suburban residents lived in concentrated areas of apartments that were both relatively high in population density and also relatively close to shopping and services. Some sprawl is quite dense.[32]

Moving to the right across the continuum in Figure 1-6, we find the general urban zone typical of older town centers. These centers, which exist in smaller towns around the country, have good "bones"— meaning the street system is often in a grid pattern—and thus score high in terms of connectivity. In addition, these town centers also contain a mixture of uses such as law offices and small shops arrayed around a county courthouse with housing at the edge. Most often, however, such town centers score low in terms of density. Most trips to and from the town centers are made by automobile (although, at lunchtime, a lawyer or pharmacist can walk from work to a nearby restaurant).

Regional downtowns come next on the continuum. Downtowns in major cities almost always have good connectivity, very high density (at least in terms of structural densities, i.e., the density of buildings), and a rich mixture of uses. However, they almost always fail in one key respect: they have little housing, which is the main factor that determines the overall vitality of a city center. As Jane Jacobs pointed out in her classic *The Death and Life of Great American Cities*, "eyes on the street" and people out walking throughout the day and evening create a safe, inviting community.[33] Without residential use, many downtowns seem abandoned and ghostly after the working day. Some downtown areas, such as parts of Manhattan, Boston, San Francisco, Seattle, and Portland have resisted this trend and show signs of life in the evenings and on weekends. However, most downtown areas are working districts only and are places that people reach by driving from homes many miles away.

At the opposite end of the spectrum from sprawl are those communities with high density, a diverse mix of land uses in close proximity to one another, highly connected street systems, and alternatives to automobile use. Unlike most downtowns, these areas include plenty of housing, usually a mix of apartments, condominiums, and single-family housing. Most often, these areas are older communities that were built near the urban core perhaps a century ago, depending of course on the history of the city's growth. Because many types of destinations are close together and connected by a gridlike street network, walking and bicycling are practical alternatives to driving. Often, these areas are characterized by dense sidewalk networks and plentiful, well-designed crosswalks. Other amenities, such as parks and street-level retail stores, add to the pedestrian-friendly nature of the district. Finally, transit service is viable because there is a sufficiently high population density.

A simple yet roughly accurate rule is that older areas can be placed to the right on Figure 1-6, while newer ones can be placed to the left. Older neighborhoods tend to be located toward a region's core, whereas newer ones are most often built at the region's periphery. Obviously, there is some variation in this pattern; as regions expand outward from a city, new development often engulfs older towns that had been built decades beforehand as distinct outlying communities. In these cases, sprawl surrounds pockets of high density, mixed land use, and connectivity. Yet the typical core-periphery development trends can be observed on most maps of metropolitan land use patterns. For instance, Figure 1-7 shows the variation of household density across the Atlanta region, based on 2000 census data. Most outlying parts of the region are shown in the lighter colors, indicating low density, while the darker shading, indicating higher density, tends to be located closer to the region's center. Pockets of high density outside the central city indicate older town centers that have been engulfed by the growth of the metropolitan area.

Similarly, Figure 1-8 shows the distribution of employment density (the number of jobs per unit of land area). Much of the commercial development is concentrated in the region's core, where it originated historically. However, there is a trend toward pockets of higher employment density in outlying areas. These are almost always areas near intersections of the region's major highways, indicating that some developers and employers sought locations with less traffic congestion, lower development and infrastructure costs, and shorter travel times. Ironically, these major highway interchanges are now the most congested spots in many metro areas. And the mismatch of residential locations and employment, especially for poor and working-class people, remains a pressing concern with important health and equity implications (see Chapter 10).

■ FIGURE 1-7   Residential density in the Atlanta region in 2000, measured in 700-foot grid cells, using census bureau and land use data from the Atlanta Regional Commission

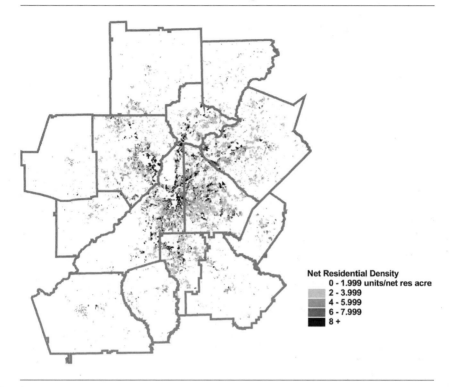

Net Residential Density
0 - 1.999 units/net res acre
2 - 3.999
4 - 5.999
6 - 7.999
8 +

SOURCE: A. Carpenter, J. Chapman, and L. Frank, the Atlanta Based SMARTRAQ Program, 2004.

THE SUBJECTIVE EXPERIENCE OF SPRAWL

The emphasis on objective measures of sprawl, especially in the context of research, should not eclipse the importance of subjective responses to urban form. In fact, subjective responses arguably launched the contemporary debate over sprawl in the first place. Writers such as Kunstler, who did not base his criticism on statistical analysis, undoubtedly played a seminal role in placing the sprawl debate on the nation's agenda. For most people, moreover, objective indicators of density and land use mix do not fully capture their sense of the term sprawl. Some people have an emotional reaction to sprawl that cannot be explained entirely by reference to density, land use mix, connectivity, or any other technically grounded factors.

■ **FIGURE 1-8**   Employment density in the Atlanta region in 2000, measured in 700-foot grid cells, using employment security data
and land use data from the Atlanta Regional Commission

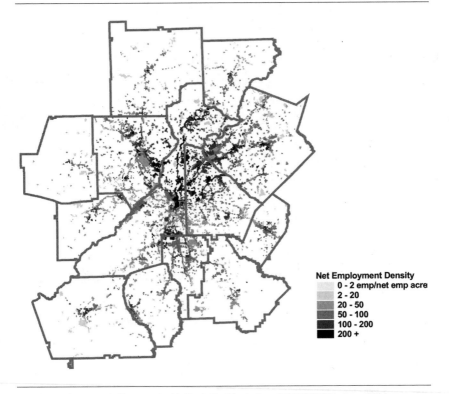

Net Employment Density
0 - 2 emp/net emp acre
2 - 20
20 - 50
50 - 100
100 - 200
200 +

SOURCE: A. Carpenter, J. Chapman, and L. Frank, the Atlanta Based SMARTRAQ Program, 2004.

These reactions may relate to the fact that the land use patterns
and transportation systems of sprawl are scaled to the automobile, and
not to the individual human being. Sprawl is designed and built to center not on the human, but on the human being *who is traveling in an
automobile*. The primary design goal is to allow vehicular traffic to
move from point to point with a minimum of difficulty and a maximum
of speed.

The "number of noticeable differences" theory of urban space,
proposed by architect Amos Rapoport,[34] focuses on the speed of the
traveler and helps explain why subjective reactions to sprawl can be so
negative. Rapoport asserts that different environments serve the needs
and interests of people who move at different speeds through those
environments. According to this theory, people in motor vehicles can

perceive fewer details in the environment, and people moving at slower speeds, such as pedestrians and bicyclists, are able to process more detail. Environments that place the automobile at the center, as sprawl certainly does, are built with the perceptual abilities of the motorist in mind. Streets and spaces that are scaled to the 40- or 50-mile-per-hour car will have enormous buildings and signage, consistent with the motorists' ability to process detail at such speeds. In contrast, environments built first and foremost for the pedestrian, including towns and cities predating the advent of the automobile, are far richer in building and streetscape detail. A good shopping street offers much to notice when walking at a regular pace, about 3 miles per hour. In contrast, walking on suburban arterials is a highly monotonous experience because there is less detail. Such practices as placing parking in the front of development increases pedestrian travel distances between commercial structures, but offers routes without the attractive, safe, and ordered qualities that accommodate and attract pedestrians. As a result, the pedestrian or bicyclist may find the street an unpleasant, inhospitable, and even dangerous place (see Figure 1-9).

■ **FIGURE 1-9**   A suburban streetscape scaled to the automobile. There is a sidewalk, but a pedestrian walking on it would find it a jarring experience.

SOURCE: Tuscon, Arizona, image by Gordon Price.

Ironically, while sprawling places may appear disordered to the pedestrian, sprawl is a highly systematic form of development. Sprawl represents a pattern that is enshrined in public policies, supported by public subsidies, and structured by commercial practice. The history of these policies is described in Chapter 2.

OVERVIEW OF THIS BOOK

This book is written for designers, planners, and architects who care about the health implications of their work, but who have little or no background in public health. It is also written for health care providers and public health professionals who care about the effects of the built environment on individual patients and entire populations, but who have little or no background in design, planning, or architecture. And it is also written for public officials, businesspeople, environmentalists, and members of the public who understand, based on experience and common sense rather than technical training, that the places we live, work, and play have a great deal to do with the way we feel.

This chapter has defined sprawl and introduced concepts very familiar to planners. Planners have probably skimmed up to this point, while health professionals have probably read more closely. Chapter 2 reviews the history of sprawl and explains how and why American cities have transformed so profoundly over the last century. Again, planners will be familiar with much of this material, but it will be new to many health professionals.

Chapter 3 introduces the field of "urban health," and places this field in the context of larger public health trends since colonial times. For health readers, the epidemiological transition and its urban manifestations will be familiar, while readers from planning and related fields will find this material new. We propose that urban health—a field that has until very recently focused on the diseases of poverty in the inner city—needs to be broadened to consider health on a systems basis, across the entire metropolis.

The next few chapters discuss specific health implications of sprawl. Chapter 4 focuses on air pollution. As discussed earlier, people in sprawling areas drive more miles per day,[35] use less transit,[36] and walk less[37] than people in traditional communities, a travel pattern that generates substantial quantities of air pollutants.[38] Automobiles and trucks emit nitrogen oxides (NOx), volatile organic compounds (VOCs), carbon monoxide (CO), particulate matter, and other toxic chemicals. Another pollutant—ozone—forms secondarily from the interaction of NOx and hydrocarbons. In general terms, the output of these pollutants is correlated with the amount of driving; longer driving distances, a characteristic of sprawl, therefore create more pollution.

Chapter 5 discusses the association between sprawl and physical activity. Land use and transportation patterns influence physical activity patterns, which in turn contribute, over the long term, to an array of health outcomes including body weight, chronic diseases, and mortality. Most Americans are less physically active than public health guidelines recommend. One solution is deliberate exercise such as team sports or jogging. However, many people are unable or disinclined to start these activities, and even when people start exercising, quit rates are high. Accordingly, public health recommendations have focused on routine activities that can be incorporated into daily patterns and sustained over time. Walking is a key form of such physical activity.

Environments that are built for and scaled to walking therefore represent an important venue for physical activity. People are more willing to walk from place to place if the distance is short and the route is safe and attractive. Sprawl inhibits walking trips because, with low proximity and low connectivity, distances are long and walking routes unavailable or unappealing. At a time when the nation faces epidemics of inactivity, obesity, and related disorders such as diabetes, this is a compelling public health issue.

Chapter 6 discusses injuries related to the heavy dependence on motor vehicles. The automobile is a relatively hazardous mode of travel, and all things being equal, more hours as a driver or passenger increase the risk of being involved in a collision, with the possibility of injury or death. Pedestrian injuries and deaths are also a serious concern in sprawling communities, where pedestrian infrastructure such as sidewalks and crossings are often deficient. Ironically, the pedestrian fatality rate is slowly declining nationally, probably because fewer and fewer people are walking. If this is a public health victory, it is one we purchase at the steep price of widespread physical inactivity. We need community designs that seduce people into traveling on foot and by bicycle, and controlling injury risks is essential to this goal.

Americans take for granted an unlimited supply of clean water for drinking and washing. However, as Chapter 7 discusses, sprawl threatens both water quantity and water quality. An adequate water supply is obviously a central part of well-being. And when water quality is threatened, serious health consequences may follow. This chapter discusses the ways in which sprawl can contribute to siltation, nonpoint source water pollution, and microbial contamination, and thereby threaten water quality.

Mental illness is one of the most common reasons for medical visits. Some patients are formally diagnosed with conditions such as depression and anxiety disorder, but many simply feel depressed, or anxious, or distressed. We know very little about the ways in which the built environment can contribute to these health burdens. However, we do know that certain aspects of sprawl, such as driving, are sources of psychological stress, and we do know that the responses can range from angry behavior to physical illness. Chapter 8 reviews these mental health issues.

There is also reason to suspect that the social costs of sprawl are experienced not just on the individual level, as psychological distress, but also on the community level, as a loss of social capital. Social capital refers to the forces that bind communities together—attitudes of trust and reciprocity, and behaviors such as civic participation and charitable giving. Several aspects of sprawl, from mathematical realities such as long driving times to abstract concepts such as income inequality, may all contribute to the erosion of social capital. This is the subject of Chapter 9.

Political scientists, when confronted with public policy decisions, famously ask whose ox is gored. Public health professionals think along similar lines. Nearly every known health hazard, from pneumococcal pneumonia to homicide, from osteoporosis to cancer, preferentially targets some groups more than others. People may be vulnerable because of social circumstances, as when they are disproportionately exposed to air pollutants or hazardous waste. People may also be vulnerable because of biological factors. Children, for example, consume more air and water in relation to their size, and have immature biological defenses compared to adults, increasing the risk of toxic exposures, while people with asthma are especially sensitive to some air pollutants. Chapter 10 discusses the disparate impact of sprawl on several "special populations," including women, children, the elderly, poor people and people of color, and people with disabilities.

Finally, because the authors are optimists and are dedicated to the design and construction of healthy places, Chapter 11 discusses a range of solutions. Many of these solutions have been proposed, codified, and implemented by advocates of "smart growth," a paradigm originally oriented toward aesthetics, quality of life, and environmental sustainability. These are of course deeply worthy goals, but we argue in Chapter 11 that smart growth can also be considered a public health paradigm. Mixed land use; a balance of density and preserved greenspace; a balance of automobile transportation with walking, bicycling, and transit; the provision of attractive and functional public spaces; the mingling of different styles and price levels of housing—these and other strategies offer the potential to increase physical activity, decrease air pollution, protect source water, control injuries, and improve mental health and social capital.

A message that runs through this book becomes explicit in the final chapter: we need to return to a tradition as old as Frederick Law Olmsted, and reunite the perspectives of urban planning and public health. We are only now realizing that the ways we have built cities and suburbs over the last half century has been extremely costly, not only in economic and environmental terms, but also to human health and well-being. Combining the expertise and vision of planners and designers with the expertise and vision of health professionals, we can assure that our children, and their children, will thrive in healthier, safer, and more wholesome and beautiful places than those we know so well.

CHAPTER 2

■ ══════════ ■

THE ORIGINS
OF SPRAWL

People came together to form cities thousands of years ago, to enjoy the benefits of company, commerce, and mutual defense. Nearly all early cities were at the water's edge, to permit transportation and trade. Early cities were compact, to make them easier to defend and to keep home, work, and other activities within walking distance of each other and the waterfront. Even when overland transportation emerged, first with horses and later with mechanized transportation, cities remained compact. For example, in the rail cities of the early 1800s, homes and businesses clustered around rail lines.

But over time, cities sprawled well beyond their original boundaries. This chapter traces the history of suburbanization, based on historian Kenneth T. Jackson's classic account, *Crabgrass Frontier.* By the early nineteenth century, Jackson explains, cities shared five features.[1] First, they were densely settled and congested. Second, there was a clear distinction between city and country. Third, there was a mixture of functions, including homes, commerce, manufacturing, recreation, and schools. Fourth, distances were short; people lived close to where they worked, a necessity when commuting was on foot. Fifth, the most fashionable and respectable addresses tended to be located close to the center of town. In fact, members of the lower classes tended to live at the edges, and sub-urb connoted moral inferiority, the lairs of prostitutes, ne'er-do-wells, and rascals. "Suburbs, then," according to Jackson, "were socially and economically inferior to cities when wind, muscle, and water were the prime movers of civilization."[2]

There was an exception to this pattern: the country homes of the wealthy. Even in the earliest cities, members of privileged classes sought the fresher air of the nearby countryside, and built country homes and retreats. This occurred in Babylon as early as 2300 BC, in Italian city-states and in London by 1500, in Paris in the 1600s, and in U.S. cities such as Boston and Philadelphia by the 1700s. However, this did not develop into modern suburbanization—"a process involving the systematic growth of fringe areas at a pace more rapid than that of core cities, as a lifestyle involving a daily commute to jobs in the center"[3]—until the earliest part of the nineteenth century, in both Great Britain and the United States.

TRANSPORTATION

The nineteenth century saw a "transportation revolution" with the introduction of successive technological innovations, including the steam ferry, the omnibus, the commuter railroad, the horsecar, the elevated railroad, and the cable car. It became practical for the first time for large numbers of people to commute to a job in the city from a residence well beyond walking distance. Perhaps the earliest commuter suburb was Brooklyn Heights, a pleasant rural rise across the East River from Manhattan. Regular steam ferry service between lower Manhattan and Brooklyn began in 1814. Thanks to easy access, attractive surroundings, cheap land, and low taxes, Brooklyn grew at a faster rate than New York for much of the nineteenth century, its population doubling almost every decade until the Civil War. By the 1840s, Walt Whitman, then a Brooklyn newspaperman, could describe a commuting scene that seems strangely familiar nearly two centuries later:

> In the morning there is one incessant stream of people— employed in New York on business—tending toward the ferry. This rush commences soon after six o'clock. . . . It is highly edifying to see the phrenzy exhibited by certain portions of the younger gentlemen, a few rods from the landing, when the bell strikes . . . they rush forward as if for dear life, and woe to the fat woman or unwieldy person of any kind, who stands in their way.[4]

Some of the modern tension between central city and suburb was also evident in the early days of Brooklyn's development. One critic noted that Brooklyn "sold nature wholesale" to developers, who then sold lots retail to homeowners. Back in Manhattan, some New Yorkers expressed concern over "the desertion of the city by its men of wealth."[5]

The steam ferry was followed by a number of other transportation innovations. Omnibus service—horse-drawn coaches on regular routes and schedules—began in New York in 1829, and appeared in Philadelphia, Boston, Baltimore, and other cities within the next decade or two, typically with a charter granted by a city government to one or more private companies. The disadvantages included very rough rides and slow speeds. Steam railroads developed beginning in the 1830s, and by the 1840s some were functioning as commuter lines. By 1849 there were 59 commuter trains arriving daily in Boston. Horse railways arose in the 1850s and 1860s as a more comfortable alternative to omnibuses. By the mid-1880s, 415 street railway companies operated nationwide over 6,000 miles of track and carried 188 million passengers per year. These also became part of integrated transportation systems, linking with omnibus, train, and ferry routes. Thus, as the nineteenth century drew to a close, urban mass transit—including extensive links to suburban locations—made commuting from outside the city a practical and attractive choice for increasing numbers of Americans.

Geographer Peter O. Muller has emphasized the importance of transportation in defining urban form.[6] He identifies four distinct eras in American urban development, as shown in Figure 2-1.

THE PULL OF THE SUBURBS

There were also deep-rooted cultural values, some rooted in European thinking, that blossomed in the United States and encouraged the growth of suburbs. These can be grouped into domesticity, privacy, and isolation.

Family and home were central in several ways. First, religious thinking highly valued the family. Second, between 1820 and 1850, "work and men left the home" and the home came to be regarded as the woman's sphere, morally superior to the outside world. Third, an increasingly industrial world raised grave concerns about the transitoriness and speed of everyday life, and domesticity came to be seen as a counterweight. Finally, business leaders were eager for people to own their own homes, to "chain" them to their mortgages. As the result of these factors, says Jackson, "The single-family dwelling became the paragon of middle-class housing, the most visible symbol of having arrived at a fixed place in society, the goal to which every decent family aspired."[7] Early postwar suburban developers, in such places as Levittown, would skillfully market these values.

■ **FIGURE 2-1**   The development of urban form in relation to transportation

Walking horsecar

Electric streetcar

Recreational auto

Freeway

SOURCE: Adapted from P. O. Muller, "Transportation and Urban Form: Stages in the Spatial Evolution of the American Metropolis" in S. Hanson, Ed., *The Geography of Urban Transportation* (New York: Guildford Press, 1995).

There were also traditional values concerning land. Land ownership had for centuries been an important marker of wealth and social position. Moreover, a love of land, and antipathy toward cities, had been a tradition, especially in England. Against this backdrop, the role of land in daily life changed during the nineteenth century. With the growth of commercial agriculture, Americans no longer needed to grow garden products for food. This contributed to a less utilitarian view of land, and the lawn came to be viewed as a picturesque setting for the family home. At the same time, an idealized view of nature arose during the nineteenth century, replacing some earlier conceptions of a hostile, dangerous natural world. The New England transcendentalists, painters of the Hudson River School, and writers such as Washington Irving and James Fenimore Cooper, promoted this newer view.

The romance with land and nature soon influenced popular culture. Catharine Beecher (1800–1878) wrote influential books and articles on housekeeping and "domestic economy" that promoted the detached, semirural cottage as the ideal family setting. Andrew Jackson Downing (1815–1852), a nurseryman, horticulturist, architectural critic, essayist, and park advocate, opposed rows of houses and championed country homes. Downing defined a bucolic lifestyle for America, and called for the use of natural landscape features, curvilinear streets, and larger lots. Calvert Vaux (1824–1895), an Englishman, came to Newburgh, New York, in 1850 to work with Downing as a landscape architect. Vaux also advocated country homes with landscaped yards, and was to go on to collaborate with Frederick Law Olmsted (1822–1903) in Central Park and other major projects.

These developments resonated with American homeowners. There had always been a strain of anti-urban thinking in the United States, initially and for many years a nation of farmers. "I view cities," Thomas Jefferson famously wrote in 1800, "as pestilential to the morals, the health, and the liberties of man."[8] Cities were increasingly unpleasant places to live, viewed as unwholesome hotbeds of disease, noise, air pollution, crime, and the "foreign born," to which suburban homes could offer a solution. "The atmosphere at WARWICK VILLA is delightful, cool, bracing and envigorating [sic]," claimed an 1873 newspaper ad for a Louisville suburban development, "NO MALARIA, coal soot, smoke, dust or factories."[9]

As the nineteenth century unfolded, these values transformed the view of the city, and established a place in the popular mind for the suburbs. "By romanticizing the benefits of private space and by combining the imagery of the New England village with the notion of Thomas Jefferson's gentleman farmer," according to Jackson, "individuals like Catharine Beecher, Andrew Jackson Downing, and Calvert Vaux created a new image of the city as an urban-rural continuum and spawned a remarkable generation of landscape architects . . . who proposed fundamental changes in the form of the metropolis. By the 1870s the word *suburb* no longer implied inferiority or derision."[10]

Suburbs Romantic and Practical

The grid was a popular configuration for cities and towns in the early eighteenth and nineteenth centuries. It seemed efficient and orderly, it packed a lot into the available space, it was scaled to pedestrians, and it facilitated development. But during the nineteenth century, criticism arose. The grid came to be associated with tenements and congestion, disconnected from the increasingly valued landscape. One solution, espoused by the City Beautiful Movement, was broad avenues. Another, which arose in the early planned suburban communities, was the winding street. In the decade before the Civil War, New York drug merchant Llewellyn S. Haskell decided to build these principles into a new suburban development, Llewellyn Park, in West Orange, New Jersey. Haskell hired Alexander Jackson Davis (1803–1892), a protégé of Andrew Jackson Downing, to design and build the project. Llewellyn Park was built as a commuter community, with lots that averaged 3 acres, curvilinear streets, an open space at the center (the Ramble), a ban on industry, and no fences. Frederick Law Olmsted, also a protégé of Andrew Jackson Downing, pursued this vision with great intensity, becoming the most prominent landscape architect and planner in the post–Civil War generation. Olmsted designed numerous suburbs, including Riverside (Chicago), Brookline and Chestnut Hill (Boston), Sudbrook and Roland Park (Baltimore), and Yonkers and Tarrytown Heights (New York). He also utilized curved roads, large lots, and extensive tree plantings. As part of his Riverside plan, he conceived of a dedicated turnpike into Chicago. Although it was never completed, this combination of suburban land use and automobile-friendly transportation planning was prophetic.

New concepts of suburban design merged with business initiatives during the nineteenth century, giving rise to many planned suburban developments. Some failed, such as Garden City, Long Island, demonstrating that not all patterns of development were commercially viable. (Garden City's developers rented rather than sold lots, and made no provision for amenities such as schools and churches.) Others, such as Mount Vernon, New York, succeeded but evolved away from their planners' visions. (Mount Vernon was initially a working-class community, a project of the Industrial Home Owners Society Number One, but original owners later sold their homes to more affluent new arrivals.) Still others, such as Vineland, New Jersey, flourished.

A special kind of suburban development in the years after the Civil War was the railroad suburb. Commuter rail service expanded greatly between 1865 and 1900 in cities such as Chicago, Philadelphia, New York, and Boston. Railroad suburbs reached their apex around 1920, but some, including such American fixtures as Philadelphia's Main Line, are still thriving. The early railroad suburbs were socioeconomically diverse, and included housing for poor and working-class people either in servant's quarters or in modest dwellings around the railroad station. Over time, a continuing challenge was the cost of railroad commuting, which remained somewhat out of reach for poor and working-class families.

Some of the advantages offered by commuter railroads were extended by trolley car systems. By the 1880s, alternatives to the slow and messy horsecar were being sought. Cable cars were installed in some larger cities in the last two decades of the nineteenth century, but these were expensive, inefficient, and prone to disconnect from their cables. Electric streetcars, or trolleys, appeared at about the same time (Figure 2-2). These were relatively fast, less expensive to build, and less expensive to operate, so lower fares were possible. Richmond, Virginia, installed the first successful trolley line in 1887, and other cities quickly followed suit. By 1903 there were 30,000 miles of street railways in the United States, almost all of it electrified. Trolleys, together with contemporary technological advances such as elevators and skyscrapers, were a major contributor to the phenomenal growth of cities from 1890 to 1950. Large numbers of workers could now converge on central locations. This, in turn, increased the value of urban real estate, an indirect spur to suburban growth.

■ **FIGURE 2-2** Early electric trolleys in Denver, 1863

SOURCE: Photo by Louis Charles McClure, courtesy of the Denver Public Library.

Trolleys also played a major role in opening up new urban corridors to development. Streetcar companies extended their lines beyond the city into open country, actively facilitating outward movement. In some cases, they built recreational destinations at the ends of the lines, such as Coney Island. More important, streetcar owners forged alliances with real estate developers, promoting large residential developments along streetcar lines, in Oakland, Los Angeles, Washington, and other cities. To assure the success of these ventures, streetcar fares were kept low, typically five cents. Indeed, the presence of trolley lines emerged as a major predictor of growth in a suburban location. "The electric streetcar was vital," writes Jackson, "in opening up the suburbs for the common man."[11]

Together, communities from Oakland to Riverside, from Brookline to the Main Line, established that there was a viable third way between dense urban dwelling and rural life. By the 1870s, a suburban home was a fashionable and increasingly popular alternative. And by the turn of the century, suburbs were a significant part of the American housing scene.

Houses in the Suburbs

Residential suburbs could not have developed without plentiful, affordable houses. In the years following the Civil War, several major factors greatly expanded the availability of affordable housing. One was inexpensive construction methods. The balloon-frame house, developed in the 1830s, was built of a small number of standardized parts and required relatively little labor and craftsmanship to construct. The resulting house was both strong and affordable. A second factor was cheap land. Land in the United States was relatively plentiful and therefore inexpensive, especially during the three decades of agricultural depression that followed the Civil War. A third factor was favorable tax policies. The pattern was established early of building infrastructure such as roads and sewers at public expense—and, in the case of outlying areas, of taxing the entire city to pay for these. And with mortgage interest deductible from taxes, people found a powerful incentive for home ownership. Finally, the rapid expansion of public utilities supported the proliferation of new homes.[12] And as immigrants increasingly arrived in the late nineteenth and early twentieth centuries, willing to make major sacrifices to achieve home ownership, the availability of affordable homes was a significant draw to the suburbs.

Suburban houses were not just built when new residents appeared, money in hand. Instead, land speculators and private developers drove much of the design and construction. Developers purchased large parcels; created subdivisions; and arranged public transportation, road construction, sewer and water service; and other infrastructure—often at public expense. These were deliberate and large-scale efforts. "The theory that early suburbs just grew, with owners turning cowpaths and natural avenues of traffic into streets, is erroneous."[13]

EXPANDING CITIES: FROM GROWTH TO NO GROWTH

During the period of rapid urban growth in the nineteenth century, cities typically grew in size as they grew in population. There were two methods available—annexation and consolidation. In annexation, a city added unincorporated land to its area; in consolidation, one municipal government absorbed another, usually adjacent, municipal government. The city of Philadelphia consolidated with the county in 1854, expanding its area from 2 square miles to 130 square miles. Major waves of annexation and consolidation occurred in St. Louis in 1856 and 1970, in Chicago in 1889, in New York in 1898 (when Brooklyn, the nation's fourth largest city, and Queens joined Manhattan), and in Detroit between 1880 and 1918.

There were several reasons for annexation. One was urban pride and boosterism. Another was the notion, championed by the business community, that large would be more efficient than small. In some cases the city government, or particular constituencies, wanted to extend greater control over outlying areas. And less affluent suburban areas needed access to the infrastructure of the city—the sewers, the schools, the water, the police force—that might have been prohibitively expensive for them.

As the years passed, suburbs developed their own identities, and by the twentieth century, voters were rejecting annexation. Racial, ethnic, and class distinctions increasingly set the suburbs apart from the city. Emerging laws allowed suburbs to maintain these distinctions; it became easy for suburban towns to incorporate, but difficult for cities to accomplish annexation. Accordingly, wealthier suburbs were more likely to remain independent than were poorer ones. At the same time, suburban services improved. This was achieved in part through the use of special service districts such as the Massachusetts District Commission (providing sewage treatment in 1889, parks in 1893, and water in

1895). As a result, annexation has become less and less common in the growth of cities. Instead, cities are bordered by a patchwork of independent suburban jurisdictions. This poses a dilemma for the governance of metropolitan areas, as they confront issues that are regional in scale and require coordinated action.

THE AUTOMOBILE AGE

Forerunners of the automobile appeared as early as the 1860s in both Europe and the United States, and automobile technology advanced rapidly in the last years of the nineteenth century. But affordable cars, especially the Model T Ford, were not mass-produced until the first two decades of the twentieth century. For several reasons, Americans were initially slow to adopt cars. Laws restricted the use of cars. Roads were poorly surfaced. Early automobiles were technically unreliable and physically uncomfortable. Finally, the absence of road signs made it difficult to navigate. But the automobile culture developed rapidly, and by the mid-1920s, automobile ownership was an essential part of normal, middle-class life.[14]

Numerous interests promoted the growth of automobiles. Road building became a publicly financed enterprise instead of, say, dependent on user fees—a major policy decision that greatly subsidized and encouraged driving. By the 1920s, a coalition of special interests including tire, oil, automobile, and road-building interests and land developers had formed and was pushing more road construction. In time, the very concept of the road changed, from an open, public space to an artery for motor vehicles.[15] Limited access expressways first appeared on a large scale between 1906 and 1911 with the construction of the Long Island Motor Parkway, and by the 1920s a large number had been built across the country.

Even as public investment flowed to road construction, mass transportation continued to be viewed as a private initiative that needed to be self-supporting (assumptions that survive and operate even today). Faced with the competition of automobiles, streetcar companies had three options: increase ridership (they tried), seek public subsidies (they were unsuccessful), and raise fares (which cities did not permit). Moreover, between 1926 and 1956, General Motors systematically bought and dismantled streetcar lines across the country, substituting buses.[16] The nation's trolley system crumbled. The number of trolley cars peaked in 1917, ridership peaked in 1923, and both declined precipitously in the 1930s. By 1985 trolleys continued to run on only a few lines in Philadelphia, Boston, New Orleans, San Francisco, Pittsburgh, and Newark.

Automobiles continued to assert a role in every aspect of middle-class life—making a living, making a home, raising the young, leisure, religion, and community activities. In rural areas, the impact was considerable. Farm life became much more convenient, even as mechanization greatly decreased the labor requirement; the farm population declined from 32 percent in 1900 to 23 percent in 1940 to 3 percent in 1980. In urban areas, cars gave rise to a downtown business boom, as mobility increased, but by the 1920s the apparent boon was yielding to the difficulty of driving and parking in downtown areas. The major benefit was to suburban areas. Undeveloped land on metropolitan fringes became prime real estate, and enormous development occurred during the 1920s. From 1920 to 1930 the suburbs of the largest ninety-six cities grew twice as fast as the core cities.[17] And by 1933, the President's Research Committee on Social Trends noted that "imperceptibly, car ownership has created an 'automobile psychology.' The automobile has become a dominant influence in the life of the individual and he, in a real sense, has become dependent upon it."[18]

Automobile-oriented destinations began to appear. Kansas City's Country Club Plaza, built in 1922 by developer J. J. Nickol, was the first regional shopping mall, and the surrounding district quickly became a prototype car-based planned suburb. It embodied three design precepts: no right angles or gridiron streets, no wanton destruction of trees, and attention to natural land contours. And as automobile suburbs developed from the 1920s on, they differed from previous suburbs in four respects. First, the overall pattern of settlement was dispersed, since proximity to trolley lines no longer defined corridors of development extending like fingers from the central city. Second, commuting patterns changed, as employment in the suburbs grew. Not all suburban residents now commuted radially, from suburb to central city; some could work locally, or commute circumferentially to other suburban locations. Third, there was a dispersion of employment, with trucks moving raw materials and finished products throughout the metropolitan region. Finally, new forms of low-density residential architecture emerged, with simpler, less expensive houses built on larger lots, forming a less dense pattern of land use.

ZONING

Chapter 1 identified three defining features of sprawl as low density, low land use mix, and low connectivity. If automobiles made low density possible, then zoning laws enshrined the separation of different land uses that typifies many metropolitan areas.

Zoning has been defined as "the practice of allocating different areas of cities for different uses, much as rooms in a house serve different functions."[19] Zoning regulations first appeared in Germany and California in the late nineteenth century, in Germany to keep abattoirs out of residential areas, and in California as a discriminatory tool to restrict Chinese laundries from certain neighborhoods. Between 1909 and 1915, Los Angeles implemented zoning regulations to separate industrial and residential areas, and in 1916, New York City adopted a zoning code that defined commercial, retail, and residential districts of the city. Proponents claimed that zoning would reduce fluctuations in real estate values, safeguard the interest of property owners, and create a more orderly and organized city. In particular, separating residential districts from noxious industrial uses was seen as an important public health strategy.

Property owners, on the other hand, challenged zoning laws as unfair restrictions on property rights. The final legal decision came in the landmark 1926 Supreme Court case of *Village of Euclid* v. *Ambler Realty Company*. Euclid, a lakeside farming community of 2,000 outside Cleveland, had adopted its first-ever zoning code in 1922. The village was divided into six use districts: single-family, two-family, apartment house, retail-wholesale stores, commercial, and industrial. The residential district included nearly half of a 68-acre parcel along Euclid Avenue owned by the Ambler Realty Company, a Cleveland firm that had planned to sell the land for industrial use. Ambler challenged the zoning code, and the case made its way to the Supreme Court. In an influential amicus brief, Cincinnati lawyer and planning pioneer Alfred Bettman justified zoning as a legitimate and effective way to control nuisances and to protect public health, morals, and general welfare. The Court agreed and validated the concept of zoning.[20]

Over the last eighty years zoning has become a standard tool in town and city planning. Its record of accomplishment is mixed. On the positive side, zoning has helped establish that private property rights must sometimes yield to the public interest and has kept some incompatible uses separated. However, many argue that zoning has not produced the high-quality living and working environments that early proponents promised. The separation of different land uses went far beyond separating abattoirs from homes; zoning came to be used to separate uses that were neither inconsistent nor noxious, such as retail stores from homes. Suburban communities have misused zoning to exclude low-income and minority families, most effectively by limiting multifamily and other affordable forms of housing, creating one of the principal legal devices for segregation by income, race, and ethnicity. Suburban policies have concentrated undesirable uses in central cities. And zoning, as a local process, is unable to address regional problems, unlike broader growth management strategies.[21]

Today, we are left with a legacy of rigid separation of different land uses. Even within categories, such as residential, different subcategories are separated; in many areas, zoning codes prohibit multifamily housing in single-family districts. Such practices lead to residential segregation by social class (see Chapter 10) and raise disturbing questions of social equity. They also thwart elderly people who want to downsize while remaining in their neighborhoods. In addition, the practical effect is to create the long distances between different uses that are a fundamental characteristic of sprawl. Low-income workers, for example, are systematically distanced from their workplaces, requiring long commutes. These long distances, in turn, contribute to a heavy reliance on automobile travel.

FEDERAL HOUSING POLICY AND SUBURBAN GROWTH

Government housing and lending policies during and after the Great Depression greatly encouraged suburbanization. Prior to the 1930s, housing was generally not regarded as a government responsibility. However, the Great Depression inflicted crippling blows on the construction industry and on homeowners, so the federal government took action. The Hoover administration supported four initiatives: long-term amortized mortgages, low interest rates, government aid to private efforts to house low-income families, and reduction of home construction costs. Legislation to implement these goals, however, was generally ineffective.

The Home Owners Loan Corporation, formed in 1933 to refinance foreclosed mortgages, signaled the entry of the federal government into mortgage lending. A year later, the National Housing Act created the Federal Housing Administration (FHA), which insured long-term residential mortgages made by private lenders. This permitted lower down payments than had ever existed and extended the repayment period from five or ten years to as long as thirty years. The long-term, self-amortizing mortgage became a path to home ownership for millions of Americans.

The FHA also established minimum standards for home construction, verified by on-site inspections, and standardized appraisal practices. It went farther, devising a system for rating neighborhoods for loan-worthiness. FHA policies hastened the decay of older urban neighborhoods in at least three ways. First, the FHA favored construction of single-family dwellings over multifamily projects. Second, repair loans were kept small and of short duration, discouraging improvement and maintenance of older, urban properties. And third, the FHA appraisal scheme undervalued older properties, introducing bias in favor of suburbs. One part of the appraisal scheme was explicit "ideal home" provisions regarding such attributes as lot size and setback from the street. In practice, racially mixed and minority neighborhoods were also devalued, the forerunner of modern loan and insurance discrimination against certain neighborhoods known as "redlining."[22] And as private lenders adopted FHA policies, the influence of these policies went far beyond government lending. By 1966, when a major policy shift finally made mortgages available to inner cities, urban flight was well under way, and the policy only made it easier for White families to flee the cities.

URBAN SPRAWL IN THE POSTWAR YEARS

As soldiers returned home from World War II, the nation faced an acute housing shortage in the face of enormous pent-up demand (Figure 2-3). Vigorous federal responses, including the Veterans Administration mortgage program and increased mortgage insurance for the FHA, helped fuel an unprecedented building boom in the postwar years. An innovative approach to homebuilding—large-scale standardized developments such as Levittown—first appeared at this time. These postwar suburban developments were located at the periphery of the cities, had relatively low density, were architecturally monotonous (both within developments and across the nation), and were economically and racially homogeneous (Figure 2-4). They offered the promise of readily available housing, within reach of working- and middle-class families. Along with this form of suburban development arose zoning restrictions, which protected residential interests in the suburbs and commercial interests in the cities.

As suburban development rapidly accelerated, and large distances needed to be traversed, the nation's automobile infrastructure developed rapidly. Beginning in 1943, the American Road Builders Association lobbied strongly for the creation of an interstate highway system.

■ **FIGURE 2-3** Postwar dreams of suburban living

SOURCE: Image courtesy of the America Historical Association.

This coalition included oil, rubber, asphalt, and construction industries; car dealers and renters; trucking and bus concerns; banks; and labor unions. The Interstate Highway Act, passed in 1956, provided for a 41,000-mile highway system. Construction was funded from a

■ **FIGURE 2-4**   Post-World War II suburban development: Levittown, Long Island, New York

SOURCE: Photo courtesy of Corbis.com.

uniquely inflexible source: nondivertible highway revenues from gasoline taxes. According to Jackson, this funding arrangement left the United States with "the world's best road system and very nearly its worst public-transit offerings."[23] An entire culture grew up around the automobile, with a panoply of icons: garages, motels, drive-in movies, service stations, shopping centers, house trailers and mobile homes, and fast-food franchises. The very form of cities began to change. Factories and offices were dispersed from traditional urban centers, and the "centerless city" appeared.

Numerous authors lamented the result. As early as 1964, Lewis Mumford wrote that when the American people voted for the Interstate Highway Act, "the most charitable thing to assume about this action is that they hadn't the faintest notion of what they were doing." Mumford lamented the "religion of the motorcar," and predicted that the exclusive dependence on cars, at the expense of other modes of transportation, would create both inefficient transportation and cultural decline.[24] And twenty years later, Kenneth Jackson seemed to give voice to Mumford's prediction: "Garish signs, large parking lots, one-way streets, drive-in windows, and throw-away fast-food buildings—all associated with the world of suburbia—have replaced the slower-paced, neighborhood-oriented institutions of an earlier generation."[25]

CONCLUSION

Sprawl, as we know it today, appears deceptively chaotic. In fact, it is a highly ordered and predictable form of development. An edifice of public and private instruments erected over the past three-quarters of a century reinforces and extends sprawl. In addition to the zoning codes discussed earlier, subdivision regulations, development financing, and housing lending policies, to name just a few such instruments, converge to the same end. Private sector practices such as the financing of commercial and residential development also contribute to the ordered replication of sprawl.

Financial institutions that lend money for development, for instance, readily lend to developers and builders of conventional sprawl, while making it very difficult for neotraditional and other alternative developers to borrow money. Banks maintain separate departments that correspond to different land uses; the department that finances residential construction does not lend for new retail developments and vice versa. As a result, no single department within a bank has the authority to make decisions about the viability of the projects that mix different uses. Departmental officials often lack the tools to evaluate the financial viability of mixed-use projects, and they do not possess the conceptual vision needed to understand how a mixed-use project would be profitable. Moreover, real estate financing is systematically biased against the kinds of long-term investments that add character to a community and that could help alleviate the worst excesses of sprawl.

The replication of sprawl through development financing is, unfortunately, even more ingrained than this one example suggests. Chris Leinberger, a commercial real estate expert, asserts that real estate financing decisions are based upon a very short time horizon, perhaps five to seven years, during which all real estate investments are expected to generate the full return on the initial investment.[26] As a result, only those developments that skimp on materials and architectural content (think of the quality of design of chain development) will be financed. Because investors refuse to value anything beyond five or seven years, developers cannot obtain financing for structures that are built to hold their value over time. Unfortunately, developments that will add value to a community over time require a good deal of initial investment; good architecture does not come cheap, nor do all of the amenities that people value such as sidewalks, plazas, public art, attractive plantings, and so on.

What does the future hold in store? Nearly twenty years ago, Jackson completed his history of the suburbs by describing a long-term cycle of urban land use, from initial development to abandonment to redevelopment. He predicted that suburbanization would eventually slow, driven by increasingly scarce and expensive fossil fuel, rising land costs, the cost of money, static building technology, new federal efforts to spur redevelopment and renovation, and the changing structure of the family. While some of these changes have begun to appear, especially with the redevelopment of numerous urban "brownfields" and failing residential areas, others of Jackson's predictions, such as the increase in gasoline prices, have not materialized. We can be sure that the population pressure of a growing country, predicted to reach nearly 600 million by the year 2100, will create stiff demand for further housing. However, some of the negative consequences of sprawl, such as congestion and the health burden discussed in this book, are already pressing issues for those who live in the suburbs. As the demand for livable alternatives rises, the history of sprawl will undoubtedly come to feature other forms of development.

CHAPTER 3

THE EVOLUTION OF URBAN HEALTH

The urban environment fostered the spread of diseases with crowded, dark, unventilated housing; unpaved streets mired in horse manure and littered with refuse; inadequate or nonexisting water supplies; privy vaults unemptied from one year to the next; stagnant pools of water; ill-functioning open sewers; stench beyond the twentieth-century imagination; and noises from clacking horse hooves, wooden wagon wheels, street railways, and unmuffled industrial machinery.[1]
—J. W. Leavitt,
The Healthiest City: Milwaukee and the Politics of Health Reform, 1982

Two hundred years ago, as the nineteenth century dawned, it must have seemed dangerous to live in one of America's major cities. The 60,000 people in New York, or the 40,000 in Philadelphia, or the 25,000 in Boston might have been proud of the emerging culture and commerce in their cities. But out their front doors and down their streets, they saw (and smelled) sordid, unhealthy places. Many might have quietly agreed with Thomas Jefferson's famous verdict that cities were "pestilential to the morals, the health, and the liberties of man."[2] With yellow fever ravaging American cities at the time, Jefferson's opinion certainly had some basis. In fact, while acknowledging the yellow fever epidemics as "great evils," Jefferson thought that they might have a salutary effect: "yellow fever will discourage the growth of great cities in our nation." Not to be outdone, the great colonial physician Benjamin Rush wrote Jefferson that he considered cities "in the same light that I do abscesses on the human body, viz., as reservoirs of all the impurities of a community."[3]

Just as the evolution of public health has been described as an "epidemiologic transition," the environmental health of cities—in fact, the very meaning of "urban health"—also evolved through history. According to the epidemiologic transition framework, countries pass through three stages of demographic and health changes as they develop. The Age of Pestilence and Famine lasted for most of human history; although birth rates were high, death rates were also high—at times extremely high—due to epidemics, famines, and war. Most people died of infectious diseases. The Age of Receding Pandemics came next, beginning in the mid-nineteenth century (in Europe and North America). Death rates fell as a result of better sanitation, nutrition, and medical advances, so population grew rapidly. Finally, during the Age of Degenerative and Man-Made Diseases, birthrates fell to about the same level as death rates, population stabilized, and cancer and cardiovascular diseases emerged as major causes of death.[4] Recent writers have suggested additional stages, such as the Age of Delayed Degenerative Diseases, to account for unexpected modern developments such as long-term disability.[5]

In the same way, health in the urban context has evolved through what we might call the "urban epidemiologic transition." Infectious diseases dominated the health profile of early cities, which did without clean water, sewage treatment, and trash collection. Sanitary improvements during the nineteenth century controlled many of these threats, but at the same time, industrialization introduced the threats of pollution. And as urban populations grew in waves during the nineteenth and twentieth centuries, sometimes at a dizzying pace, cities became foci of concentrated poverty, social dislocation, and crime.

None of these problems has disappeared, although all have been tamed to some extent. Infectious diseases continue to spread in cities, as the HIV epidemic and recent outbreaks of SARS illustrate. Industrial pollution continues to challenge some cities, although at levels well below those of fifty or a hundred years ago. And the problems of poverty and social dislocation continue to plague the poor parts of every city. In the rapidly growing cities of the poor nations of the world, of course, each of these problems persists, often in tragic proportions.

This chapter traces the history of urban environmental health problems from the early days of American cities to the present. It is a history that unfolded against a backdrop of profound physical and demographic changes in cities. And it is a history that set the stage for a new set of urban health concerns, growing out of the land use and transportation patterns known as sprawl.

URBAN PESTILENCE AND FILTH

As Europeans began to settle North America, health was one of the great attractions. The New World had bracing fresh air, plenty of open land, pure water, and a merciful lack of disease—all a sharp contrast with the crowded, pestilential cities of Europe. In 1630 John Winthrop extolled New England with these words: "Here is sweet aire faire rivers and plenty of springes and the water better than in Eng[land] here can be noe want of any thinge to those who bring meane[s] to raise out of the earth and sea."[6] A visitor to New York in 1670 wrote of the ideal climate, the seasonable showers, "a sweet and pleasant air, and . . . such Influences as tend to the Health both of Man and Beast."[7]

But as early settlements grew into established towns, the health consequences of more concentrated and varied human activity became clear. "Compared to modern cities," notes historian John Duffy, "colonial towns were odorous and lacked effective water, sewer and street-cleaning systems."[8] All residents of cities confronted these problems, but for the poor, the lack of sanitation could be far more awful. Most early-nineteenth-century urban residents, writes historian Charles Rosenberg, "lived in tiny unventilated apartments, often with whole families—and perhaps a few boarders—occupying the same room, a condition deplored by physicians and moralists alike. The most miserable and degraded lived in unfinished cellars, their walls a mat of slime, sewage, and moisture after every rain. Houses adjoined stables, abattoirs, and soap factories; their front yards were the meeting place of dogs, swine, chickens, and horses."[9]

Beginning in the late eighteenth century, and continuing through the Civil War, the growth of cities far outpaced their ability to manage sanitary problems. These problems fell into several categories: garbage, commercial activity, sewage, water, air, and housing.

Garbage (including dead animals and manure)

In colonial towns and cities, horses provided the transportation, and cows, pigs, sheep, and goats provided food. Stables, dairies, and pigsties were located throughout business and residential areas. Dogs and cats ran wild. When alive, all these animals deposited vast quantities of manure—an average of 22 pounds per horse per day, or (assuming one horse for every ten or twenty people in the city) 1 or 2 pounds of horse manure per person.[10] When they died, there were carcasses to contend with, on the streets and in vacant lots. In addition to the manure and dead animals, there was refuse from households and from a wide range of businesses, from butchers to tanneries.[11]

Both humans and animals were recruited in early efforts to collect and remove trash. As early as 1666, Boston appointed a scavenger to impound stray cows and horses, and to remove dead animals and other carrion from the streets.[12] New York followed in 1695,[13] and by the eighteenth century all major towns had such an official. Citizens were required to sweep up the streets in front of their homes and place the contents in the scavengers' carts. However, whether because of graft, inadequate funding, or inefficiency, the scavengers often did not arrive. New Yorkers came to call the decomposing piles of filth in their streets "corporation pie" as an ironic tribute to the city government.[14] Some cities had to supplement ineffective, public trash collection arrangements with requirements for private action. In Washington, for example, two 1809 ordinances addressed what must have been current practices. One forbade citizens from cleaning fish in the streets, and the second required owners to remove the carcasses of their dead animals from streets and public places within twenty-four hours.[15] When trash was picked up, either by scavengers or by responsible citizens, it often made it no farther than vacant lots and nearby waterways.

Hogs were an important adjunct to human efforts at trash collection. Running wild in the streets, they performed "Herculean service" in eating trash (in the words of Frances Trollope).[16] Packs of dogs, goats, and geese also helped. Charleston even passed a law protecting turkey buzzards, which swooped in obligingly to eat carrion from the streets.[17]

But these efforts did not keep the cities clean. The *Pittsburgh Gazette* sarcastically editorialized in 1800: "some folks have no objection to the smell of warm tripe and garbage, to wading through puddles of green stagnant water, or to skating over dabs of ordure. What if a few citizens should be carried off by fluxes and fevers? It would be of no consequence, as our population is rapidly increasing."[18] Long-skirted ladies had to suffer the indignities of trailing their hems through liquefied manure.[19] Years later, major cities had still not managed to clean up the streets. In 1864, the inspector of New York City's Eleventh Ward wrote:

> As a rule, the streets are extremely dirty and offensive, and the gutters obstructed with filth. The filth of the streets is composed of house-slops, refuse vegetables, decayed fruit, store and shop sweepings, ashes, dead animals, and even human excrements.

These putrefying organic substances are ground together by the constantly passing vehicles. When dried by the summer's heat, they are driven by the wind in every direction in the form of dust. When remaining moist or liquid in the form of "slush," they emit deleterious and very offensive exhalations. The reeking stench of the gutters, the street filth, and domestic garbage of this quarter of the city, constantly imperil the health of its inhabitants. It is a well-recognized cause of diarrheal diseases and fevers.[20]

By the late 1800s, New York City's offal contractors were removing as many as 15,000 dead horses from the city's streets each year.[21] By modern standards, these solid waste problems are almost inconceivable.

The "Noxious Trades"

Early industry was another source of filth. Many workshops and factories were located close to (and sometimes within) homes. Historian John Duffy writes of the tribulations caused by "nuisance industries such as tanning, bone boiling, slaughtering, butchering, fishmongering, cloth dying, and starch making." For example, he writes,

> slaughterers and butchers drained the blood from slaughtered animals into gutters or drains and piled entrails, refuse, and hides outside their places of work until the fat-burners, bone-boilers, and tanners could come to take them away. The hides, complete with bits of flesh, the entrails, and other refuse were eventually hauled away to the establishments of other tradesmen, who then piled them on their own premises.[22]

Dairies generated large quantities of cow manure; even if they could sell it, as they often did, neighbors had to put up with the smell and the flies. Tanneries laid out skins to dry, emitting penetrating odors, accumulating pools of animal fat and chemicals, and attracting more insects.[23] And metalworkers released toxic fumes into their neighborhoods.

Milwaukee provides an interesting example of nuisance industries within a city. Both slaughterhouses and breweries discharged their wastes directly into waterways that ran through the city. The 1874 annual report of the city's health department described the perpetually turbulent water of Burnham's Canal, which flowed into the Menominee River and then into Lake Michigan. The water was "thick, inky, putrid . . . in a state of violent commotion, produced by the fermentation existing at the bottom. . . . The water, grains, cow manure, and other filthy matter was thrown by the power and explosive force of the gas generated many feet into the air . . . [resembling] some great subterranean explosive power."[24]

At a time when working people commuted by foot, distances from home to work were short, and people lived close to all manner of noxious trade. Organic waste material was common in many businesses, and trash collection was erratic. The results could be repulsive.

Sewage

Sewage disposal emerged as a challenge soon after the first towns were established in the New World. Early colonists used privy pits and cesspools, which often overflowed in the low-lying land of coastal settlements. In their homes they used slop buckets, which were emptied into the nearest street, ditch, or waterway. The earliest "sewers" were nothing more than open drainage ditches. In 1644, within twenty years of the founding of New Amsterdam (now New York), the first sanitary regulation attempted to address what must have been a problem already. It banned anyone from depositing filth and ashes, and provided "that no one shall make water" within the fort.[25]

During the eighteenth century, human waste management remained an individual responsibility. When collective efforts were made, they usually consisted of groups of neighbors collaborating to dig drainage ditches. As urban populations grew,

> [t]hese drains, or open sewers, soon became receptacles for every type of filth, all of which drained into the slips in the harbor. The solid material was deposited on the bottom of the slip; and when the tide was out, the stench, particularly in the summer, was almost unbearable.[26]

By the early nineteenth century, growing populations had made the problem of human waste disposal more pressing. "Overflowing cesspools and privies were a constant aesthetic outrage and menace to health. In many slum areas one privy often sufficed for twenty or more families. As a result, slum residents resorted to using tubs and bowls, which were simply emptied into the gutters."[27]

As the nineteenth century progressed, more and more cities installed water distribution systems. Ironically, these aggravated the sewage disposal problem. When water was supplied before there were effective ways to carry off wastewater, there were large volumes of contaminated water to contend with. The options were limited; wastewater could be dumped into the gutter, poured into a cesspool, or collected by a scavenger. Many households continued to use privies, which remained a serious sanitary problem. "In the poorer districts," writes Duffy,

> landlords were reluctant to spend money to have them emptied, with the result that they frequently overflowed. And even when this was not the case, the very emptying of privies created nuisances. Scavengers responsible for this task frequently overloaded their carts and bumped through the rough city streets, scattering their nauseous loads, or else left a trail of the carts' liquid contents as they passed. Large hospitals and hotels frequently poured the contents of their privies into the street gutters or open drains. Scavengers usually unloaded their cargoes of human wastes into the nearest water body or onto the most accessible piece of empty land. . . . [P]rivies remained a major health hazard and aesthetic offense until the advent of effective sewer systems during the late nineteenth century.[28]

Exposure to human waste was to have profound health consequences during the nineteenth century, as cholera and other diarrheal diseases, which are transmitted through contact with human waste, swept through the country repeatedly.

Clean Water

In early towns and cities, people drew their water from shallow wells or from the nearby rivers and streams. However, with even modest population growth, compounded by the absence of systematic sewage treatment and waste disposal, these sources quickly became contaminated. Before long only the poor used wells, and those who could afford it purchased water brought by wagon from pure springs and wells in the surrounding countryside (a situation that prevails in the cities of poor countries today). In addition to clean water for drinking, there was another reason to think of a reliable water supply—the need to fight fires.

It was during Boston's yellow fever outbreaks in the last decade of the eighteenth century that the city chartered the Boston Aqueduct Corporation to bring water from Jamaica Pond to the city (Figure 3-1). Although the germ theory of disease was not yet accepted, the supply

■ **FIGURE 3-1**   Boston in the 1700s. More wholesome than European cities, but with shallow wells, no sewage management, and no solid waste disposal.

SOURCE: Photo courtesy of the Bettman Archive at Corbis.com.

of fresh water was hailed as a way to control the "putrid and pestilential fevers, and other fatal diseases," that ravaged the city.[29] In 1799, Philadelphia began construction of its Centre Square Waterworks, to carry water more than a mile from the Schuylkill River through wood, and later cast iron, pipes. In New York, Assemblyman Aaron Burr obtained a charter for the Manhattan Company, a private firm that was to hold a monopoly on piped water for the next quarter of a century. It was not until 1842 that the Old Croton Aqueduct was completed, providing a reliable source of clean water for the city. As the nineteenth century progressed, more and more cities constructed waterworks—45 in 1830, 84 in 1850, 244 in 1870, 599 in 1880[30]—enabling citizens to rely on piped water rather than contaminated wells. But periodic cholera outbreaks provided a grim reminder that even piped water was not always clean. The first technique introduced for water purification was sand filtration, but as late as 1880 there were only three such systems in the United States.[31] Clean water continued to be a challenge until well into the twentieth century.

Air Quality

Air pollution is generally considered a by-product of the industrial age. Indeed, the intense use of fossil fuels that marked the industrial revolution in the nineteenth century greatly intensified the problem of dirty urban air. But even early colonial towns and cities had less than pristine air, thanks to a combination of rotting trash, swamp gas from poorly drained areas, and biomass combustion. Because diseases were attributed to "miasmas," the malodorous air was considered a health hazard and not merely a nuisance.

By 1704, a Charleston ordinance dealing with garbage removal and slaughterhouses began by noting that "[t]he air is greatly infected and many maladies and other intolerable diseases daily happen."[32] At the 1874 meeting of the American Public Health Association, Dr. Edward H. Janes spoke of the foul air in crowded parts of the city: "It is this odor which indicates the commencement of that condition known as crowd-poisoned atmosphere, and which, if allowed to increase, furnishes the specific germs which develop typhus, ship or jail fever."[33] Dr. Richard McSherry informed the Baltimore Academy of Medicine in 1882 that the city desperately needed cleaner air, since the city's polluted air from a "vast collection of decomposable refuse" and thousands of privy pits and cesspools was so bad "that adults grow ill and children die of it by the thousands, especially during the summer heats, with each recurring year."[34] Until the end of the nineteenth century, the concern for air quality was primarily geared to risk of infection.

Inadequate Housing

The rapid growth of American cities from 1800 to 1850, including a wave of immigration in the 1840s, led to a crisis of crowding and poor housing. As early as 1830, the urban slum was firmly established.[35] By the middle of the nineteenth century, builders in older cities such as New York were constructing housing on every inch of available space in certain districts. Conditions in these dwellings could be horrific. One sanitary inspector in Cincinnati, in 1865, told of a two-story tenement that housed 102 people, all sharing a single privy.[36] Jacob Riis's 1890 illustrated essay on squalid conditions in New York tenements, *How the Other Half Lives*, offers lasting testimony of the shocking conditions (Figures 3-2 and 3-3).

Contemporary observers recognized the association of poor housing with ill health. New York's city inspector, in his 1860

SOURCE: Jacob Riis image courtesy of the Bettman Archive at Corbis.com.

report, took note of excess mortality in some parts of the city, and wrote that

> [t]he causes of this excessive mortality . . . are readily traceable to the wretched habitations in which parents and children are forced to take up their abode; in the contracted alleys, the tenement house with its hundreds of occupants, where each cooks, eats, and sleeps in a single room, without light or ventilation, surrounded with filth, an atmosphere foul, fetid, and deadly, with none to console with or advise them, or to apply to for relief when disease invades them.[37]

A Milwaukee health officer echoed this view in his 1872 report: "This slaughter of innocents is found, chiefly, in crowded parts of the city, where families are massed together, in filthy, dark, ill-ventilated tenements, surrounded by dirty yards and alleys, foul privies, and imperfect drainage."[38]

■ FIGURE 3-3   Bandit's Roost, a squalid alley in late-nineteenth-century
New York

SOURCE: Jacob Riis image courtesy of the Bettman Archive at Corbis.com.

Particularly worrisome was the crowding that occurred in basements, which were often liable to flooding. A ward inspector during
New York's 1864 sanitary inspection described these homes:

> This submarine region is not only excessively damp, but is liable to
> sudden inroads from the sea. At high tide the water often wells up
> through the floors, submerging them to a considerable depth. In
> very many cases the vaults of privies are situated on the same or a
> higher level, and their contents frequently ooze through the walls
> into the occupied apartments beside them. Fully one-fourth of

these subterranean domiciles are pervaded by a most offensive odor from this source, and rendered exceedingly unwholesome as human habitations. These are the places in which we most frequently meet with typhoid fever and dysentery during the summer months.[39]

The early cities, then, posed a wide variety of health threats, known collectively as sanitary problems: garbage, the "noxious trades," sewage, contaminated water and air, and crowded, substandard housing. Together, these exposures led to high rates of infectious diseases, making early cities far less healthy than rural areas.

The Results: A Plethora of Infections

Infectious diseases struck early cities with appalling regularity. Yellow fever outbreaks occurred from the late eighteenth century through the first part of the nineteenth century. Cholera epidemics raged in waves during the nineteenth century (Figure 3-4). Smallpox ravaged urban populations until vaccination was broadly accepted in the early twentieth century. Typhus and typhoid were frequent. Cadwallader Colden, a physician in Philadelphia and New York, sought an explanation for the frequent outbreaks of fevers in the unhealthy city environment. He attributed the fevers to the effects of "noxious vapors from stagnating filthy water" on the "animal oeconomy [sic]," postulating that different kinds of miasmas arose from different kinds of filthy water or putrefying substances. Colden also pointed out that country children died at much lower rates than city children, which he attributed to the unsanitary conditions and dangerous miasmas of the city.[40]

The period 1793–1806 was the yellow fever era. Small outbreaks of yellow fever had occurred in the mid–eighteenth century, ending with the last one in Philadelphia in 1762. After more than thirty years without it, the first of the major yellow fever epidemics broke out in 1793, also in Philadelphia. It spread rapidly through the small but crowded city. The first cases occurred in early August, the first definite diagnosis was made on August 19, and by the end of August there were several hundred deaths. Within weeks, President Washington and most federal, state, and city officials had fled. The death toll remained at several hundred per week until well into the autumn, and surpassed 5,000—more than 10 percent of the city's population, a literal *deci*mation—by the time cold weather arrived and the epidemic abated. Yellow fever returned to Philadelphia in 1794, when it also reached Baltimore and New Haven. New York City had a full outbreak in 1795, and the major coastal cities suffered a yellow fever outbreak each summer until 1820.

The reaction was grim. A Philadelphia citizens group wrote at the time that "if the fever shall become an annual visitant, our cities must be abandoned, commerce will desert our coasts, and we, the citizens of this great metropolis, shall all of us, suffer much distress, and a great proportion of us be reduced to absolute ruin."[41]

The legacies of this era included quarantine stations, local public health agencies (then called "committees on health" or "boards of health"), local health officers, and marine hospitals, the forerunner of today's U.S. Public Health Service. After the 1820s, yellow fever ceased to be a major problem in cities north of Virginia, but it worsened in southern cities, peaking at midcentury.

By 1830, "with slum dwellers crowded together in damp, filthy housing, in some cases lacking even elementary sanitary facilities, and in all cases drinking highly polluted water, the stage was set for the first of the great Asiatic cholera epidemics."[42] These epidemics occurred in 1832, 1849, and 1866. Charles E. Rosenberg, in his classic history *The Cholera Years*, shows that the successive epidemics did more than take

■ **FIGURE 3-4**   Epidemics in ninteenth century cities and towns. This 1832 sign announced that cholera had overwhelmed a local cemetery.

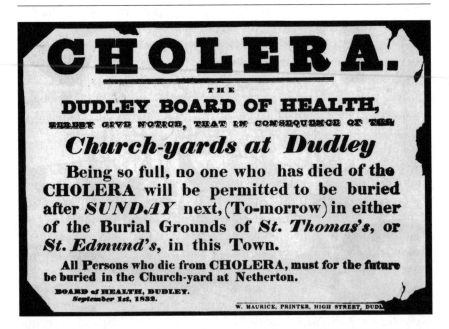

SOURCE: Bettman Archive at Corbis.com.

the lives of thousands of urban dwellers. They also signaled a loss of innocence and piety regarding urban life: "America was no longer a city set upon a hill."[43] In August 1849, as cholera ravaged the nation's cities, an Indiana minister wrote, "There is something radically wrong in the construction of our cities and villages. The Creator never designed that man should be deprived of the air, and light of heaven. Imperfect ventilation, impure water, and a crowded population, necessarily induce fevers and pestilence. . . . "[44]

Tuberculosis, known as "the sorrow of the cities,"[45] was recognized by the mid–nineteenth century as a major killer of urban residents. An 1872 textbook, *On the Treatment of Pulmonary Consumption by Hygiene, Climate, and Medicine*, advised that "the vitiated air breathed in cities, in the close crowded workshops, and in the closer and still more crowded sleeping rooms, gradually weakens constitutional powers, and constitutes one of the principle predisposing causes of Phthisis."[46] Typhoid, too, continued to plague the cities. Philadelphia lost more than 4,000 residents to the disease in the decade of the 1860s and over 6,000 by the decade of the 1880s.[47]

Cities, then, were incubators of infectious disease, from their origins as early settlements in the New World, through their rapid growth in the eighteenth and nineteenth centuries. Sanitary improvements in the nineteenth century began to tame this problem, thanks in part to some of the same technologies that heralded the dawn of the industrial revolution.

INDUSTRIAL POLLUTION IN CITIES

With the harnessing of fossil fuels and the rapid development of industry in the nineteenth century, industrial pollution became a hallmark of cities. This was not entirely new; some of Europe's older cities that relied on coal had for centuries suffered its consequences. In 1659, British intellectual and horticulturist John Evelyn wrote that London was immersed in "such a cloud of sea-coal, as if there be a resemblance of hell on earth."[48]

Pittsburgh, with its ready supply of coal to power foundries and forges, led the way in the United States. As early as 1800, a European traveler approaching the city wrote that "we were struck with a peculiarity nowhere else to be observed in the States: a cloud of smoke hung over it in an exceedingly clear sky."[49] In 1826 a city report stated that "the atmosphere is darkened with a 'sulphurous canopy' which nearly conceals the place from view" and gives the traveler "a dark and melancholy aspect of men and things (Figure 3-5)."[50]

■ **FIGURE 3-5**   Pittsburgh, 1890. Approaching visitors could see the "sulphurous canopy" for miles.

SOURCE: Photo courtesy of the Bettman Archive at Corbis.com.

Oil joined coal as a heavily used fossil fuel, and also contaminated city streets and properties, creating "ecological wastelands" as early as the Reconstruction era.[51] Most industrial waste was dumped into streams, rivers, and harbors, carrying on the tradition established with sewage, dead animals, garbage, and other refuse.[52] In 1864 Pittsburgh petitioned the Pennsylvania legislature to make it "a penal act to empty the chemicals and residium from the distillation of carbon oil into the Allegheny River."[53] Across the state, in Philadelphia, the growing chemical industry had contaminated the once-pristine Schuylkill River as it flowed through the industrial districts of Conshohocken, Norristown, and Manayunk. In 1883 the chief of the Philadelphia Water Bureau, in his annual report, described the Schuylkill as a "natural sewer," whose pollution was "as diversified as the occupation of the people: sewerage, chemical, wool-washing, dye stuff, butcher and brewery refuse—there is almost nothing lacking."[54] The situation was similar in Massachusetts industrial centers such as Lowell, Lawrence, and Springfield. A state board of health report in 1876 noted that "fluid refuse from . . . factories . . . some of it very poisonous, produced in the processes of cleaning and preparing the manufactured article . . . forms the chief element in the pollution of these streams," making the water "not merely repulsive or suspicious, but more or less dangerous for family use."[55]

By the end of the century, industry was well established in most major cities. The Great Lakes, praised as "sweet water seas" by the early explorers, were heavily contaminated near the major shore cities of Buffalo, Cleveland, Detroit, Chicago, and Milwaukee. Novelist Frank Norris, in his 1903 novel *The Pit: A Story of Chicago*, described the industry that drove Chicago: "factories, their smoke blackening the sky, clashed and flamed . . . and converters of forges belched into the air their tempest breath of molten steel."[56] Although Norris wrote of this industrial cacophony with Sandburg-like admiration, the spectacle came at a price; his main character, a transplant from a small town in western Massachusetts, had to lament "the black murk that closed every vista of the business streets" and "the soot that stained linen and gloves each time she stirred abroad."[57] In *The Turmoil* (1915), Booth Tarkington described an unnamed "heaving, grimy city," probably his native Indianapolis, as a "dirty and wonderful city nesting dingily in the fog of its own smoke."[58] As late as 1969, the Cuyahoga River in Cleveland, "choked with debris, oil, scum, and floating organic sludges,"[59] caught fire, leaving an enduring image of urban industrial water pollution.

One artifact of the industrial age was the large-scale production of lead-based paint, and later, leaded gasoline.[60] Lead had of course been known since ancient times. But exposure increased greatly in the 1920s, when leaded paint began to be widely used in homes and apartments. The lead poisoned painters and other workers as it was applied, and children when it eventually deteriorated and came loose as chips or dust. We now know that millions of IQ points were lost over the

■ **FIGURE 3-6**   "Black Tuesday," St. Louis, November 28, 1939. Periods of especially intense air pollution affected many cities during the industrial era.

SOURCE: Missouri Historical Society.

decades,[61] and other effects of lead exposure on generations of urban residents—kidney damage, hypertension, gastrointestinal pain, joint pain—cannot be quantified.

In recent years the acute problems of industrial pollution have been much improved. Some industries have cleaned up their operations; others have closed; and still others have relocated from cities or even departed the country. But the industrial age had another impact on cities: it attracted people. Starting in the nineteenth century, and continuing through the twentieth century, cities grew explosively, as migration from rural areas and from other countries brought millions of new workers and their families. Cities became places of crowding and social dislocation, home to a whole range of problems that came to be understood as the "urban crisis" of the late twentieth century.

THE SOCIAL PATHOLOGY OF CITY LIFE

Colonial seaport cities in the United States featured deep social and class distinctions.[62] As early as 1700 the New York City Council noted that "the Crys of the poor and Impotent for want of Reliefe are Extreamly Grevious,"[63] and an official report in Boston fifty years later described the impoverished homes where "scenes of Distress we do often behold! Numbers of Wretches hungry and naked shivering with Cold, and, perhaps, languishing with Disease."[64] According to Jackson Turner Main's statistical examination of the social structure of revolutionary America, one of every three people in the northern colonies could be termed poor by the end of the revolutionary period, and by the early eighteenth century poorhouses in the largest towns were filled.[65] During the nineteenth and early twentieth centuries, immigrants and members of ethnic minorities crowded into poor urban neighborhoods. Later in the twentieth century, wrote Michael Harrington, came "a new type of slum. Its citizens are internal migrants, the Negroes, the poor whites from the farms, the Puerto Ricans. They join the failures from the old ethnic culture and form an entirely different kind of neighborhood."[66]

Harrington may have been right about the ethnic transformation of poor urban neighborhoods, but the associated social problems were not new. What *was* new was their visibility, and the dominance they assumed in defining urban life. During the nineteenth and twentieth centuries, as sanitary challenges were met and as industrial pollution was managed, the toxicity of cities—the factors that most threatened residents' health and well-being and even helped drive migration out of the cities—came overwhelmingly to revolve around social circumstances.

The central parts of cities became pockets of concentrated poverty, reversing a pattern that had characterized urban life for centuries, and

as the twentieth century progressed, entire neighborhoods lost virtually all employment opportunities.[67] Racial and ethnic conflicts simmered, and at times erupted into violent riots, in cities across the country. Urban racial tensions in the early twentieth century exploded in the
"Red Summer" of 1919, with riots in Chicago, Charleston, Knoxville,
Nashville, Omaha, and more than a dozen other cities. The pattern
continued in the second half of the century with repeated high-profile
urban catastrophes: the Watts riots of 1965, the summer of 1967 when
no fewer than 130 riots swept American cities, the 1992 south-central
Los Angeles riots following the acquittal of police charged in Rodney
King's beating, and riots in Cincinnati in 2001 following a police shoot-
ing. Urban crime rates remained high for much of the twentieth century; in the final years of the century, they continued to increase until the
mid-1990s.[68]

By the 1960s the "urban crisis" had entered popular awareness.
"Increasingly," wrote one observer in 1963, "central cities are tend-
ing to become ghettos for the racially and economically underprivi-
leged, so that divisions between city and suburb are becoming ones of
race and class."[69] Indeed, many of the racial tensions that have
plagued the United States throughout its history seemed to play out
on the stage of the nation's cities. Cities seemed "less in the midst of
municipal difficulties," declared a 1978 article in *Harper's Magazine*,
"than in the path of the Four Horsemen of the Apocalypse." Indeed,
the article continued, the cities were "writhing in poverty, arson, and
decay."[70]

The 1960s saw successive federal efforts to understand America's
urban problems: the National Commission on Urban Problems (the
Douglas Commission), the President's Commission on Urban Housing (the Kaiser Commission), and the National Advisory Commission
on Civil Disorders (the Kerner Commission). Major federal initiatives
addressed urban problems: the Housing and Urban Development Act
of 1968, the Model Cities Program of 1966, and the Fair Housing Act
of 1968. But the cyclic pattern of capital flight, declining services, and
rising taxes continued. Crime rates remained high in many cities,
school quality declined, racial tension simmered, and high-poverty
neighborhoods expanded. By the 1990s, 40 percent of urban children
were living in poverty.[71] Some cities approached bankruptcy.

These factors gave new meaning to the term "urban health." People living in inner cities—in "an environmental jungle characterized by
personal insecurity and tension," as the Kerner Commission graphically put it[72]—faced formidable threats to health: the diseases of poverty

from infant mortality to diabetes to strokes, an appalling level of violence, and epidemic waves of substance abuse. Beginning in the 1980s, the HIV epidemic targeted the urban poor. These problems were aggravated by inadequate access to health care, also a disproportionately urban problem. By the 1990s, 78 percent of people living in medically underserved counties were in urban areas.[73] Observers described the "urban health penalty"—a complex of environmental conditions such as deteriorating housing, inadequate access to nutritional food, and scant medical care, and health consequences such as untreated hypertension, cardiovascular disease, intentional and unintentional injuries, and infectious diseases (see Table 3-1).[74] A widely discussed 1990 article in the *New England Journal of Medicine* revealed that men in Harlem had a lower life expectancy than men in Bangladesh.[75] In the city of Atlanta in 1995, of every 1,000 babies born, 119 were classified as low birth weight and 12.4 died within a year, while in the remainder of the Atlanta metro area the corresponding figures were 79 and 7.8.[76] Homelessness—frequently accompanied by mental illness—became concentrated in cities.[77]

Urban health was increasingly seen as part of a complex web of social and environmental conditions. Studies of "urban ecology" described interacting features of disadvantaged urban neighborhoods—unemployment, female-headed households, households on welfare, low educational levels, and disintegrating housing. These, in turn, were associated with child abuse, violence, substance abuse, HIV infection, family stress, a breakdown of social support networks, and community instability, interacting with each other in a synergistic or "syndemic" fashion.[78] A literature of urban health arose, focusing on these conditions and on how to provide health care to the victims.[79]

■ **TABLE 3-1** Examples of the urban health penalty in the twenty-five largest U.S. cities, 1993

Disease	Incidence in large cities cases/100,000/year	U.S. incidence cases/100,000/year	% difference
Tuberculosis	12	10	20
Syphilis	22	10	120
Gonorrhea	434	172	152
AIDS	61	40	52

SOURCE: D. P. Andrulis and N. J. Goodman, National Public Health and Hospital Institute, *The Social and Health Landscape of Urban and Suburban America* (Chicago: American Hospital Association Press, 1999), p. 243.

The Future of Urban Health

Urban health, then, had come full circle. In colonial times infectious disease dominated the health profiles of cities, and in the industrial era pollutants became a prominent concern. Social problems and their impact on health had always been a reality of urban life, but seemed to take center stage during the twentieth century. These problems were environmental as well as social. The conditions of urban life promoted the transmission of infectious diseases, and contaminants such as lead paint in substandard housing continued to threaten health.

Cities have been engines of economic growth, homes to waves of immigrants, and centers of cultural and intellectual development. But a ribbon of anti-urban bias has stretched throughout American history. Cities have been viewed as unwholesome, morally degrading, and unhealthy. From the public health point of view, cities have indeed been hazardous. The major dangers of cities—infectious diseases, industrial pollutants, and social conditions that threatened health—coexisted for long periods, as they do today in the poor cities of the developing world.

The historical legacy of these problems helped fuel the exodus from central cities, and contributed to the deconcentration of cities known as sprawl. Sprawl, in turn, had its own impact on health, suggesting that "urban health" in the future will be a broader, more varied field. In addition to the traditional health challenges of cities, public health will confront a range of sprawl-related health challenges, as the following chapters discuss.

CHAPTER 4

■══════════■

AIR QUALITY

────────────

Sprawl means driving. We drive the long distances that separate home, work, stores, and other destinations. Trucks carry the goods we need over the same long distances. Today's automobiles emit 99 percent fewer hydrocarbons, 96 percent less carbon monoxide, and 95 percent fewer nitrogen oxides, compared to the automobiles of the 1960s,[1] but these gains have been largely offset by the steady increase in the number of vehicles on the roads and in the miles they are driven. This chapter explores the links that connect sprawl, travel patterns, air quality, and health.

LAND USE, TRANSPORTATION, AIR QUALITY, AND HEALTH: A MODEL

This chapter traces a sequence of steps: sprawl leads to more driving, which increases overall vehicle emissions, which degrades air quality, which threatens health. This sequence is illustrated in Figure 4-1. At the top of the figure, two kinds of pollutant sources are depicted, anthropogenic (human-made) and biogenic (natural). Anthropogenic emissions come from mobile, stationary, and area sources. Mobile sources include automobiles and trucks, as well as off-road equipment such as bulldozers, locomotives, boats, and airplanes. Stationary sources, also called point sources, include power plants and factories; these have been subject to state and federal regulations for years, and emissions profiles have improved substantially. Area sources range

■ **FIGURE 4-1** A conceptual model linking sprawl, travel, air pollution, and health.

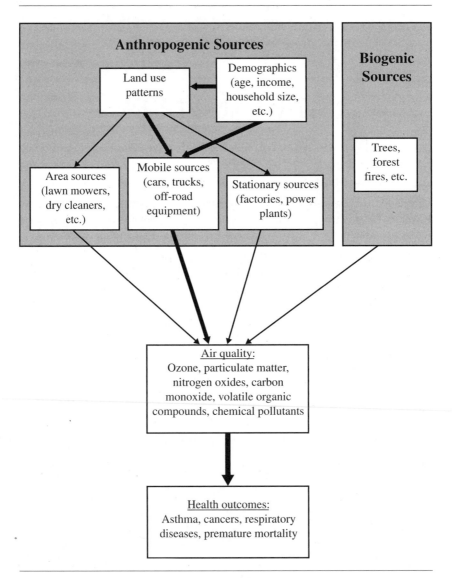

from airports to unpaved roads, from agricultural feedlots to forest fires, from fireplaces to lawnmowers.

As the model illustrates, land use patterns affect each category of anthropogenic emissions—their location, their quantity, their dispersion in the air, and how people are exposed. For stationary sources such as power plants and industrial facilities, zoning codes and other land use regulations may restrict them to designated industrial corridors, away from heavily populated areas. (A significant exception, of course, occurs when polluting industries are located near poor communities, a phenomenon that raises profound questions of social and economic equity.[2] Chapter 10 discusses this issue further.) Therefore, the air quality effects of stationary sources across a region are determined in part by the spatial distribution of these sources, such as where industry sits with respect to prevailing wind patterns and population centers. Emissions from area sources are similarly affected by land use. The people who live closest to area sources such as airports are heavily exposed to air pollution (and to other undesirable contaminants such as noise). Zoning and subdivision codes often require large lots, implying large lawns that require frequent maintenance using small two-stroke engines, which are notorious polluters.

However, the major impact of land use patterns on air pollution relates to mobile source emissions. Driving increases with sprawl and decreases with denser, more compact development, a relationship discussed in detail in Chapter 1.

Mobile, stationary, and area sources combine to release a variety of air pollutants, sometimes against a background of naturally occurring pollutants. These emissions largely determine air quality over urban areas. The emission patterns, and the air quality that results, can vary on a daily basis with changes in weather. Ozone, for example, forms in the atmosphere when oxides of nitrogen (NOx) and volatile organic compounds (VOCs) interact in the presence of heat and sunlight, so ozone is usually at its worst in summer months. For mobile sources, emission patterns vary with vehicles, trip characteristics, fuel types, and other factors.

Characteristics of the community—the ages of its residents, their incomes, their family structures—also affect the amount of driving. All other factors being equal, for instance, higher income usually predicts higher vehicle ownership rates and more driving. This directly increases mobile source emissions, but there are indirect effects as well. Higher incomes are generally associated with larger houses and lots, meaning that wealthier people tend to live in neighborhoods that require more frequent and longer driving trips.

Finally, air quality has a direct influence on health, contributing to mortality, respiratory and cardiovascular disease, cancer, and perhaps even birth defects. The fact that poor air quality threatens health has, of course, long been recognized; this understanding was the basis of the landmark Clean Air Act of 1970 and subsequent amendments, and continues to play a central role in determining clean air standards. Yet despite the long-standing recognition that air quality and health are linked, health research continues to uncover new relationships between the two. This research has led the U.S. Environmental Protection Agency (EPA), the agency responsible for enforcing the Clean Air Act, to tighten exposure limits for several pollutants, most recently ozone and particulate matter.

TRAVEL BEHAVIOR, EMISSIONS, AND AIR QUALITY

As described in Chapter 1, the relationship between sprawl and driving is well established, although there is some debate over specific details. There is much less debate about the second link in our chain: the link between driving and air pollution. This section reviews the kinds of air pollutants that come from tailpipes, and the patterns of their emissions.

Air pollution is not a single entity. Instead, it is a mixture of numerous kinds of specific pollutants, a mixture that varies from place to place. Polluted air in Atlanta has a different composition than polluted air in Los Angeles. Each pollutant has its own characteristic sources, behavior in the atmosphere, and fate.

Mobile sources are an important source of air pollutants—in heavily trafficked areas, often the predominant source. Vehicles contribute to air pollution in two ways: combustion and evaporation. Combustion is the major source of air pollution. When fuel is burned, both the fuel and the surrounding air undergo oxidation. If the fuel is carbon-based, like gasoline or diesel fuel, the oxidation products include carbon monoxide (CO) and carbon dioxide (CO_2). If the fuel contains sulfur, as many fossil fuels do, then oxides of sulfur (SOx) also result. And since the air is about 80 percent nitrogen, some nitrogen is also inevitably oxidized, forming oxides of nitrogen (NOx).

Combustion also directly releases small particles (particulate matter, or PM) that contain carbon, ammonium, sulfates, nitrates, organic chemicals, water vapor, and metals; these particles form the smoke that can be seen emerging from factory smokestacks, tailpipes, and home chimneys. Among mobile sources, diesel engines are especially active PM emitters. Particulate matter continues to form and change in the atmosphere, as molecules of gas, water vapor, and other materials combine, and larger particles break into smaller ones. As a result, PM varies in size and chemical composition. The most hazardous particles are the smallest ones—those under 10 microns in diameter (PM_{10}), and especially those under 2.5 microns in diameter ($PM_{2.5}$). In fact, the very smallest particles, those with a diameter under 0.1 micron (ultrafine particles) may prove to be the most dangerous, because they penetrate deep into the lungs, and perhaps because of their chemical composition. Motor vehicle emissions are the major source of these small particles.[3] Lead was previously added to gasoline as an anti-knock agent, and it was released with other emissions. While this is still a serious problem in some other countries, lead is no longer added to gasoline in the United States.

Evaporation is the other way motor vehicles can contribute to air pollution. Fuel is a complex mixture of hydrocarbons, including aromatic and aliphatic compounds. These compounds can evaporate when fuel is being handled, such as during a fill-up, or simply when fuel is being stored. Some components of fuel evaporate readily, and are classified as volatile organic compounds (VOCs). Since the VOCs are generally carbon-based molecules, they are also referred to as hydrocarbons. Another category of chemicals—air toxics—can also be found in fuels, and can also evaporate; examples include benzene, methanol, and formaldehyde. But evaporation is not the only way VOCs and air toxics enter the atmosphere; they also result from combustion.

Finally, some pollutants are not emitted by motor vehicles, but form in the air from precursor chemicals. A key example of such a "secondary pollutant" is ozone (often called, with some imprecision, "smog"). Ozone is a product of chemical reactions involving NOx and hydrocarbons, in the presence of heat and sunlight. As a result, cities that experience high levels of ozone follow a predictable pattern; the ozone is highest during the warm summer months, peaks in the late afternoon, and is higher on weekdays (when heavy traffic produces copious ozone precursors) than on weekends. An example of summertime ozone tracing from Atlanta is shown in Figure 4-2. The other major secondary pollutant is particulate matter (PM). As noted earlier, PM is both a primary pollutant, when emitted from tailpipes and smokestacks, and a secondary pollutant that can form and change once in the environment.

Human activities such as driving are not the only source of air pollutants. Several of the major air pollutants can also be traced to natural sources. Nitrogen oxides come from volcanoes, oceans, biological decay, and lightning strikes, and sulfur dioxide comes from volcanoes, biological decay, and forest fires; globally, these natural sources rival and may even exceed anthropogenic sources. Natural sources of particulate matter include volcanoes, dust storms, and unpaved roads. Volatile organic compounds are naturally produced by vegetation. For

BOX 4-1
Exposure Chambers on Wheels: Air Pollution Inside Cars, Trucks, and Buses

Air pollution from cars and trucks is a problem alongside busy streets, and across entire metropolitan regions, especially in sprawling areas where people drive vast numbers of miles. Even while traveling in their vehicles, drivers and passengers can be exposed to unusually high levels of pollution.

Studies in the United States and Asia have clarified the dimensions of this problem.[1] Much of the focus has been on volatile organic compounds (VOCs) such as benzene, styrene, toluene, 1,3-butadiene, and formaldehyde, some of which are carcinogenic. These chemicals can evaporate from gasoline, they can be present in exhaust fumes from nearby vehicles, and they can even off-gas from items in the vehicle such as air fresheners, upholstery, and dry-cleaned clothing. The levels of VOCs inside automobiles vary greatly. Factors associated with higher exposures include heavy traffic, older cars (especially those without catalytic converters), cars with very warm interiors (such as a car that has been sitting in the sun), driving with the windows closed, smoking in the car, and using the car heater. On the other hand, exposures are much lower when driving with the windows open or with the air conditioner on, and when driving on a rural road. In some circumstances, levels of VOCs inside vehicles can be several times higher than outdoor levels, even levels measured alongside the road. Commuting can therefore account for a large portion of a person's total exposure to VOCs. Certain unusual conditions, such as carburetor malfunction, can lead to greatly increased exposures inside a car. And VOCs are not the only pollutant to concentrate inside vehicles; carbon monoxide can behave similarly.

A 2001 study by two environmental groups, the Natural Resources Defense Council and the Coalition for Clean Air, produced especially worrisome findings. These groups tested levels of diesel exhaust (including "black carbon" and $PM_{2.5}$) in California school buses. They found that diesel exhaust in the school buses reached levels up to four times higher than in cars traveling nearby. Levels were especially high in the back of the bus, when the windows were closed, and when the bus was driving up or down a hill (compared to driving on level ground or idling). The authors pointed out that diesel exhaust is a well-known respiratory toxin and carcinogen. In fact, they calculated that based on observed exposure levels, children's lifetime risk of cancer was elevated twenty-three to forty-six times above the level the EPA considers "significant."[2] These results were replicated in Connecticut in 2002,[3] and in California in 2003.[4] School buses offer important advantages on a regional scale, since one school bus trip can replace dozens of automobile trips, but cleaner bus technology would go a long way to reducing emissions and health risks.

The conclusion is clear: extensive driving, a key aspect of sprawl, creates air pollution that not only threatens the health of all those within the affected air shed, but may pose special risks for those who spend much of their time in vehicles.

1. Chan CC, Ozkaynak H, Spengler JD, Sheldon L. Driver exposure to volatile organic compounds, CO, ozone, and NO2 under different driving conditions. *Environment Science and Technology* 1991;25:964–72; Chan CC, Spengler JD, Ozkaynak H, Lefkopoulou M. Commuter exposures to VOCs in Boston, Massachusetts. *Journal of Air and Waste Management Association* 1991;41:1594–1600; Weisel CP, Lawryk NJ, Lioy PJ. Exposure to emissions from gasoline within automobile cabins. *Journal of Exposure Analysis and Environmental Epidemiology* 1992;2:79–96; Lawryk NJ, Lioy PJ, Weisel CP. Exposure to volatile organic compounds in the passenger compartment of automobiles during periods of normal and malfunctioning operation. *Journal of Exposure Analysis and Environmental Epidemiology* 1995;5(4):511–31; Jo WK, Choi SJ. Vehicle occupant's exposure to aromatic volatile organic compounds while commuting in an urban–suburban route in Korea. *Journal of Air and Waste Management Association* 1996;46:749–54; Duffy BL, Nelson AF. Exposure to emissions of 1,3-butadiene and benzene in the cabins of moving vehicles and buses in Sydney, Australia. *Atmospheric Environment* 1997;31:3877–85; Park JH, Spengler JD, Yoon DD, Dumyahn T, Lee K, Ozkaynak H. Measurement of air exchange rate of stationary vehicle and estimation of in-vehicle exposure. *Journal of Exposure Analysis and Environmental Epidemiology* 1998;8(1):65–78; Jo WK, Park KH. Concentrations of volatile organic compounds in the passenger side and the back seat of automobiles. *Journal of Exposure Analysis and Environmental Epidemiology* 1999;9(3):217–27; Fedoruk MJ, Kerger BD. Measurement of volatile organic compounds inside automobiles. *Journal of Exposure Analysis and Environmental Epidemiology* 2003;13:31–41.

2. Solomon GM, Campbell TR, Feuer GR, Masters J, Samkian A, Paul KA. *No Breathing in the Aisles: Diesel Exhaust Inside School Buses.* New York and Los Angeles: Natural Resources Defense Council and Coalition for Clean Air, February 2001. Available: http://www.nrdc.org/air/transportation/schoolbus/sbusinx.asp (accessed December 2, 2003).

3. Wargo J, Brown D, Cullen M, Addiss S, Alderman N. *Children's Exposure to Diesel Exhaust on School Buses.* North Haven, CT: Environment and Human Health, 2002. Available: http://www.ehhi.org/pubs/children_diesel.html (accessed December 2, 2003).

4. Fitz DR, Winer AM, Colome S, et al. Characterizing the Range of Children's Pollutant Exposure during School Bus Commutes. Final Report to the California Air Resources Board, Contract No. 00-322. Department of Environmental Health Sciences, UCLA School of Public Health, and College of Engineering, UC Riverside. October 2003. Available: ftp://ftp.arb.ca.gov/carbis/research/schoolbus/report.pdf (accessed December 2, 2003).

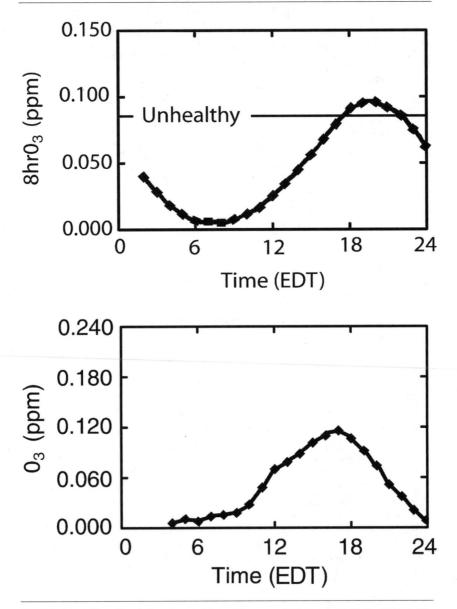

■ FIGURE 4-2 Ozone levels in Atlanta on a summer day, in ppm. The upper panel shows the eight-hour running average, and the lower panel shows hourly readings, from the same day. Note that the running average peaks later and at a lower level than the hourly readings.

SOURCE: Adapted from Georgia Department of Natural Resources, Environmental Protection Division, Air Protection Branch, Ambient Monitoring Program, http://www.air.dnr.state.ga.us/amp.

example, many plants and trees produce isoprene, a five-carbon molecule that can probably trigger asthma. Isoprene, in turn, is assembled into larger molecules such as terpenes, which give pine and spruce trees their characteristic aroma. In some places, these naturally occurring hydrocarbons can be a significant contributor to ozone formation.

The principal air pollutants are shown in Table 4-1. As the table shows, mobile sources are among the most important sources of many pollutants nationally. Automobiles and trucks account for more than three-quarters of carbon monoxide emissions, over half of NOx emissions, nearly half of VOC emissions, nearly a third of air toxics, and about a fifth of the nation's output of particulate matter. The EPA does not produce such estimates for ozone, but since ozone is formed from NOx and VOCs, which derive heavily from cars and trucks, it must be considered a transportation-related pollutant as well. In areas that have relatively heavy traffic, and relatively little industry, the relative contribution of traffic to air pollution is substantially greater than Table 4-1 shows.

■ TABLE 4-1   Major air pollutants, United States, 1999

Pollutant	Contribution of cars and trucks (percent)*
Carbon monoxide (CO)	77%
Sulfur oxides (SOx)	7%
Nitrogen oxides (NOx)	56%
Particulate matter (PM_{10})	25%†
Ozone	
Lead	13%
Volatile organic compounds (VOCs)	47%
Air toxics (e.g., benzene, formaldehyde, methanol, etc.)	31%
Carbon dioxide (CO_2)	30%

* Proportions refer to anthropogenic sources only. In some cases, natural sources account for a substantial proportion of total contributions. See text.

† This figure refers only to *directly emitted* particulate matter. The true contribution of cars and trucks to PM levels is higher than 19 percent, since other pollutants, such as NOx, combine to form PM in the atmosphere after they are released. The figure shown is for PM_{10}; the corresponding figure for $PM_{2.5}$ is 28 percent.

SOURCES: For all pollutants other than air toxics and carbon dioxide: EPA (United States Environmental Protection Agency), *National Air Quality and Emissions Trends Report, 1999* (EPA-454/R-01-004). Office of Air Quality and Standards, U.S. EPA, Research Triangle Park, NC, March 2001. Available at: http://www.epa.gov/oar/aqtrnd99/. For air toxics: EPA, *Toxic Air Pollutants,* available at http://www.epa.gov/airtrends/toxic.html. Further detail can be found in EPA, "The Projection of Mobile Source Air Toxics from 1996 to 2007: Emissions and Concentrations" (EPA-420/R-01-038). U.S. EPA, Research Triangle Park, NC, August 2001. Available at: http://www.epa.gov/otaq/regs/toxics/r01038.pdf. For carbon dioxide: EPA, *National Air Pollutant Emission Trends: 1900-1998* (EPA-454/R-00-002). Office of Air Quality and Standards, U.S. EPA, Research Triangle Park, NC, March 2000. Available at: http://www.epa.gov/ttn/chief/trends/trends98.

The precise relationships among motorized travel, emissions, and air quality are complex. The patterns of emissions that result from driving, and the impact they have on air quality, vary considerably. Many factors play a role, including the characteristics of the vehicle, the trip, the type of pollutant, the meteorological conditions, and the scale at which air quality is measured (local or regional).

Vehicle characteristics: Different vehicles produce different quantities of pollutants, depending on engine size, fuel used (gasoline or diesel), maintenance status, age, and driving habits. Often, agencies calculate emissions based on fleet averages, which assume an "average" vehicle for the region and assign this vehicle's emissions profile to all trips. Unfortunately, there is significant variation in the distribution of vehicle types across demographic groups and, significantly, across space as well; it may not be reasonable to apply the same vehicle profile across a metropolitan area.[4]

Trip characteristics: Emissions vary by different trip characteristics, only some of which may be included in regional emissions models. Different pollutants are emitted in greater or lesser quantities depending on the vehicle's average speed, the trip's length (VMT), the duration of the trip (VHT), the acceleration characteristics of the vehicle at intersections, engine characteristics, and roadway conditions. For example, as shown in Figure 4-3, per-mile emissions of CO and VOCs are highest at very low speeds, while per-mile NOx emissions are highest at very fast speeds. Another example is the "cold start." Automobiles pollute most when cold, as their catalytic converters do not operate at peak efficiency until they reach ordinary operating temperature.[5] As a result, the first few miles of a trip following a cold start may result in as much pollution as the next 10 miles or so (in one study, over 50 percent of carbon monoxide [CO] and VOC emissions).[6] (See Figure 4-4.)

Pollutant characteristics: Different vehicle, trip, and meteorological conditions affect the production of each type of pollutant differently. In addition, primary pollutants such as carbon monoxide are more localized, whereas secondary pollutants such as ozone are regional in nature.

Meteorological conditions: Weather contributes to air pollution levels in complex ways. During the era when coal was the primary fuel for heating and industrial uses, layers of cold air could trap large amounts of coal-produced soot and pollutants over cities, creating deadly respiratory conditions for residents, as happened on a sporadic basis in London and major American cities at midcentury. Now, the worst weather for air pollution tends to be sunny and warm conditions, which contribute to ozone formation.

Scale issues: Different pollutants form, remain in the air, and dissipate at different scales. In general, a pollutant that is emitted directly from a tailpipe or smokestack reaches its maximum concentration close to the point of emission, and decreases with distance from that point.

■ **FIGURE 4-3**   Vehicle emissions for NOx, VOCs, and CO, by average travel speed, Seattle area, 1996

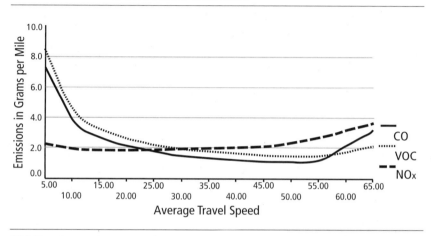

SOURCE: L. Frank, B. Stone, Jr, and W. Bachman, "Linking Land Use with Household Vehicle Emissions in the Central Puget Sound: Methodological Framework and Findings," *Transportation Research Part D* 2000;5(3):173-96.

■ **FIGURE 4-4**   Hydrocarbon emission rates for a hypothetical trip

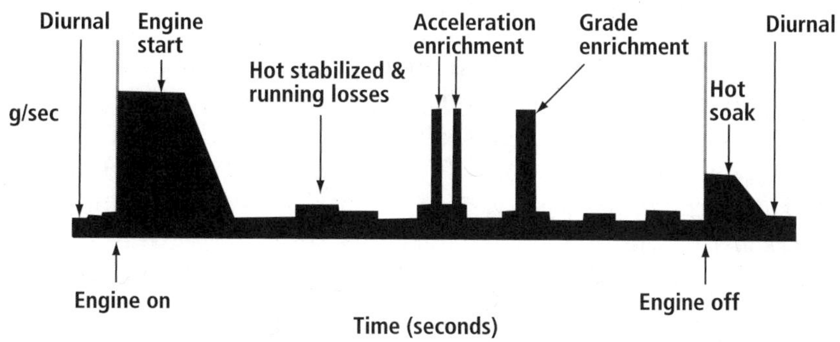

SOURCE: W. Bachman, J. Granell, R. Guensler, and J. Leonard, "Research Needs in Determining Spatially Resolved Subfleet Characteristics," *Transportation Research Record* 1998;1625:139-146.

The decrease may be rapid, if the pollutant is removed from the air by chemical or physical processes, or it may be gradual, if the pollutant remains airborne for some time. On the other hand, a pollutant that is secondarily formed from precursors may reach its highest levels some distance downwind of the source. For example, CO is a deadly pollutant in enclosed areas where engines are left running, such as garages, and CO may also reach unhealthy levels alongside busy roadways. At a regional level, however, CO is diluted and rarely represents a widespread health problem. NOx also tends to be concentrated near roadways, and to fall to background levels within relatively short distances (NO more strikingly than NO_2). In contrast, ozone is formed over large areas as miles-wide plumes containing NOx and hydrocarbons move downwind, forming ozone as they move. In fact, ozone levels are often lower in central cities than in suburbs, because of downwind formation and because the ozone in central cities is scavenged (or consumed) by the formation of nitric oxide originating from traffic.[7]

Investigators in several countries have carefully measured pollutant levels alongside streets and in homes to determine the exposures associated with traffic. One study, in Amsterdam, found that people who lived near busy streets (defined as carrying more than 10,000 vehicles per day) were exposed to two- to threefold higher levels of "black smoke" (a measure of particulate matter), NOx, and carbon monoxide, compared to people who lived near a less busy street. In fact, the only pollutants that did not fit that pattern were ozone and SOx.[8] A more detailed study, also in Amsterdam, compared homes on busy main streets with homes on lightly traveled side streets, measuring both outdoor air and indoor air. Levels of both PM and VOCs were higher near the busy streets, both outside homes and indoors.[9] Studies in Los Angeles showed that PM levels fell with increasing distance from a busy highway; 30 meters (98 feet) downwind from the highway, the total PM level was several times higher than background levels, and closely reflected the traffic density, but by 300 meters (980 feet) away, the PM level was indistinguishable from background.[10] A study in Poland, the United Kingdom, the Netherlands, and the Czech Republic demonstrated dramatic variations in NOx levels at locations just blocks apart from each other.[11] Finally, a study of Dutch elementary schools examined nitrogen dioxide (NO_2) exposure.[12] As the degree of "urbanization" increased, the exposure to NO_2 increased. Similarly, as the volume of traffic near the school increased, the exposure to NO_2 increased. Figure 4-5 shows the results of another Dutch study; both

■ **FIGURE 4-5**   Black smoke and NO$_2$ concentrations measured at different distances from the roadside in Delft, Netherlands, at high exposed times (upper line), low exposed times (lower line), and all times (middle line)

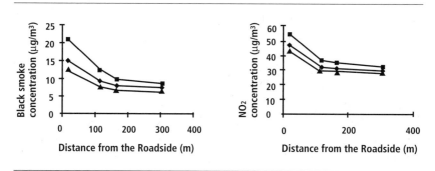

SOURCE: M. C. Roorda-Knape, N. A. H. Janssen, J. de Hartog, P. H. N. Van Vliet, H. Harssema, and B. Brunekreef, "Traffic Related Air Pollution in City Districts near Motorways" *Science of the Total Environment,* 1999;235:339-41.

black smoke and NO$_2$ levels decline for 100 or 200 meters (about 350 to 650 feet) from the school, before reaching background levels. Overall, then, being near busy roads (even indoors) can increase a person's exposure to PM, NOx, hydrocarbons, and CO. In contrast, ozone and SOx vary on a much larger scale, so roadside locations are not notably worse than places away from roads.

The scale issues pose interesting challenges. If sprawl leads to more driving, and if driving contributes to air pollution, then alternatives to sprawl offer a way to reduce air pollution exposure. But if one of those alternatives is greater density, the result could be paradoxical. On a regional scale, less driving would lead to less pollution, an improvement that would be especially marked for regional-scale pollutants such as ozone. But on a very localized scale—alongside a street in a particular neighborhood—greater traffic density could increase exposure to pollutants, especially locally scaled pollutants such as particulate matter and air toxics. This dilemma emphasizes that strategies to control air pollution exposure must extend beyond land use changes; they must be linked to other strategies, such as cleaner vehicle technology, improved access to transit, and provision of bicycle trails, to avoid unwanted results.

Not many studies have investigated the link between land use patterns and mobile source emissions.[13] One study[14] assessed the air pollution produced by drivers in various Seattle neighborhoods according to neighborhood characteristics. The investigators studied how various aspects of urban form, such as density, connectivity, and land use mix, predicted NOx, CO, and VOC emissions. As shown in Figures 4-6 and 4-7, conditions typical of sprawl—low density, low land use mix, and disconnected street networks—consistently predicted greater air pollution emissions. These relationships held true after controlling for demographic variables such as household size, number of vehicles, and income.

Interestingly, urban form may have unexpected effects on motor vehicle emissions. As urban planner Randall Crane points out, communities that are high in density, land use mix, and connectivity might result in decreased VMTs and increased foot and bike trips, but more short car trips.[15] This view is based on microeconomic theory, that greater convenience and ease of access will increase all sorts of trips. In turn, more frequent automobile trips imply more cold starts of automobile engines. According to this argument, if denser neighborhoods result in more frequent short automobile trips, they might increase emissions of CO and VOCs. These are theoretical claims, and real-world evidence will be required to sort them out.

■ **FIGURE 4-6** Household emissions by home tract street connectivity

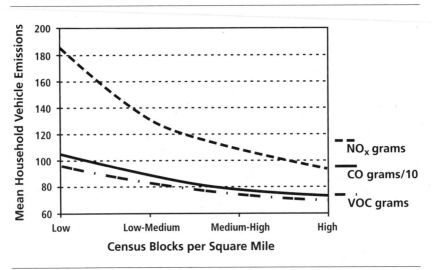

SOURCE: Puget Sound Transportation Panel (PSTP).

■ FIGURE 4-7 Household emissions by home tract household density

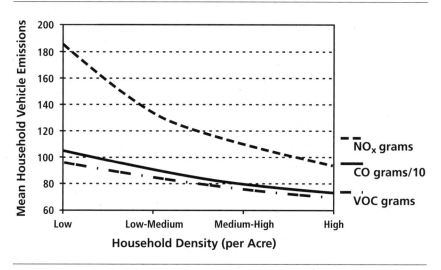

SOURCE: Puget Sound Transportation Panel (PSTP).

AIR QUALITY AND PUBLIC HEALTH

The third link in our chain connects air quality and health. Clean air is important for good health, and air pollution threatens health in a variety of ways. A vast literature on the health consequences of air pollution has developed in recent years, and is far more extensive than we can cover in this chapter. Instead, we provide a brief overview, with a focus on motor vehicle-related pollution.

One challenge in describing these health effects is that the various pollutants tend to occur together. In a smoggy city, the air typically contains high levels of ozone, PM, NOx, and other contaminants. Therefore, it is difficult to pinpoint which specific pollutant is the culprit when pollution makes people sick. One solution is to rely on experimental studies, in which animals or human volunteers are exposed to high levels of a single pollutant at a time. Such studies are informative, but only about short-term effects. Another solution is to carry out epidemiological studies in different settings with different mixes of air pollutants. In theory, if one city has high ozone and low PM, and another city has high PM and low ozone (or if one city has high ozone at some times of the year and high PM at others), then comparative studies should be able to tease out the effects of each pollutant. However, such pure study situations are rare. In any event, it is likely that different pollutants work together to cause health effects.

Similarly, it is difficult to say whether a specific particle came from a car, a truck, a factory, or a power plant, and it is impossible to attribute a molecule of ozone to precursors (NOx and hydrocarbons) from a specific source. In general, we know that mobile sources are a major contributor to NOx, VOCs, CO, and air toxics, and in heavily trafficked areas, to PM (especially fine PM) as well. The more cars and trucks are driven, the greater their relative and absolute contribution to air pollution in an area. But our statements about the health effects of pollutants are not unique to the pollutants that come from cars and trucks.

Air pollution threatens human health in four principal ways. The two most important are by increasing mortality and by threatening respiratory health. In addition, air pollution can damage cardiovascular function and increase cancer risk. There is evidence for some other health effects as well.

Mortality

During the first week of December 1952, London was engulfed by a thick cloud of polluted air, the result of intensive burning of high-sulfur coal in homes, factories, and power plants, and weather conditions that concentrated the resulting emissions. This was not the first time the world had known such a disaster; for example, similar events had occurred in Belgium's Meuse Valley in 1930, and in Donora, Pennsylvania, in 1948. But the London smog was perhaps the best studied, both at the time and in later years. Approximately 3,000 excess deaths occurred in London during that December, and according to a recent reanalysis, a total of 12,000 excess deaths may have occurred during the ensuing months.[16] While some early observers theorized that the excess deaths represented "harvesting"—deaths among elderly or ill people who would have died a few days or weeks later anyway—later analysis confirmed that the pollution killed many people who would not otherwise have died any time soon. It became clear that the kind of pollution seen in London—thick with particulate matter and SOx—could be deadly.

In recent decades, as pollution levels in many cities declined, the idea that tiny airborne particles could be fatal might have faded into oblivion. But careful studies have revealed that even current levels of PM are responsible for lives lost. In one line of research, "ecologic studies," investigators compare death rates in places with differing levels of PM. For examples, the Six Cities study followed death rates in Steubenville, Ohio; Watertown, Massachusetts; Harriman, Tennessee; St. Louis, Missouri; Topeka, Kansas; and Portage, Wisconsin. Steubenville had high PM levels, Portage's were low, and the other cities were intermediate between the two. Over more than a decade of follow-up, death rates in Steubenville were 26 percent higher than in Portage, and the intermediate cities had mortality rates higher than Portage's, but lower than Steubenville's, after accounting for factors such as income and age. Three causes of death accounted for the excess: cardiovascular disease, pulmonary disease, and cancer.[17] Similar findings emerged from other ecologic studies. The largest of these was the American Cancer Society's Cancer Prevention II study, involving approximately half a million adults in dozens of metropolitan areas during the 1980s and 1990s.[18] Several smaller cohort studies provide additional supporting evidence.

Another line of research relies on "time-series" studies. In these studies, daily fluctuations in PM (and other pollutants) in particular locations are correlated with daily changes in mortality. These studies have several advantages: PM levels change considerably from day to day due to weather; the same people are followed over time, so they serve as their own controls; and the studies are practical, since data collected for other purposes are readily available.[19] One of the largest of these studies followed day-to-day fluctuations in PM over a five-year period in twenty-nine European cities that were home to 43 million people.[20] The investigators noted a clear association between PM exposure and death rates; when PM levels rose, mortality rose for about a day. Overall, an increase in the PM_{10} concentration of 10 µg/m^3 was associated with an increase in the city's mortality rate of 0.6 or 0.7 percent (depending upon the statistical model used). The impact of the PM exposure was higher among elderly people, and in cities where the NOx was high and where the climate was warm and dry. Time-series studies in the United States (e.g., the National Morbidity, Mortality, and Air Pollution Study, or NMMAPS)[21] have shown a similar relationship between PM exposure and mortality.

These proportional increases in mortality seem small, but when they operate on large numbers of people, the overall effect can be enormous. In 1996, the Natural Resources Defense Council applied mortality data on PM exposure to the U.S. population, focusing on 239 U.S. cities for which PM records were available. They estimated that approximately 64,000 people die prematurely each year due to PM exposure—a higher number than die from motor vehicle crashes and homicides combined.[22] Put differently, high levels of PM exposure are estimated to shorten average life expectancy by as much as one or two years.[23] Mobile sources are an important contributor to these public health burdens.

Researchers continue to address several questions about the association between air pollution and mortality. First, although PM is clearly associated with mortality, are any other pollutants also implicated? Some studies suggest a role for sulfates, and others a role for ozone, although this evidence is not consistent.[24] Second, over what time scale do particulates cause death? Time-series studies point to an effect occurring over one to two days, and ecological studies demonstrate trends over the course of years. In recent studies, investigators have found that the long-term impact of PM exposure, over weeks and even months, outweighs the deaths that occur within a few days of exposure.[25] These results emphasize that PM does not simply kill people who were about to die anyway.

Third, which kinds of particles, and from which sources, are most deadly? Are particles that contain metals, sulfates, or certain organic chemicals especially hazardous, as some evidence suggests? How important are motor vehicles in the PM story, compared to other sources such as power plants? While these are not easy questions to answer, some recent evidence points to a major role for motor vehicles. In a follow-up of the Six Cities study, investigators were able to distinguish the contributions of different PM sources; they concluded that PM from mobile sources contributed three times more to mortality than did PM from coal combustion, and PM from "crustal sources" such as road dust did not contribute to mortality.[26] This suggests that motor vehicles account for a large proportion of PM-related mortality. Recent research from the Netherlands supports this conclusion. In a large prospective cohort study, living near a major road increased the cardiopulmonary mortality by 41 percent compared to living on a road with little traffic, again implying an important role for vehicle-related emissions.[27] In another Dutch study that examined PM-related mortality, the association was considerably stronger among people living near busy roads, suggesting that vehicle emissions were an important source of fatal PM exposure.[28] Overall, it is clear that cars and trucks are a major contributor to PM-related mortality.

Finally, what are the biological mechanisms by which particulates cause death? Some of the excess deaths relate to respiratory causes among people with chronic obstructive pulmonary disease or pneumonia. The particulates might inflame the airways in these people, triggering fatal flares of their disease. It seems more difficult to envision how inhaling tiny particles could trigger a fatal cardiovascular event such as a heart attack, but several explanations have been suggested.

Perhaps the particles act on nerve endings in the lungs and affect the autonomic nervous system in ways that predispose to heart arrhythmias. (Researchers are studying heart rate variability as a possible marker of this effect.) Perhaps inflammatory changes occur in the lungs, leading to higher circulating levels of certain proteins (such as fibrinogen and C-reactive protein), more viscous blood, and a higher probability of heart attacks. Perhaps inflammatory changes occur throughout the body, making atherosclerotic plaques more likely to rupture. Perhaps blood vessels constrict following exposure to PM, increasing the risk of heart attacks. There is evidence for all of these theories, from both human and animal studies, and research is ongoing.[29]

Respiratory Health

Although air pollution can cause deaths, a far more common outcome is disease, especially of the respiratory system. This can be seen in many ways: more symptoms such as coughing and wheezing, greater use of respiratory medications, increased absence from school or work for respiratory disease, increased diagnosis of asthma, impaired lung development in children, more visits to clinics or emergency departments for respiratory disease, and more hospital admissions for respiratory disease. As this list suggests, some of the respiratory responses to air pollution occur within hours of exposure, while others are seen over the course of years.

Short-term responses to pollutants have been studied in animals, in human volunteers in exposure chambers, and in populations exposed to pollutants. A vast body of evidence documents that air pollutants damage respiratory health.[30] Ozone is well recognized as an irritant to the airways. Within hours of exposure to ozone, some people will experience coughing, wheezing, and shortness of breath. Although people with asthma are especially susceptible, people with no apparent predisposition can also respond with these symptoms. People vary greatly in their sensitivity to ozone, at least in part for genetic reasons.[31] Similar responses can occur with exposure to NOx and SOx.

One measure of this response is school absenteeism. As shown in Figure 4-8, school absenteeism rises with rising levels of PM, SOx, and ozone. Of note, this effect is seen when ozone levels reach just 20 ppb (parts per billion), well within permissible limits.

The role of cars and trucks in these symptomatic responses is also well established. On a regional scale, motor vehicles are a principal contributor to PM and NOx emissions and to ozone formation. And on a local scale, living on streets with heavy traffic is associated with acute (and chronic) respiratory symptoms, including cough and sputum production in children and adults.[32]

Short-term reactions to air pollution can also be seen in other ways: abnormal lung function as measured by lung function tests, and rates of emergency department visits and hospital admissions. Again, people with asthma are especially susceptible, as are children, the elderly, and people with lung diseases. But even healthy athletes are susceptible. For example, a 1998 study measured the lung function of day hikers before and after they climbed New Hampshire's Mount Washington. These were fit, healthy people, but some suffered decreases in airflow and lung volume on days when ozone levels rose above 40 ppb.[33] There are numerous studies showing increases in emergency department visits within one or two days of when ozone levels rise. An especially interesting study illustrates the link with motor vehicles. During the Atlanta Olympic games in 1996, morning peak traffic flow decreased by 22 percent, one-hour peak ozone levels decreased by 28 percent (these two were significantly correlated), and various measures of acute asthma decreased between 11 percent (for emergency hospital admissions) and 44 percent (for urgent care through health maintenance organizations).[34] These outcomes, too, are clearly related to motor vehicle traffic.

Long-term health damage from air pollution exposure has also become increasingly evident. For example, a series of studies in Los Angeles has tracked children and adults who live in communities with different pollutant levels. These studies have shown that lung growth in children was significantly reduced with increasing exposure to NOx, PM, and acid vapor.[35] In fact, when children moved from less polluted to more polluted areas, their lung growth rates declined, and when children moved from more polluted to less polluted areas, their lung growth rates improved.[36] Consistent with these findings, another study found that college freshmen who had grown up in high-ozone areas had lower measured airflow than their classmates who had grown up in lower-ozone areas.[37] Studies also showed that children who play

■ FIGURE 4-8 Relationship between concentrations of (a) particulate matter ≤10 μm in diameter (PM$_{10}$), (b) sulfur dioxide, and (c) ozone and illness-related school absenteeism; ppb indicates parts per billion.

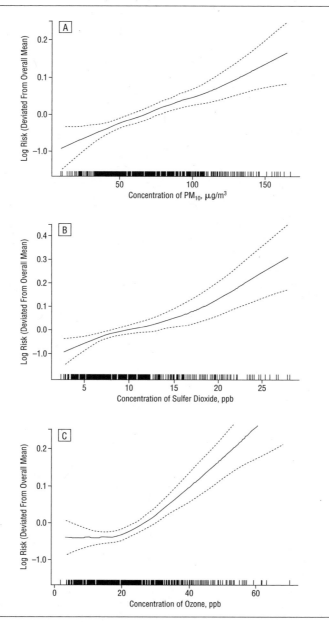

SOURCE: H. Park, B. Lee, E.-H. Ha, J.-T. Lee, H. Kim, and Y.-C. Hong, "Association of Air Pollution with School Absenteeism Due to Illness," *Archives of Pediatric and Adolescent Medicine,* 2002;156:1235-39.

BOX 4-2
From Local Sprawling to Global Warming?

Global climate change may pose one of the biggest health challenges of the coming century. Since the beginning of the Industrial Revolution, people have burned vast amounts of fossil fuels, including coal, oil, gasoline, and diesel fuel. These fuels are carbon-based, so their combustion releases carbon dioxide. Carbon dioxide (together with other emissions such as methane and nitrous oxide) acts as a greenhouse gas, trapping heat in the earth's atmosphere. A warmer atmosphere, in turn, leads to a cascade of other events: less stable and stormier weather, melting of polar ice caps and rising ocean levels, changes in agriculture, and others.[1]

These changes could have profound consequences for human health. Warmer weather will mean more heat waves, causing hundreds of deaths in affected cities. Warmer weather also promotes formation of some air pollutants, such as ozone. With severe weather events such as monsoons, floods, and hurricanes, people are injured and displaced, and hunger and disease can follow, especially in poor areas. As tropical climates expand from the equator into temperate zones, tropical diseases are expected to expand their ranges as well. Malaria, dengue fever, and schistosomiasis are some of the diseases expected to increase worldwide with climate change.[2]

What does this have to do with sprawl? The United States is the world's largest contributor to greenhouse gases, in both absolute and per capita terms. With 5 percent of the world's population, the United States contributes over 20 percent of the world's greenhouse gases. Of these emissions, about 32 percent comes from the transportation sector. Each gallon of gasoline burned produces about 20 pounds of CO_2. Industry was a larger greenhouse gas emitter in 1990, but with reductions in industrial emissions and with transportation emissions increasing by about 2 percent per year, transportation was by 2000 the largest source.[3]

Which vehicles emit the most CO_2 emitters depends upon several factors: the age and performance characteristics of each vehicle, the fuel burned, the number of vehicles of each type on the road, and how far they are driven. As the following table shows, cars and trucks account for the vast majority of CO_2 emissions in the transportation sector, and their combined emissions (especially the light truck category, including sport-utility vehicles) grew steadily from 1990 to 2001.[4] More energy-efficient vehicles, use of alternative fuels, and system efficiencies can all help limit these emissions, but less driving could also make a significant contribution.[5]

■ Transportation–related CO_2 emissions (teragrams)

Vehicle Type	1990	2001
Cars	600.3	632.7
Light trucks	306.2	460.0
Other trucks	203.9	298.3
Buses	7.5	8.6
Aircraft	176.9	183.9
Boats	48.6	58.3
Locomotives	28.1	34.3
Other (motorcycles, construction equipment, agricultural machinery, etc.)	102.0	115.8
Total	**1473.5**	**1791.9**

SOURCE: EPA (United States Environmental Protection Agency), "Inventory of U.S. Greenhouse Gas Emissions and Sinks: 1990-2001" (USEPA #430-R-03-004). Washington: Office of Atmospheric Programs, U.S. Environmental Protection Agency, April 2003.

1. IPCC (Intergovernmental Panel on Climate Change). *Climate Change 2001* (4 Volumes). Geneva: IPCC, 200 1. Available: http://www.ipcc.ch/pub/reports.htm (accessed December 2, 2003).
2. Haines A, Patz JA. Health effects of climate change. *Journal of the American Medical Association* 2004;291(1):99–103; McMichael AJ. Health consequences of global climate change. *Journal of the Royal Society of Medicine* 2001;94(3):111–14.
3. United States Environmental Protection Agency. Inventory of U.S. Greenhouse Gas Emissions and Sinks: 1990-2001. USEPA #430-R-03-004. Washington, DC: Office of Atmospheric Programs, U.S. Environmental Protection Agency, April 2003.
4. Ibid.
5. Greene DL, Schafer A. *Reducing Greenhouse Gas Emissions from U.S. Transportation*. Philadelphia: Pew Center on Global Climate Change, May 2003. Available: http://www.pewclimate.org/docUploads/ustransp%2Epdf (accessed December 2, 2003).

sports—which involves deep and rapid breathing outdoors during high-ozone times of the day—are at increased risk of developing asthma if they live in high-ozone areas.[38] (The special risks of air pollution for children are discussed further in Chapter 10.) Findings like these emphasize that long-term exposure to air pollution, including the pollutants that derive from motor vehicles, can have lasting effects on respiratory health.

Other Health Effects

Air pollution exposure threatens health in a variety of other ways, beyond shortening life and contributing to respiratory disease. One target is the cardiovascular system, which was discussed in the section on mortality. But mortality is not the only indicator of cardiovascular harm. When patients with coronary artery disease are exposed to PM, their exercise stress tests show an increased level of ischemic changes.[39] Higher PM levels are associated with increased hospital admissions for ischemic heart disease, congestive heart failure, and strokes.[40] Air pollution is a respiratory toxin in many respects.

Could air pollution exposure be associated with cancer? Several components of air pollution are considered probable human carcinogens. These include diesel exhaust,[41] 1,3-butadiene,[42] and aldehydes such as formaldehyde,[43] all of which come at least in part from motor vehicles. Epidemiologic observations link exposure to air pollution with cancer, especially lung cancer.[44] For example, in the American Cancer Society's Cancer Prevention II study, which found a link between $PM_{2.5}$ exposure and cardiopulmonary mortality, every increase of 10 µg/m^3 of $PM_{2.5}$ also increased the risk of lung cancer death by about 14 percent, after controlling for smoking and other risk factors.[45] Smoking is clearly the predominant risk factor for lung cancer, but traffic-related air pollution appears to contribute to this risk as well.

Finally, some evidence suggests that air pollution may play a role in adverse birth outcomes, such as low birth weight and preterm birth. One study, which reviewed data from the California Birth Defects Monitoring Program for a seven-year period, found an association between air pollution exposure during the second month of pregnancy and risk of cardiac ventricular septal defect (for carbon monoxide) and aortic artery and valve defects, pulmonary artery and valve anomalies, and conotruncal defects (for ozone).[46] This is an area that requires much more research.

CONCLUSION

We began this chapter by proposing three links: between land use patterns and travel behavior, between travel behavior and vehicle emissions, and between air quality and health. Sprawl leads to increased driving, as described in Chapter 1. As cars and trucks cover longer and longer distances, they produce large quantities of air emissions. And these emissions threaten the public's health, increasing mortality, and raising the risk of respiratory disease, cardiovascular disease, and cancer. Indirectly, by contributing to global climate change, motor vehicle emissions also threaten health in other ways.

Coping with air pollution in sprawling areas is a vexing challenge. Throughout the year, but especially on high-ozone days, people should be encouraged to walk or bicycle to work and school instead of driving. This behavior reduces the volume of traffic, helps diminish air pollution, and offers the additional benefits of physical activity. But in a polluted area, a person who walks or bikes home from work—prolonging the exposure time, breathing unconditioned air, and breathing at a higher rate than during driving—sustains a greater exposure to pollution than he or she would while driving. There are other dilemmas that face health professionals. For example, after-school sports are a wonderful way to promote children's health. But the afternoon hours are when ozone levels reach their peak, and the exposure can endanger children.

The only answer to these dilemmas, in the long run, is primary prevention: controlling levels of air pollutants. Reducing emissions from automobiles and trucks can be achieved, in part, by consolidating growth into centers, reducing the need for automobile travel. However, the resulting higher densities could increase traffic congestion and worsen pollution exposures in centers, so land use changes will need to go hand in hand with cleaner vehicles, and a shift to travel within centers by foot, bicycle, and transit.

Outdoor air should be clean enough through the day, and throughout the year, to permit people to be physically active without threatening their health. This will require technical advances, behavior changes, and policy changes, and much of this effort will need to focus on the land use and transportation patterns of sprawling metropolitan areas.

CHAPTER 5

■ ══════════ ■

PHYSICAL ACTIVITY, SPRAWL, AND HEALTH

A century ago, physical activity was woven into the fabric of life. Most jobs required physical exertion. Much of the population was agricultural, and farm life consisted of long days of hard work. Factory work, construction work, and even many service jobs required strenuous exertion. People walked to get from place to place, they used stairs instead of elevators and escalators, and household chores—cleaning, cooking, gardening, and repair work—were acts of manual labor.

In just a few generations, the built environment has changed profoundly, and with it, the levels of physical activity in daily life. With changes in technology and migration from the countryside to metropolitan areas, agricultural labor now accounts for less than 5 percent of the workforce. Machines have replaced muscle power, transforming manufacturing and construction work. In a "postindustrial" economy, the typical job now involves sitting at a desk or computer terminal. Conveyor belts move us through airports, escalators move us up and down in stores, and elevators take us from lobbies to upper floors. At home, washing machines, dryers, dishwashers, blenders, vacuum cleaners, leaf blowers, gasoline-powered lawn mowers, and countless other appliances have eased the physical burden of household work. And as detailed in Chapters 1 and 2, changes in land use have radically changed the way we travel. Different land uses are separated from each other by large distances. The transportation infrastructure is increasingly planned and built for automobiles rather than for pedestrians. Travel by foot or bicycle has given way to driving.

The result is a nation of sedentary people. According to the Behavioral Risk Factor Surveillance System (BRFSS), an annual national survey, more than half of American adults are not physically active on a regular basis, and just over one in four reports no leisure-time physical activity at all.[1] In 2000, only 26.2 percent of adults were classified as meeting recommended levels of physical activity (defined as any physical activity for at least thirty minutes per day at least five days per week, or vigorous physical activity for at least twenty minutes at least three days per week). In 2001, when the recommended level of physical activity had been slightly redefined and the BRFSS questions changed, the proportion of adults meeting recommended levels of physical activity rose, but only to 45.4 percent (ranging from a low of 28.9 percent in Kentucky to a high of 55.8 percent in Wyoming). Among children aged nine to thirteen, the pattern is similar: 61.5 percent participate in no organized physical activity when not in school, and 22.6 percent engage in no free-time physical activity.[2]

Sedentary lifestyles have emerged as a pressing public health challenge, because some of the consequences—overweight, type 2 diabetes, and other conditions—have reached epidemic proportions. Public health advocates have worked hard to promote more physical activity, and researchers have worked hard to identify what factors will help in this effort. Clearly, there are many such factors. In their 1999 book, *Physical Activity and Behavioral Medicine*,[3] Sallis and Owen proposed an ecological model that included six categories: demographic and biological factors (such as age, gender, race, and socioeconomic status); psychological, cognitive, and emotional factors (such as knowledge, attitudes, beliefs about exercise, and stress levels); behavioral attributes and skills (such as past history of physical activity); social and cultural factors (such as family and social support); physical environment factors (such as the presence of sidewalks and attractive scenery); and physical activity characteristics (such as intensity). The ecological model predicts that these categories of factors interact in complex ways. While all these factors are important, our focus in this chapter is on the physical environment. In particular, we ask whether sprawl—the combination of low density, low land use mix, low connectivity, and automobile dependence—may contribute to sedentary lifestyles. More broadly, we ask how the built environment can be designed to promote physical activity, and thereby to promote health.

The Varieties of Physical Activity

To consider the relationship between sprawl and physical activity, we need to understand the categories of physical activity. Three dimensions are especially relevant: recreational versus utilitarian activity, moderate versus intense activity, and activity as it varies among different groups of people.

Physical activity may be either recreational or utilitarian.[4] Recreational physical activity—a jog in the park, a game of tennis—is carried out with the intention of getting exercise. In contrast, utilitarian physical activity is activity done for a purpose, such as walking to the store, to the theater, or to work. The primary purpose of such a trip is to arrive at the destination, and the physical activity it involves is incidental. Physical activity done at work—lifting boxes, carrying tools, and so on—is also utilitarian, and for some people, it accounts for the majority of physical activity. (Some activities, such as gardening, have both recreational and utilitarian qualities.)

The distinction is important because the impetus for recreational physical activity is very different than the impetus for utilitarian physical activity. Recreational physical activity, or exercise, requires a high level of motivation, and even people who begin exercise programs often do not sustain them. Utilitarian physical activity, on the other hand, is secondary to other goals. For this reason, it may be easier to build into a daily routine and maintain over time. A person who walks three blocks from home to the subway each morning, rides to the station near his office, walks the final two blocks to his office, and reverses the commute at the end of the day, walks at least ten blocks a day (and even more if he walks to lunch or on errands at midday). Even if he gets no "exercise" at all, his daily routine includes a fair level of physical activity.

The built environment influences both recreational and utilitarian physical activity. Environments that provide facilities for active recreation, such as nearby parks, multiuse trails, and even appealing sidewalks or public spaces for evening strolls, may promote recreational physical activity. On the utilitarian side, environments that facilitate commuting by foot, bicycle, or transit (most transit riders are also walkers, since they have to travel to and from the transit stops) help incorporate walking or bicycling as a daily routine. Environments that locate stores, theaters, and other destinations within walking distance of home and work have the same potential, a strategic opportunity since nonwork trips account for the majority of trips people make.

Another important distinction is between moderate and vigorous physical activity. Moderate physical activity is defined as activity that raises the heart rate to 50 to 69 percent of its maximum capacity, whereas vigorous physical activity raises the heart rate to at least 70 percent of its maximum. A person's maximum heart rate is commonly estimated by subtracting his or her age from 220. For example, a fifty-year-old person's estimated maximum heart rate would be 220 - 50 = 170 beats per minute. The 50 percent and 70 percent levels would be 85 and 119 beats per minute, respectively.

Brisk walking, bicycling, and even gardening qualify as moderate physical activities.[5] Current recommendations are for a half hour of moderate physical activity on at least five days per week,[6] although some experts have suggested higher levels.[7] Moderate physical activity is as beneficial as vigorous exercise in preventing cardiovascular disease, assuming that equivalent levels of energy are expended.[8] Contrary to popular opinion, such activity does not need to be accumulated in one activity session, such as a gym workout. Multiple episodes during that day, as short as eight or ten minutes, offer the same benefit. This has implications for built environment design; places designed so that people walk on multiple occasions during the day may go a long way toward helping them reach recommended levels of physical activity.

A final distinction is not between different kinds of physical activity, but among different groups of people. Different people are active (or inactive) in different ways. Much research in recent years has characterized the physical activity patterns, and the reasons for inactivity, among various populations. Studies have examined physical activity patterns according to gender, age, and race and ethnicity.[9] Generally, these studies have suggested that inactivity is higher among members of minority groups, poor people, and women. Members of these groups cite a wide range of constraints on physical activity. Some pertain to life circumstances, such as being too busy; juggling competing demands from job, family, or friends; being physically tired or ill; and major life changes or traumas. Poor people cite economic constraints to physical activity. Other constraints pertain more to the environment, including safety concerns, weather and environment, and a lack of facilities and opportunities to be physically active.

Those who want to promote physical activity through community design, then, face several questions. What design features promote utilitarian physical activity, which may be the most sustainable strategy? What design features promote recreational physical activity among those who might otherwise not exercise? How much physical activity results from various design interventions? And how should strategies be tailored to meet the needs of different groups of people?

THE HEALTH BENEFITS OF PHYSICAL ACTIVITY

These questions matter because physical activity is good for health, and being sedentary threatens health both directly and indirectly. A sedentary lifestyle increases the risk of cardiovascular disease, stroke, and all-cause mortality,[10] whereas physical activity prolongs life.[11] Men in the lowest quintile of physical fitness have a two- to threefold increased risk of dying overall, and a three- to fivefold increased risk of dying of cardiovascular disease, compared to men who are more fit.[12] Among women, walking ten blocks per day or more is associated with a 33 percent decrease in the risk of cardiovascular disease.[13] The risk of low physical fitness is comparable to, and in some studies greater than, the risk of hypertension, high cholesterol, diabetes, and even smoking.[14] Physical fitness prevents cardiovascular disease and prolongs life among people with diabetes, and the benefits are greatest among those with the highest blood sugar levels.[15] Physical activity also appears to be protective against cancer,[16] cognitive decline in the elderly,[17] depression,[18] osteoporosis,[19] and a range of other common diseases.

In addition to its direct effects on health, lack of physical activity is also a risk factor for being overweight. Weight gain has reached epidemic proportions in the United States (and in some other industrialized countries). While weight gain is a complex phenomenon, it is based on some simple algebra: more calories are consumed than burned. In theory, the epidemic of obesity could result from more food intake, from less exertion, or from both. Food intake indeed plays a crucial role, prompted by low-cost, calorie-intensive, supersized portions that are aggressively marketed.[20] Food is a subject with much media appeal; magazines, newspapers, radio talk shows, television shows and ads, and billboards are full of weight loss supplements and miraculous new diets, suggesting that better eating will solve the problem of overweight. But physical activity is also a crucial part of the equation. This was graphically demonstrated in a *British Medical Journal* article on obesity in Britain that asked the provocative question, "gluttony or sloth?" (Figure 5-1). The article showed that from 1950 to 1990, obesity steadily increased, even as gluttony peaked and declined. Sloth, on the other hand, increased in tandem with obesity, suggesting an important causal role.[21]

Gluttony and sloth together have contributed to a rapid increase in the prevalence of overweight in recent years. In 1960, 24 percent of Americans were overweight (defined as a body mass index, or BMI, above 25 kg/m^2), and by 1990 that proportion had increased to 33 percent.[22] During the same interval, the prevalence of obesity (defined as a BMI above 30 kg/m^2) nearly doubled.[23] According to data from the Behavioral Risk Factor Surveillance System (BRFSS), this trend continued during the 1990s, with the prevalence of obesity rising from

■ **FIGURE 5-1**   Obesity trends compared to "gluttony" on the left (measured as energy intake and fat intake) and to "sloth" on the right (measured by car ownership and television viewing)

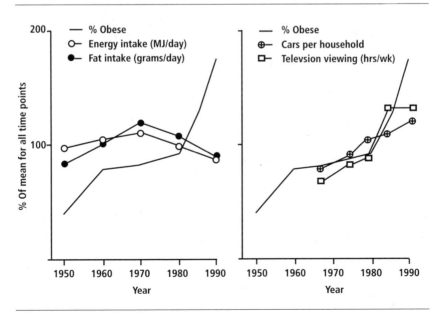

SOURCE: A. M. Prentice and S. A. Jebb, "Obesity in Britain: Gluttony or Sloth?" *British Medical Journal* 1995;311:437-39.

12.0 percent in 1991 to 19.8 percent in 2000.[24] By 2001, the prevalence of obesity among adults had reached 20.9 percent.[25] These trends are dramatically displayed on maps prepared by the Centers for Disease Control and Prevention (CDC), which trace the advance of the obesity epidemic on a state-by-state basis (Figure 5-2).

Being overweight is itself a well-established risk factor for a number of diseases.[26] People who are overweight die at as much as 2.5 times the rate of non-obese people,[27] and an estimated 300,000 Americans die preventable deaths each year as the result of being obese.[28] Being

■ **FIGURE 5-2** Obesity among adults by state. Obesity is defined as a Body Mass Index of greater than 30, corresponding to a weight of about 185 pounds for a height of 5'6", 210 pounds for a height of 5'10", and 230 pounds for a height of 6'1". The states in white (in the 1991 map) are missing data. The shades of gray correspond to the obesity prevalence percentage shown in the legend. The percentages span from below 10 percent to 25 percent or higher.

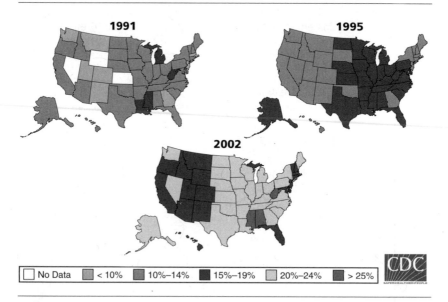

SOURCES: U.S. Obesity Trends 1985 to 2002, Division of Nutrition and Physical Activity, National Center for Chronic Disease Prevention and Health Promotion, U.S. Centers for Disease Control and Prevention (CDC). Available (including year-by-year maps) at http://www.cdc.gov/nccdphp/dnpa/obesity/trend/maps/index.htm. Data drawn from: A. H. Mokdad, M. K. Serdula, W. H. Dietz, B. A. Bowman, J. M. Marks, and J. P. Koplan, "The Spread of the Obesity Epidemic in the United States," 1991-1998, *JAMA* 1999;282:1519-22; A. H. Mokdad, B. A. Bowman, E. S. Ford, F. Vinicor, J. S. Marks, and J. P. Koplan, "The Continuing Epidemics of Obesity and Diabetes in the United States," *JAMA* 2001;286:1195-1200.

overweight increases the risk of high blood pressure, osteoarthritis, high cholesterol and other lipid abnormalities, asthma (perhaps only in women[29]), ischemic heart disease such as angina and heart attacks (as much as fourfold), and gall bladder disease.[30] Obesity increases the risk of type 2 diabetes by as much as fortyfold,[31] and by 2001, the diabetes epidemic had advanced to the point that 7.9 percent of adults in the United States reported the disease.[32] A recent report from the American Cancer Society's Cancer Prevention Study II, which has followed more than 1 million Americans since 1982, showed a dramatic relationship between body weight and risk of cancer.[33] As shown in Figure 5-3, people in the highest category of body weight had significantly increased risks of a wide range of cancers, including common sites such as colon–rectum, prostate, and breast. (For these sites, even a small increase in relative risk translates to a large increase in the number of cases, and a large burden of excess disease across the population.) Obesity is associated with depression, perhaps through genetic traits that predispose to both conditions, and perhaps through such mechanisms as low self-esteem.[34]

Overall, then, both inactivity and its first cousin, overweight, are major public health challenges in the United States. Can we identify some features of sprawl that aggravate these problems and, more important, some design solutions that would help get people more physically active and healthier?

PHYSICAL ACTIVITY AND THE BUILT ENVIRONMENT

In November 2003, the *Atlanta Journal-Constitution* profiled a sixty-seven-year-old retired couple, Carolyn and Norman Daniels, who had recently moved to a neighborhood on the Silver Comet Trail, a popular multiuse trail near Atlanta.[35] Both reported routinely using the trail, Norman on his bicycle and Carolyn on foot. For each of them, the regular activity was new, and both gave credit to the nearby trail. "I hadn't used that bike in how many years?" Norman wondered aloud to his wife and the reporter. "Six or seven or eight?" Carolyn, who had exercised only occasionally on a stationary bike in her bedroom, was walking three times each week with other women in the neighborhood. "I like to walk with the girls," she said. "We just enjoy running our mouths. It's more sociable." As this story showed, a convenient, attractive trail could motivate previously sedentary people to become active.

Cancer mortality among (a) men and (b) women in relation to body weight. In each case, the highest weight category (shown by the Body Mass Index in parentheses) is compared to the reference category. The number above each line is the relative risk of dying of that cancer.

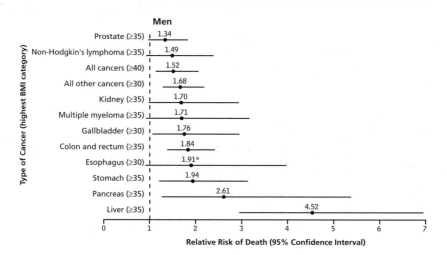

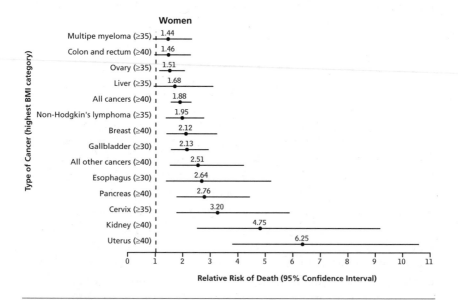

SOURCE: E. E. Calle, C. Rodriguez, K. Walker-Thurmond, and M. J. Thun, "Overweight, Obesity, and Mortality from Cancer in a Prospectively Studied Cohort of U.S. Adults," *New England Journal of Medicine* 2003;348:1625-38.

It also made clear that other factors—such as the company of friends—played an important role.

What features of community design encourage physical activity? In particular, what environmental factors get people out of cars for utilitarian trips, and motivate inactive people to start exercising? To what extent are these factors found in sprawling areas? In recent years, more and more evidence has become available to help answer these questions.[36]

Frank, Engelke, and Schmid[37] identify three dimensions of the built environment that help organize answers to these questions: land use patterns, design characteristics, and transportation systems. Each of these has a distinct role in shaping activity. Land use patterns operate at a large spatial scale, and determine the arrangement of physical activities across the metropolis. Design characteristics operate on a smaller spatial scale. Examples include the architecture or buildings; the width, tree canopy, and placement of sidewalks; and the vistas in a park; which when taken collectively create a sense or feeling of place. Transportation systems connect different land uses, and define the relative ease and convenience of walking, bicycling, transit, and driving.

Pikora and colleagues in Australia[38] proposed a further framework, related primarily to design characteristics, for classifying the determinants of walking and cycling. They identified four categories: functional factors, safety factors, aesthetic factors, and destination factors. Functional factors relate to the physical attributes of the street or path, such as path continuity and design, street type and width, and traffic volume. Safety factors include crossing aids, lighting, and the level of passive surveillance of the path or sidewalk. Aesthetic factors include cleanliness, maintenance, the presence of trees, and architecture. And destinations are such places as parks, transit nodes, stores, and restaurants. In interviews with experts, they asked which of these factors seemed most important in determining people's walking and bicycling behavior, for both recreational and utilitarian purposes. The experts identified several factors as being most important. These included safety factors, attractiveness of the streetscape, the presence of destinations (for walking), and the presence of a continuous route and traffic safety (for bicycling). The relative importance of these factors will need to be confirmed by further research.

Research has identified many determinants of physical activity. These include overall neighborhood design features, density, land use mix, the presence and quality of sidewalks and footpaths, enjoyable scenery, the presence of other people who are physically active, and safety.

Overall Neighborhood Design

The overall form of a neighborhood seems to have an effect on residents' levels of physical activity. For example, rural residents generally report less leisure-time physical activity than urban residents.[39]

Many studies in the transportation literature have compared the frequency of walking in "high-walkable" and "low-walkable" neighborhoods. The high-walkable neighborhoods are characterized by high density, high land use mix, high connectivity, good walking infrastructure, pleasing aesthetics, and safety, whereas the low-walkable neighborhoods lack most or all of these features. People in both kinds of neighborhoods keep travel logs to record their travel behavior. In general, people in high-walkable neighborhoods record more walking trips per week, sometimes by a factor of four or five, especially for utilitarian trips such as errands and going to work.[40]

In one such study, Saelens and colleagues compared the levels of physical activity in high-walkable and low-walkable neighborhoods of San Diego by asking people in a neighborhood of each type to complete surveys and wear accelerometers.[41] People in the high-walkable neighborhood (which featured higher density, land use mix, connectivity, aesthetics, and safety) averaged 194.8 minutes of moderate activity per week, and those in the low-walkable neighborhood averaged only 130.7. In addition, 35 percent of people in the high-walkable neighborhood were overweight, as compared to 60 percent in the low-walkable neighborhood. SMARTRAQ, a study of land use, transportation, and public health in Atlanta found that the proportion of obese White males declined from 23 percent to 13 percent as neighborhood residential density increased from less than two to more than eight dwellings per acre.[42]

Studies of sprawl on the scale of entire metropolitan regions reveal similar findings. One of the largest such studies was performed by Ewing and colleagues.[43] These investigators looked at physical activity patterns in nearly 400,000 people who lived in 448 U.S. counties and 83 metropolitan areas, as reported in the BRFSS over three years (1998–2000). Each county or metropolitan area was scored on a "sprawl index," based on density, land use mix, degree of "centering," and street accessibility. There was a clear relationship between the degree of sprawl and the amount of walking; more sprawl was associated with less walking. More sprawl was also associated with less leisure-time physical activity, although this relationship did not reach statistical significance. Interestingly, the investigators went a step further and looked at related health outcomes such as obesity, hypertension, diabetes, and coronary heart disease. As the level of sprawl increased, so did hypertension, body weight, and the probability of being obese. More sprawl also tended to predict a higher prevalence of diabetes and coronary heart disease, but these relationships were weaker, and did not reach statistical significance.

A commonly used question in studies of predictors of physical activity is deceptively simple: "Do you have access to places to be physically active?" This is not solely a question about neighborhood design, since a person may answer yes because of an exercise bike in the basement or membership in a health club 20 miles away. Moreover, a yes answer reflects the person's *perception* of access, which could be influenced by proximity, safety, and numerous other factors. However, part of "having access to places to be physically active" probably reflects neighborhood facilities. Not surprisingly, a positive answer to this question is a strong predictor of being physically active. For example, in a survey of nearly 1,800 adults in North Carolina, those who answered yes to this question were more than twice as likely to be physically active in their leisure time, and to be getting recommended levels of physical activity, as those who answered no.[44] This finding suggests that access to venues for physical activity—whether they be parks, trails, or sidewalks—is a design feature that may promote physical activity.

An interesting approach is to consider housing age as an indicator of overall neighborhood design. Older neighborhoods, especially those built before the widespread adoption of automobiles in the 1920s, are likely to be pedestrian-oriented in many ways, including the presence of sidewalks, pedestrian-scaled scenery, and mixed land uses. Berrigan and Troiano, researchers at the National Institutes of Health, took this approach in analyzing data from the Third National Health and Nutrition Examination Survey (NHANES).[45] Among the nearly 15,000 respondents they studied, people who lived in a home built after 1973 were significantly less likely to walk a mile or more at least twenty times per month than people who lived in an older home.

Overall, it appears that certain kinds of neighborhoods—older places, with a less sprawling quality, and with accessible nearby destinations— are places where people are more active. What specific attributes of such places encourage their residents to be physically active?

Neighborhood Density

Research in the transportation field has long shown that higher density is associated with more walking. For example, Ross and Dunning analyzed results from the 1995 National Personal Transportation Survey.[46] In the least dense areas, with fewer than 100 housing units per square mile (equivalent to less than one unit per 6.4 acres), only 3.3 percent of trips were on foot or bicycle. In contrast, the densest areas had over 3,000 units per square mile (4.7 units per acre), and 14.9 percent of trips were on foot or bicycle, a difference of nearly fivefold.

Land Use Mix

Similarly, the mix of different land uses has been consistently associated with more walking. For example, in the Puget Sound Transportation Panel, a study of 1,680 Seattle area households between 1989 and 1994, a high level of land use mix in a neighborhood predicted more walking for both shopping trips and commuting to work.[47] In a study of the 1990 San Francisco Bay Area Travel Surveys, a similar finding emerged.[48] It stands to reason that when different kinds of destinations are within easy walking distance, people will be more likely to walk to them.

Nearby Sidewalks and Footpaths

Many studies have suggested that access to sidewalks and footpaths is associated with more walking. This is true for both utilitarian and recreational walking. For example, a Canadian study[49] examined walking to work in twenty-seven neighborhoods in three provinces, ranging from urban to suburban to small town settings. The proportion of people who walked to work varied from less than 2 percent to over 40 percent, and the suburban neighborhoods had the lowest proportion of walkers (and the highest proportion of automobile drivers). Simply having sidewalks available predicted walking to work, but so did several specific design features that were felt to "meet pedestrians' needs": continuous uninterrupted routes, multiple route choices, easily navigated topography, and crossing lights. (There were other predictors of walking to work, including the number and variety of nearby destinations; links to transit; and an environment that was interesting, attractive, and varied, but not too complex or overwhelming.)

On the recreational side, a statewide survey in Georgia asked adults about their access to "places where people can walk for exercise or recreation, such as trails, parks, sidewalks, and treadmills," and about their exercise patterns.[50] There was a direct relationship between having a convenient place for exercising and achieving recommended levels of physical activity. People who lived within ten minutes' walk of a park had a 51.8 percent probability of meeting physical activity recommendations, compared to 36.7 percent among people without such a nearby park. A walking or jogging trail within ten minutes was associated with a 51.6 percent probability of meeting physical activity recommendations, compared to 40.2 percent without such a nearby trail. Overall, among people who reported a place to walk within ten minutes of home, 41.5 percent were meeting physical activity recommendations, while among those without such a place, the proportion was only 27.4 percent.

Other studies[51] have shown that accessible, well-built sidewalks and trails predict walking. It almost goes without saying that the sidewalks and trails are used more when they are close to where people live. For example, a survey of more than 400 adults in Arlington, Massachusetts, focused on the Minuteman Trail in that town, found that every quarter mile in distance from the trail decreased use of the trail by almost 50 percent.[52] In an Australian study, although streets and public open spaces were far more commonly used for exercise than health clubs, swimming pools, and other formal facilities, the use of these informal settings was far more sensitive to distance.[53] As a person's home distance from a park increased, the person became much less likely to use the park, emphasizing the importance of designing and building such amenities in residential areas. Not all studies show an association between the presence of sidewalks and more physical activity,[54] perhaps because, in at least some settings, other factors play a more important role.

Enjoyable Scenery

People are more likely to get out and be active in places that are attractive and aesthetically appealing. This may involve natural beauty, with the presence of trees, riverfronts, or distant views, or it may simply involve well-designed streets and parks. In the U.S. Women's Determinants Study, which included over 2,000 women evenly distributed among White, Black, Hispanic, and Native American participants, having enjoyable scenery was a predictor of leisure-time physical activity.[55] Similarly, in the 1996 Physical Activity Survey in New South Wales, Australia, over 3,300 adults were interviewed.[56] Three statements in the interview evaluated the aesthetic qualities of their neighborhoods: "Your neighborhood is friendly," "Your local area is attractive," and "You find it pleasant walking near your home." The probability of having walked for exercise in the last two weeks was nearly twice as high if the combined scores for these statements were high compared to if they were low. These findings resonate with recent research suggesting that "green exercise"—physical activity in natural settings—may offer benefits above and beyond simply burning calories on a treadmill.[57] Attractive natural settings may not only attract people to exercise in them, but also provide special benefits to those who take advantage of them.

Other People Who Are Physically Active

People seem to like being physically active in environments where others are doing the same. This may involve companions with whom to walk (as exemplified by Carolyn Daniels earlier in this chapter), or simply enjoying the sight of others on the sidewalk or in the park. In a survey of over 3,200 randomly selected Australian households, for instance, adults aged sixty and over were queried about their level of physical activity and associated personal and environmental factors. Observing others in the neighborhood being physically active was one of the factors that predicted being physically active (although it just missed statistical significance).[58] Similarly, in the Women's Determinants Study described previously, "frequently seeing others exercise" was associated with being physically active; interestingly, this effect was strongest among African American women.[59] These results suggest that public venues such as sidewalks and parks (and perhaps sports clubs), which offer the appeal of other people, might encourage physical activity.

Safety

People are most comfortable being physically active when they can do so in places that they perceive to be safe. In the BRFSS, for example, people were asked, "How safe from crime do you consider your neighborhood to be?" They answered on a four-point scale: "extremely safe," "quite safe," "slightly safe," and "not at all safe." In nearly all subgroups of respondents, physical inactivity increased as the responses moved from "extremely safe" to "not at all safe." The gradient was particularly striking for elderly people and for women.[60] Similar findings emerged in the Australian study described above,[61] where "footpaths perceived as safe for walking" nearly doubled the probability of being physically active, but not in the U.S. Women's Determinants Study.[62] Environments perceived as low in crime are environments that may promote physical activity.

Together, these design features offer guidance in designing communities that promote physical activity. Such communities are relatively dense; they contain various kinds of places including homes, stores, restaurants, and recreational destinations; and they are well supplied with sidewalks, paths, and other settings for activity. They offer appealing scenery that attracts people out of their homes, into parks, and onto paths. Other people can also be seen getting physical activity, and (perhaps related) crime is uncommon. Some studies also suggest additional features, such as absence of nearby heavy traffic, absence of busy streets that impede access to parks and paths, and good lighting. Together, these features paint a picture of communities very different than the usual sprawling suburbs. Sprawl, it appears, may undermine public health not only by fostering excessive reliance on automobiles, but also by incorporating design features that discourage physical activity.

LIMITS TO WHAT WE KNOW

There are limits to the conclusion that sprawl inhibits physical activity. First, sprawl is not the only culprit in the modern epidemics of inactivity, overweight, diabetes, and related conditions. Many factors other than community design help determine people's activity levels. The ecological model discussed earlier[63] predicts that features of the physical environment interact with social, attitudinal, and other factors to determine physical activity patterns. Indeed, many such factors have been identified, including self-efficacy, social support, and others.[64]

Reflecting this complexity, the U.S. Task Force on Community Preventive Services was able to identify very few evidence-based environmental approaches to increasing physical activity in communities.[65] In 2002, the task force recommended six interventions, of which two were informational (community-wide campaigns and point-of-decision prompts to encourage use of stairs), three were behavioral and social (school-based physical education, social support interventions such as buddy systems, and personal health behavior change programs), and only one used environmental and policy approaches. This one recommended creating or enhancing access to places for physical activity, together with informational outreach activities. Based on currently available evidence, environmental factors that promote physical activity are only one part of a much larger set of considerations.

Current travel patterns remind us that attitudes and preferences (as opposed to environmental design) have a great deal to do with travel behavior. A substantial proportion of trips, especially nonwork trips, traverse a "walkable" distance of less than a quarter mile, yet many of these trips are made by automobile.[66] According to survey research, the average American is willing to walk less than a quarter mile, and in some cases as little as 400 feet, for errands. The 1983–84 National Personal Transportation Survey suggested that 70 percent of Americans would walk 500 feet for daily errands, 40 percent would walk one-fifth of a mile, and only 10 percent would walk a half mile.[67] Another study found that people were willing to walk between 400 and 1,200 feet for typical trips.[68] The preference for driving over walking, even when walking is feasible, is by now deeply ingrained. Therefore, the design features that provide for walking—nearby destinations, density, good sidewalks, attractive scenery, and so on—will need to be complemented by changes in public attitudes if walking and bicycling are to become more widespread. More research is needed to clarify how the distance we are willing to walk is impacted by the design features discussed in this chapter.

Not only are environmental interventions only one part of the solution to physical inactivity, but in most studies their impact is relatively modest. For example, in the large study by Ewing and colleagues that showed an association between sprawl and physical activity,[69] the difference between the most- and least-sprawling areas corresponded to less than a 12 percent difference in the probability of getting any leisure-time physical activity. While studies at a finer scale might show more pronounced effects, the magnitude of these effects, taken in isolation, may remain limited.

Another limit is that we do not understand how to implement the best design features. There is no simple formula for deploying design features that are shown to promote physical activity. There is no guarantee that, say, increasing the density of a neighborhood will result in more physical activity among its residents. Research has identified specific design features that promote physical activity, but there is still much to understand about how to incorporate them into both new and existing neighborhoods, how they work in combination, and the optimal ways to combine them. Urban planner Michael Southworth has pointed out that even in New Urbanist communities, which give careful attention to mixed use, public open space, and sidewalks, attempts to create pedestrian access to parks, schools, civic facilities, and shops and services "cannot be said to be entirely successful."[70] Design principles that combine these features, and perhaps traditional urban characteristics such as mixed income housing and commercial and industrial spaces, may be needed to create the "urbanity" that will get people to walk.

Finally, our conclusions about what neighborhood features get people to walk are limited by the cross-sectional design of most available studies. In these studies, the walking habits of people in different kinds of neighborhoods are compared at a single point in time. If there is an association between walkable neighborhoods and walking (as there generally is), it is not clear in which direction the causal arrow points. People walk more in neighborhoods that offer mixed use, sidewalks, and other pedestrian attractions; but this may well be because walkers preferentially move to such neighborhoods, while couch potatoes who want to minimize their walking opt for auto-dependent suburbs instead. Ideally, we would randomly assign people to walkable communities or conventional sprawling suburbs, and observe whether walking behavior differed afterward. But since randomized trials of residential location are impossible, creative approaches to research will be needed. For example, cross-sectional studies of people in different types of neighborhoods might control for their stated preferences with regard to walking. Similarly, before–after studies of new sidewalk networks or parks, or before–after studies of people who relocate, might reveal the impact of neighborhood design on residents' activity levels. Such approaches have already begun to confirm the findings of cross-sectional studies.[71]

CONCLUSION

Inactivity and overweight, and associated conditions such as diabetes, have emerged as major public health challenges of this century. These problems have emerged in tandem with urban sprawl. (Of course, concurrent trends such as dietary changes and television and computer infatuations cannot be ignored.) There is growing evidence that the physical features of urban sprawl discourage physical activity, and thereby contribute to these epidemics.

There is an alternative. In some countries, a combination of more walkable built environments and different social attitudes results in dramatically more walking than in the United States. As shown in Figure 5-4, more than 30 percent of trips in the urban areas of the Netherlands, Denmark, Sweden, Austria, Germany, and Switzerland are made on foot or on bicycle. The walkable qualities of European cities are well known, and much appreciated by visitors, who sometimes return to the United States waxing lyrical about the opportunities to walk on their vacations and lamenting the lack of similar environments back home.

▟ FIGURE 5-4   Proportion of trips in urban areas made by walking and bicycling in North America and Europe, 1995

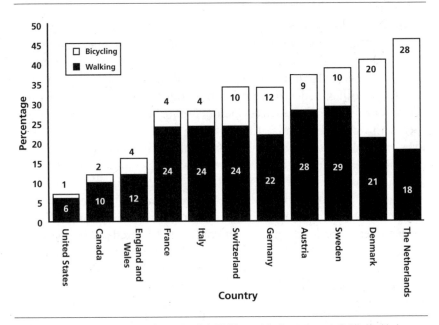

SOURCE: J. Pucher and L. Dijkstra, "Promoting Safe Walking and Cycling to Improve Public Health: Lessons from the Netherlands and Germany," *American Journal of Public Health* 2003;93(9):1509-16.

There is much we still need to learn. Sprawl is clearly not the only, or even the primary, force behind physical inactivity and its health consequences. And better design will clearly not be the only solution. But better design, design that improves on sprawl in ways that seduce people out of their cars and onto sidewalks and bicycle paths, may be a critical part of increasing physical activity and promoting public health. The market will increasingly demand such neighborhoods, and health evidence increasingly confirms their value.

CHAPTER 6

■━━━━━━■

INJURIES AND DEATHS
FROM TRAFFIC

Strategies which reduce the need for car travel or substitute car travel with safer forms of transport would substantially reduce population death rates.[1]

—I. Roberts, 1993

In every American city, a disturbing ritual marks the morning radio news. At regular intervals, a traffic report tells listeners where cars have crashed and which of the collisions have resulted in injuries or deaths. The report also mentions "rubbernecker" delays, debris in the road, breakdowns, and police chases. For most listeners, this is background chatter, hardly noticed or remarked upon (although a lucky few hear the news at the right time and place, and can change their commuting routes to avoid traffic congestion).

Imagine a different morning routine. Imagine that the radio, each morning, announced how many new cases of anthrax had been diagnosed in the city, and how many had been fatal. We would be horrified. We would wonder what diabolical force had imposed such a risk, and we would ask how we might protect ourselves.

But automobile travel is part of the fabric of our lives, especially in sprawling areas. If automobile travel involves some risk of death and injury, for both vehicle occupants and pedestrians, then all things being equal, more driving will lead to more deaths and more injuries. Of course, all things are not equal; the safety of vehicles themselves, the design of roadways, and the ways drivers behave, all vary. In this chapter, we consider the role of sprawl in injuries and fatalities related to automobiles. We begin with a discussion of motor vehicle crashes and their impact on drivers and passengers, and follow this with a discussion of pedestrian injuries and fatalities. Finally, we put the injury risk in perspective, by considering the risk of leaving home more generally.

MOTOR VEHICLE CRASHES

Automobiles claim more than 40,000 lives each year in the United States.[2] Automobile crashes are the leading cause of death among people from one year to twenty-four years old, cause about 3.4 million nonfatal injuries each year, and cost an estimated $200 billion annually.[3] The death toll has slowly declined from about 50,000 per year in the 1960s, thanks to engineering improvements, law enforcement, and public education, but the public health toll remains enormous.

The automobile is a relatively dangerous way to travel. Depending upon the assumptions used, a mile of automobile travel is between 30 and several hundred times more likely to result in the traveler's death than a mile of bus, train, or airplane travel.[4] The National Safety Council uses such data to calculate the "odds of dying" while traveling. According to these figures, the lifetime odds of dying as an automobile driver or passenger are 1 in 242, compared to 1 in 179,003 as a bus passenger, 1 in 119,335 on a train, and 1 in 4,608 on a plane.[5]

According to the American College of Emergency Physicians, "Traffic crashes are predictable and preventable, and therefore are not 'accidents.'"[6] What are the factors that predict automobile crashes? Could some of them have to do with sprawl?

The "three Es" that have helped decrease car crash injury and fatality rates—engineering, enforcement, and education—are well known. These include more crashworthy automobile features, such as crumple zones; restraints, such as seat belts and air bags; advances in road design, such as separating opposing lanes of traffic; imposition and enforcement of speed limits; and laws and social marketing that promote seat belt use and discourage drunk driving. Additional measures, such as improvements in emergency medical care, have helped decrease injuries and deaths from car crashes.

However, even with these advances, the sheer number of vehicle miles traveled (VMTs) and vehicle hours traveled (VHTs) means that people are heavily exposed to the hazards of the road. The epidemiologic concept of "time at risk" is relevant here. As explained in Chapter 1, sprawl implies more time spent in the car. More time in a car, in turn, means greater exposure to the dangers of the road, implying a higher probability of a motor vehicle crash.[7] Despite better cars, better roads, and perhaps better drivers, the huge amount of driving keeps the absolute toll of automobile crashes high.

A second aspect of roadway injury risk in sprawling areas has to do with the drivers themselves. People who need to combine long commutes, or long hours chauffeuring their children, with full work and home schedules, are often tired, busy people. Fatigue and driving are a dangerous combination. Indeed, large numbers of drivers are driving sleepy,[8] especially commuters and long-distance drivers.[9] Fatigue, in turn, is an important risk factor for traffic crashes, and falling asleep at the wheel may account for as many as one in five crashes.[10]

A more recent development is talking on cellular telephones while driving. With more and more time spent on the road, and with more and more people using that time to speak on the telephone (at least one in twenty according to recent roadside observations, with higher numbers during rush hour commuting),[11] a potent new risk has been introduced. Cellular phones offer many benefits,[12] but it is clear that drivers are less attentive to the road while talking on cell phones,[13] and that this is associated with an increased risk of crashes and deaths.[14]

In addition to the amount of time spent on the roads and the attributes of drivers in sprawling areas, a third aspect of sprawl is the quality of roads. Sprawl implies a particular configuration of road types. Suburban developments with "loop and lollipop" roadways connect to "feeder" roads that combine high speed, high traffic volume, and frequent "curb cuts" for entering and exiting stores and other destinations.[15] These are features associated with automobile crashes. In automobile-dependent areas, moreover, roads can become highly congested. Congestion increases the risk of collisions.[16] (This problem is not limited to sprawling areas, of course; congestion also occurs in dense urban settings.)[17]

In residential subdivisions, street widths are typically scaled to permit rapid, unimpeded automobile travel, resulting in relatively wide streets. A 1998 study in Longmont, Colorado, reviewed approximately 20,000 police reports of car crashes, to determine what features of residential street design were associated with crash risk. When numerous features were considered—street width, trees, building height, curb cuts, and others—street width was by far the strongest predictor of crash risk. (The only other predictor of crashes was street curvature.) The safest street width was approximately 24 feet, and streets of standard suburban width, 30 feet, were substantially riskier.[18]

These observations would predict that sprawling metropolitan areas, where people spend more time in automobiles, would have higher automobile fatality rates. Data from the National Highway Traffic Safety Administration (NHTSA) suggest exactly that pattern, although with some exceptions.[19] In general, denser cities, which require shorter trip distances and rely more on walking and public transportation, have lower automobile fatality rates (including drivers and passengers, but excluding pedestrians) than more sprawling cities: 2.45 per 100,000 population per year in San Francisco, 2.30 in New York, 3.21 in Portland, 6.67 in Chicago, and 5.26 in Philadelphia, compared with 10.08 in Houston, 16.15 in Tampa, 12.72 in Atlanta, 11.35 in Dallas, and 9.85 in Phoenix.[20] (There are notable exceptions to this pattern, such as 5.79 per 100,000 population in Los Angeles and 10.93 per 100,000 in Detroit.)[21]

Reid Ewing and colleagues performed a more systematic study of this relationship.[22] They considered 448 metropolitan counties in the 101 most populous metropolitan areas in the United States, and ranked each one using a sprawl index that included measures of density and street accessibility. After controlling for factors such as age, income, and household size, they found a strong relationship between sprawl and traffic fatalities (including both pedestrian and vehicle occupant fatalities). For every one point decrease in the sprawl index (on a scale that ranged from about 60 for very sprawling areas to over 200 for very compact areas), the traffic fatality rate increased by 1.49 percent. In the most sprawling counties in the nation—Geauga County (outside Cleveland, Ohio), Clinton County (outside Lansing, Michigan), Fulton County (outside Toledo, Ohio), Goochland County (outside Richmond, Virginia), and Yadkin County (outside Greensboro, North Carolina)—the traffic fatality rates were nearly 10 times higher than in the most compact counties. If Geauga County had the same traffic fatality rate as New York, then each year, the families of fifteen people in that county would be spared the grief of losing a loved one.

Motor vehicle fatality rates vary widely by racial and ethnic group, especially among males, raising important equity concerns. The rate among Black men is 32.5/100,000 person-years, compared to 10.2 among Hispanic men and 19.5 among White men. Among women, the corresponding figures are 11.6, 9.1, and 8.5. Motor vehicle fatality rates are also higher among people who have low incomes and educational levels, and/or who are unemployed.[23] The explanations for these disparities are complex. Racial and ethnic groups may differ in behavior, in how much time they spend in cars, in the age and condition of their cars, in the roads they use, and in the emergency medical care available, among other factors. Whatever the reasons, when death rates vary this dramatically by racial and ethnic group, preventable factors must be contributing. In this case, less exposure—an approach to land use and transportation that enables people at high risk to decrease their risk—may offer important advantages.

Planners and traffic engineers are faced with competing demands. They need to increase traffic flow to achieve greater efficiency, and they need to slow traffic down and reduce traffic to improve safety. The solutions to these challenges are complex, but it is clear that limiting sprawl—creating "live-work-play" communities that decrease automobile dependence, and offering safe and attractive public transportation alternatives—could help decrease the public health burden of motor vehicle injuries and deaths.

PEDESTRIAN INJURIES AND FATALITIES

On December 14, 1995, seventeen-year-old Cynthia Wiggins rode the public bus to her job at the Walden Galleria mall in suburban Cheektowaga, New York, outside Buffalo. The bus did not stop at the mall itself, so Cynthia had to cross a heavily used seven-lane roadway on foot to complete her trip to work. On that day, she had made it across six lanes when a dump truck crushed her.[24] Her death received national media attention; it was seen as exemplifying inadequate mass transit links, pedestrian-hostile roadways, and the disproportionate impact of these factors on members of minority groups.

Each year, automobiles cause about 6,000 fatalities and 110,000 injuries among pedestrians nationwide. Pedestrians account for about one in eight automobile-related fatalities.[25] Sadly, a mile of walking or biking is more dangerous than a mile of driving, in terms of fatality risk. In 2001, a mile of walking was 23 times more likely to kill a pedestrian, and a mile of biking was 12 times more likely to kill a bicyclist, than a mile of driving was likely to kill a car occupant.[26]

In sprawling areas, the problem seems to be especially worrisome. For example, a study in Atlanta showed that as that city sprawled in recent years, the pedestrian fatality rate increased even as the national rate declined slightly (see Figure 6-1). The most dangerous stretches of road were those built in the style that typifies sprawl: multiple lanes, high speeds, no sidewalks, long distances between intersections or crosswalks, and roadways lined with large commercial establishments and apartments blocks.[27] Across the country, the pattern seen for driver and passenger fatalities is repeated for pedestrian fatalities, with

■ **FIGURE 6-1**   Pedestrian fatality rates (per 100,000 population per year) by year in Cobb, Fulton, DeKalb, and Gwinnett Counties, Georgia, and in the United States, 1994–1998

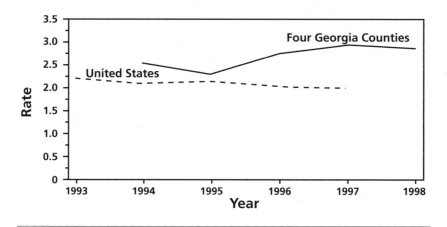

SOURCE: R. Hanzlick, D. McGowan, J. Havlak, M. Bishop, H. Bennett, R. Rawlins, et al., "Pedestrian Fatalities—Cobb, DeKalb, Fulton, and Gwinnett Counties, Georgia, 1994–98," *Morbidity and Mortality Weekly Report* 1999;48:601-05.

lower annual rates in denser cities: 2.22 per 100,000 population in New York, 2.52 in Chicago, 2.57 in Philadelphia, and 1.89 in Portland, compared with 3.03 in Dallas, 4.08 in Phoenix, 6.60 in Tampa, and 3.61 in Atlanta. However, this pattern is not as consistent as for driver and passenger fatalities, and there are exceptions—for example, 2.61 per 100,000 population in Houston, 2.60 in Los Angeles, 3.86 in San Francisco, and 4.73 per 100,000 in Detroit.[28]

For those concerned with the public health implications of sprawl, preventing pedestrian injuries and fatalities is a vexing challenge. It may make sense to recommend that people drive less and walk and bike more, in terms of promoting physical activity, reducing air pollution, and other health goals. But if the roads in sprawling areas are pedestrian hostile, and if there are few sidewalks and paths, then walking in these areas could entail more risk than benefit.

Pedestrian and bicyclist injury and fatality rates are decreasing, not only in the United States but also in other industrialized nations (see Figure 6-2).[29] This is a pyrrhic victory, since it results from the regrettable fact that people are walking less. A recent British study of children's "independent mobility" demonstrates a steep decline in children's exposure to traffic, related to less walking. For example, 80 percent of seven- and eight-year-old English children were permitted

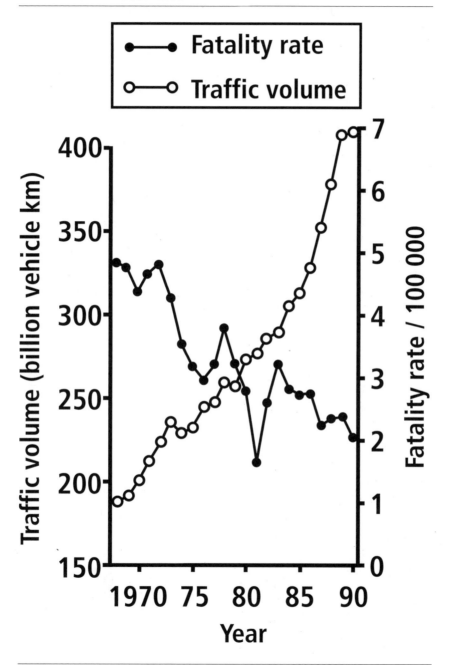

FIGURE 6-2 Child pedestrian death rates and traffic volume in Britain, 1967–1990

SOURCE: I. Roberts, "Why Have Child Pedestrian Death Rates Fallen?" *British Medical Journal* 1993;306:1737-39.

to travel to school unaccompanied in 1971, but by 1990 that proportion had declined to 9 percent. The leading reason parents gave for restricting their children's unaccompanied travel was traffic danger.[30] In the United States, CDC researchers analyzed data from the 1999 nationwide HealthStyles survey.[31] Among respondents who had school-age children, only 19 percent reported that their children had walked to or from school, and 6 percent reported that their children had biked to or from school, at least once a week during the preceding month. The two leading barriers reported to walking or biking to school were distance and traffic; while "safety" was not offered as a perceived barrier, the concern with traffic is presumably a safety concern (see Figure 6-3). Parents who keep their children from walking to school because of safety concerns have some basis for their belief. The more children are exposed to traffic on their way to school (as measured by how many intersections they cross), the higher their risk of being hit by a car.[32] Certainly, not walking or biking is an effective way to reduce pedestrian injuries and fatalities; but, just as certainly, the loss of physical activity exacts public health costs (see Chapter 5).

How might sprawl contribute to pedestrian injuries and fatalities, and what are the prospects for public health improvements? Two aspects are potentially important: the quantity of driving, and the design of walking and biking routes.

■ **FIGURE 6-3** Percentage of HealthStyles Survey respondents reporting barriers to their children walking and biking to school, 1999 (N = 611)

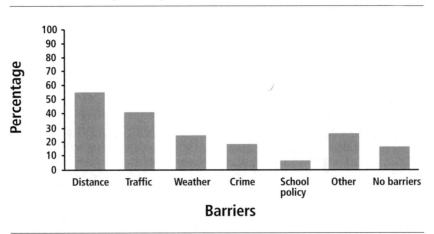

Barriers

SOURCE: A. M. Dellinger and C. E. Staunton, "Barriers to Children Walking and Biking to School—United States, 1999," *Morbidity and Mortality Weekly Report* 2002;51(32):701-04.

Just as for automobile crashes, less driving is likely to make pedestrians and bicyclists safer. An unintended experiment in New Zealand demonstrated this point. Following the 1973 energy crisis, the New Zealand government restricted automobile use. This policy remained in place for seven years, and effectively limited traffic volume. During that time, child pedestrian mortality decreased 46.4 percent.[33] In a long-term study of child pedestrian deaths in the United States, a similar pattern emerged; during years when traffic volume fell, so did pedestrian fatality rates.[34]

Design is also important. Sprawling areas rely heavily on driving for transportation, and infrastructure is designed and built accordingly. Roadways designed to move large numbers of vehicles quickly are usually unfriendly to pedestrians, and alternative routes, such as sidewalks and bicycle paths, are often omitted.

At a very local scale, sprawl may offer safe environments for a certain kind of pedestrian use: small children at play. Cul-de-sacs in suburban subdivisions offer families the prospect of safe play environments for their children, because of the lack of through traffic. But that means a lack of connectivity—one of the defining features of sprawl. The safety of cul-de-sacs for small children may be transitory, for at least two reasons. As children grow older, and as their territories expand, they need to travel to friends' houses and other destinations. The available options—walking or biking on pedestrian-hostile roads, or relying on automobiles—bring hazards of their own (and if the teenagers lack a way to get around, that too has costs, as discussed in Chapter 10). Second, on the larger scale of a metropolitan area or a region, the lack of connectivity requires high levels of driving, and as noted earlier, more driving implies more risk for drivers, passengers, and pedestrians.

Much is known about what design features place pedestrians at risk. As shown in Table 6-1, some of these features are typical of dense urban neighborhoods, such as curb parking (because children dart out into traffic from between parked cars) and high population density. High speeds and high traffic volume, typical of busy roads, are also important risk factors. It is very important to note that children are not only hit by cars while walking to school or other destinations; playing in streets, especially in urban areas, is also a common way to be exposed to traffic hazards.[35] When children have protected play areas such as parks, they are less exposed to traffic hazards.

Several kinds of environmental modifications offer great promise in protecting pedestrians and bicyclists. These can be divided into three categories: separating pedestrians from vehicles, making pedestrians more visible and conspicuous to drivers, and reducing vehicle

■ TABLE 6-1 Neighborhood features that increase the risk of pedestrian injuries.

Design feature	References
High traffic volume	Mueller et al., 1990;[a] Stevenson et al., 1995;[b] Roberts et al., 1995;[c] Agran et al., 1996;[d] Posner et al., 2002[e]
High density of curb parking	Roberts et al., 1995;[f] Agran et al., 1996[d]
High speeds	Mueller et al., 1990;[a] Roberts et al., 1995;[c] Agran et al., 1996;[d] Stevenson et al., 1995;[b] Giese et al., 1997[g]
Number of streets crossed during routine travel	MacPherson et al., 1998[h]
Housing or population density (including multifamily residences)	Rivara and Barber 1985;[i] Joly et al., 1991;[j] Braddock et al., 1991;[k] Bagley 1992;[l] Agran et al., 1996[d]
Absence of a park or play area near the home	Mueller et al., 1990;[a] Joly et al., 1991;[j] Bagley 1992[l]
Presence of crosswalks (where there is no traffic light)	Herms 1972;[m] Stevenson et al., 1995;[b] Zegeer et al., 2001;[n] Koepsell et al., 2002[o]

a. Mueller BA, Rivara FP, Shyh-Mine L, Weiss NS. Environmental factors and the risk of childhood pedestrian-motor vehicle collision occurrence. *American Journal of Epidemiology* 1990; 132:550-60.

b. Stevenson MR, Jamrozik KD, Spittle J. A case-control study of traffic risk factors and child pedestrian injury. *International Journal of Epidemiology* 1995;24:957-64.

c. Roberts I, Norton R, Jackson R, Dunn R, Hassall I. Effect of environmental factors on risk of injury of child pedestrians by motor vehicles: A case-control study. *BMJ* 1995;310:91-94; Roberts I, Marshall R, Lee-Joe T. The urban traffic environment and the risk of child pedestrian injury: A case-crossover approach. *Epidemiology* 1995;6(2):169-71.

d. Agran PF, Winn DG, Anderson CL, et al. The role of the physical and traffic environment in child pedestrian injuries. *Pediatrics* 1996;98:1096-1103.

e. Posner JC, Liao E, Winston FK, Cnaan A, Shaw KN, Durbin DR. Exposure to traffic among urban children injured as pedestrians. *Injury Prevention* 2002;8(3):231-35.

f. Roberts et al., The urban traffic environment.

g. Giese JL, Davis GA, Sykes RD. The relationship between residential street design and pedestrian safety. ITE Annual Meeting Compendium, 1997 (January): 1097-1104. Available from ITE as document CD 2/AHA97K97.

h. Macpherson A, Roberts I, Pless IB. Children's exposure to traffic and pedestrian injuries. *American Journal of Public Health* 1998;88:1840-43.

i. Rivara FP, Barber M. Demographic analysis of child pedestrian injuries. *Pediatrics* 1985;76:375-81.

j. Joly MF, Foggin PM, Pless IB. Les déterminants socio-écologiques du risqué d'accident du juene piéton. *Revue d' Epidémiologie et de Santé Publique* 1991;39:345-51.

k. Braddock M, Papidus G, Gregorio D, et al. Population, income and ecological correlates of child pedestrian injury. *Pediatrics* 1991;88:1242-47.

l. Bagley C. The urban setting of juvenile pedestrian injuries: A study of behavioral ecology and social disadvantage. *Accident Analysis and Prevention* 1992;24:673-78.

m. Herms BF. Pedestrian crosswalk study: Accidents in painted and unpainted crosswalks. *Highway Research Record* 1972;406:1-13.

n. Zegeer CV, Stewart JR, Huang H, Lagerwey P. Safety effects of marked vs. unmarked crosswalks at uncontrolled locations: Analysis of pedestrian crashes in 30 cities (with discussion and closure). *Transportation Research Record* 2001;1773:56-68.

o. Koepsell T, McCloskey L, Wolf M, Moudon AV, Buchner D, Kraus J, Patterson M. Crosswalk markings and the risk of pedestrian-motor vehicle collisions in older pedestrians. *Journal of the American Medical Association* 2002;288(17):2136-43.

speeds.[36] Pedestrians can be separated from vehicles in time, such as with pedestrian-activated crossing signals, favorable traffic signal timing or no-right-on-red laws; and/or they can be spatially separated from vehicles, such as with pedestrian overpasses, wide sidewalks on both sides of the street, and pedestrian refuge islands in the middle of wide streets. In some cities, motor vehicles are banned from designated streets or entire zones, a strategy that has been widely used in Europe. Similarly, infrastructure for pedestrians and bicyclists, such as the extensive path systems in Holland and Germany, help prevent injuries from motor vehicles.[37] Pedestrians can be made more conspicuous to drivers in several ways; examples include increased roadway lighting, raised intersections and crosswalks, and "bulb-outs" that extend the sidewalk corners into the street. And vehicle speeds can be reduced with traffic circles, narrowed traffic lanes, curving or zigzag roadways, raised intersections, and speed bumps. In some Dutch cities, the *woonerf* (street for living) is designed for sharing by pedestrians, bicyclists, and motor vehicles, which are limited to "walking speed."[38] These techniques are collectively known as "traffic calming."[39]

Sometimes, techniques that attract and protect pedestrians are seen as inconvenient or even hazardous to automobiles. In Georgia, for instance, the State Department of Transportation prohibits placing trees, benches, and other fixed objects within 8 feet of a curb. In practical terms, this precludes trees in the buffer zone between sidewalk and street. "To a traffic engineer's way of thinking," an *Atlanta Journal-Constitution* article wryly explained, "sidewalks are auto recovery zones where drivers have space to correct course if they've veered off. Trees would ensure the driver came to an abrupt end before getting the car back on the road."[40] Of course, an automobile that uses a sidewalk to correct course may mow down pedestrians in the process. Careful thinking about such assets as trees along sidewalks needs to take into account the safety of both pedestrians and drivers, as well as other health outcomes such as increased physical activity (if the trees attract more people to walk).

Not all safety design solutions are intuitive, and it is important to collect evidence on what works. For example, when investigators at the University of Washington studied intersections at which older pedestrians were killed, they found that the presence of marked crosswalks (where there was no traffic light) more than tripled the risk, presumably because the crosswalks give a false sense of security.[41] On the other hand, there is good evidence that single-lane traffic circles, sidewalks, exclusive pedestrian signal phasing, pedestrian refuge islands, and roadway lighting can help prevent pedestrian injuries and fatalities.[42]

There is growing evidence that *more* walking and bicycling are associated with *lower* rates of injuries and fatalities to pedestrians and cyclists. In countries where walking and bicycling are far more common than in the United States, such as Holland and Germany, pedestrians and cyclists are killed at far lower rates (on either a per trip basis or a per person basis) than in the United States.[43] In observational studies of intersections in Sweden[44] and Ontario,[45] heavier pedestrian and bicycle traffic predicted lower rates of collisions with automobiles. Recently, this relationship was confirmed in studies of California cities (see Figure 6-4), Danish towns, and European countries.[46] There is a happy irony here. Sprawl decreases foot and bicycle trips in both relative and absolute terms, and this may help account for decreased injury rates among pedestrians and cyclists. But a major increase in foot and bicycle trips, with all that entails—greater awareness among drivers, and better roads and paths—also decreases the injury risk to pedestrians and cyclists. And, of course, the latter strategy also offers additional advantages, such as physical activity and cleaner air.

■ **FIGURE 6-4** Risk of injury to pedestrians and bicyclists in sixty-eight California cities in 2000, according to the proportion of work trips made on foot or bicycle. The per capita injury rate among pedestrians and cyclists decreases as the proportion of work trips made by these modes increases.

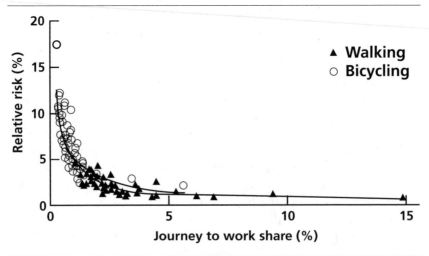

SOURCE: P. L. Jacobsen, "Safety in Numbers: More Walkers and Bicyclists, Safer Walking and Bicycling," *Injury Prevention* 2003;9:205-09.

Poorly designed roadways, of course, do not tell the entire story of pedestrian injuries. More than half of pedestrian and bicyclist injuries do not involve a car, and 31 percent of bike and 53 percent of pedestrian injuries occur off streets, on parking lots, paths, and even sidewalks.[47] The vast parking lots that surround malls and other locations often feature disorderly, speeding cars but no safe footpaths, so this comes as no surprise.

Poor children have higher pedestrian fatality rates than wealthier children.[48] This must relate, in large part, to the environments in which poor children live and play—neighborhoods with many of the unsafe features shown in Table 6-1. High density, heavy traffic, and lack of safe play areas and nearby parks are factors. Could it be that poor children endanger themselves through their behavior? Pless and colleagues at Montreal Children's Hospital examined a broad set of risk factors for childhood pedestrian and bicycle injuries, and found that behavioral factors played very little role.[49] Children who were fidgety, who were reported as having abnormal behavior, and who suffered from family disruption or disadvantage were at increased risk, but environmental factors played a far greater role than these personal and family characteristics. When children's environments are changed, and when these changes are accompanied by comprehensive safety programs that include training, supervised recreational activities, and similar measures, child pedestrian injury rates appear to decline.[50]

THE RISK OF LEAVING HOME

People care a great deal about safety when they choose where to live.[51] In a 1999 survey by the National Association of Home Builders, the neighborhood crime rate was the leading reason people cited for their choice of neighborhood; more than 80 percent of respondents rated it as very important, a far higher proportion than for such features as transportation options and shopping.[52] This is a principal factor encouraging sprawl; many people view urban neighborhoods as hotbeds of crime, and suburbs as a safe haven.

This view was challenged by William H. Lucy, a professor at the University of Virginia School of Architecture.[53] Lucy analyzed the risk of dying from two causes—traffic crashes and murders by strangers—in fifteen medium and large metropolitan areas over a fifteen-year period. Like Ewing and colleagues, Lucy found that the risk of dying in traffic was highest in the most sprawling counties (as measured by population density). In each metropolitan area studied, the risk of dying in traffic in the suburbs was far higher than the risk of being murdered by a stranger in the central city. (Even in central cities, the traffic fatality rate was generally higher than the stranger homicide rate.) As Lucy concluded, "homicides are not nearly so great a danger as traffic fatalities."[54] The risk of dying in traffic, he noted, is "largely unrecognized as a danger to be factored into residential location decisions."[55]

Injuries remain a major public health problem, and those related to driving—crashes that injure and kill drivers and passengers, and incidents that injure and kill pedestrians—form one of the largest categories. Sprawl plays a role. For automobile crashes, the extensive driving and the kinds of roads on which people drive are important threats to safety. For pedestrians, the absence of safe walking and biking routes also threatens safety, and even the good news—falling pedestrian fatality rates in recent years—is built on bad news, the decline in walking and biking. Designing safe communities means providing alternatives to driving, and safe routes for nonmotorized travel.

CHAPTER 7

WATER QUANTITY AND QUALITY

WITH STEVE GAFFIELD

WATER AND HEALTH: AN OVERVIEW

Clean water is essential for our health. Just as the planet's surface is 78 percent water, so, too, is the composition of the human body at birth. Cultures and civilizations have risen with water availability and collapsed with droughts, and water is becoming a natural resource that rivals petroleum in its importance to the prosperity and civil security of all the inhabitants of an increasingly crowded world. Cosseted in the convenience and abundance of the industrialized world, it is easy to forget that the water we drink originates not at the faucet, but in the planet's rivers, lakes, or underground aquifers. Protection of these waters, and the land from which they flow, is an important part of ensuring a healthy future for our society.

In the United States, we generally take clean water for granted because we have state-of-the-art treatment plants and laws designed to protect drinking water safety. Early in each of our lives an adult grabbed our hand, pulled us back from a puddle, and admonished us: "Don't drink that water, it is dirty." As one of our earliest life experiences, we internalized the lesson that dirty water could make us sick. As we grew older, we learned the diseases that come from dirty water—hepatitis, cholera, and typhoid—and why it was important to keep human waste away from water supplies. Probably no single health intervention, not antibiotics or vaccines, has had the massive life-benefiting impact of the development of effective water treatment techniques over the last century.[1] Even today, severe diarrhea from contaminated drinking water kills nearly 2 million children each year in developing countries without adequate water treatment.[2]

For water to sustain human health, two conditions are necessary: the water must be clean, and there must be an adequate supply. Clean water, in turn, means an absence of two kinds of contaminants: microbial contaminants and chemical contaminants.

Microbial Contamination

Microbial contaminants can take several forms. Bacteria such as *Salmonella typhi* (the cause of typhus), *Vibrio cholera* (the cause of cholera), *Escherichia coli*, *Campylobacter jejuni*, and various species of *Shigella* have been scourges of humanity for centuries. Water with one or more of these bacteria has typically been contaminated by fecal material from humans or animals. Viruses can also contaminate water; examples include rotavirus, a common cause of childhood diarrhea; norovirus and Norwalk virus, which also cause gastroenteritis; and hepatitis A virus. Finally, parasites such as *Giardia intestinalis* and *Cryptosporidium parvum*, which cause giardiasis and cryptosporidiosis, respectively, can also contaminate water.

Even with the benefits of modern technology, these infectious agents collectively cause many water-related illnesses each year in the United States. Official public health statistics from 1991 to 2000 record 123 outbreaks of waterborne illness in the public and private water systems of forty-one states and three U.S. territories, affecting over 430,000 Americans, and causing 653 hospitalizations and 58 deaths.[3] However, the true extent of waterborne disease is thought to be at least 3 or 4 times greater, since many outbreaks are never detected and many cases never diagnosed.[4] Of the approximately 99 million cases of acute gastrointestinal illnesses involving diarrhea or vomiting that occur each year, costing billions of dollars,[5] between 6 and 40 percent may be related to drinking water.[6] Rotavirus alone is responsible for approximately 50,000 hospital admissions among children each year.[7] A 1993 outbreak of cryptosporidiosis in Milwaukee's drinking water supply sickened 403,000 people[8] and killed at least 50 people with compromised immune systems.[9] Waterborne illnesses can be caused not only by drinking contaminated water, but also by eating produce irrigated with untreated water, by eating seafood caught in contaminated water bodies, and by swimming or other recreational contact.[10]

Elderly people, children, and those with compromised immune systems are especially vulnerable to contaminated water. When drinking water becomes unusually turbid, even when drinking water standards are still met, hospital visits for gastrointestinal illness rise among members of these groups.[11] For more than a year before the 1993 Milwaukee outbreak, increases in that city's drinking water turbidity were associated with increases in doctor visits for gastrointestinal illnesses, and the increase in visits was twice as large for children as for adults.[12] And during outbreaks of cryptosporidiosis, people with compromised immune systems comprise a large share of the severe illnesses and deaths.

Chemical Contamination

Water can also be contaminated by chemicals. The magnificent solvent properties of water mean it can easily be polluted by both "point" and "nonpoint" sources. Point sources, which pollute water directly from a single spot, such as a factory drainpipe, were the major cause of water pollution in the United States before the Clean Water Act was passed by Congress in 1972. This law led to extensive construction of sewage treatment plants and environmental enforcement, which have greatly reduced point source pollution. However, nonpoint sources—runoff from farms, parking lots and streets, golf courses, and similar expanses of land—remain a serious source of chemical contaminants, including pesticides, metals, nitrates, radionuclides, and a wide range of organic chemicals, even including pharmaceuticals.

Another source of chemical contaminants, ironically, is the process used to disinfect water. Chlorine used for water treatment can react with organic sediment in river and lake water to form disinfection by-products (DBPs) such as halomethanes and haloacetic acids. These chemicals are linked to cancer of the bladder and other sites, miscarriages and birth defects, including neural tube defects and cleft palate, low birth weight, kidney and immune system disorders, and neurotoxic effects.[13]

Water Scarcity

Anyone gazing across the Great Lakes might feel that fresh water is a limitless resource. But less than 3 percent of the world's water is fresh water, and of this, more than two-thirds is frozen in the polar ice caps. If the world's entire water supply were one gallon, then the available fresh water would amount to just a few tablespoons.

Available sources of clean water are under growing pressure from a changing climate, population growth, increasing per capita use of water, and destructive land use patterns. This is especially true in the United States, whose citizens are very heavy consumers of water. In 1997, per capita water use was 382 liters per person per day in the United States compared to 278 liters in Japan, 153 liters in the United Kingdom, and 129 liters in Germany.[14] The heavy demand for water by a growing population and changing land use patterns is already straining water supplies in parts of the country where water has always been considered to be plentiful. For example, after years of rapid growth, Frederick, Maryland, is so short of water that it has instituted a moratorium on new developments and has implemented a plan to allocate water among different users patterned after plans used in the arid western United States.[15] Alabama, Georgia, and Florida are locked in a "water war" over the scarce water resources of the Apalachicola-Chattahoochee-Flint river basin, and years of negotiations collapsed in 2003, requiring federal court intervention.[16] As we look to the future, climate change is likely to cause more evaporation from rivers and lakes and more droughts, punctuated by intense storms.

THE HYDROLOGY OF SPRAWL

To understand how land use patterns, including sprawl, may affect water, we need to understand certain aspects of the hydrological cycle (see Figure 7-1). Rainwater that falls can soak into the ground, where it percolates down into groundwater (a process called "recharging"), or it can flow along surfaces and enter bodies of water such as streams and lakes.[17] When rainwater soaks into the ground in forested areas, some of the water is taken up by trees. Some of this water sustains tree growth, and some undergoes evapotranspiration, an important process because it has a cooling effect. (Part of the urban heat island effect results from the removal of trees from urban centers.) Surface water and groundwater are not entirely separate, since much surface water is fed by groundwater aquifers (e.g., from springs), and since surface water can percolate into groundwater. Over half of Americans receive their drinking water from surface water sources, and the remainder depends on groundwater.[18]

Natural recharging of groundwater is essential to maintain the water supply for those who depend on groundwater. It is also essential to maintain groundwater quality. In many parts of the country, groundwater supplies are being depleted, raising concerns for households and

■ **FIGURE 7-1** An overview of the hydrologic cycle.

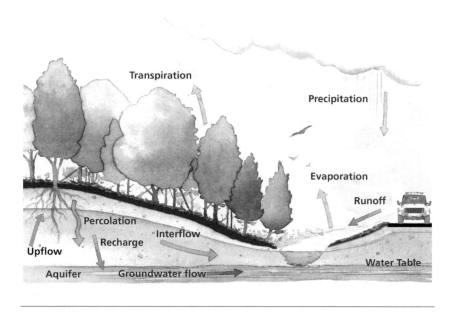

farmers. In addition, when groundwater levels fall, geochemical balances shift, and can result in contamination of groundwater by such chemicals as arsenic.[19] As groundwater levels drop, springs feeding streams and wetlands dry up, damaging habitats that help preserve ecological diversity and provide high-quality resources for recreation and contemplation.

Land use patterns affect this process in several ways. Some kinds of land cover, such as forests, promote absorption of groundwater. These areas have porous soils that function like hydraulic "shock absorbers," absorbing a large proportion of most rainfall.[20] These soils also provide valuable filtering services, removing microbes and chemical pollutants as rainwater percolates downward to replenish underground aquifers. In contrast, surfaces such as pavement and rooftops allow virtually no rainwater to be absorbed, favoring runoff instead.[21] Figure 7-2 shows this process schematically. In the developed area on the right, trees have been replaced by impervious surfaces, including rooftops, a driveway, and roads. More rainwater runs off, and less soaks into the ground to recharge groundwater and to be taken up by trees, compared to the forested scene on the left.

■ **FIGURE 7-2** Schematic view of water balance before and after development. Note the decrease in evapotranspiration and soil absorption, and the increase in surface runoff that accompany development.

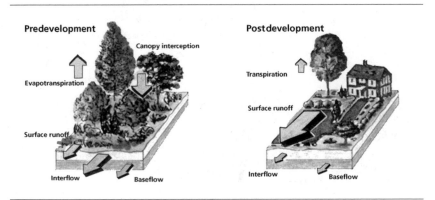

SOURCE: Center for Watershed Protection, http://www.cwp.org/. Impacts of Urbanization Slideshow CD-ROM (1999) Center for Watershed Protection, Ellicott City, Maryland.

The relationship between impervious surfaces and runoff has been well studied (Figure 7-3). In one study, about 4 percent of rainfall on undeveloped grassland was lost as runoff, compared to 15 percent on suburban land.[22] In a study of land use changes in suburban Indianapolis over nearly twenty years,[23] an 18 percent increase in impervious areas resulted in an estimated 80 percent increase in annual average rainwater runoff. According to both empirical data[24] and hydrologic modeling,[25] development densities greater than about 10 to 20 percent lead to dramatic increases in runoff. A similar pattern is seen for melting snow.[26] This effect is so well established that impervious surface has been suggested as a key environmental indicator, much like air quality.[27]

While sprawling residential and commercial lots may each have a smaller proportion of impervious surface than lots in dense cities, the total impervious area across a community may be very high.[28] This is largely due to roads and parking lots, which can account for more than 60 percent of impervious surfaces in sprawling areas.[29] In sprawling areas, large lawns may compensate somewhat for the impervious surfaces, since the lawns absorb some runoff from roofs, driveways, and parking lots. However, lawns and other "green spaces" in suburban areas are often so compacted that they generate up to 90 percent as much runoff as pavement.[30]

■ **FIGURE 7-3**   The relationship between impervious surfaces in a watershed and runoff of rainwater. The "runoff coefficient" is the proportion of rainfall that is lost as runoff. As more and more of the surfaces become impervious, more and more rainwater runs off into streams and rivers, with accompanying siltation and nonpoint source pollution.

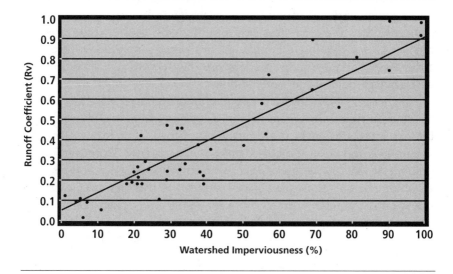

SOURCE: T. Schueler, *Controlling Urban Runoff: A Practical Manual for Planning and Designing Urban BMPs,* Washington, DC, Metropolitan Washington Council of Governments; 1987.

The impact of sprawl on runoff probably differs from place to place depending on rainfall patterns, soil properties, topography, and the existing rural land use that is being converted to suburban uses. One study estimated that a new low-density development in the outskirts of Chicago would produce ten times more stormwater runoff than a comparable redevelopment in the inner city.[31] Numerous studies predict similar results elsewhere. However, other researchers have noted that converting farmland to low-density development can actually reduce some nonpoint source pollution, due to the large amounts of runoff produced by some farms.[32]

By diverting rainwater from being absorbed by soil and toward runoff, sprawl may contribute to depletion of groundwater. In a recent report, the Natural Resources Defense Council, Smart Growth America, and American Rivers identified some of the nation's most sprawling cities as measured by land development.[33] These organizations then estimated the amount of groundwater recharge lost due to runoff, based on a model that used U.S. Geological Survey data. The results suggested vast losses. For example, Atlanta was estimated to be losing between 56.9 and 132.8 billion gallons of water per year, Orlando between 9.2 and 21.5 billion gallons, and Houston between 12.8 and 29.8 billion gallons. Groundwater recharge is a very difficult process to measure, and other investigators have not been convinced that urban development reduces groundwater recharge.[34] Increased pumping of groundwater to serve growing populations, rather than loss of recharge, may account for observed declining groundwater levels. In either case, these problems underscore the need for conservation and wise management of our water supplies.

Increased runoff also has major effects on waterways. Because of the intense runoff during storms, streams carry huge volumes of water known as "storm surges" (Figure 7-4). These high flows carve out streambeds and undermine the banks of the streams. Moreover, development of land in the watershed can result in erosion; at a fresh construction site on a rainy day, there is typically a trail of mud flowing off the site. Stripping the protective vegetation cover from construction

■ FIGURE 7-4 Stream flow before and after development. Note the greater runoff volume after a storm, the higher and more rapid flow, and the lower base flow that accompany development.

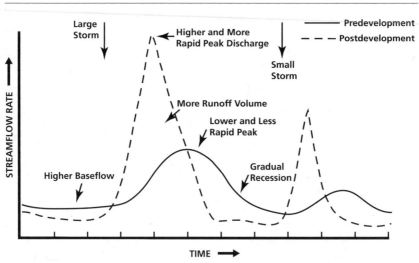

SOURCE: Center for Watershed Protection, http://www.cwp.org/. Impacts of Urbanization Slideshow CD-ROM (1999) Center for Watershed Protection, Ellicott City, Maryland.

■ **FIGURE 7-5** Changes in stream and floodplain morphology with development. Note the carving out of the streambed, the expansion of the floodplain limit, and the diminished low-flow level following development.

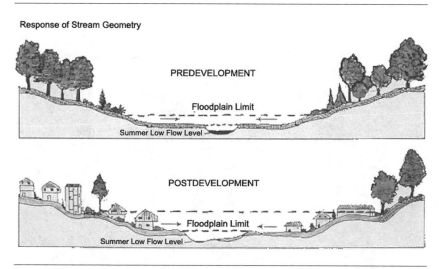

Response of Stream Geometry

SOURCE: Center for Watershed Protection, http://www.cwp.org/. Impacts of Urbanization Slideshow CD-ROM (1999) Center for Watershed Protection, Ellicott City, Maryland.

sites accelerates soil erosion up to 40,000-fold.[35] As soil and silt are carried into waterways, they coat the streambeds, altering stream ecology. Large amounts of sediment reduce the "life span" of dams, shorten reservoir life, raise the cost of water treatment, and degrade final water quality. These changes in stream characteristics can last for many years after the initial disturbance, threatening structures built near floodplains (Figure 7-5).

These destructive changes to waterways do not directly threaten human health. However, the effects of sprawl on water quality pose a more direct health concern.

SPRAWL AND WATER QUALITY

Sprawl may contribute to both microbial and chemical contamination of water (Figure 7-6). On the microbial side, several related phenomena are important. First, stormwater runoff includes large loads of waste from pets and wildlife and nutrients from such sources as fertilizers,[36] and streams and rivers downstream from developed areas typically have

■ FIGURE 7-6 Warnings like these on the Chattahoochee River are necessary in many urban and suburban streams, due to nonpoint source pollution. Better riparian protection, with ample stream buffers and less impervious surface, could protect stream quality.

SOURCE: Photo by Howard Frumkin.

higher bacterial counts after rainfall.[37] These contaminants are rapidly dumped unfiltered into storm sewers and streams, contributing to nearly 4,000 beach closings each year due to unsafe water quality. Studies show a strong relationship between large rainfalls and outbreaks of waterborne disease,[38] clearly implying a link between polluted runoff and health.

High levels of runoff after heavy rainfall contribute to microbial contamination of water in another way: through sediment. Sediment in waterways is more than a problem of appearance; it reduces the effectiveness of drinking water treatment systems. Soil particles can protect organisms such as *Giardia* and *Cryptosporidium* from coming into contact with chlorine used for purification, preventing adequate disinfection. *Cryptosporidium* organisms are difficult to treat effectively, and a 1995 study found that 13 percent of samples of drinking water were still contaminated with *Cryptosporidium* oocysts after treatment with chlorine.[39] This may have been an important factor in the 1993 cryptosporidiosis outbreak in Milwaukee. Although the treated water from Lake Michigan met all safety standards, it became more turbid during spring rains and snowmelt and may have been contaminated by cattle or human sewage.[40]

A third link between sprawl and microbial contamination arises in low-density exurban areas, where homes commonly rely on private wells and septic systems maintained by homeowners. Approximately 42 million people in rural and suburban areas use their own private water supplies, which are typically shallow wells.[41] These wells are not covered by the Safe Drinking Water Act and are especially vulnerable because they are rarely monitored.[42] Suburban homeowners on recently developed farmland may not realize that agricultural chemicals can remain in the soil for decades and can contaminate the shallow groundwater tapped by their wells.[43] While small septic systems can control microbial intrusion into groundwater fairly effectively when they are well maintained,[44] homeowners—unaware of the potential for groundwater contamination, and with little incentive beyond cosmetics to maintain their septic systems—may neglect them. As a result, contamination is common.[45]

Sprawl may also contribute to microbial contamination of water through an indirect route: by competing for infrastructure dollars. Expansion at the urban fringe requires the development of new water infrastructure, sometimes at the expense of maintaining existing systems in other parts of the community. Drinking water and wastewater infrastructure in the United States is already strained, and investment in maintenance and repair of public systems has been inadequate for decades.[46] Leaks in water and sewer lines are common in aging systems, and may go unrepaired for lack of funds.[47] (On the positive side, leaks in pipes may help maintain groundwater recharge, even in areas with much impervious surface.)[48]

A pressing need is to upgrade the 950 aging sewer systems in the United States that carry both sewage and stormwater to treatment plants in the same pipelines.[49] During storms, the combined flows overwhelm the capacity of the pipes and treatment plants, and the excess volume—including untreated human sewage—is discharged directly to streams and rivers, a process known as "combined sewer overflow" or CSO. Not surprisingly, high concentrations of bacteria have been measured below CSOs in river water and in the sediments of rivers and storm drains. These accumulations provide a reservoir of bacteria that can continue to contaminate the water between storms.[50] When new development increases the impervious surfaces in a watershed, and green space is not set aside to help absorb rainfall, buffer runoff, and protect streams, there is additional strain on these sewer systems.

Sprawl also contributes to chemical contamination of waterways.[51] Nonpoint source pollution is now the major source of water contamination in the United States. Parking lots and roadways accumulate a wide range of chemical contaminants: oil and antifreeze that drip from cars, gasoline spilled at filling stations, lead particles from wheel balances, other metals such as copper and cadmium, household chemicals, and others. Pesticides and herbicides are applied to lawns. These substances are carried across impervious surfaces by rainwater and end up in streams and rivers. Studies of the movement of polycyclic aromatic hydrocarbons,[52] organic waste,[53] and lead and zinc[54] suggest that suburban development is associated with high loading of these contaminants in nearby surface water.

Pesticide and herbicide runoff is a particular concern. While this problem is primarily associated with rural agricultural land, lawn care can also be a major source of these chemicals in stormwater. The U.S. Geological Survey found that insecticides were present at levels above those thought to harm wildlife in sediment from 40 percent of the urban streams tested and in fish tissue samples from 20 percent of the sites.[55]

Automobile and truck use contributes to water pollution in several ways beside runoff from roadways and parking lots. First, the gasoline additive MTBE has leaked from thousands of underground gasoline storage tanks and contaminated groundwater. MTBE can be tasted in water down to parts per billion, the human tongue and nose being nearly as sensitive as million-dollar chemical analyzers. Second, the heavy use of cars and trucks contributes to air pollution, and the resulting air pollutants can contaminate surface water. Vehicle exhaust is an important source of nitrogen and petroleum compounds.[56] Nitrogen contributes to eutrophication of lakes and harmful algal blooms. Polycyclic aromatic hydrocarbons (PAHs), petroleum compounds in exhaust, are known carcinogens in laboratory animals and humans. In a study of six reservoirs near major American cities, the U.S. Geological Survey found that PAH concentrations in the sediments increased with traffic volume and reached levels up to 100 times higher than thresholds set to protect aquatic ecosystems. Motor vehicles, then, are a substantial contributor to water pollution.[57]

CONCLUSION

What is good for trout is good for humans. The same water source that provides gentle runoff into the oxygenating riffle of rock in a streambed and that nourishes the plants and insects in the life cycle of a stream is also likely to be of good and usable quality for human use. Streams destroyed by erosion, siltation, riprap, and contamination are less likely to provide water that can be used for drinking without expensive engineered cleanup.

During the 1990s, New York City faced a difficult decision. For more than a century, the city had drawn its drinking water from upstate sources (Figure 7-7). Because these were pure sources, the city had not installed a filtration system. However, increasing concerns about water purity, related in part to upstate development, led to calls for filtration of the water. Filtration plants would have cost $6 billion to install and $300 million each year to operate. Instead, the city developed a detailed plan for protecting the Catskill–Delaware watersheds. This included purchasing large tracts of land as buffers against development. The cost of this plan was $1.4 billion over ten years—a prudent business decision, and a splendid illustration that watershed protection is human health protection.[58] Growth and development that balance density with green space and that limit impervious surfaces, as discussed in Chapter 11, can protect water quantity and quality,[59] and are part of a strategy for places that are safe and healthy for people.

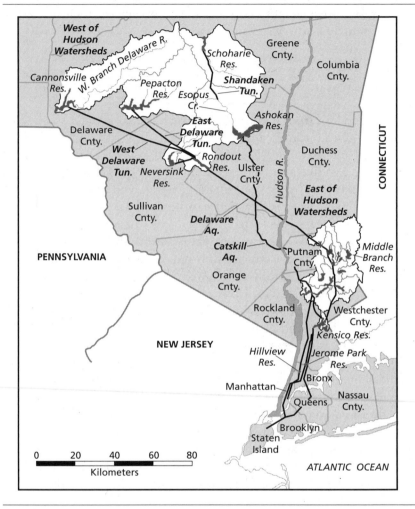

■ FIGURE 7-7 The watersheds that provide drinking water to New York City. By protecting these upstream watersheds, New York protects its drinking water and saves money on filtration.

SOURCE: National Research Council, *Watershed Management for Potable Water Supply: Assessing the New York City Strategy,* Washington, DC, National Academy Press; 2000. Available at http://gateway2.ovid.com/ovidweb.cgi-29#29.

CHAPTER 8

■=======■

MENTAL HEALTH

─────────

Most Americans live in suburban habitats that are isolating, disag-gregated, and neurologically punishing. . . . Placed in such an envi-ronment even a theoretically healthy individual would sooner or later succumb to the kind of despair and anomie that we have labeled "depression.". . . The emotional toll of the American Dream is steep. What we see all over our nation is a situational loneliness of the most extreme kind. . . .

    This pervasive situational loneliness, of being stuck alone in your car, alone in your work cubicle, alone in your apartment, alone at the supermarket, alone at the video rental shop—because that's how American daily life has come to be organized—is the injury to which the insult of living in degrading, ugly, frightening, and monotonous surroundings is added. Is it any wonder that Americans resort to the few things available that afford even a semblance of contentment: eating easily obtainable and cheap junk food and popping a daily dose of Paxil or Prozac to stave off feelings of despair that might actually be a predictable response to settings and circumstances of our lives? . . .

    How depressing.[1]

—James Howard Kunstler,
"Big and Blue in the USA," 2003

Kunstler's words evoke a mental health disaster. If sprawl presents us with ugly, degrading environments, if the lifestyles that evolve in sprawling places are lonely and "neurologically punishing," and if many people respond by feeling anxious and depressed, then we need to rethink our communities urgently and thoroughly.

But is Kunstler right? Perhaps the chance to live at the edge of the city, and to calm down and relax while commuting home from work, is a wonderful tonic. On July 26, 2002, the sports section of the *Atlanta Journal-Constitution* carried a curious front-page story.[2] "Brave Commute," declared the headline, "Reliever's drive to work is 90 miles." In a tone at once respectful and incredulous, the story told of Atlanta Braves pitcher Chris Hammond, who made his home on a 218-acre farm in Wedowee, Alabama, 90 miles from Turner Field. In a city where commuting hassles dominated local concerns, Hammond's epic commute was indeed news.

But for Hammond, the trade-off was worth it. "He and his wife Lynne moved their family there two years ago seeking a simpler life. . . ," the *Journal-Constitution* story recounted, "when living the typical baseball player's life became too harsh." While most of his teammates "fight the interstates and maddening bumper-to-bumper traffic" to get home, "Hammond prefers the scenic route"—a route that was described in rhapsodic terms: "The hazy, stifling city atmosphere gives way to the humid, earthen country air in the summertime. The senses signal the transition: the pungent odor of chicken houses and pig farms. The sight of red barns and country cemeteries. Wooden houses, abandoned and ramshackled with crimson-rusted roofs, stand hidden in fields overgrown in wild grasses."

Hammond himself was clear on the pleasures of his commute. "I enjoy driving by myself," he explained. "It gives me time to relax. Especially driving in the country. So many beautiful things to look at. No graffiti on buildings. Just cows in the pastures. The one hour and twenty minutes it takes me to get there is really stress-free."

THE MENTAL HEALTH BENEFITS OF SPRAWL

Chris Hammond's story reminds us that sprawl may benefit mental health in at least three ways. First, it offers an escape from crowding. Second, it offers sanctuary from life stress. Third, it offers the prospect of contact with nature.

In an age of large homes on large lots, it is easy to forget the incredible crowding of the cities of yesteryear. Urban tenements, according to a turn-of-the-twentieth-century report, were places "in which thousands of people are living in the smallest space in which it is possible for human beings to exist—crowded together in dark, ill-ventilated rooms, in many of which the sunlight never enters and in most of which fresh air is unknown."[3] Such conditions, of course, bred infectious diseases, but the overcrowding was also a significant stressor, as demonstrated by both animal studies and human data.[4] In overcrowded situations, physiological markers of stress such as blood pressure and stress hormones rise, immune function declines, and aggressive behaviors increase. It is no surprise that one of the original motivations for suburban migration was to escape the crowding of cities.[5] Given the alternative, the lower density of the suburbs must be counted as an early mental health benefit.

A second mental health benefit of suburban living may be one that vacation planners know well: the sense of peaceful refuge, the sanctuary from the hassles of daily life. "Getting away from it all," whether on vacation or simply at the end of a workday, offers much potential for stress relief.

And once at home, the suburban resident may enjoy a third mental health benefit: contact with nature. People like trees, birds, and flowers. These pleasures can be more accessible in suburbs than in very dense urban areas. And contact with nature may be more than aesthetically pleasing; it may reduce stress, improve attention, and relieve depression.[6] Studies show that simply having views of nature can decrease clinic visits,[7] speed healing after surgery,[8] and help control pain during invasive medical procedures.[9] If these kinds of benefits can come from a backyard, then nature contact represents one of the benefits of sprawl.

THE MENTAL HEALTH COSTS OF SPRAWL

Sprawl may also carry mental health costs. For example, who benefits by "getting away from it all"? Escaping to a suburban home may offer more to men than to women, since women still bear a disproportionate share of household responsibilities—amounting to between twenty-five and forty-five hours per week, according to various studies.[10] At the same time the nation's cities have sprawled, working hours have increased, both individually and on a household basis. For two-career households, if the woman has a full-time job, the travel time of a long commute, and the burden of household duties, including transporting children to school and after-school activities, the hours spent behind the wheel each week are likely to contribute significantly to stress.

And what of the nature contact available in suburban locations? That nature may be a highly constructed one—a carefully laid out grassy lawn with a limited number of trees, and perhaps a garden.

While this is a restorative environment for many people, it comes at a cost. When thousands of acres are developed as suburban housing, with no preservation of forest, field, and farm, then large parks and natural areas become much less accessible. We gain some opportunities for nature contact even as we lose others.

In fact, the pleasant backyard is only one part of suburban sprawl. The highways and broad feeder roads, the vast parking lots, and the rows of big-box stores are a prominent part of the landscape as well. And for many people, these aspects of the environment are anything but a mental health asset. Country roads seem to be better for mental health than thoroughfares cluttered with road signs and billboards, strip malls and body shops, and large parking lots. In one study, volunteers looked at films of both country roads and commercial roads.[11] They showed less stress and quicker stress recovery when viewing the rural road scenes than when viewing the commercial roadway scenes.

Psychologists, geographers, architects, and planners have much to say about the form, scale, and speed of the environments we inhabit, and of how they make us feel.[12] The high speeds of suburban boulevards, on which everything rushes by quickly; the large scales of big-box stores and vast parking lots; the absence of tranquil and attractive "places of the heart" in daily travels: could these features undermine mental health, or at least forfeit important opportunities to promote it?

Finally, we need to consider the archetypal experience of living in a sprawling area: driving. Aside from the truncated access to large tracts of natural land, aside from the time pressure, aside from the alienating quality of some suburban landscapes, driving itself is a cardinal feature of sprawl, and one of the best understood in terms of its impact on mental health.

DRIVING AND MENTAL HEALTH

Researchers have known for years that driving may have effects on physiology and mood, and may even affect mental health.

The Stress of Driving: Acute Changes in Mood and Physiology

In the decades after World War II, physiologists and physicians increasingly came to view stress as a medical concern. At the same time, automobiles became more and more a central fixture in modern life, so it was no surprise that stress researchers turned their attention to driving.

They studied drivers under various conditions, both on roads and in simulators. They found that driving caused "physiologic arousal"—a combination of elevated heart rate, electrocardiographic changes, increases in serum cortisol and catecholamine levels, and self-reports of anxiety, agitation, and similar feelings. In the language of stress researchers, the "stress" of driving resulted in "strain" among drivers.

Investigators in Germany pioneered the use of remote electrocardiographs, attaching EKG leads to radio transmitters (called telemetry) and collecting data on drivers as they drove.[13] Their studies found that driving increased the heart rate, especially on city streets and during "critical situations" such as passing and sudden stops, and most markedly among inexperienced drivers. In London, investigators conducted similar experiments, asking volunteers to drive their cars for about twenty minutes on familiar streets, from Middlesex Hospital through Piccadilly Circus and Trafalgar Square, and back to the hospital, while wearing "radioelectrocardiographs." They also found that the heart rate increased while driving.[14] And in the United States, investigators in Minnesota studied long-distance drivers[15] and investigators in Philadelphia studied city drivers,[16] and all reached similar conclusions: driving increased the heart rate.

But a higher heart rate is not necessarily cause for concern. After all, the heart rate increases with excitement, exercise, and other triggers that are not considered dangerous. Does it matter if driving increases heart rates?

Investigators also found other signs of stress. In the German studies, not only did heart rate increase, but there were also electrocardiographic changes such as ST segment depressions and T-wave inversions that suggest ischemia (inadequate blood flow to the heart).[17] In fact, when the German investigators focused on patients known to have coronary artery disease, approximately half the patients showed pathological EKG changes while driving.[18] And in the English studies, when the drivers with heart disease showed an increase in their heart rates, they also showed an increase in ectopic heartbeats and pathological changes on their cardiograms. Moreover, occasional patients developed angina and left ventricular failure while driving. The Minnesota investigators found that situations such as passing and sudden stops caused not only an increase in the heart rate, but also T-wave flattening, and concluded that "there is a significant myocardial involvement in the stress of driving an automobile, even in some apparently healthy drivers."[19]

Additional studies confirmed the notion that driving is a stressor. In Philadelphia, physicians studied drivers before and after two hours of city driving, and found that urinary levels of catecholamine and corticosteroids increased, indicating a stress response.[20] In Miami, after driving their cars across the city for forty-five minutes, university student volunteers had higher blood pressure, higher heart rates, and lower frustration tolerance than controls.[21] In an unusual study in Toronto, drivers reported on their feelings by cellular phone as they drove.[22] Higher levels of congestion caused considerable stress, expressed by terms such as "frustrated," "distressed," "uneasy," and "losing my temper."

Over several decades, these and other studies[23] clearly established that driving could be a cardiovascular stressor. But what is it about driving that is stressful?

Several factors seem to contribute. One is the personality a driver brings to driving. Features such as neuroticism, absentmindedness, and aggression and hostility are associated with higher levels of driving stress. Life circumstances, such as a high level of daily hassles and background stress, also contribute. Attitudes toward driving, such as disliking driving and feeling anxious while driving, are associated with higher levels of driving stress. And certain driving situations, such as driving on a tight schedule, driving in uncontrollable or threatening situations, or driving in ways that tax drivers' abilities to their limits, also increase stress.[24] Interestingly, in an Australian study, the factors that predicted stress also predicted a high risk of collisions.[25]

Among professional drivers, such as truck and taxi drivers, some additional factors may operate. According to the standard Karasek model, workplace stress results from a combination of high demand and low decision latitude.[26] Belkić and colleagues in Sweden[27] suggest some additional factors that may increase stress among professional drivers: underload (referring to tasks that are more monotonous than interesting), extrinsic time pressure, unpleasant driving conditions, the consequences of error, and conflict uncertainty.

It seems clear that driving causes physiologic arousal, with many of the changes that have come to be known as the "stress response." These changes are seen in both nonprofessional and professional drivers, under a variety of driving conditions. Although personality features and life experiences help determine the level of strain a driver experiences, the root exposure—driving—emerges as an important source of stress.

The Stress of Commuting

For many of us driving has become one of the most frustrating activities we regularly engage in.[28]

—M. Joint,
"Road Rage," 1997

If driving can be stressful, then commuting—a twice-daily drive, at the most congested times of the day—can be a chronic and persistent source of stress. Research over several decades has investigated the links between commuting and stress.[29] Researchers have identified several aspects of commuting that result in stress, including commute impedance, unpredictability, and loss of control.

"Commute impedance" refers to factors such as traffic jams, road construction, or long trip distances that delay the commuter's arrival at work or home.[30] Research has shown that commute impedance causes stress among commuters. For example, studies of commuters in Irvine, California, showed that longer commutes predicted higher blood pressure and more self-reported "tense" and "nervous" feelings.[31] The stress also seemed to extend to other health outcomes. During follow-up studies, commuters with more commute impedance (as measured by such factors as the total number of changes between surface streets and expressways) had more sick days out of work, more self-reported colds and flu,[32] and even more days in the hospital.[33] In a study of government employees commuting to work near Washington,[34] high-impedance drivers had significantly higher blood pressures and decreased task performance compared to the low-impedance drivers. In contrast, high impedance did not predict an increased heart rate or higher hostility or anxiety levels. Interestingly, single-occupancy vehicle drivers reported significantly more hostility and anxiety than did carpool drivers.

But there is more to commute impedance than obstacles on the road. Commuters may *feel* blocked in their efforts to get to work, out of proportion to the actual delays they confront. Novaco and his colleagues distinguished "subjective impedance" (SI) from "physical impedance" (PI), to get at the notion of the driver's perception of delay.[35] Drivers seem to perceive impedance when they face traffic congestion (especially during the afternoon commute, perhaps because that trip seems to eat into personal time),[36] obstacles on surface streets, and unpleasant encounters during their trip. While SI and PI are closely correlated, they are not identical, suggesting that individual factors play an important role. Some people take long commutes in stride, whereas others are relatively distressed by short commutes. The disparity is gender related; women are more likely to have high SI with low PI, while men are more likely to have low SI with high PI,[37] consistent with research showing that gender affects the amount of strain resulting from a given stress. Interestingly, in Novaco and his colleagues' research, although SI did not predict residential satisfaction or job satisfaction, it was strongly associated with "mood at home in the evening," including such states as "negative mood" and "dysphoria."[38] This suggests that commuting stress may spill over into family life, and overall well-being, in important ways.

Commute impedance may also cause stress that spills over to work and causes increased absenteeism. Several studies have demonstrated that longer commutes predict more lost work days,[39] more late arrivals at work,[40] and higher employee turnover,[41] although not all studies have supported this conclusion.[42] In the follow-up study of Irvine commuters, job satisfaction decreased as the freeway mileage in the commute increased.[43] Koslowsky and Krausz, at Israel's Bar-Ilan University, surveyed 682 nurses to investigate the impact of commuting stress. They found a strong association between the length of the commute and the level of strain the nurses experienced.[44] In turn, the commute strain predicted decreased job satisfaction, decreased job commitment, and a greater intention to leave the job. The effect was seen in nurses who drove to work, but not in those who commuted by public transit. Not only did automobile commuting stress the nurses, but the spillover effect on their attitudes toward work was substantial.

Another stressor in commuting is unpredictability.[45] As psychologist Avraham Kluger explains, an unpredictable commute is one that varies widely from day to day due to heavy traffic, bad weather, time of day, school buses, traffic crashes, and similar factors.[46] In a study of New Jersey commuters, while longer trips were more stressful than shorter ones as reflected by higher levels of resentment, worry, fear, and somatic symptoms, Kluger found that the day-to-day variability of the commute was an even more powerful stressor.[47]

Still another potential stressor in commuting is loss of control. As a contributor to commuting stress, loss of control overlaps with impedance and unpredictability,[48] and also dovetails closely with our understanding of workplace stress. In the workplace, loss of control is a principal cause of stress.[49] But the workplace is not the only place where this may occur. In fact, feeling a loss of control is a well-recognized component of occupational stress among professional drivers such as bus drivers,[50] and the job factors that engender loss of control, such as roadway congestion and time pressure, also confront commuters.

Koslowsky combined the components of commuting stress into a three-stage model (see Figure 8-1).[51] In this model, the first stage is physical impedance, the second is subjective impedance, and the third

■ **FIGURE 8-1**   A model of commuting stress. "Impedance" refers to obstacles during the commute, which cause stress. The stress, in turn, causes strain.

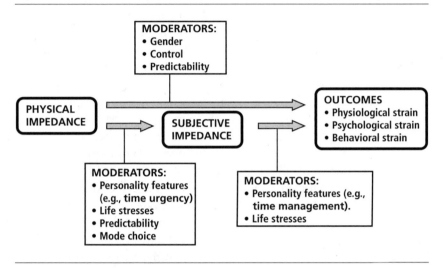

SOURCE: Adapted from M. Koslowsky, "Commuting Stress: Problems of Definition and Variable Identification," *Applied Psychology: An International Review* 1997;46(2):153-73.

consists of physiological, psychological, and behavioral outcomes, with moderators operating throughout. While the psychology and physiology of stress are complex, and people vary considerably in their responses to stimuli, it is clear that the simple fact of a difficult commute—the physical impedance that forms the starting point for the model—plays a crucial role.

The public seems to understand that driving in general, and commuting in particular, are stressful and possibly unhealthy. In fact, a considerable popular literature has arisen, both in printed form and on the Web, offering assistance to drivers in managing stress.[52] Serious suggestions have been made that commuters need specialized mental health services.[53] Among both commuters themselves and those who observe and care for drivers, there is a sense that commuting is a substantial source of stress.

The stress of commuting needs to be put in perspective in three ways. First, there is evidence that some people, at least some of the time, enjoy long commutes (remember the story of Atlanta Braves pitcher Chris Hammond that began this chapter). Some commuters indicate that the commute is their only opportunity to have "quiet time" for themselves.[54] In a busy life, an interval of downtime sandwiched between work demands and home demands, with the opportunity to listen to the radio or simply relax, may be restorative for some people, especially those with relatively uncongested commutes. Second, the amount of strain that results from the stresses of commuting, and the medical effects of this strain, differ from person to person. Early studies focused on the role of type A behavior in mediating the impact of commuting,[55] and more recent work has focused on personality traits such as coping style.[56] Life circumstances, and especially life stresses, also seem to play a major role in mediating driving stress.[57] As with many potentially hazardous exposures, commuting does not affect everybody in the same way. Third, automobile commuting is not the only form of commuting that can be stressful. Train and bus commuting have also been linked to increased heart rate, catecholamine excretion, and other indicators of stress,[58] perhaps because of the need to keep on schedule, crowding, physical discomfort, and/or the lack of control. However, the evidence suggests that automobile commuting is more stressful, for more people, than these other forms of travel.[59]

Stress-Related Morbidity among Commuters

What are the results of driving stress? What happens to suburban commuters who confront long drives on busy roads, year after year? We have evidence on three health outcomes in relation to the stress of driving in general, and commuting in particular: cardiovascular disease, back pain, and collisions.

As early as 1929, when driving was first becoming widespread, there were reports of cardiac death during driving.[60] Some of these events may have been coincidental, and some may have been triggered by ambient carbon monoxide on roadways.[61] However, the stress of driving may well have contributed. More recently, studies of professional drivers such as truck drivers, bus drivers, and taxi drivers, have consistently shown an increased risk of cardiovascular disease, despite selection against these disorders at the time of hiring and during medical follow-up.[62]

Another manifestation of stress is musculoskeletal symptoms, especially back pain and neck pain. Commuting may contribute to these outcomes not only through stress, but also through biomechanical mechanisms, including prolonged sitting in a fixed position, ergonomically incorrect seats, and/or prolonged exposure to whole-body vibration. Research in the occupational health field documents

■ TABLE 8-1 Neck and back pain in relation to annual driving distance

Annual km driven	Odds ratio for neck pain (95% confidence interval)	Odds ratio for back pain (95% confidence interval)
5,000	1	1
5,000–10,000	0.99 (0.45–2.2)	1.40 (0.65–3.04)
10,000–15,000	1.48 (0.75–2.93)	1.89 (0.96–3.73)
15,000–30,000	1.74 (1.01–2.99)	2.23 (1.29–3.85)
30,000–50,000	2.10 (1.24–3.54)	2.18 (1.28–3.72)
>50,000	2.43 (1.36–4.34)	2.79 (1.54–5.07)

SOURCE: T. Skov, V. Borg, and E. Orhede, "Psychosocial and Physical Risk Factors for Musculoskeletal Disorders of the Neck, Shoulders, and Lower Back in Salespeople," *Occupational & Environmental Medicine* 1996;53(5):351-56.

that professional drivers have an increased risk of back pain.[63] If exposure to driving is a risk factor for back pain among people who drive for a living, then commuting—which also exposes people to prolonged driving—might confer some of the same risk.

Studies do reveal a link between automobile commuting and back pain. In a case-control study of herniated lumbar intervertebral disc patients in Connecticut, driving was found to be a risk factor—not only professional driving (defined as spending more than half of one's work time driving), but also other driving.[64] Patients with herniated discs averaged 10.2 hours per week of driving, while control patients averaged 8.3 hours per week of driving.[65] In a French questionnaire study of over 1,000 working people, time spent in a car was a significant predictor of low-back pain.[66] Most recently, in a Danish questionnaire study of 1,306 salespeople, neck, shoulder, and back pain were related not only to occupational stressors such as high job demands, overwork, and lack of social support, but also to driving long distances (Table 8-1).[67]

Life stress in general has been shown to be a risk factor for traffic crashes.[68] More specifically, the stress of driving may be linked to crashes in two ways. First, driving stress leads to behaviors that predispose to crashes, such as speeding, weaving, and tailgating.[69] Second, stress seems to be a direct risk factor for crashes,[70] perhaps because stressed drivers are less alert, less reactive, or otherwise less capable behind the wheel.

Aggressive Driving

The car is an extension of personal space, often people's second most valuable possession, their main access to freedom, and a statement of self through the choice of vehicle, colour, make, model, and of course, the way they drive. A car is like a second home, and with this comes territorial beliefs and feelings which, when threatened, lead the owner to respond in a territorial and sometimes aggressive fashion. A car also provides the owner with protection, unusual power, easy escape and a degree of autonomy. It is perhaps for these reasons that an individual encased in an automobile seems to have a lower threshold for hostility.[71]

—G. Fong et al.,
"Road Rage: A Psychiatric Phenomenon?" 2001

Most drivers are familiar with aggression on the roads, having seen it in others and perhaps displayed it themselves. Why should we care about aggressive driving? First, aggressive behavior is itself an important mental health outcome, with broad implications for health and social functioning. Second, aggressive behavior is a risk factor for collisions and for acts of violence.[72]

Aggressive driving is common. In a pioneering 1968 study, psychologist Meyer Parry surveyed 382 drivers on a major road into London. The questionnaire asked about several aggressive driving behaviors, from the relatively benign to the more hazardous. When asked about swearing out loud at other drivers, 50 percent of men and 38 percent of women reported doing so. Fifteen percent of men and 11 percent of women reported that, at times, they felt they "could gladly kill another driver." Thirteen percent of men and 2 percent of women reported that on occasion they had tried to edge another car off the road, 9 percent of the men and 1 percent of the women reported that they had been in a fight with another driver, and 7 percent of the men and 2 percent of the women reported that they had deliberately driven at another vehicle in anger.[73] In a 1975 study in Salt Lake City, drivers reported similar levels of aggression while driving, although unlike in Britain, females outdid males on some responses (see Table 8-2). For example, 12 percent of men and 18 percent of women sampled reported that, at times, they "could gladly kill another driver."[74]

In a 1980 Dutch study,[75] Hauber observed the reactions of 966 drivers when a pedestrian crossed at an intersection as they approached in their cars. He defined aggressive behavior as any of three actions: failure to stop for the pedestrian, angry gestures or language, or horn blowing. Overall, 25 percent of the drivers displayed such behavior, with the proportion rising to 33 percent among young male drivers. Other factors associated with aggressive behavior included the gender of the pedestrian (males elicited more aggression than females), afternoon as opposed to morning driving (perhaps due to accumulated tension from the day, and/or driver impatience to get home after work), and commercial as opposed to private drivers (perhaps due to more time driving).

■ TABLE 8-2 Self-reported hostility while driving, Salt Lake City, 1975 (percentage of drivers[a])

Questionnaire item	Male	Female
I am easily provoked when driving.	23	18
I lose my temper when another driver does something silly.	40	41
I have been known to flash my lights at others in anger.	50	15
I get annoyed if the traffic lights change to red as I approach them.	23	23
I make rude signs at other motorists when I am provoked.	15	11
At times, I've felt that I could gladly kill another driver.	12	18
If someone suddenly turns without signaling, I get annoyed.	58	92
I swear out loud at other drivers.	23	41
I swear under my breath at other drivers.	77	56
I have given chase to a driver who has annoyed me.	12	4
If the driver behind me has his lights shining in my mirror, I pay him back in some way.	23	12
I am usually impatient at traffic lights.	19	7

[a]n = 26 males, 27 females.

SOURCE: C. W. Turner, J. F. Layton, and L. S. Simons, "Naturalistic Studies of Aggressive Behavior: Aggressive Stimuli, Victim Visibility, and Horn Honking," *Journal of Personality and Social Psychology* 1975;31:1098-1107.

Interestingly, Hauber evaluated the same drivers in a nondriving situation by "telephone manipulation"—calling their homes with two successive wrong numbers. Again, he assessed aggressive behavior, this time noting such responses as becoming verbally abusive, banging down the telephone receiver, and exhibiting marked irritation. Only 11 percent of those reached by phone became aggressive, less than half the proportion that became aggressive while driving. Something about driving seemed to bring out the aggression in people.

In early 1995, the Automobile Association in Great Britain commissioned a survey of 526 drivers.[76] (The report of this survey does not describe how the participants were selected and recruited.) Remarkable proportions of the respondents reported both having behaved aggressively and having been subject to aggressive behavior, as shown on Table 8-3. This study asked about the kinds of roads on which aggressive incidents occurred, and found that 46 percent had occurred on "main roads," 26 percent on divided highways, 23 percent on minor roads, and 4 percent in parking lots.

More recent surveys have shown evidence of continuing frustration and aggression on the roads. In national telephone surveys in 1999 and 2001, large numbers of respondents reported both engaging in aggressive behaviors while driving (Table 8-4) and being on the receiving end

TABLE 8-3 Self-reported aggressive driving behavior among English drivers, 1995 (percentage of respondents[a])

| | Percentage of drivers who report | |
	Being the victim of this behavior	Committing this behavior toward other drivers
Aggressive tailgating	62	45
Flashing headlights when annoyed	59	22
Aggressive or rude gestures	48	12
Deliberately obstructed or prevented from maneuvering the car	21	6
Verbal abuse	16	5
Physical abuse	1	<1
None of these	12	40

[a]n = 526

SOURCE: M. Joint, "Road Rage," *Aggressive Driving: Three Studies* Washington AAA Foundation for Traffic Safety, March 1997. Available at http://www.aaafoundation.org/pdf/agdr3study.pdf. Accessed June 23, 2002.

TABLE 8-4 Self-reported aggressive driving behaviors among U.S. drivers, 1999 (percentage of respondents)[a]

How often do you . . .	Never	Rarely	Sometimes	Often
Say bad things to yourself about other drivers	15.3	22.9	39.5	22.1
Complain or yell about other drivers to a passenger in your vehicle	25.5	22.2	39.0	13.1
Give another driver a dirty look	41.8	17.6	32.7	7.7
Honk or yell at someone through the window to express displeasure	61.1	17.9	17.9	2.9
Keep someone from entering your lane because you are angry	80.2	12.9	5.9	0.8
Make obscene gestures to another driver	83.7	9.2	6.1	0.8
Think about physically hurting another driver	89.0	5.4	4.4	1.1
Make sudden or threatening moves to intimidate another driver	94.6	4.0	1.1	0.1
Follow or chase another driver in anger	96.5	3.2	0.3	0.0

[a]n = 1,508

SOURCE: R. W. Snow, "Monitoring American's Attitudes, Opinions, and Behaviors," 1999 National Highway Safety Survey, Mississippi State University, Social Science Research Center, January, 2000. Available at www.ssrc.msstate.edu/publications/srrs2000-1.pdf. Accessed July 18, 2002.

■ **TABLE 8-5** U.S. drivers reporting being the victims of aggressive behavior, 2001 (percentage of respondents)[a]

Percentage of drivers reporting that within the last year, another driver . . .	Rural	Small town	Small city	Large city	Total
Tailgated you	69.1	61.3	70.3	69.8	66.8
Made an obscene gesture at you	39.7	37.1	44.9	44.3	41.8
Cut you off	32.0	33.7	38.6	48.0	38.1
Made a threatening move with car	25.4	23.5	30.0	25.9	26.4
Followed or chased you in anger	9.9	6.4	9.9	11.5	9.4
Got out of car to argue with you	5.8	5.8	4.2	8.3	5.9
Deliberately hit you with his car	1.7	0.9	1.1	2.6	1.5

[a]n = 1,394

SOURCE: R. W. Snow, "Monitoring American's Attitudes, Opinions, and Behaviors," 2001 National Highway Safety Survey, Mississippi State University, Social Science Research Center. January, 2002. Available at http://www.ssrc.msstate.edu/publications/2001NationalHighwaySafetySurvey.pdf. Accessed July 18, 2002.

of such behavior (Table 8-5). A similar survey, conducted for the National Highway Traffic Safety Administration in 1998, found somewhat lower but comparable numbers.[77] In the NHTSA survey, people were asked why they engaged in aggressive behavior. The two leading reasons cited were being rushed or behind schedule (23 percent), and heavy traffic or congestion (22 percent)—common experiences on the crowded roadways of sprawling areas. Moreover, 30 percent of the NHTSA respondents perceived that aggressive driving—their own and others'— was increasing over time (and only 4 percent thought it was decreasing).

More recently, researchers at Johns Hopkins University[78] surveyed 218 women employed by a telecommunications company. This was a stable, professional population; 67 percent of the respondents had more than a high school education, 76 percent were parents, and the average job seniority was eighteen years. Among these women, 56 percent admitted to driving aggressively, 41 percent reported yelling or gesturing at other drivers while commuting, and 25 percent reported taking out their frustrations from behind the wheel of their cars. In a nationwide survey of 880 drivers in 2001, 28.7 percent reported that when they are running late and approach a red light, they speed up to beat the light rather than slow down and prepare to stop. Among those who reported this behavior, 69 percent gave as their reason being "in a rush" or wanting "to save time." However, red light running was not the prime response to frustration while driving. Weaving in and out of traffic, gesturing angrily at other drivers or pedestrians, tailgating, and speeding were all more closely linked to increasing frustration than was red light running.[79] Aggressive behavior while driving appears to be a widespread problem.

What causes aggressive driving behavior? Or, put more colorfully, what makes "an apparently perfectly normal, mild-mannered individual turn into an antisocial road maniac?"[80] A large body of literature addresses this question, most of it focusing on characteristics of the drivers.[81] Psychologists at Colorado State University have even developed a Driver Anger Scale, based on the concept that driver anger is a measurable personality trait.[82] Not surprisingly, risk factors for aggressive driving include male gender, young age, alcohol drinking, aggressive personality features, and life stress.[83] Some people seem to feel gratified, and even to have fun, when they drive aggressively.[84] Observers focused on law enforcement have emphasized the role of reduced levels of traffic enforcement,[85] pointing out that courts are more lenient toward aggressive drivers than toward aggressors who use other weapons.[86] To some extent, aggressive driving may simply reflect aggressive behavior in society more generally.[87]

Several psychological explanations have been offered. Perhaps the automobile evokes territorial feelings, leading drivers to defend aggressively against perceived invasions.[88] Hines postulated that something in the interaction of driver and automobile unlocks aggressive tendencies. "In many cases," he wrote, "the car seems to sharpen dispositions and reduce inhibitions. Apparently cautious individuals may take chances. Few people would shake their fist at another pedestrian, yet many would make aggressive or derisory gestures to other drivers. Perhaps they feel safer in the car, less accessible and unlikely to be called to account."[89] And Novaco emphasized the role of media images in spurring aggressive behavior among drivers. "The symbolization of the automobile," he pointed out, "has commonly incorporated aggressive themes, reflected in car names and marketing images. Both cars and trucks are often used by their drivers as instruments of dominance, and the road serves as an arena for competition and control."[90] Indeed, some people may feel that their automobile reflects and projects their image, what Connell and Joint call the "egoic aspect of driving," leading to heightened sensitivity to perceived insults.[91]

Could sprawl contribute to aggressive driving? Relatively little research has looked at environmental factors, such as road conditions, as predictors of aggressive behavior. Congestion is likely to be a contributor. Hennessy and Wiesenthal, in their cellular phone interviews of Toronto drivers, found that congested traffic doubled the frequency of aggressive behaviors, including horn honking, hand gestures, tail-gating, flashing high beams, and swearing at other drivers.[92] Shinar proposed that the main cause of aggression on the roads is traffic con-gestion, based on the "frustration–aggression" psychological model.[93] Lajunen and colleagues surveyed 270 British drivers to identify situa-tions that aroused anger.[94] Three sets of factors emerged: having their progress impeded, reckless driving by other drivers, and hostility in other drivers. The first of these factors, impedance, certainly occurs with congested roads. When it comes to aggression, concluded British researchers Connell and Joint, "Congestion is . . . undoubtedly an issue."[95] This view has reached the popular literature as well. In a hor-tatory 2000 book entitled *Road Rage and Aggressive Driving: Steering Clear of Highway Warfare*, the authors explain the role of congestion as follows: "Because it inconveniences, delays, and frustrates drivers, con-gestion increases the number of crashes due to aggressive driving. Peo-ple experience time pressure when they can't predict travel time accu-rately; they feel caged or trapped with no way out, and some become incensed. . . . "[96]

However, British and Finnish researchers reached a different con-clusion in a 1999 study, which compared drivers in Britain, Holland, and Finland.[97] In this study, the researchers assessed the amount of exposure to congested driving by asking drivers how often they drove during rush hour, and how often they drove on country roads. There was no association between rush-hour driving and aggressive behavior (as indicated by angrily blowing their horns, chasing another driver "to give a piece of your mind," and otherwise expressing hostility). More-over, the more congested countries (Britain and Holland) did not have more aggressive rush-hour behavior than sparsely populated Finland. "In general," concluded the investigators, "the relationship between exposure to congestion as measured by frequency of rush-hour driving, and aggressive violations was weak. . . . "

Perhaps some features of sprawl other than traffic congestion lead to aggressive driving. A 1999 study by the Surface Transportation Pol-icy Project,[98] a Washington nonprofit group, focused on aggressive driving, defined as speeding faster than 80 miles per hour, tailgating, failing to yield, weaving in and out of traffic, passing on the right, mak-ing improper and unsafe lane changes, and/or running stop signs and red lights. Using this definition, they found that aggressive driving was a factor in 56 percent of fatal crashes (excluding crashes in which drugs or alcohol were a factor). In a comparison of seventy metropolitan areas, the investigators found that higher rates of transit use, higher rates of commuting by foot, and fewer miles of highway per capita, all predicted lower aggressive driving death rates. Among large cities, the highest aggressive driving death rates were in Riverside–San Bernardino (California), Tampa–St. Petersburg, Phoenix, Orlando, Miami, and Las Vegas, while the lowest were in Boston, New York, Minneapolis, Pittsburgh, Norfolk–Virginia Beach, and Cleveland, suggesting a higher risk in more sprawling cities. But as in the British-Finnish findings, roadway congestion was not associated with the aggressive driving death rate. The investigators concluded "aggressive driving death rates are much higher in places with uncontrolled sprawl development," but that "metropolitan areas with high congestion levels were no more likely to have high aggressive driving death rates than areas with less congestion." Certain community attributes, in particular the presence of higher density, mixed land uses, and transportation alternatives such as mass transit and sidewalks, seemed to offer protection against deadly aggressive driving.

Road Rage

The pinnacle of aggressive driving, when emotions, words, and reckless driving erupt in violent acts, has come to be known as road rage. While aggressive driving behavior had been recognized for decades, the term "road rage" came into use during the 1980s, initially in the United States, and later in Australia and Great Britain, to reflect what was perceived as an epidemic of these incidents on the roads. The *Oxford Dictionary of New Words* defines road rage as "A driver's uncontrolled aggressive behavior, apparently caused by the stresses of modern driving."[99] A report issued by the American Automobile Association Foundation for Traffic Safety[100] offers a definition of aggressive driving that in fact fits better as a definition of road rage: an instance when "an angry or impatient driver tries to kill or injure another driver after a traffic dispute." By the 1990s, *Time* magazine wrote (with some hyperbole), "It's high noon on the country's streets and highways. This is road recklessness, auto anarchy, an epidemic of wanton carmanship."[101]

Accounts of road rage are not difficult to find, and they range from the tragic to the comic. In Massachusetts in 1994, Donald Graham, a fifty-four-year-old church deacon and bookkeeper, became embroiled in a heated, ongoing traffic dispute with Michael Blodgett, forty-two, as they drove on Interstate 95. After several miles, they both pulled onto an access road and got out of their cars. Graham took a crossbow from his trunk and skewered Blodgett with a 29-inch arrow, killing him.[102] In September 1999, twenty-one-year-old Shaun Mohr was driving his Isuzu Rodeo on Interstate 275 near Cincinnati, when he came up behind a Dodge Colt driven by twenty-seven-year-old Kraal Wiggins. The two men jockeyed for position, and Mohr eventually passed Wiggins. As Wiggins pulled up behind Mohr, Mohr slammed on his brakes, Wiggins struck Mohr from behind, and Mohr lost control of his vehicle. It rolled several times, throwing his passenger, twenty-one-year-old Tiffany Frank, from the vehicle and seriously injuring her.[103] In January 2000, thirty-eight-year-old Chris Duron got into a dispute with another driver as they drove in the high-occupancy vehicle lane of Interstate 75 south of Atlanta. Both drivers stopped their cars, and Duron ran toward the other car, prompting his rival to shoot him. When police arrived, Duron's engine was running, his driver's door was open, his lights and radio were on, and his body lay 30 feet from his car.[104] A few days later, Sara McBurnett was picking up her husband at the airport in San Jose, California. In rainy weather and bumper-to-bumper traffic on the airport approach road, she accidentally bumped a sport-utility vehicle in front of her. The driver left his vehicle, approached her car, grabbed her small dog through an open window, and threw it into oncoming traffic, where it was killed.[105]

The most unlikely perpetrators may be involved. In 1995, Robin Ficker, fifty-two, a prominent attorney and former Maryland state legislator, bumped his Jeep into a newer Jeep driven by Caroline Goldman, who was six months pregnant, as they drove in the upscale town of Potomac. When she asked him why he had done it, he struck her in the face, breaking her glasses and giving her a black eye.[106] And in Salt Lake City in 1997, forty-one-year-old Larry Remm Jr. honked at seventy-five-year-old J. C. King for blocking traffic. Mr. King took umbrage, and followed Mr. Remm's car until it pulled off the road. He commenced his attack by hurling his prescription bottle at Mr. Remm, and followed this with what *U.S. News & World Report* dubbed "a display of geriatric resolve": smashing Remm's knees with his 1992 Mercury.[107]

Attention to road rage is certainly increasing, as judged by press coverage, popular books, and Web site discussion. However, data do not clearly establish that the incidence of road rage is increasing. One of the difficulties is the variable definition of road rage used in different investigations. The broadest definitions include many kinds of aggressive driving behavior, even name-calling. Narrower definitions are restricted to deliberate attacks, sometimes further limited to attacks on strangers (excluding, say, domestic disputes that play out on the roads). Available data sources, ranging from police reports to newspaper accounts, are highly inconsistent.

In the only available longitudinal study in the United States, conducted for the AAA Foundation for Traffic Safety study,[108] the investigator collected reports of road rage incidents from across the United States for the period 1990 through 1996. Data sources included newspapers, police reports, and insurance reports; as a result, an observed increase may have been due, at least in part, to increased reporting rather than to a true increase. During this time, the annual tallies increased by 51 percent, from 1,129 per year to approximately 1,800 per year. (The final year's count was extrapolated from eight months of data.) In a total of 10,037 recorded incidents, there were 12,610 injuries and 218 deaths. The reasons for assaults were disclosed in a series of quotations taken from crime reports. In one case, a man was shot to death "because he was driving too slowly." In another case, a woman was shot because "the bitch hit my new Camaro." There were assaults because "He cut me off," because "She was driving too slowly," because "She wouldn't let me pass," and because "She kept crossing lanes without signaling; maybe I overreacted but it taught her a lesson." "I never would have shot him," mused one driver, "if he hadn't rear-ended me." Various weapons were used, including guns (in 37 percent of cases), the vehicle itself (in 35 percent of cases), knives, clubs, tire irons, baseball bats, fists, and feet. Perpetrators were disproportionately young and male. In some cases, the incidents involved domestic disputes that played out on the roads, and in other cases, there was apparently an overlay of racism.

Investigators at the Crime Research Center at the University of Western Australia studied road rage in that country during the interval 1991 to 1995, using a narrow definition: "impulsive driving related violence between strangers," as recorded in state police data.[109] This definition excluded attacks on cars by "thumping or banging and also such matters as obscene language or gestures, flashing lights, tailgating, lane hopping, and queue jumping into parking bays," which were considered acts of incivility rather than criminality. By definition, the aggressor and the victim had to be unacquainted with each other. During the study period, the annual number of road rage incidents rose, although it comprised a fairly stable proportion of all stranger assaults (about 10 percent). However, when measured against the state population, and against the number of registered vehicles, there was an upward trend, especially in the Perth metropolitan area where traffic congestion and clogged roads had become common. Five common triggers for acts of road rage emerged: encounters with slow drivers; other drivers cutting in or passing; gender bias, with males attributing driving incompetence to females; collisions between vehicles; and competition for parking spaces. Risk factors for committing road rage included being young and male, afternoon hours, and Aboriginal ethnicity (of either driver or victim). In addition, more time driving was associated with a higher risk of road rage. These investigators interpreted their results in terms of violence theory, pointing to several aspects of driving that facilitate violence: defending territory, enhancing reputation, anonymity, some cognitive distortions on the part of offenders, and the physiological arousal that accompanies driving.

Similar findings have emerged in Britain. In a search of English newspapers during 1996, 255 articles describing 60 separate incidents of road rage were retrieved.[110] Of these, 22 involved assault, almost all with weapons, and 29 injuries and 12 deaths resulted. In the 1998 British Crime Survey, over 4,500 people answered questions about crime during the preceding twelve months.[111] Of these, 54 percent of those who had driven reported having been the victim of some form of road rage. Most were limited to verbal abuse or gestures, but 9 percent had been forced to pull off the road, and 3 percent reported that another driver had left his or her car and threatened violence. In a 2001 study, 131 patients in medical office waiting rooms in England were interviewed about road rage. They were asked whether they had been involved in an act of road rage during the previous five years as victim, perpetrator, or both, and they completed psychological questionnaires. These investigators defined road rage broadly, as "responding verbally or physically in a threatening manner" to another driver's behavior. Just over half of the sample reported experiencing an incident of road rage—29 percent as victim, 12 percent as perpetrator, and 11 percent as both. The study focused on personal risk factors rather than on environmental or situational ones. Road rage perpetrators tended to be younger, less-experienced drivers, and members of "manual" social classes. They showed an increase in psychiatric morbidity, with elevated scores on the Aggression Questionnaire, in particular on the anger and physical aggression subscores.[112]

What disinhibits drivers, escalating aggressive driving to the intentional, directed acts that we recognize as road rage? Why is the term "road rage" familiar, while there is no such thing as "sidewalk rage"? Perhaps the underlying stress of driving, the anonymity of roadway disputes, and the rapid pace at which disputes develop, combine to facilitate acts of road rage. As in the driving stress literature, risk factors include personal attributes such as age, gender, personality structure, and life stress. In some cases, alcohol plays a role. For example, a review of thirty-six years of records in Marion County, Oregon, revealed five deaths from road rage. In all but one, alcohol intoxication played a role.[113] The factors that contribute to driving aggression—time spent driving and traffic impedance—may also contribute to episodes of road rage. In several ways, then—the sheer quantity of driving, the challenges of commuting on congested roads, perhaps the associated effects of life stresses—sprawl may contribute to road rage.

It is clear that driving is a stressful activity, at least in the physiological sense of the word. For nearly fifty years, data have indicated that many people experience increased blood pressure, increased levels of catecholamines and cortisol, and other systemic responses to driving. It is also clear that in some people, under some circumstances, driving elicits aggression, which can be dangerous to themselves and others. These facts alone suggest that driving may pose a mental health risk, and that limiting or offering alternatives to driving may offer mental health benefits. But there is much that remains unknown. What is the trend over time in driving aggression and in acts of road rage? What are the contributions of particular patterns of driving, such as commuting, and of particular road designs? What individuals are at highest risk? Can alternative transportation options, such as sidewalks, bicycle paths, and mass transit, help control the mental health consequences of driving?

SPRAWL AND MENTAL HEALTH: THE BIG PICTURE

It seems reasonable to hypothesize that anger and frustration among drivers are not restricted to their cars. Fortunately, most people restrain themselves and do not commit acts of road rage. But what becomes of the anger? When angry people arrive at work in the morning or at home in the evening, what are the implications for work and family relations? If parents become distracted and hostile while driving their children to school, can they have "quality time" together? To the extent that social ties are frayed by the long and difficult automobile commutes of sprawling cities, the mental health consequences may be extensive.[114] Some of the implications of these questions are explored in Chapter 9.

While the main focus of this chapter has been on stress, anger, and aggression, there is much more to mental illness. The various mental illnesses are an enormous cause of suffering and expense. They account for 15.4 percent of lost Disability-Adjusted Life Years (DALYs) in countries like the United States, second only to cardiovascular disease.[115] Moreover, there is evidence that some mental illnesses have been increasing, in tandem with the postwar growth of urban sprawl. Could there be a link? Three conditions merit special mention: depression, anxiety, and attention deficit disorder.

Depression is an increasingly important mental illness. Three percent of adults in the United States suffer an episode of major depression every year, and over the course of a lifetime, 5.2 percent are affected.[116] Major depression alone accounts for 6.8 percent of lost DALYs in developed countries, more than any other single disease except ischemic heart disease.[117] Depression incidence varies considerably from place to place, suggesting environmental contributions,[118] and the incidence seems to be increasing.[119]

Sprawl might contribute to depression in several ways. First, by limiting regular opportunities for physical activity, sprawl may deprive people of one of the most effective "treatments" of depression.[120] Second, by limiting opportunities for interpersonal contact, sprawl may aggravate social isolation, a risk factor for depression.[121] Third, if beautiful, natural environments can raise the spirits, could ugly suburban roads do the opposite? The quotation that begins this chapter, from social critic James Howard Kunstler, makes an eloquent case for this effect. Suburban roads confront us, Kunstler writes, with the "fantastic, awesome, stupefying ugliness of absolutely everything in sight—the fry pits, the big-box stores, the office units, the lube joints, the carpet warehouses, the parking lagoons, the jive plastic townhouse clusters, the uproar of signs, the highway itself clogged with cars." "And naturally," Kunstler continues, "this experience can make us feel glum about the nature and future of civilization."[122]

Anxiety is also an important mental health issue, and one that commonly coexists with depression.[123] According to the Surgeon General's 1999 report, approximately 16 percent of adults suffer from an anxiety disorder during any given year. Most of these are phobias, but panic disorder, obsessive–compulsive disorder, post-traumatic stress disorder, and other anxiety disorders are included as well. Among children and adolescents, anxiety disorders are the most common mental disorder, with a prevalence of 13 percent.[124] Could the factors discussed earlier in this chapter—the stress of driving, commutes that feature time pressure and unpredictability, contact with aggressive thoughts and behaviors in self or others, social isolation—contribute to anxiety as well?

Attention deficit–hyperactivity disorder (ADHD) is the most commonly diagnosed behavioral disorder of childhood, occurring in approximately 3 to 5 percent of school-age children.[125] The causes of ADHD are unknown; although genetic predispositions probably play a small role, environmental factors are thought to be important. Little is known about which environmental factors may contribute to ADHD. But if children have limited opportunities for physical activity in communities that discourage walking and biking, might this be a factor?

The questions raised here are speculative, and we have little evidence to help answer them. But they are perhaps the most important questions we face about the mental health consequences of sprawl. As the built environment continues to evolve, and as mental disorders continue to loom large in absolute and relative terms in our nation's health profile, we need to remain alert to possible links between sprawl and mental health.

CHAPTER 9

■ ══════ ■

SOCIAL CAPITAL, SPRAWL, AND HEALTH

W̲hat binds us together as communities and as a society? What helps us connect with each other where we live, work, and play? People have discussed concepts like social networks, reciprocity, and trust for many centuries. In recent years, the term "social capital" has become popular, and a lively debate has arisen over the importance of social capital in modern life. This chapter considers the relationships among sprawl, social capital, and health.

WHAT IS SOCIAL CAPITAL?

For many centuries, social scientists and commentators have studied the ways in which people live together. Alexis de Tocqueville, in *Democracy in America* (1835, 1840) famously commented on the national urge to affiliate. "Americans of all ages, all stations of life, and all types of disposition," he wrote, "are forever forming associations."[1] More than a century later, the idea of "psychological sense of community"[2] became central to the discipline of community psychology. Sense of community is defined as "a feeling that members have of belonging, a feeling that members matter to one another and to the group, and a shared faith that members' needs will be met through their commitment to be together."[3] There are four aspects of the sense of community: membership, influence, integration and fulfillment of needs, and shared emotional connection.[4] Community psychologists, human ecologists, and

— 161 —

sociologists have distinguished communities of place, such as neighbor-hoods, from communities of interest, such as professional associations, networks of friends and relatives, and church groups.[5] In studying how neighborhoods function, some have focused on cohesion, including such components as use of physical facilities, personal identification with the neighborhood, social interaction, and values consensus.[6]

Political scientists and anthropologists have described a similar concept, "civil society." This refers to the world of voluntary, purpose-ful associations distinct from government, where citizens come togeth-er according to their interests, beliefs, and goals—the Rotary Club, a church, a bowling league, or the Boy Scouts.[7] By pursuing private ini-tiatives for the common good, these organizations are thought to fill three roles: socialization, or building citizenship skills and the motiva-tion to use them; public and quasi-public functions such as caring for the needy and promoting cultural life; and fostering democratic debate by giving voice to interest groups and even helping them oppose gov-ernment actions.[8] Critics point out that civil society is not necessarily good; it includes "a bewildering array of the good, the bad, and the out-right bizarre," often pursuing narrow self-interests, and sometimes inimical to democratic function.[9]

The great observer of urban life, Jane Jacobs, focused on the most informal kind of civil society: "casual public contact at a local level," on the streets and parks of cities and towns. In *The Death and Life of Great American Cities*, she extolled the small and quotidian dramas of sidewalk life—"people stopping by at the bar for a beer, getting advice from the grocer and giving advice to the newsstand man, comparing opinions with other customers at the bakery and nodding hello to the two boys drinking pop on the stoop, eyeing the girls while waiting to be called for dinner, admonishing the children, hearing about a job from the hardware man and borrowing a dollar from the druggist, admiring the new babies and sympathizing about the way a coat faded." These are valuable, she wrote, because they create conviviality and trust, "a feel-ing for the public identity of people, a web of public respect and trust, and a resource in time of personal or neighborhood need."[10]

Jacobs was writing about what we now call social capital. This term was apparently introduced as early as 1916 by a West Virginia school official, L. J. Hanifin, to refer to "those tangible substances [that] count for most in the daily lives of people: namely good will, fellowship, sym-pathy, and social intercourse among the individuals and families who make up a social unit." Hanifin thought of these assets as beneficial at both the individual level and the community level, and argued that they were important for successful schools.[11] Social analyst Pierre

Bourdieu[12] and sociologist James Coleman,[13] among others, reintroduced the term social capital in the 1980s, and Harvard political scientist Robert Putnam brought it to public attention, especially with his book *Bowling Alone* (2000).

Putnam has defined social capital as "connections among people—social networks and the norms of reciprocity and trustworthiness that arise from them."[14] This definition highlights two components of social capital: social networks, reflecting behaviors and actions that can be readily observed; and norms and attitudes, which are less tangible. Kenneth Newton, professor of politics and government at the University of Southampton, England, emphasizes the transformative power of social capital. It is "a social force," he writes, "that binds society together by transforming individuals from self-seeking and egocentric calculators, with little social conscience or sense of mutual obligation, into members of a community with shared interests, shared assumptions about social relations, and a sense of the common good."[15] In fact, some commentators emphasize the functional outcome of social capital as part of its definition. For example, Stolle and Rochon define it as "the networks, norms and values that link citizens to each other and that enable them to pursue their common objectives more effectively."[16] For social commentator Francis Fukuyama, trust—a central part of social capital—is a critical stepping-stone to prosperity.[17] In other words, social capital has both relational and material aspects.[18]

The concept of social capital can be teased apart in other ways. Perhaps the most important is the distinction between bridging (or inclusive) social capital and bonding (or exclusive) social capital. Bridging social capital, dubbed "sociological WD-40" by Putnam, is outward looking and cross-cutting, useful for building extensive networks and diffusing information. Examples include the civil rights movement and ecumenical religious organizations. Bonding social capital, dubbed "sociological superglue" by Putnam, is inward looking. It reinforces the exclusive identities of homogeneous groups, building solidarity and reciprocity among members. Examples are ethnic fraternal organizations, church-based women's groups, and fashionable country clubs.[19]

Putnam also distinguishes between "thin" and "thick" trust. Thin trust is defined as trust in the "generalized other," a person with whom one has little personal experience, but shares some social networks and expectations of reciprocity. Thin trust is a general inclination to give most people—even strangers—the benefit of the doubt. We demonstrate thin trust when we yield to another driver in traffic, or hold the elevator door open for a stranger. Thick trust, on the other hand, is embedded in personal relations that are strong, frequent, and nested in wider networks. If a customer forgets his wallet, but the neighborhood cleaner lets him take his clothes home and pay "whenever you come back in" because he has been a customer for many years, thick trust is at work. Thin and thick trust characterize different relationships and serve different purposes.[20]

Social trust may also be "horizontal" or "vertical." Horizontal trust is trust in people at a similar social position, whereas vertical (or hierarchic) trust is trust in institutions and political authorities. For example, trusting one's neighbors is an instance of horizontal trust, while trusting the police to take care of crime is an example of vertical trust. Putnam asserts that horizontal trust represents more productive social capital than vertical trust.

Not all associations are alike. For example, participating in Mothers Against Drunk Driving (a cause-oriented volunteer organization) may produce different social capital, in quantity or quality, than belonging to the American Psychological Association (a professional association). In other words, social capital is context dependent.[21] Moreover, social capital is unevenly distributed, and not all groups have access to all forms of social capital. Schulman and Anderson call attention to the "dark side" of social capital, recognizing that access to social capital depends on the social standing of the people and groups who attempt to access it.[22] Another dark side of social capital is its use for malevolent, antisocial purposes. Groups like the Ku Klux Klan, and individuals like Timothy McVeigh, depend on networks of trust and reciprocity, but these are hardly social goods.[23]

How is social capital measured? If researchers wish to track levels of social capital over time, or ask, as we do in this chapter, whether social capital is higher in some environments than in others, they need ways to quantify it. Several approaches are commonly used.[24] First, researchers measure attitudes such as confidence in public institutions, trust in other people, and optimism, using questionnaires or interviews. For example, the General Social Survey conducted almost every year by the National Opinion Research Center asks respondents whether they believe "most people can be trusted" and whether they believe "most of the time people try to be helpful." Second, researchers measure behaviors such as voter turnout, newspaper readership, membership in voluntary organizations, and church attendance. Surveys are useful in assessing behaviors; the General Social Survey, for example, asks about participation in church groups, sports groups, hobby groups, fraternal organizations, and labor unions. In addition, behaviors such as voting and organizational membership can be directly observed and measured. Structural variables, a third indicator of social

capital, are neither attitudes nor behaviors. Instead, they are characteristics of an individual or a relationship such as family size or the presence of parents in the home.[25] Of note, social capital is usually viewed
as a property of networks or communities, so measurements are often
made at the community scale; an example is the extent to which neighborhood sidewalks are cleared after a snowstorm.[26] However, other
measurements of social capital focus on different scales, from the individual to the state or even the national level. This can introduce confu-
sion into the use of the concept.

THE DECLINE OF SOCIAL CAPITAL

For much of the last century, observers have described a decline in
sense of community or, more recently, in social capital. From social scientists like Émile Durkheim (1858–1917) to novelists like D. H.
Lawrence (1885–1930), commentators watched the development of
industry, the growth of large cities, and other aspects of modernization,
and mourned the loss of community that these trends seemed to her-
ald. Not only did the prototypical rural village dwindle, but society
became more mobile; people flocked to anonymous cities, large institutions eclipsed local governance, and impersonal human relations
supplanted the conviviality of the past.[27] Psychologist D. E. Poplin
echoed at least a century of American thought when, in 1972, he
lamented the loss of "the common bonds, which seem no longer to
typify the social life of modern communities."[28]

But nowhere was the case more forcefully made than in Putnam's
Bowling Alone. Putnam documents declines, from the 1950s to the end
of the century, in a wide range of indicators, including citizen participation in campaign activities; voter turnout for presidential elections;
public expression; membership in national and local associations; participation in the PTA; attendance at club meetings and church services;
union membership; frequency of social visits; card playing; participation in bowling leagues; philanthropic and charitable giving; community projects; and perception of honesty, morality, and trustworthiness.
The picture is not a consistent one. There have been increases in other
plausible indicators of social capital, such as the number of political
organizations with regular paid staff; the number of national nonprofit
organizations; attendance at sporting events (as a spectator); volunteer-
ing; and tolerance for racial integration, civil liberties, and gender
equality. However, the overall trend seems to be downward.

If social capital has declined, a great many factors might have contributed. People spend more time in front of televisions and computers. There are more two-career families. People are under more time and money pressure. Could urban sprawl have played a role? Before considering this question, we preview the health implications of social capital, to confirm that social capital is indeed a health issue.

DOES SOCIAL CAPITAL AFFECT HEALTH?

Does it matter if social capital is diminishing? It certainly does, if social capital brings some of the benefits that have been attributed to it: better functioning government, more prosperity, less crime. Here, we are concerned with a particular benefit, good health. Is social capital good for health?

For many years, social bonds have been recognized as an important component of good health. Loneliness and isolation are toxic, and social relationships are healthy.[29] Research has focused on two broad aspects of the social environment: structural features and social support.[30] Structural features refer to both the types and the number of relationships people have, sometimes called the density of relationships or the extent of social networks. Social support refers to how social relationships function, such as the amount of emotional support provided at a time of need. Of course, social relationships are not the same as social capital. Social capital is a feature of communities, corresponding at the individual level to a person's network of social relationships. But since an essential feature of social capital is social networks, and since both draw on trust and reciprocity, health data on social networks are likely to be informative about the broader concept of social capital.

People with strong social networks live longer. Long-term follow-up studies involving thousands of people, in Tecumseh, Michigan;[31] Alameda County, California;[32] Evans County, Georgia;[33] and elsewhere,[34] have consistently confirmed this finding. Interestingly, the effect seems to be stronger for men than for women. The excess mortality among those with few social contacts comes from cardiovascular disease, stokes, injuries, and suicide.[35]

Cross-sectional studies have also revealed that social capital prolongs life. For example, Kawachi and colleagues at Harvard University compared the mortality rates in thirty-nine states with different levels of social capital.[36] Their ratings were based on four items from the General Social Survey, conducted by the National Opinion Research

Center: membership in groups and associations, perceived fairness (the response to "Do you think most people would try to take advantage of you if they got a chance, or would they try to be fair?"), social trust (the answer to "Generally speaking, would you say that most people can be trusted or that you can't be too careful in dealing with people?"), and perceived helpfulness (the response to "Would you say that most of the time people try to be helpful, or are they mostly looking out for themselves?"). Their analysis controlled for factors such as income, age, race, and education.

The results were striking. As the level of a state's social capital decreased, the overall age-adjusted mortality increased. Figure 9-1 shows this relationship with regard to social mistrust. The same pattern held for the other three markers of social capital, and when the investigators looked at specific causes of death such as infant mortality, heart disease, stroke, and cancer. A one-unit increase in the average per capita group membership, for example, was associated with a decrease in the annual age-adjusted overall mortality rate of 66.8 deaths per 100,000 population.

■ **FIGURE 9-1** Mortality in U.S. states as a function of social capital

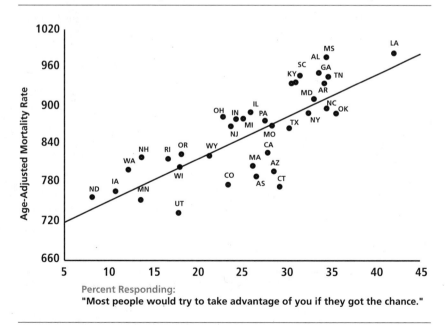

SOURCE: I. Kawachi, B. P. Kennedy, K. Lochner, and D. Prothrow-Stith, "Social Capital, Income Inequality, and Mortality," *American Journal of Public Health* 1997;87:1491-98.

Gerry Veenstra, a sociologist at the University of British Columbia, conducted a similar study in Saskatchewan.[37] His unit of analysis was smaller than a state; he focused on the province's health districts, which range in size from 11,000 to 220,000 people. Veenstra created a social capital index for each health district, based on the number of clubs and associations in each, the amount of public participation in the clubs and associations (from National Population Health Survey data), and recent voter turnout. The results, as shown in Figure 9-2, were similar to Kawachi's: more social capital meant lower age-adjusted mortality.

Could social capital not only lower mortality but also improve overall health status? Results have been mixed. In state-by-state comparisons, Kawachi and his Harvard colleagues found such a relationship (see Figure 9-3).[38] However, in a survey of over 500 people in Saskatchewan's thirty health districts, Veenstra[39] found different results. Higher income and more education predicted better overall health, an expected finding, but social capital for the most part did not. People who attended church regularly and who reported good work relationships were healthier, but socializing with family and friends,

■ FIGURE 9-2 Mortality in Saskatchewan Health Districts as a function of social capital

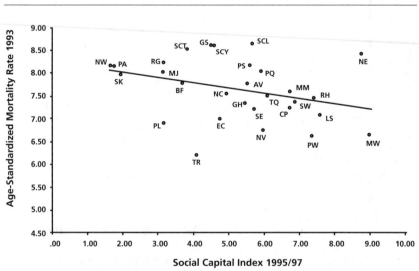

SOURCE: G. Veenstra, "Social Capital and Health (Plus Wealth, Income Inequality and Regional Health Governance)," *Social Science and Medicine* 2002;54:849-68.

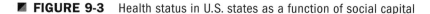

■ **FIGURE 9-3**   Health status in U.S. states as a function of social capital

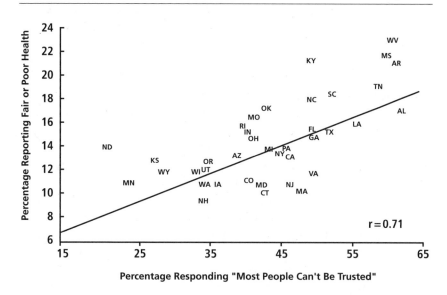

SOURCE: I. Kawachi, B. P. Kennedy, and R. Glass, "Social Capital and Self-Rated Health: A Contextual Analysis," *American Journal of Public Health* 1999;89(8):1187-93.

participating in clubs or associations, performing acts of civic participation such as voting, trusting others from the local scale to the national scale, identifying with communities, and feeling committed to the common good of those communities were all unrelated to health status. Veenstra's survey sample—several hundred people—may have been too small to demonstrate a benefit of social capital on overall health.

Social capital has been shown to confer many other health benefits. In a Swedish study, men with lower levels of "attachment" (emotional support from very close friends and family) and "social integration" (the support provided by an extended network) were more likely to develop coronary artery disease; the effect was stronger than for any other predictor except smoking.[40] Patients with strong social support have less extensive coronary artery disease than more socially isolated patients (although perhaps only among type A patients).[41] People who live alone die at higher rates after heart attacks than those who live with other people.[42] The link between social networks and cardiovascular health seems to be stronger in men than in women.[43]

However, not all studies of cardiovascular health have shown benefits from social capital. In a study of Kaiser Permanente members in Portland, Oregon, those who were more socially connected developed cardiovascular diseases at similar rates as those with fewer social ties, with few exceptions. However, once the diseases had developed, people with strong social ties survived significantly longer. The investigators concluded that social networks seemed more effective at promoting recovery from an illness than in preventing the onset of new disease.[44] Still other studies have shown no link between heart disease and social networks,[45] or have shown an equivocal relationship.[46] Interestingly, some studies indicate that family problems can increase the risk of angina, perhaps because of the stress they can introduce.[47] This suggests that social capital at the family level may have both positive and negative consequences, so studies that include both family- and community-level measures may give a mixed picture of health benefits. While social connectedness appears to protect against heart disease, the full nature of the benefits is not understood.

In contrast, social connectedness is clearly good for mental health. Research in public health and psychology shows that loneliness leads to depression, and people with strong social networks, beginning with immediate family members and extending to friends, are less likely to be depressed.[48] In the Saskatchewan study described earlier,[49] health districts with higher social capital had fewer inpatient and outpatient mental health visits, and lower use of alcohol and drug abuse services. While there is some evidence that strong social networks can also have a downside, such as anxiety in close-knit communities (a social form of "cabin fever"),[50] the weight of evidence suggests that social networks benefit mental health.

Finally, social capital benefits health in a variety of other ways. Social capital is associated with decreased violent crime,[51] less frequent binge drinking,[52] lower teen birth rates,[53] and more leisure-time physical activity.[54] Although many health outcomes remain to be studied, it appears that social capital offers a wide range of health benefits.

What are the mechanisms by which social capital might improve health? Several answers are possible.[55] First, social relationships might be directly good for health, perhaps by boosting immune, neuroendocrine, and/or cardiovascular function.[56] Second, people living in communities with high social capital might enjoy superior access to health information and health services. Third, people living in communities with high social capital may behave in healthier ways. For example, a Swedish study found that social participation, including attendance at study groups, classes, and organizational meetings, writing letters to the editor, and similar activities, was strongly associated with leisure-time physical activity.[57] Finally, moving from the community scale to the state or national scale, high social capital may lead to policies that protect health, such as more inclusive health insurance plans or stricter regulation of environmental hazards. At present, even without a full understanding of the mechanisms, we can conclude that social capital—and the networks of social relationships that comprise it—is good for health. Therefore, if sprawl diminishes social capital, then sprawl may threaten health.

DOES SPRAWL UNDERMINE SOCIAL CAPITAL?

In the postwar years, as Americans flocked to the suburbs, one of the strongest attractions was the promised sense of community. Indeed, writes Putnam, the "postwar wave of suburbanization produced a frontier-like enthusiasm for civic engagement."[58] Whyte observed an almost frantic pace of socializing, a "hotbed of participation," in Park Forest.[59] "You belong in Park Forest!" urged a 1952 ad. "The moment you come to town you know you're welcome, you're part of the big group, you can live in a friendly small town instead of a lonely big city, you can have friends who want you—and you can enjoy being with them. Come out. Find out about the spirit of Park Forest."[60] "Come out to Park Forest where small-town friendships grow," urged another ad, "and you still live so close to a big city."[61]

In his pioneering study of Levittown (now called Willingboro), New Jersey, sociologist Herbert Gans described "the beginnings of group life": initial casual meetings that blossomed quickly into bridge groups, weekly and even daily "coffee-klatsches" and mahjong games, and a multitude of more formal organizations such as service clubs, veterans' groups, and religious groups.[62] More than 50 percent of the subjects Gans interviewed reported that moving to the suburbs had increased their level of organizational activity.[63] In their study of Levittown, Long Island, Rosalyn Baxandall and Elizabeth Ewen[64] describe the many social organizations that formed during the 1950s: babysitting co-ops, joint shopping trips (since many women did not drive), Tupperware parties, service on the school board and PTA, the Little League, and others. There was apparently no absence of social capital in the early days of the suburban boom.

Moreover, many national surveys, especially during the postwar decades, found that suburban residents reported high levels of personal happiness, social activity in their local areas, and satisfaction with the social, physical, and lifestyle features of their communities.[65] To some extent, this comes as no surprise; similar and socially compatible people might be attracted to live in the same neighborhoods, and large travel distances might encourage people to look nearby for their social contacts.

However, other observers have criticized the culture of the suburbs, accusing these communities of lacking any real sense of community. As early as 1938, Lewis Mumford, in *The Culture of Cities*, called suburbia "a collective effort to lead a private life."[66] Kenneth Jackson,[67] the historian of suburbanization, concluded that "A major casualty of America's drive-in culture is the weakened 'sense of community.'" Similarly, planner Reid Ewing[68] believes that "strong communities of place, where neighbors interact, have a sense of belonging, and have a feeling of responsibility for one another, are harder to find" in suburbs than in traditional small towns or cities. This criticism rode a wave of antisuburban writing in the postwar years, a "critical onslaught of monumental, and largely nonsensical, proportions" in the words of one skeptical historian[69] that blamed suburban life for "overconformity, conservatism, alcoholism, sexual promiscuity, racial prejudice, and even momism."[70] But despite the occasional rhetorical flourish, the idea that sprawl might undermine social capital has persisted.

How could this be? First, and most simply, urban sprawl restricts the time and energy people have available for civic involvement. A commuter who arrives home at 6:30 after a grueling fifty-minute commute, feeling tired, depleted, and irritable, is not likely to go back out for a 7:30 meeting of the PTA or the neighborhood association. As early as the 1950s, sociological studies in Coburg, a suburb of Eugene, Oregon,[71] and in Claremont, outside Los Angeles,[72] showed that commuters in suburban communities participated less than noncommuters in voluntary associations. The Claremont study showed a direct relationship between longer commutes and less community participation, leading the author to a blunt conclusion: "Usually the commuter participates very little in community affairs." In *Bowling Alone*, Robert Putnam reports that commute time is more important than almost any other demographic variable in predicting civic involvement. He writes that *"each ten additional minutes in daily commuting time cuts involvement in community affairs by 10 percent*—fewer public meetings attended, fewer committees chaired, fewer petitions signed, fewer church services attended, and so on" (italics in original).[73] It is striking, as Putnam points out, that the "civic penalty" in communities with high levels of commuting falls not only on the commuters, but on their neighbors, including retired people and others outside the workforce. Not only weekday evening meetings suffer low attendance; so do Sunday morning church services. The erosion of social capital related to commuting seems to pervade entire suburban communities.

Second, sprawl could undermine social capital by reducing opportunities for spontaneous, informal social interaction. Purely residential suburbs have few if any "great good places"—the "cafes, coffee shops, bookstores, bars, hair salons, and other hangouts at the heart of a community" where people traditionally gathered to schmooze.[74] Certainly, people in their cars are less likely to mix and mingle than people on the sidewalk. In fact, as discussed in Chapter 8, driving might actually engender hostility and mistrust, at least in some drivers under some circumstances. So spontaneous, informal social interaction might well occur, but in the form of honking or shouting at the driver in the next car!

Third, sprawl privatizes the public realm. As G. Scott Thomas has written, "Suburbanites reject the underlying tenets of city life, believing in decentralization, not density, and placing a higher value on the individual than on the community."[75] People who work out in their basements rather than jog on public trails, or relax in their backyards rather than stroll or picnic in parks, may have little feeling for parks and other public assets. By sanctifying the private realm, sprawl may undermine people's support for public initiatives. In fact, recent political science research[76] documents a pattern of voting that reflects these values. Suburban voters prefer limited government programs. Relative to urban and small-town voters, they place little emphasis on such social goals as eliminating discrimination and reducing poverty, and tend to reject initiatives such as park acquisition and mass transit. (In contrast, suburban voters generally support funding for education and highway construction, which may benefit them more directly.)

Fourth, sprawl segregates us into relatively homogeneous communities by social class and race. Political scientist J. Eric Oliver[77] suggests that in homogeneous suburban communities, social conflicts between citizens are transformed into conflicts between political institutions. This reduces the incentives for people to become personally involved in the political process, reducing levels of civic participation. As Putnam writes, sprawl is "especially toxic for bridging social capital."[78]

Finally, sprawl might undermine social capital by disrupting continuity of community life as people age. A homogeneous neighborhood of four-bedroom houses and large lots might appeal to a family with small children. But when the children have grown up and left for college and the couple wants to downsize, the neighborhood offers no options. Typically, the now middle-aged parents will sell their house and move to a different neighborhood that offers smaller houses, apartments, or condominiums. This discontinuity—the systematic departure of families after about twenty years of living in a neighborhood—cannot be good for social capital.

What does the evidence show? In 1998, the Transit Cooperative Research Program[79] reviewed and synthesized approximately 500 publications concerning the costs of sprawl. The report concluded that sprawl weakens households' connection both to their immediate neighbors and to the larger metropolitan community. It went further, identifying specific features of sprawl that might be related to a weakened sense of community. The conclusions are shown in Table 9-1.

These conclusions provide a clear reminder that not all suburbs are alike. Specific features of community design, they suggest, may either promote or undermine the sense of community. Similarly, because suburbs have evolved and diversified considerably during the last half century, and vast changes in other social forces have also occurred, we would expect that the effects of sprawl on social capital might vary from place to place and over time. This is indeed what the evidence shows, in nine studies conducted over the last quarter century.

In one investigation, psychologist Thomas J. Glynn[80] studied the sense of community in two demographically similar suburban Maryland towns, Greenbelt and Hyattsville. At the time, Greenbelt had a population of 18,000. Although mostly residential, it had a small-town

■ **TABLE 9-1** Features of sprawl that weaken sense of community

Feature of sprawl	Contribution to weakening the sense of community
Leapfrog development	Strong
Low density Unlimited outward extension Transport dominance by motor vehicles Highly fragmented land use governance Great variance in local fiscal capacity Widespread commercial strip development Reliance on filtering for low-income housing	Moderate or minor
Land uses spatially segregated No central ownership or planning	None

SOURCE: R. W. Burchell, N. A. Shad, D. Listokin, H. Phillips, A. Downs, S. Seskins, J. S. Davis, T. Moore, D. Helton, and M. Gall, *The Costs of Sprawl—Revisited.* Transportation Research Board; Transit Cooperative Research Program. Report 39. Washington DC: National Academy Press, 1998.

feeling, with well-defined boundaries and a central mall area from which the residential areas radiated, connected by a network of walkways. Hyattsville had a more sprawling quality. Its 16,000 residents were spread over a large area, with no identifiable geographic or business center. Most travel in Hyattsville required a car or public transportation. Glynn surveyed residents in each community, using an extensive 133-item questionnaire. He measured the sense of community using the responses to 60 items such as "There are people in this community, other than my family, who I really care about" and "My role in this community is to be active and involved." He also measured a factor he called "community satisfaction" using response to 6 items such as "The atmosphere is more relaxed here, compared to other communities in the area."

Two important findings emerged. First, the sense of community was significantly higher in Greenbelt than in Hyattsville. Second, the two strongest predictors of a person's sense of community were the number of neighbors he or she could name, and the number of years he or she expected to remain in the community. The same two factors predicted community satisfaction, as did a positive response to the statement that "a car is not necessary to get around in this community." These findings suggest that walkability and the opportunity to get to know neighbors—two neighborhood attributes that may be closely linked—are important determinants of sense of community and community satisfaction.

During the 1980s, anthropologist M. P. Baumgartner[81] spent a year interviewing residents of an affluent New York City suburb. On the surface, it was a harmonious place, characterized by tolerance and the absence of confrontation. However, beneath this she found a pervasive disconnectedness—transient and fragmented relationships, weak family and communal ties, and indifference. Baumgartner felt that this "culture of avoidance" signaled a "moral minimalism" reflecting the erosion of traditional social bonds.

Jack Nasar and David Julian,[82] city and regional planning researchers at Ohio State University, surveyed residents in three suburbs of Columbus, Ohio. They used a short questionnaire, which they had adapted from Glynn's earlier work. The questions they included are shown in Table 9-2.

These researchers hypothesized that mixed land use might increase the sense of community. Neighborhoods that combined homes, stores, parks, recreational destinations, schools, and other uses, they reasoned, would increase walking, which would encourage casual social contacts, building the sense of community. Because Upper Arlington, Ohio, one of the suburbs they studied, included a range of

■ **TABLE 9-2**   Questions to measure psychological sense of community

1. I am quite similar to most people who live here.
2. If I feel like talking, I can generally find someone in this neighborhood to talk to right away.
3. I DON'T care whether this neighborhood does well. [*]
4. The police in this neighborhood are generally friendly.
5. People here know they can get help from others in the neighborhood if they are in trouble.
6. My friends in this neighborhood are part of my everyday activities.
7. If I am upset about something personal, there is NO ONE in this neighborhood to whom I can turn. [*]
8. I have NO friends in this neighborhood on whom I can depend. [*]
9. If there were a serious problem in this neighborhood, the people here could get together and solve it.
10. If someone does something good for this neighborhood, that makes me feel good.
11. If I had an emergency, even people I do not know in this neighborhood would be willing to help.
12. What is good for this neighborhood is good for me.
13. Being a member of this neighborhood is like being a member of a group of friends.
14. We have neighborhood leaders here that you can trust.
15. There are people in this neighborhood other than my family who really care about me.

[*] indicates reverse scoring

SOURCE: J. L. Nasar and D. A. Julian, "The Psychological Sense of Community in the Neighborhood," *Journal of the American Planning Association* 1995;61:178-84.

land use patterns, they could test the mixed-use hypothesis. They conducted twenty-five interviews in each of four neighborhoods with different levels of land use mix—with one, two, three, and four kinds of uses. As predicted, they found that the single-use residential neighborhood had less sense of community than the neighborhoods with multiple uses. This supports the notion that social capital may flourish more in mixed-use neighborhoods than in the purely residential neighborhoods found in many sprawling suburbs.

Georjeanna Wilson and Mark Baldassare, social ecologists at the University of California, Irvine, studied the attitudes of Orange County residents based on results from the county's 1990 Annual Survey.[83] Orange County is a part of metropolitan Los Angeles that experienced rapid growth, increasing density, and increasing ethnic diversification during the 1980s. It includes cities such as Anaheim, Garden Grove, and Santa Ana, as well as large expanses of dispersed, suburban-style housing. The investigators defined "sense of community" as a positive response to the question, "In general, would you describe your city or community as one which has a sense of community, or not?"

They found that several factors predicted a sense of community, including satisfaction with the level of civic involvement and satisfaction with the level of privacy from neighbors' homes. In contrast, correlates of "urbanization," such as larger city size, higher population density, and greater ethnic diversity, were associated with a lower sense of community. (The survey was conducted at a time of rapid community change, with growing density and ethnic diversity, so these latter responses may reflect the difficulty of adjusting to these changes, and may not apply to suburbs in different circumstances.) But the core findings of the study make intuitive sense. People dislike too much density, and to the extent that sprawl protects privacy, it may promote a sense of community. But if long commutes, home recreation, or other features limit residents' civic participation, then sprawl may also undermine the sense of community.

Scandinavian researchers have also studied how neighborhood design affects social capital, focusing on an outcome they called "neighboring." In 1992, two researchers surveyed more than 1,000 people in various neighborhoods of the city of Bergen, Norway.[84] There were relatively dense, turn-of-the-century downtown neighborhoods with brick buildings, postwar neighborhoods outside the central city with detached four-family wooden houses, and 1970s suburbs. The participants completed a questionnaire called the Multidimensional Measure of Neighboring, which groups responses into four categories: supportive acts of neighboring, neighborhood attachment, neighbor annoyance, and weak social ties. In this study, several aspects of the built environment strongly predicted neighboring, including visible open space near the home, dwelling density that was not too high, and the availability of semiprivate and open places such as porches, gardens, and parks. The authors noted that well-laid-out, well-equipped, and well-maintained public spaces near home promote outdoor time, which in turn may promote social interactions.

Jeanne M. Plas and Susan E. Lewis, psychologists at Vanderbilt University, wondered whether town design could influence the sense of community, and studied the New Urbanist town of Seaside, Florida, as a case study.[85] Seaside, built in the early 1980s, was designed to offer "the new town, the old ways." The town is a network of narrow streets, footpaths, and charming houses with generous front porches no more than 20 feet from the street, built around a central public area with stores, restaurants, and other community facilities. In extensive open-ended interviews with residents, visitors, and workers at Seaside, these researchers looked for a link between design features and the sense of community people felt. Without prompting, more than half of their respondents mentioned features that had been designed with social interaction in mind: the footpaths, the proximity to the central public area, the availability of public spaces such as parks, the ambiance of the town's grocery store, the beach pavilions with sitting areas, and the wide porches. The most often mentioned factor was the "devaluing of the automobile that results in few cars on the streets." The authors acknowledged that Seaside is a highly unusual place—an upscale resort community whose members share "demonstrated interest in family, political, social responsibility, and environmental concerns"—so findings there may not be generalizable. Nevertheless, they concluded that their results "provide very strong support for the hypothesis that environmental factors may be crucial for the development of sense of community in urban communities."

Lance Freeman,[86] an urban planner at Columbia University, also hypothesized that sprawl might affect social capital. To investigate this hypothesis, he analyzed data from Atlanta, Boston, and Los Angeles, drawn from the Multi City Survey of Urban Inequality. The measures of sprawl were neighborhood residential density and automobile dependence (the proportion of people in the neighborhood who drive to work alone). The indicator of social capital was neighborhood social ties, as reflected by the answer to the question, "From time to time, most people discuss important matters with other people. Looking back over the last six months, who are the people, other than people living in your household, with whom you discussed matters important to you?" The interviewers followed up by asking if any of the first three people mentioned lived in the same neighborhood. Freeman controlled for factors such as age, gender, race/ethnicity, income, education, length of time at present residence, family structure, neighborhood poverty rate, and the city.

Freeman found that residential density did not predict the probability of having a neighborhood social tie. However, the proportion of residents driving to work alone was strongly associated with having a neighborhood social tie. Interestingly, he also found that some demographic factors (being female, having children, and being more educated) increased the probability of neighborhood social ties, while others (being African American or Asian, being currently employed, and living in Atlanta or Boston as opposed to Los Angeles) decreased this probability. These findings suggest that automobile dependence, a defining feature of sprawl, is associated with a decline in social capital. They also remind us that social capital is a complex phenomenon, relating to a variety of social and situational variables.

Kevin Leyden,[87] a political scientist at West Virginia University, compared the attitudes of people living in traditional, mixed-use, pedestrian-oriented neighborhoods with those of people living in modern automobile-dependent subdivisions, in Galway City, Ireland. He surveyed 750 residents of this rapidly growing city. Interestingly, commutes are no longer than twenty minutes, even in the new suburban developments, so the most salient difference between the communities was probably neighborhood design rather than commuting. To assess a neighborhood's walkability, Leyden listed nine possible destinations, including a local store, a church, a park, and a school, and asked respondents to check off those to which they could walk. He also measured possible confounding variables, including age, whether there were children in the home, television watching, attendance at church services, years lived at the current address, educational attainment, and commitment to a political party. To measure social capital, Leyden asked his respondents about how well they knew their neighbors, about the extent of their political participation, about how much they trusted other people, and about how socially active they were.

Leyden found that living in a walkable, mixed-use neighborhood was strongly and significantly associated with each of the four aspects of social capital. Other factors were associated with social capital—age in a positive direction and watching television in a negative direction—but these did not have as strong an effect as neighborhood form. Attending religious services and living more years in the neighborhood were associated with knowing one's neighbors, and having a child in the home had mixed effects. This is strong evidence that mixed-use, walkable neighborhoods contribute to social capital, as measured by knowing one's neighbors, participating in political life, trusting other people, and being socially active.

There is further evidence that walkability promotes social capital. Hollie Lund, a professor of planning at California State Polytechnic University, Pomona, compared two neighborhoods in Portland, Oregon.[88] The neighborhoods were similar in important ways: household income, length of residence in the neighborhood, access to a commercial area, highway access, transit access, and topography. But they differed in important ways as well. One was a "traditional neighborhood," built in the early 1900s, with small lots, a gridiron block pattern of narrow streets, a network of tree-lined sidewalks, and nearby stores. The other was a "modern suburban neighborhood," with larger lots, a disconnected, curvilinear roadway pattern with wide traffic lanes, and a commercial area separated from the homes by a five-lane arterial road and large parking lots. Using a survey, Lund assessed people's perceptions of walking, their walking behavior, and their social capital. The social capital questions were drawn from Nasar and Julian's Psychological

Sense of Community Scale,[89] shown in Table 9-2, with items such as "People here know they can get help from others in the neighborhood if they are in trouble" and "If someone does something good for this neighborhood, that makes me feel good."

Lund found that the strongest predictors of psychological sense of community were positive attitudes toward walking: a perception of opportunities for social interaction, a safe walking environment, and an interesting walking environment. Interestingly, the number of destination walking trips did not predict sense of community, but the number of strolling trips did. Lund concluded that the sense of community was higher among traditional neighborhood residents than among modern suburban residents. She recognized that people who value social interaction and walking may have self-selected into the traditional neighborhood, but since the two neighborhoods shared similar attitudes toward transit and toward the environment, bias probably did not account for the results.

Despite some inconsistencies, this body of evidence suggests that the way a neighborhood is built can have a major impact on the social interactions of the people who live there. In particular, walkability, public spaces, and mixed use are associated with improvements in social capital, while automobile dependence, absence of public spaces, and low density seem to have a negative impact. This has not always been true, since postwar suburban neighborhoods were by some accounts rich in social capital, and it is unlikely to be true in all suburban neighborhoods. But the weight of evidence suggests that sprawl is part of the complex of social forces that have undermined social capital over the last few decades.

THE ROLE OF INCOME INEQUALITY

No human settlement is exempt from differentiation by race and class. But in dense cities and small towns partial integration often exists through the sharing of some common facilities, and the geographic distance between groups is not large. In low-density environments, where geographic distances between racial and class groupings are greater, the functional segregation of such groups is accentuated.[90]

—D. Popenoe,
"Urban Sprawl: Some Neglected
Sociological Considerations," 1979

Income inequality—the disparity in income between the wealthiest and poorest strata of society—is closely related to social capital. In recent years, researchers have linked greater income inequality to poorer health. Could this have anything to do with sprawl?

Income inequality is the skew in income distribution across a society. It is quantified in several ways. One approach is to measure the share of total income earned by the bottom 50 percent of households. These earnings would account for 50 percent of total income if income were equally distributed. In the United States, the share of income earned by the bottom 50 percent of households ranges from 17.5 percent in Louisiana (the most unequal) to 23.6 percent in New Hampshire (the most egalitarian).[91] Another approach is to compute the "decile ratio" of household incomes, the ratio of income in the top 10 percent of households to income in the bottom 10 percent of households.[92] Another common approach is the Robin Hood Index, the proportion of aggregate income that would need to be redistributed from rich to poor to achieve an equal distribution of incomes.[93] In the United States, the overall Robin Hood Index is 30.22, ranging from 34.05 percent in Louisiana to 27.13 percent in New Hampshire.[94] Still another approach is the Gini coefficient, which reflects the difference between the observed cumulative income distribution and a hypothetical equal distribution of incomes. The Gini coefficient for the United States is 0.43, ranging from 0.50 for Louisiana to 0.38 for Minnesota.[95] The Robin Hood Index and the Gini coefficient are not equivalent; the Gini coefficient is more sensitive to the income in the lowest stratum, reflecting extreme deprivation, while the Robin Hood Index tends more to reflect inequality across the entire income spectrum.

Poverty has long been recognized as a risk factor for poor health. But beginning in the 1980s, researchers in Europe and the United States showed that the level of income inequality in a society, separate and apart from the effects of poverty, also predicts poor health.[96] For example, in a study comparing the fifty states, the Robin Hood Index predicted total mortality, infant mortality, coronary heart disease, cancer, and homicide.[97] Each one-point increase in the Robin Hood Index was associated with a total mortality increase of 21.68 deaths per 100,000 people. This effect persisted even after controlling for poverty. A similar study compared the 100 counties of North Carolina, and found that income inequality predicted total mortality rates, even after controlling for income.[98] Other studies in the United States,[99] Great Britain,[100] and cross-nationally[101] have verified these findings, not only for mortality but also for self-rated overall health,[102] although occasional studies have been negative,[103] and in some cases the results depend on the measure of income inequality that is used.[104]

What does this have to do with social capital? As it turns out, there may be a very direct link. Researchers have hypothesized that income inequality is bad for health because it diminishes social capital. Kawachi and his colleagues found that both income inequality and diminished social capital predicted increased mortality, but when they conducted a path analysis to determine the most likely causal pathways, income inequality exerted its effect through a decrease in social capital. "As income inequality increases," they explained, "so does the level of social mistrust, which is in turn associated with increased mortality rates."[105] Similarly, in a study of more than 300 U.S. cities, the cities with the highest income inequality had the highest mortality rates, but this effect diminished when the investigators controlled for civic participation. This result, again, suggested that income inequality exerted its effects on mortality, in part, by undermining social capital.[106] Similar findings emerged from a study of teen birth rates. After conducting extensive path analysis, the authors concluded that "income inequality appeared to affect teen birth rate through its impact on social mistrust, which was strongly associated with birth rate."[107]

This is not the only theory as to how income inequality might be bad for health.[108] Income inequality might also be a marker for disinvestment in human capital, such as decreased school funding, which could in turn contribute to poor health. In fact, states with the highest income inequality tend to have the lowest educational budgets (as a proportion of total state budget), the worst scores on standardized tests, and the highest dropout rates.[109] Alternatively, income inequality may directly stress people by leading them to "look over their shoulders" constantly, comparing themselves with others, and worrying about their place in the social pecking order. Evidence from both humans and primates suggests that this may occur. Among captive monkeys, those that are socially subordinate have higher blood pressure, higher cortisol levels, higher cholesterol levels—physiologic signs of stress—than those that are socially dominant.[110] And when their social status is experimentally manipulated, their coronary artery atherosclerosis increases. Interestingly, in one experiment, the dominant monkeys forced into a subordinate status showed a 44 percent increase in their atherosclerosis, but the subordinate monkeys forced into a dominant status showed a 500 percent increase, compared with monkeys that did not change their social status.[111] This suggests that social position has important effects on health; that being subordinate is more stressful than being dominant, but that maintaining any position within a hierarchy may have physiologic costs.

Could sprawl aggravate income inequality? Or could sprawl enshrine income inequality solidly in daily life, or make it more blatant than it might otherwise be? Indeed, suburban neighborhoods are often more homogeneous, in terms of income, than traditional small towns or urban neighborhoods.[112] This might be expected to blunt the effects of income inequality, since people might be less likely to encounter, and compare themselves, with others above or below them on the social ladder. On the other hand, across a region, suburban residential patterns might confront people regularly with reminders of their social standing, especially at a time (as during recent decades) of rapidly increasing income inequality. A scene like the one pictured in Figure 9-4 might appear to be a tasteless joke, since we do not segregate ourselves by social status this explicitly. Or do we? Figure 9-5, a

■ **FIGURE 9-4** A caricature of residential segregation by social class

SOURCE: Photo simulation by Charles Dobson.

■ **FIGURE 9-5**   Suburban roadside housing advertisements

SOURCE: Photo by Dr. Howard Frumkin.

photograph taken alongside a busy suburban Atlanta road, depicts a grimly effective means test, and those driving the road view a daily reminder of where they stand (and where others stand) on the social ladder.

CONCLUSION

Social capital is the glue that helps bind communities together. It consists of attitudes such as trust and reciprocity, and behaviors such as social networking and civic participation. Urban sprawl seems to undermine social capital. Much of this effect may occur in direct ways—an absence of sidewalks and public places where one can encounter neighbors, an absence of "great good places" as destinations for socializing, a shortage of time with family and friends due to long commutes. Perhaps there is an additional contribution if sprawl reinforces the effects of income inequality. In any case, the decline in social capital is worrisome, since social capital is an important contributor to good health. It seems to take a "village" not only to raise a child, but also to support an adult, and to look after the elderly. In sprawling regions, with little that resembles a village either architecturally or socially, and with deficits in social capital, we may forfeit critical opportunities to promote health across the life span.

CHAPTER 10

HEALTH CONCERNS OF
SPECIAL POPULATIONS

A central question about every public health hazard is this: Who is most at risk? For almost every hazard, some people bear more risk than others. The disparity may relate to differences in exposure, or differences in susceptibility, or both. Some groups are disproportionately exposed to hazards because of social circumstances (e.g., poor communities near hazardous waste sites), behavior (e.g., children placing things in their mouths), or other reasons. Once exposed, some groups are especially susceptible because of genetic predispositions, underlying illnesses, or even age. In recent years, progress on the human genome has highlighted the role of biological susceptibility, and the Environmental Justice movement has clarified the role of social circumstances in disproportionate exposures.

Sprawl is no exception. Many of the health effects of sprawl are distributed unequally across different populations, and some people bear more risk than others (see Figure 10-1). In this chapter, we review some of the disproportionate impacts of sprawl on several "special populations." (We use the term *special populations* advisedly, because in the aggregate, the members of these populations comprise a majority of Americans!) These populations include women, children, the elderly, the poor, and people with disabilities.

WOMEN

In sprawling communities, where distances are large and most travel is by automobile, family life involves a great deal of chauffeuring.

▨ FIGURE 10-1   This roadside design, especially the walking route, is inappropriate for (a) children, (b) elders, (c) people in wheelchairs, (d) blind people, and (e) all of the above.

SOURCE: Photo by Dr. Howard Frumkin.

Taking children to school, play dates, or soccer games; taking elderly parents to the doctor; running errands to the grocery store, post office, or bank—this collective burden falls disproportionately on women. A 1999 report by the Surface Transportation Policy Project, *High Mileage Moms*, found that two-thirds of all chauffeur trips are made by women.[1] In 1995, the report found, married women with school-aged children were averaging more than five automobile trips per day, 21 percent more than the average for men. On the way home from work, 61 percent of women made at least one stop for an errand, compared to 46 percent of men. Among women, 50.4 percent of trips were made for chauffeuring, compared to 41.1 percent among men. The average woman was spending sixty-four minutes per day in the car, a figure that rose to sixty-six minutes for married women with school-aged children and seventy-five minutes for single mothers.

The image of the suburban "soccer mom" in a minivan turned out to reflect long hours at the wheel providing transportation and delivery services.

The health implications for women of this heavy load of driving have not been fully documented. As discussed in Chapter 6, more time driving, all things being equal, increases the risk of a collision. As described in Chapter 8, driving is a substantial source of stress, and women seem to experience higher levels of subjective stress than men, given similar levels of traffic congestion.[2]

"Like many women with children," wrote newspaper columnist Linda Baker, at the time the mother of three- and five-year-old children, "I spend a good portion of every week strapping my kids in and out of car seats, negotiating back-seat squabbles while changing lanes, and scooping up wayward preschoolers as they skip dangerously through one of an infinite number of parking lots." In analyzing the effects of this lifestyle, Baker noted that "the stress women incur from driving their kids around town is tremendous, if not yet quantifiable. Ask any mother; road rage is a tame descriptor when you're stuck in traffic with a screaming child in the back seat."[3] For women in sprawling areas, faced with a large burden of driving, sprawl must seem very much a women's health issue.

CHILDREN

Many of the impacts of sprawl fall disproportionately on children. These include air pollution, physical inactivity, and injuries, as well as threats to mental health and social capital.

Air Pollution

Children breathe more rapidly than adults, inhale more air relative to body weight, and have narrower airways. They play outside where ozone and other pollutant levels are highest, and while playing, they breathe more rapidly and deeply, increasing their intake of air. Their developing lungs are susceptible to any exposures that may impede lung growth. And asthma is highly prevalent among children. As a result, air pollutants pose a special threat to children.[4] Two pollutants, ozone and particulate matter, are especially important.

Ozone causes both short-term and long-term respiratory damage to children. Dozens of studies have documented that children's respiratory symptoms, medication use, school absenteeism, emergency department visits, and hospitalizations all increase within a day or two of ozone level peaks. In addition, long-term studies have implicated ozone exposure in impaired lung growth and possibly in the onset of asthma. For example, in a study of freshmen at the University of California, Berkeley, students who had grown up with higher ozone exposure (primarily in the Los Angeles basin) had diminished air flow in their small airways compared to students who had grown up breathing cleaner air (primarily from the San Francisco Bay area).[5] In the California Children's Health Study, McConnell and colleagues followed more than 3,500 children in twelve Los Angeles area communities for up to five years.[6] Student athletes in high-ozone communities had more than 3 times the risk of developing asthma compared to their counterparts in low-ozone communities. The authors concluded that outdoor exercise in the setting of high ozone could contribute to the development of asthma in children.

Cars and trucks, especially diesel vehicles, are also a source of particulate matter (PM), another air pollutant that targets children. Some of the effects of PM resemble the effects of ozone: respiratory irritation, symptoms such as cough and sputum production,[7] and asthma attacks.[8] Proximity to road traffic appears to pose a special risk for children. In a study in Erie County, New York,[9] for example, children under age fifteen living within 200 meters of roads with heavy truck traffic were at increased risk of asthma hospitalization. A Dutch study[10] revealed that children attending school within 100 meters of a freeway reported cough, wheeze, runny nose, and doctor-diagnosed asthma significantly more often than children without this exposure. Similar findings have been reported from many locations. PM exposure, like ozone exposure, has been linked to impaired lung growth in children.[11] PM exposure may be related to low birth weight,[12] infant mortality,[13] and other early childhood health problems. Therefore, the two major vehicle-related air pollutants, ozone and PM, pose special risks for children.

Physical Activity

Sprawl limits physical activity in children as well as in adults. In fact, children may have fewer options than adults. A child who is unable to walk or bike to school, and whose school is reducing or eliminating physical education programs, may have few opportunities for regular physical activity, while a determined adult in a similar predicament can at least join a sports club or drive to a safe place to exercise. As noted in Chapter 5, the obesity epidemic that has swept the nation during recent decades has fallen heavily on children. The prevalence of over-weight among children has more than tripled since the 1960s; approximately one in ten preschoolers, and one in seven school-age children, are now overweight.[14] The increase is particularly striking among Black and Hispanic children; approximately one in four teenagers in these groups is overweight.[15]

In sprawling areas, it is nearly impossible for most children to walk or bike to school. According to data from the National Personal Transportation Survey, half of U.S. children are driven to school in a private vehicle, approximately one-third travel by school bus, and fewer than one in seven trips to school is made on foot or bicycle.[16] In the 1999 nationwide HealthStyles survey, as discussed in Chapter 6, only 19 percent of parents reported that their child had walked to school at least once a week during the preceding month, and 6 percent reported that their child had biked, together accounting for only 14 percent of all school trips.[17] In one of the few state-level studies of travel behavior to school, similar findings emerged. A statewide telephone survey in Georgia collected data on 1,656 children in nearly 1,000 households. Of these, 43.3 percent were driven to school in a private vehicle, 48.9 percent rode a bus, and only 4.2 percent walked most days of the week. In a subset of 315 children who lived within a mile of school, 41.9 percent were driven in a private vehicle, 33.4 percent rode a school bus, and 18.6 percent walked.[18]

In children, as in adults, inactivity is dangerous in and of itself, and it also contributes to the risk of being overweight. Children who are physically inactive tend to have lower self-esteem.[19] Children who become overweight confront psychosocial challenges such as rejection by other children.[20] They also face increased risks of diabetes[21] during childhood, and of adult diseases such as hyperlipidemia and perhaps sleep apnea, polycystic ovaries, and orthopedic ailments.[22] Moreover, overweight children tend to become overweight adults, predisposing to a wide range of adult disease.[23]

Sprawl, of course, does not fully explain the inactivity and over-weight that plague American children. Dietary changes such as super-size portions of high-calorie foods, behavioral changes such as more television and computer "screen time," and programmatic changes such as cutbacks in school-based physical education all contribute. However, the inability to walk or bike to school or to other destinations such as after-school activities is an important factor. The health consequences are especially worrisome for children.

Injuries

Automobile crashes are a leading cause of death among young people. In 2000, 2,831 children under sixteen years of age were killed in traffic crashes, including 2,151 who were passengers, 524 who were pedestrians, and 193 who were on bicycles. That same year, 332,000 children under sixteen years of age were injured in traffic crashes, including 24,000 who were pedestrians and 20,000 who were bicyclists. Children comprise 23 percent of the population, and account for 5 percent of vehicle passenger fatalities, 11 percent of pedestrian fatalities, 25 percent of bicyclist fatalities, and 31 percent of nonfatal pedestrian injuries. On an average day, 8 children are killed and over 900 are injured in motor vehicle crashes.[24]

The epidemiology of pedestrian injuries among children has been well studied. Risk factors include male gender, age five to nine, and poverty, but also several factors that relate directly to land use and transportation decisions: high traffic volume and speed, absence of play space, on-street parking, and possibly one-way streets.[25] In studies in Long Beach, California, large boulevards were riskier than residential streets[26] and denser census tracts were safer than those with low density.[27] However, the impact of residential density is complex. In a study of childhood pedestrian injuries in Memphis, Rivara and Barber found that high residential density predicted childhood pedestrian injuries, possibly because the densest neighborhoods in this study were also the poorest.[28] And in parts of Baltimore where children were driven home, rates of pedestrian injury were significantly lower than in walking neighborhoods.[29] The influence of the built environment also appears to be mediated by activity patterns. For example, a study in Philadelphia suggested that children face a higher risk of pedestrian injuries when playing, or when walking on nonroutine trips, than when walking to school, irrespective of street design.[30] In general, heavy, fast-moving traffic, in the absence of safe, protected areas for play, threatens children's safety.

As discussed in Chapter 6, the solutions to these children's health threats include not only education but also traffic law enforcement and engineering improvements to roads and automobiles. Design solutions such as traffic calming, and providing public spaces where children can play safely away from traffic—features that remain uncommon in many sprawling residential areas—will go a long way toward protecting children.[31]

Mental Health and Development

> *It is not alone the desire to try and use his power that prompts the boy at this age to seek adventure high and low, far and wide, it is particularly the . . . need of his unfolding innermost life, the desire to control the diversity of things, to see individual things in their connection with a whole, especially to bring near that which is remote, to comprehend [the world] in its extent, its diversity, its integrity; it is the desire to extend his scope step by step.[32]*
>
> —Freidrich Froebel,
> *The Education of Man*, 1826

Exploring the environment is an integral part of normal child development.[33] Infants and toddlers explore on a very localized scale; their boundaries reach to the edges of the crib or high chair, and later to the edges of the home or yard, never too far from their parents. During middle childhood, exploration may extend to the immediate neighborhood, and for children in more rural areas, to nearby woods, fields, and streams. During adolescence, a child's "home range" expands still farther, to other neighborhoods, stores (or nowadays malls), recreational facilities, and other destinations.[34] This developmental continuum has been called the "cradle-room-house-doorstep-neighborhood sequence."[35]

A child benefits in many ways from exploration.[36] Part of the developing sense of self involves place identity, gained through exploration.[37] Children build their "cognitive maps"—their knowledge of the world and their ability to navigate it successfully—through exploration.[38] And through exploration, children develop competence, mastery, adaptability, independence, and new skills.[39] Children cultivate their imaginations, and form lifelong memories, by finding and being in "secret spaces."[40] The outdoors seems to be an especially important setting for exploration.[41]

A child also benefits from diverse and varied experiences in daily life and while exploring. In particular, encountering different kinds of people is developmentally healthy. Wholesome child development, hypothesized psychologist Urie Bronfenbrenner in his classic *Ecology of Human Development*, is "enhanced when the settings occur in cultural or subcultural contexts that are different from each other, in terms of ethnicity, social class, religion, age group, or other background factors."[42] Sprawling communities—places that are socially homogeneous and where children's social exploration is constrained by demographic realities—are a far cry from the developmental ideal.

Modern suburbs offer children, especially those in the preteen and teen years, less freedom to roam than traditional communities. Adults who grew up in the 1950s and 1960s recall that when they arrived home from school as children, they would be sent outside, unrestricted except for orders to be back in time for dinner. Today's children are kept on a shorter leash. Spencer and Woolley, in their recent review of children's environmental psychology, write, "Parents in some communities now so restrict their children that it [the concept of a child's home range] has effectively ceased to have an application."[43] Gaster, in a study in New York, found that "children's access to their neighborhood ha[s] declined substantially since the 1940s."[44]

Many factors contribute to this trend, including parental fear of crime[45] and traffic, and two-career families in which neither parent is home during the afternoons. However, the physical arrangement of sprawling communities—things separated by large distances, with menacing major roads acting as boundaries[46]—helps narrow the child's range.

Another important factor in children's ability to explore is the availability of destinations. Purely residential developments with large lots and large distances between things offer few opportunities for children to make their way to destinations, and few social gathering places. This aspect of the built environment may be especially relevant for older children, who are otherwise ready to roam their neighborhoods. For a child of five or six years old, a home with a sizeable yard and perhaps a cul-de-sac street offer plenty of opportunities to explore, and a play date with one or two other children rounds out the adventure. In fact, the parents, comfortable with the safety of such a neighborhood, may permit more exploration for their children than would their urban counterparts. However, a teenager would likely find neighborhoods with few destinations available (except by car) restrictive and even suffocating. The image of the bored suburban teenager is a media fixture.

Two early studies[47] found that suburban children had larger home ranges than urban children, defined as mean distance traveled to selected destinations such as playgrounds, libraries, and lessons. However, these studies did not describe the children's mode of travel. The suburban children may have traveled as passengers in their parents' automobiles, while urban children walked or traveled by subway or bus. If so, the larger home range in the suburbs would reflect longer travel distances, but less independence, compared to circumstances in dense, mixed-use settings.

Author Herb Childress spent a year with teenagers in pseudonymous Curtisville, California, population 15,000, studying the role of the built environment in their lives.[48] Curtisville's population had increased tenfold since World War II, mostly in sprawling residential subdivisions of single-family homes on wide cul-de-sacs—in Childress's words, "car-oriented housing, developments held beyond easy walk of work, stores, or neighbors."[49] He described a community with few destinations appropriate for teenagers, and few ways for the youth to get to those that did exist. The community design, he concluded, contributed to emotional shallowness and alienation. "Teenagers are defined out of existence in Curtisville," he wrote, "because their concerns and interests are counter to those of the people who matter."[50]

Sprawl, then, seems unfit to nurture or sustain the normal development and exploration of children, at least those older than eight or ten years of age. Child-friendly design, with high connectivity, safe pedestrian infrastructure, and rich opportunities to interact with many kinds of people, could do much to promote the growing independence and self-sufficiency of children.

Social Capital

Finally, social capital is beneficial for children. If "it takes a village" to raise a child, is social capital a defining feature of a successful village? Architect Phillip Langdon argues that the social networks in traditional communities offer much to children: the neighbor who notices when a child falls off his bike, comforts him, and walks him home, or the neighbors who notice a child's misbehavior and help monitor and correct it. In contrast, he writes, "The typical suburban subdivision of the last few decades tries in the main to *withdraw* its children from society's difficulties, inadvertently leaving them without the skills and judgment to manage unfamiliar situations." Langdon also cites the advantages to children of diverse housing types, so that children get to know a broad range of adults. As a mother in Kentlands, a New Urbanist town, told him, "I've always thought it's very important for our children to know lots of adults other than us—to have other role models, models of decent human beings—and that certainly has happened here."[51]

Langdon may well be right.[52] For example, children who live in environments high in social capital have fewer behavior problems,[53] are less likely to drop out of school,[54] and are more likely to attend college and go on to earn a higher income[55] than children in circumstances with low social capital. In a recent study of children at risk of child abuse and neglect,[56] the children with the best developmental and behavioral outcomes were those with the highest neighborhood social support, personal social support, and church attendance. Some of this research can be hard to interpret (e.g., the benefits of social capital can be difficult to disentangle from the effects of family strengths and weaknesses),[57] but overall, it appears that communities with high levels of social capital are good places for children to grow up. To the extent that sprawling communities forfeit social capital (see Chapter 9), this deficit may have worrisome consequences for children.

THE ELDERLY

Life expectancy in the United States has increased dramatically over the last century, from forty-nine years in 1900 to seventy-six years by 2000. As a result, the sixty-five-and-older population has for years been the fastest-growing segment of the population. During the decade of the 1990s, the sixty-five-and-older population slipped from this rank, due to the low birth rate during the Great Depression, but a population boom of elders is expected between 2010 and 2030 as baby boomers reach retirement age.[58] Among those over sixty-five, the fastest-growing segment is the "oldest old"—those over eighty-five.

Today's elders are healthier and more active than ever before. However, aging inevitably takes a toll, and large numbers of elders eventually develop disabilities such as limitations in vision, hearing, and/or mobility.[59] Many need assistance, if not at the level provided by nursing homes, then at least with such tasks as shopping and cleaning. Two aspects of sprawl are especially relevant to the health and well-being of the elderly: mobility and community.

During the summer of 2003, two tragedies involving elderly drivers shook the nation. First, an eighty-six-year-old driver plowed into a farmers market near Los Angeles, killing ten people. A week later, a seventy-nine-year-old man lost control of his car and injured three people at a farmers market in Flagler Beach, Florida. These incidents served as a reminder that elderly people may lose the ability to drive safely. However, in many communities driving is essential and alternatives are nonexistent.[60] Elders who want to walk to stores, houses of worship, medical offices, and recreational and cultural facilities need these destinations to be close to home—a defining feature of mixed-use communities—and they need safe, well-maintained sidewalks. Even pedestrian-friendly environments may not adequately accommodate the elderly. For example, crossing signals are typically timed for younger people who walk briskly rather than for slow, elderly walkers.[61] Those who want to ride need bus or trolley systems that serve both their homes and their destinations. Such amenities are rare in sprawling areas, where land use mix and density are low.

The ability to walk offers more than safe and convenient access to services. It also directly promotes the health of elders.[62] Elderly people who are physically active enjoy protection from some of the most ruinous ailments of old age—coronary heart disease,[63] depression,[64] osteoporosis and fractures,[65] falls,[66] and a variety of inflammatory conditions.[67]

Social capital, and the community resources it brings, are a special concern for the elderly, for whom social isolation is a common predicament and depression an all-too-common affliction. Social networks not only help prevent and ameliorate depression in the elderly; they also predict better cognitive function.[68] Longitudinal studies of aging in Sweden, France, and the United States have found that social networks help prevent the onset of dementia.[69] In a prospective study of elderly people in New Haven during the 1980s, called EPESE (Established Populations for Epidemiologic Studies of the Elderly), more extensive social networks significantly reduced the risk of becoming disabled from "activities of daily living" (ADLs), and enhanced recovery if such a disability did occur. Interestingly, connections with relatives and friends played a role, while connections with children or a confidant did not. The researchers concluded that "being 'embedded' in a social network of relatives and friends reduces risk for ADL disability, and enhances recovery from ADL disability."[70]

By undermining the social capital available to elders, sprawl may deprive them of these health benefits. One way this occurs is by precluding "aging in place." Although many elders would prefer to stay put,[71] the burden of maintaining a large home and lawn, the difficulty of getting around (especially if driving becomes impossible), and perhaps financial realities, can require a move. In traditional neighborhoods with a variety of housing options, empty nesters can move to a nearby smaller home or apartment. In contrast, homogeneous residential developments offer few choices nearby for older adults who want to downsize. As a result, they need to uproot, severing social ties and depriving the community of their continued presence. Land use and transportation that obviate this need would promote residential continuity across the life span for those who want it, helping reinforce social capital and the health benefits it brings.

POOR PEOPLE AND PEOPLE OF COLOR

Inner-City Poverty and Disease

Racial discrimination has been part of the history of sprawl at least since the Great Depression. As described by historian Kenneth Jackson, the Home Owners Loan Corporation (HOLC) of 1933, which created the modern mortgage, also standardized appraisal methods. City blocks were rated not only according to factors such as the age, density, and type of construction, but also according to explicit racial criteria.[72] The underwriting manual required housing agencies "to determine whether incompatible racial or social groups are present, for the purpose of making a prediction regarding the probability of the location being invaded by those groups."[73] Even one Black family could earn an entire neighborhood the lowest loan rating.[74] Neighborhoods with minority residents were colored red on four-colored "Residential Security Maps," greatly devaluing them, and giving rise to the term *red-lining*. While HOLC mortgages were issued in all strata of neighborhoods, private lending institutions were far more reluctant to invest in "definitely declining" or "hazardous" neighborhoods.[75]

The Federal Housing Administration (FHA), created in 1934, continued and extended discriminatory policies. FHA insurance went preferentially to single-family houses and to new construction instead of urban, multifamily dwellings. Repair loans were small and had short terms. And FHA appraisals were less formulaic than those of the HOLC; they permitted personal bias regarding the ethnic composition of the neighborhood to play a role. Together, these factors "hastened the decay of inner-city neighborhoods by stripping them of much of their middle-class constituency."[76]

These trends contributed to a progressive hollowing out of urban areas, with Whites departing for the suburbs and Blacks remaining behind. By the 1960s, economist John F. Kain had identified a "spatial mismatch": Blacks were trapped in the inner city by housing discrimination, while the job base was increasingly moving outward.[77] As more prosperous households shifted increasingly to suburban locations, the employment that went with them—in restaurants, theaters, dry cleaners, service stations, grocery stores—was increasingly inaccessible to those in the inner city. Over the next few decades, racial discrimination in housing may have diminished, but economic segregation was profoundly embedded in the way metropolitan areas were expanding. "Sprawl is related to poverty and inequality," wrote political economist Paul Jargowsky, "mainly because sprawl creates a greater degree of separation between the income classes."[78] For those left behind—often without automobiles—public transit rarely provides affordable, efficient access to suburban jobs.[79]

As a result, inner-city neighborhoods have seen a steady concentration of poverty.[80] With the poverty comes an array of social and health problems: high levels of unemployment, drug and alcohol abuse, domestic and gang violence, unsafe sex, and related maladies. The catastrophic consequences of these conditions for people living in the inner city have been well documented. In New York City's central Harlem, where 96 percent of the population is Black, men and women die at 3 times the rate of the U.S. White population, and the odds of reaching age sixty-five are lower than in Bangladesh. The excess deaths are attributable primarily to cardiovascular disease, cirrhosis, homicide, and cancer.[81] In a group of welfare applicants and recipients in New York City who abused drugs or alcohol, the incidence of tuberculosis was 15 times higher than that of the general population of New York City; the rate of AIDS was 10 times as high; and the death rate was 5 times as high, suggesting a tangled complex of disease risks.[82] In fact, the mutually reinforcing urban epidemics of substance abuse, HIV, and violence have been dubbed a "syndemic,"[83] and this dreadful profile has become emblematic of inner-city health.

If "sprawl and central city decline are part of one unified process of metropolitan change,"[84] then the shameful burden of disease and death among the inner-city poor—the "urban health penalty"[85]—must be counted among the health consequences of sprawl.

Effects of Sprawl on the Poor

If we expand our focus from the inner city to the entire metropolitan area, poor people and people of color are disproportionately affected by mechanisms other than urban poverty. Air pollution and injury are two examples.

Air pollution related to motor vehicle use in sprawling areas targets poor people and people of color for at least two reasons: disproportionate exposure, and higher prevalence of underlying diseases that increase susceptibility. Members of minority groups are relatively more exposed to air pollutants than are Whites, independent of income and urbanization.[86] Environmental Protection Agency (EPA) data show that Blacks and Hispanics are more likely than Whites to live in air pollution nonattainment areas.[87] And as asthma continues to increase, asthma prevalence and mortality remain higher in minority group members than in Whites.[88] The prevalence of asthma in 1999 was 53.6

per 1,000 in Whites and 65.5 per 1,000 in Blacks, a 22 percent excess in Blacks, and asthma mortality is nearly 3 times higher in Blacks than in Whites.[89] Black children are 64 percent more likely than White children to have asthma.[90] Similarly, asthma prevalence is more than 3 times higher among Puerto Rican children than among non-Hispanic children.[91] Among Medicaid patients, Black children are 93 percent more likely, and Latino children 34 percent more likely, than White children to have multiple hospitalizations for asthma.[92] While some of this excess is related to poverty, the excess persists after controlling for income.[93] Both exposure to air pollution, and susceptibility to its effects, appear to be concentrated disproportionately among the poor and persons of color.

Pedestrian injuries and fatalities demonstrate a striking pattern nationwide, with rates several times higher among Black and Hispanic people than among White people. In Atlanta, for instance, pedestrian fatality rates during 1994–1998 were 9.74 per 100,000 for Hispanics, 3.85 for Blacks, and 1.64 for Whites.[94] In suburban Orange County, California, Latinos comprise 28 percent of the population but account for 43 percent of pedestrian fatalities.[95] In the Virginia suburbs of Washington, DC, Hispanics comprise 8 percent of the population but account for 21 percent of pedestrian fatalities.[96] Travis County, Texas, which includes Austin and its suburbs, showed the same pattern, with members of minority groups accounting for 37 percent of the population but 52 percent of pedestrian deaths. From 1980 to 1996, the pedestrian death rate there was 2.2 per 100,000 for Whites, 3.9 for Blacks, and 5.1 for Hispanics. Among children and the elderly, the racial and ethnic disparities were even more pronounced.[97] The reasons for this disproportionate impact are complex, and may involve the probability of being a pedestrian (perhaps related to low access to automobiles and public transportation), road design in areas where members of minority groups walk, and behavioral and cultural factors such as being unaccustomed to high-speed traffic. Whatever the mechanisms, the stark disparity reflects a disproportionate impact of sprawl on poor people and people of color.

PEOPLE WITH DISABILITIES

People with disabilities are also poorly served by sprawl. Transportation systems designed for cars instead of pedestrians are unfriendly to pedestrians, and doubly so to those with special transportation needs. People in wheelchairs need sidewalks and paths that are sufficiently wide and level to allow safe and convenient passage, with curb cuts at appropriate locations. People with visual impairments need Audible Pedestrian Signals (APSs) at intersections to let them know when it is safe to cross.[98] Crossing signals need to be timed to allow people with disabilities enough time to reach the other side. In some cases, traffic-calming measures designed to protect most pedestrians, such as round-abouts, pose special challenges for those who are blind. Careful planning is needed to provide safe and convenient mobility for all, and design guidelines are available.[99] This requires not only an awareness of the needs of people with disabilities, but a broader orientation to safe, nonmotorized travel.

CONCLUSION

Urban sprawl is a set of physical arrangements—the way space is used in metropolitan areas, and the way people travel from place to place. But urban sprawl is also a social arrangement, which both results from and defines human attitudes and behavior. Questions of equity and fairness are fundamental to a consideration of sprawl, as they are fundamental to the field of public health. Women assume a disproportionate share of the driving in sprawling areas, raising their risk of automobile collisions and exposing them to stress. Poor people and people of color, disenfranchised by economic barriers and discrimination, are further disenfranchised by some of the features of sprawl, with serious consequences for their economic opportunity, health, and well-being. People who cannot drive, and who are especially dependent on good pedestrian infrastructure and transit—children, the elderly, people with disabilities—are deeply disenfranchised in a world that is built for automobiles. These groups, too, pay with diminished opportunity, health, and well-being. Creating healthy places, places that correct some of the worst features of sprawl, is not only a general public health strategy but also a targeted strategy to promote and protect the health of vulnerable populations, a health policy to achieve equity and fairness.

CHAPTER 11

■ ═════ ■

FROM URBAN SPRAWL
TO HEALTH FOR ALL

In the late 1940s, as the world began to recover from the devastation of World War II, the fledgling United Nations formed the World Health Organization (WHO). The WHO constitution proclaimed that "the enjoyment of the highest attainable standard of health" was "one of the fundamental human rights of every human being," and defined health broadly as "a state of complete physical, mental and social well-being and not merely the absence of disease or infirmity." Thirty years later, in 1977, the WHO adopted "Health for All" as a goal, in recognition of continuing health disparities across the world.

At the same time this lofty vision of human health emerged during the latter half of the twentieth century, a radical change was occurring in American cities and towns (and, increasingly, in the cities and towns of other developed countries): sprawling development into surrounding countryside. In this book, we have described many ways in which sprawl might undermine "health for all": by contributing to air pollution; by inhibiting physical activity; by increasing the risk of automobile crashes, by increasing anger, loneliness, and isolation; by undermining social capital. We have shown that certain groups—children, the elderly, the urban poor—are especially vulnerable to some of the hazards of sprawl. But if some design decisions are toxic, then the reverse is also true: some design decisions are healthy. In this chapter, we consider a set of design strategies that offer healthy alternatives to sprawl, part of a path toward the WHO vision of health for all.

Who are the "all" whose health is at issue? It is all of our contemporaries, but it is also those who will follow—our children, and their

children, and their children. The demographic realities are inescapable. According to the Bureau of the Census, the U.S. population
is projected to grow to 570 million people—a near doubling of the current population—by 2100.[1] Metropolitan areas will continue to grow
at rates faster than the nation as a whole. "No growth" is not an option;
the challenge is how to grow in ways that are healthy, socially just, and
environmentally sustainable.

Many of the necessary growth strategies are captured by the
term Smart Growth. Smart Growth is well known in the worlds of
architecture and planning, but it has not often been embraced as a
public health strategy. We hope to help correct that oversight. In
this chapter we make the case that Smart Growth, like water purification and vaccination campaigns, fits squarely within the tradition
of public health.

HEALTHY PLACES

The idea that places can be designed and built to promote health is not
new. As described in Chapter 2, the engineers who created water and
sewer systems in eighteenth-century cities had a clear notion that
urban infrastructure could protect the public's health. Later, the mid-
nineteenth century ushered in a remarkable chapter in the history of
urban design, a time when, to quote one account, "the medical community had greater influence on the physical shape of the city than at
any other time in America's history."[2] By then, the theory that disease
was caused by miasmata (noxious vapors) had found wide acceptance.
Certain places were felt to concentrate harmful miasmata, and planners
and physicians agreed that proper site selection, design, and hygiene
could mitigate these risks. Their actions were often shrewd and sensible, even if their underlying theories would not withstand the test of
time. Dr. John Henry Rauch (1828–94), who served Chicago as an
early member of the board of health and as sanitary superintendent
after the Civil War, successfully advocated land use policies—for example, abolishing urban cemeteries in favor of rural burying grounds and
establishing large urban parks—on the basis of public health. At the
same time, preeminent landscape architect Frederick Law Olmsted
(also head of the U.S. Sanitary Commission during the Civil War) was
advancing design principles such as low-density urban and suburban
neighborhoods, large and small parks, and tree-lined boulevards and
promenades, all thought to be healthy alternatives to overcrowded

cities. And in Great Britain, the Health of Towns Association built on the work of leading sanitarian Edwin Chadwick. With active chapters from Edinburgh to Liverpool to Plymouth, the association successfully pushed for sanitary regulations, housing standards, paved streets, and public water and sewer systems.[3]

The intellectual heirs of Rauch, Olmsted, and Chadwick have made important contributions in recent years. Thomas McKeown, professor of social medicine at Birmingham University, showed that many of the health advances of the nineteenth and twentieth centuries resulted not from better medical care, but from "upstream" improvements such as better urban infrastructure—better housing, neighborhoods, water, food, and transport.[4] Psychiatrist Leonard Duhl, working at the National Institute of Mental Health in the 1960s and later at the University of California, Berkeley, championed an approach to mental health that went beyond clinical services, calling for wholesome urban design and active community involvement.[5] Trevor Hancock, a physician and epidemiologist working in Canada, helped expand this view to include both mental and physical health.[6]

In 1987, the World Health Organization Regional Office for Europe initiated its Healthy Cities Project (www.who.dk/healthy-cities). This movement took a holistic approach, defining a healthy city as "one that is continually creating and improving those physical and social environments and strengthening those community resources which enable people to mutually support each other in performing all the functions of life and achieving their maximum potential."[7]

Through the project, approximately 50 cities around the world have formally joined the Healthy Cities Network by committing to a portfolio of activities, and more than 1,000 cities have undertaken selected healthy city initiatives. Mayors and political leaders from affiliated cities have met at the end of each five-year cycle of the Healthy Cities Project and have issued "declarations" affirming the importance of healthy city principles, including design and planning that promote health. In October 2003, for example, the Belfast Declaration for Healthy Cities espoused a range of initiatives from social justice to good government. It included a commitment to "building safe and supportive cities sensitive to the needs of all citizens, actively engaging urban planning departments and promoting healthy urban planning activities."[8] Corresponding initiatives in the United States have included the Healthy Communities movement, launched in 1989 by the National Civic League with federal support, and its successor, the Coalition for Healthier Cities and Communities, founded in 1994 and including at one time more than 1,000 cities.[9] All of these initiatives have advanced the vision of cities and communities as health-enhancing places. Smart Growth has a distinguished lineage, not only in urban planning and architecture, but also in the health sciences.

Smart Growth

Smart Growth is a simple term but a complex idea. It refers to a set of land use and transportation principles that in many ways are the opposite of sprawl. One definition of Smart Growth comes from the Smart Growth Network, which was formed in 1996 by the Environmental Protection Agency and several nonprofit and government organizations (see www.smartgrowth.org). The network grew to include more than thirty organizations, including professional associations such as the Institute of Transportation Engineers, the American Planning Association, and the International City–County Management Association; trade associations such as the National Association of Realtors and the Urban Land Institute; and nonprofit groups such as American Farmland Trust, the National Trust for Historic Preservation, and the Rails to Trails Conservancy. The network's Ten Principles of Smart Growth are shown in Table 11-1. A more elaborate statement of Smart Growth principles comes from a group of planners and architects who were convened in 1991 by the Local Government Commission. This group issued the Ahwahnee Principles, named for the hotel in Yosemite National Park where the authors met. These principles are shown in Table 11-2.

■ **TABLE 11-1** Smart Growth Principles (from the Smart Growth Network)

1. Mix land uses.
2. Take advantage of compact building design.
3. Create a range of housing opportunities and choices.
4. Create walkable neighborhoods.
5. Foster distinctive, attractive communities with a strong sense of place.
6. Preserve open space, farmland, natural beauty, and critical environmental areas.
7. Strengthen and direct development toward existing communities.
8. Provide a range of transportation choices.
9. Make development decisions predictable, fair and cost effective.
10. Encourage community and stakeholder collaboration in development decisions.

SOURCE: Anonymous *Getting to Smart Growth: 100 Policies for Implementation.* Washington: Smart Growth Network and International City/County Management Association, 2002.

◪ TABLE 11-2   The Ahwhanee Principles

Community principles

1. All planning should be in the form of complete and integrated communities containing housing, shops, work places, schools, parks, and civic facilities essential to the daily life of the residents.
2. Community size should be designed so that housing, jobs, daily needs, and other activities are within easy walking distance of each other.
3. As many activities as possible should be located within easy walking distance of transit stops.
4. A community should contain a diversity of housing types to enable citizens from a wide range of economic levels and age groups to live within its boundaries.
5. Businesses within the community should provide a range of job types for the community's residents.
6. The location and character of the community should be consistent with a larger transit network.
7. The community should have a center focus that combines commercial, civic, cultural, and recreational uses.
8. The community should contain an ample supply of specialized open space in the form of squares, greens, and parks whose frequent use is encouraged through placement and design.
9. Public spaces should be designed to encourage the attention and presence of people at all hours of the day and night.
10. Each community or cluster of communities should have a well-defined edge, such as agricultural greenbelts or wildlife corridors, permanently protected from development.
11. Streets, pedestrian paths, and bike paths should contribute to a system of fully connected and interesting routes to all destinations. Their design should encourage pedestrian and bicycle use by being small and spatially defined by buildings, trees, and lighting; and by discouraging high-speed traffic.
12. Wherever possible, the natural terrain, drainage, and vegetation of the community should be preserved with superior examples contained within parks or greenbelts.
13. The community design should help conserve resources and minimize waste.
14. Communities should provide for the efficient use of water through the use of natural drainage, drought tolerant landscaping, and recycling.
15. The street orientation, the placement of buildings, and the use of shading should contribute to the energy efficiency of the community.

Regional principles

1. The regional land-use planning structure should be integrated within a larger transportation network built around transit rather than freeways.
2. Regions should be bounded by and provide a continuous system of greenbelt/wildlife corridors to be determined by natural conditions.
3. Regional institutions and services (government, stadiums, museums, etc.) should be located in the urban core.
4. Materials and methods of construction should be specific to the region, exhibiting a continuity of history and culture and compatibility with the climate to encourage the development of local character and community identity.

(continued)

■ **TABLE 11-2**   The Ahwhanee Principles *(continued)*

Implementation principles
1. The general plan should be updated to incorporate the above principles.
2. Rather than allowing developer-initiated, piecemeal development, local governments should take charge of the planning process. General plans should designate where new growth, infill, or redevelopment will be allowed to occur.
3. Prior to any development, a specific plan should be prepared based on these planning principles.
4. Plans should be developed through an open process and participants in the process should be provided visual models of all planning proposals.

SOURCE: Local Government Commission, 1991. Available at http://www.lgc.org/ahwahnee/principles.html.

Other terms overlap to some extent with Smart Growth. New Urbanism is an architectural and planning movement that emerged during the 1980s and 1990s. Its principles—walkable neighborhoods, a range of housing choices, a mix of land uses, participatory planning, revitalization of urban neighborhoods—are laid out in the sumptuous *Charter of the New Urbanism*[10] and on the Web site of the Congress for the New Urbanism, www.cnu.org. Traditional Neighborhood Development is a related term, used to describe compact, mixed-use, transit-oriented, pedestrian-friendly developments reminiscent of pre–World War II neighborhoods.

Whatever the definition, most Smart Growth strategies include mixed land use, decreased automobile dependence balanced by transportation alternatives (walking, bicycling, and transit), and increased density balanced by preservation of green spaces. Many of these design and planning principles are implemented at the local level, at the scale of buildings, neighborhoods, and communities. However, there are also state and national aspects of Smart Growth, many of these in the policy arena. For example, transportation projects such as highways and mass transit are typically regional in scale and heavily supported by federal funds. The features of Smart Growth, from local level issues to federal policies, are described in the following sections.

Design Features

At the local scale, Smart Growth entails higher density than is customary in sprawling suburbs. Instead of 1 or 2 acres per home, there might be 5 or 10 or many more homes per acre. The density is accomplished with a mix of housing types and sizes—single-family detached homes, townhouses, apartments above retail stores, and other arrangements. Typically, this density is balanced by greenspace—farmland, forest, parks, or riparian corridors that remain unbuilt, and that provide access to nature for people who live in the area. There is an emphasis on walkability, with wide, tree-shaded sidewalks on both sides of the streets, and on mixed land use, with destinations such as stores, schools, theaters, and offices near homes. These two features combine to make walking attractive: there are nearby places to go, and safe, appealing ways to walk there. (A sprawling suburb with sidewalks but no destinations is unlikely to seduce anybody into walking, and a cluster of nearby buildings unconnected by walking routes is equally uninviting.) Connectivity is high in Smart Growth neighborhoods. Gridlike street arrangements offer many routes from point A to point B. There is a range of transportation alternatives, often designed at the neighborhood scale. Bicycle lanes on streets, bicycle (or "multiuse") paths off streets, and transit stations all help provide practical alternatives to automobile travel. Finally, Smart Growth development is aesthetically pleasing at the local scale. Generous sidewalks, storefronts with interesting windows on the sidewalk, benches for resting, and attractive views all provide a pleasant walking experience. Large parking facilities are kept off the street, often behind buildings, although parallel parking on the street may be used as a buffer between the sidewalk and traffic lanes and as a traffic-calming strategy. In residential neighborhoods, houses are placed close to the street, and may be fronted with generous porches, bringing life and conviviality to the streets, and further enhancing the experience of walking.

Development Regulations

Development regulations are largely the domain of local governments. They range from more localized efforts such as building codes to larger-scale zoning and subdivision regulations.

Building codes prescribe the bulk, scale, massing, and style of structures. Smart Growth building codes contribute to a pedestrian-friendly realm at the street level. Appropriate scaling of buildings, continuity of building materials, and a coherent design "vocabulary," all help establish a sense of place for a community, creating environments where people like to live, work, play, and travel.

Zoning codes prescribe certain locations as "appropriate" for certain uses, such as residential, commercial, industrial, recreational, or open space, and regulate such parameters as density, lot coverage, and building setbacks. As described in Chapter 2, zoning began in the 1910s and 1920s as an effort to protect public health, safety, and welfare (although these goals are usually not defined by zoning ordinances)[11] and to enforce social norms.[12] While zoning has helped separate truly incompatible land uses such as noxious industries and homes, it has failed to deliver on its loftier promises of producing high-quality, livable environments.[13] In fact, zoning can stand in the way of Smart Growth; in most places, it would now be illegal to build the charming neighborhoods of Charleston, Annapolis, or Georgetown due to restrictions on narrow streets, mixed land uses, and other design features.

Innovative zoning codes are therefore a part of achieving Smart Growth. For example, recently modified zoning codes in Austin, Texas, Davidson, North Carolina, Hercules, California, and Kentlands, Maryland, permit (and in some cases require) Traditional Neighborhood Development, with gridlike streets, appealing streetscapes with sidewalks and pedestrian amenities, unusually low parking requirements, and a mix of housing types and land uses (including small-scale commercial uses integrated into residential areas). Redmond, Washington, adopted a community development guide with mixed-use and live/work codes, allowing housing and service establishments in suburban employment districts, commercial areas, and downtown neighborhoods. Some cities use "performance-based zoning" to stimulate pedestrian-friendly environments. In this approach, the permissible area of floor space built per unit of land area (the floor area ratio, or FAR) is increased when developers agree to build ground level retail, public plazas, sidewalk treatments, and other public realm amenities. Seattle and other cities have encouraged transit-oriented development (TOD) by prohibiting uses that are not compatible with transit near proposed light-rail stations. Washington Township, New Jersey, promulgated Town Center Zoning and Design Regulations, requiring streets that "have been specifically designed to provide a sense of enclosure, enhance neighborhood character, visually terminate in specific locations, and provide physical and visual access to public places." And many cities and towns have lowered the parking requirements for buildings, required attractive streetscapes and other design features, and even specified good signage, in an effort to scale the built environment for pedestrians.[14] Such local zoning initiatives, by promoting Smart Growth, are likely to promote physical activity, diminish air pollution, reduce the risk of vehicular injuries, and otherwise advance public health.

Subdivision regulations operate at a larger scale than zoning, governing the layout and form of entire communities. When a large parcel of land is being developed, it is typically subdivided into smaller parcels. The process of subdividing or "platting" land and laying out streets, lots, and other land uses, is controlled by subdivision regulations. Subdivision regulations are particularly critical to Smart Growth, since they govern street network design, open space placement, and connections with adjacent developments.

Regionalism

One of the most formidable barriers to Smart Growth is the fragmented nature of governance in metropolitan areas. A large metropolitan area may have dozens or even hundreds of public entities, including city and county governments, school systems, utility districts, transit agencies, law enforcement agencies, and others. In this setting, making regional-scale decisions about land use and transportation is effectively impossible. As a result, recent years have seen great interest in metropolitan governance.[15] Oregon's Greater Portland Metropolitan Service District, established in 1978, is an elected body that oversees regional transportation and land use planning, and operates the mass transit system, parks, and cultural facilities. Minnesota's Metropolitan Council, established in the early 1990s, oversees all regional land use, transit, and sewer planning for the Twin Cities metropolitan area. The Georgia Regional Transportation Authority, established in 1999, oversees transportation planning, operates some transit, and exercises authority over some land use decisions, in the Atlanta metropolitan area. Regional bodies like these can facilitate coordinated decisions about transit investments, direct development toward areas that are already developed and away from "greenfields," and promote Smart Growth in other ways.

Growth Management

Smart Growth advocates recognize that population growth is a reality, and distinguish between Smart Growth and "no growth." Nevertheless, managing growth—limiting where and how it occurs—is an important part of Smart Growth. Many states and metropolitan areas have experimented with growth management. One strategy emphasizes pricing schemes, such as impact fees, charges for connecting to infrastructure such as sewer and water lines, and toll roads. Another emphasizes the coordination and management of infrastructure, such as integrated land use and transportation planning. And a third relies on land use regulations such as urban growth boundaries. Oregon offers what is perhaps the best-known example of growth boundaries. In 1973, that state's Land Conservation and Development Act required urban growth boundaries around all cities in the state, and mandated comprehensive land use planning at both the local and the metropolitan levels. While the results have been widely debated, it appears that the strategy has successfully stimulated infill development, transit use, and walkable community design in cities such as Portland, while containing sprawl and protecting undeveloped land. On the other hand, critics argue that housing prices in Portland have risen steeply, that affordable housing is scarce, that planners have been inflexible in revising the boundaries, and that some sprawl has continued to occur.[16]

Land Conservation

Land conservation is an important part of Smart Growth. Building at greater density offers an opportunity to set aside farmland, forests, and other undeveloped land. This serves many purposes: watershed protection, species protection, recreational opportunities, protecting farms and historic properties, preserving beauty. Many states have become active in acquiring land for conservation purposes, often in collaboration with nongovernmental organizations such as the Trust for Public Land and the Nature Conservancy. New Jersey voters, for example, approved a 1998 constitutional amendment that dedicated $1 billion over ten years to preserve open space. Such efforts help balance residential development with other land uses.

Infrastructure Spending

Smart Growth requires patterns of infrastructure spending that differ from conventional investments. In part, this means limiting subsidies that contribute to sprawl, such as large public expenditures on roads, parking facilities, and infrastructure in exurban areas. In contrast, investments in existing infrastructure, such as aging urban sewer and water lines, and in new infrastructure, such as pedestrian facilities and transit, contribute to Smart Growth and to associated health benefits.[17]

Financing

Developers who want to build Smart Growth projects must obtain financing, which often poses a challenge. Banks and other lenders are accustomed to making loans for conventional projects, defined by conventional and rather formulaic criteria. For example, a "neighborhood center" is a 12- to 15-acre retail location, anchored by a 50,000- to 70,000-square-foot supermarket/drug store, and featuring in-line national chain stores. The buildings occupy 20 percent of the land area and are set back from the street; the balance of land is dedicated to surface parking lots. At least 20,000 people, demographically matched to the supermarket chain, live within a 3-mile radius, and traffic flow past the center reaches at least 20,000 cars each day, preferably in the "going home" direction. With acceptable formulas defined to this level of detail, and with successful alternative models not yet very common, lenders are reluctant to back Smart Growth projects. When they do make loans, they often charge higher interest rates, making the projects financially riskier for the developers. A sizeable Smart Growth project may involve blocks of housing, retail space, and office space, together with parking garages (at about $10,000 per space); these are enormously expensive projects to build. Moreover, lenders focus on short-term returns, using discounted cash flow methodologies, while the value of Smart Growth projects may not be fully realized for some years. The solutions to these challenges—creative financing, matching different investors with different kinds of returns, educating lenders, and showcasing financially successful models of Smart Growth—are slowly emerging at banks and real estate investment companies around the country.[18]

Just as sprawl can be encouraged by federal policy, policy decisions at the federal level can also support Smart Growth. "Federal and state policies, taken together," writes Bruce Katz of the Brookings Institution, "set the 'rules of the development game' that tend to facilitate the decentralization of the economy. . . . "[19] Transportation policy, tax policy, and environmental policy can all set the stage for Smart Growth initiatives.

Transportation, Tax, and Environmental Policy

Federal and state transportation policy, as reflected in spending priorities, has a profound impact on patterns of metropolitan development. Transportation policies generally support the expansion of road capacity at the edges of metropolitan areas, contributing to continued sprawl. Several changes in transportation policy would support public health by promoting Smart Growth. First, a shift in emphasis away from highway construction and toward such alternatives as mass transit, sidewalks, and multiuse trails would help promote more consolidated development and healthier forms of travel.[20] Second, policy instruments could promote less polluting motor vehicles. Examples include tax breaks for cleaner vehicles, regulatory requirements for cleaner vehicles, and withholding of federal highway funds for metropolitan

areas with poor air quality. Third, existing federal and state requirements for sidewalks and multiuse trails could be made more flexible.
For example, if federal funds are used to support construction of multiuse trails, these trails are currently required to be 12 feet in width and
made of impervious surfaces such as asphalt or cement. Environmentalists object to building what are essentially one-lane roads through
sensitive areas such as riparian zones. More flexibility could make such
trails more acceptable to greater numbers of people and communities.
As another example, some state departments of transportation regulations discourage trees alongside roadways, considering them "fixed
immobile objects" that could pose a risk to motorists. However, tree-
lined sidewalks are very attractive to pedestrians. More flexibility in
such regulations could promote walking instead of driving.

Federal transportation policy is associated with huge federal
appropriations. The multiyear federal transportation bills—the 1991
Intermodal Surface Transportation Efficiency Act (ISTEA), the 1998
Transportation Equity Act for the 21st Century (TEA-21), and its
emerging successor—offer many opportunities to promote walking
and bicycling, and to balance road-building with transit. Advocacy
groups such as the Surface Transportation Policy Project and public
health partners have called for shifts in these bills to support the kinds
of transportation strategies consistent with Smart Growth.[21]

Tax policy, primarily a federal prerogative but also a state function,
represents another way to promote Smart Growth and the corresponding health benefits. The tax benefits of homeownership appear spatially neutral, but in reality they favor higher income households and
suburban communities.[22] Tax policies that favor homes consistent with
Smart Growth principles—those in denser areas, near transit, and/or
on existing rather than new infrastructure, for instance—would balance the traditional tax incentives that encourage sprawl.

Federal environmental policy also offers opportunities to support
Smart Growth. An ironic example is the development of brownfields.
Brownfields are unused former industrial sites, often in urban areas.
These sites may be contaminated with chemical residues of past use,
but may be strategically located and ripe for development.[23] One set of
environmental health concerns pertains to the risk of exposure to hazardous chemicals, and federal environmental policy—often in the context of Superfund activity—has focused on this risk. However, the
health benefits of urban redevelopment have not often been considered. "Cleaning up a brownfield site," writes Rutgers University Professor Michael Greenberg, "may do more than rid a neighborhood of a

degrading eyesore; it may also signal the beginning of a physical and spiritual renewal of a neighborhood and its people by creating afford-able housing, a school, a playground, or a community facility."[24] If this redevelopment proceeds in accordance with Smart Growth principles, yielding safe, walkable streets, reducing commutes, and providing affordable housing, then considerable health benefits may result. Fed-eral policy that balances the health risks and benefits of brownfield redevelopment resonates with health-based Smart Growth initiatives.

LIMITS TO SMART GROWTH

Opponents and skeptics have raised numerous arguments against Smart Growth. First, some argue that the public doesn't want Smart Growth. Second, some view Smart Growth as coercive because it lim-its consumer choice. Third, some argue that Smart Growth can exacer-bate traffic congestion and related problems, which are better solved through other approaches to community and regional development. Fourth, some accuse Smart Growth projects of being isolated enclaves, not integrated into regional transportation and land use strategies. Finally, some argue that Smart Growth encourages "gentrification," the displacement of urban poor and minority residents by wealthier new arrivals.

The conventional wisdom is that sprawl simply reflects market preferences: Americans want large suburban homes, and builders and developers sell products to meet that demand. As one author argues, "Americans overwhelmingly prefer a single-family detached home on a large lot in the suburbs, and that's the type of housing they want their neighbors to live in as well."[25] Indeed, recent reviews of consumer preference surveys suggest that most Americans favor suburban loca-tions, single-family detached homes, low density, and ease of automo-bile use, and are unwilling to pay more for homes that are closer to work and other destinations.[26] However, there are significant excep-tions to these findings, exceptions that may expand in importance in coming years.

First, substantial minorities of Americans—ranging from 10 or 15 percent to more than 50 percent, depending upon the question and the survey—prefer alternatives to suburban design, such as sidewalks, nar-rower streets, shared recreational areas, higher density, and alternative housing styles such as townhouses and condominiums.[27] Second, at least half of respondents indicate that they would like less automobile dependence and more opportunities to walk.[28] For example, a random national survey conducted in 2000 for Smart Growth America found a striking level of interest in Smart Growth features.[29] In this survey, 78 percent favored Smart Growth when it was defined as "giving priority to improving services, such as schools, roads, affordable housing, and public transportation in existing communities, rather than encouraging new housing and commercial development in the countryside." Similar findings emerged when specific features of Smart Growth were queried. As shown in Figure 11-1, a majority favored walking more over driving to all destinations, and as shown in Figure 11-2, a majority thought that traffic congestion is best solved through transit or walkable community design rather than new road-building. Third, demographic shifts already underway will promote these trends. As the baby boom generation ages, older homebuyers with buying power will comprise a larger share of the market. These buyers greatly value walkability, and prefer denser neighborhoods where services and amenities are close at hand.[30]

In fact, the market demonstrates that plenty of consumers choose Smart Growth when the choice is available. In many locations—greenfield developments such as Florida's Seaside and Virginia's Reston Town Center, and infill projects such as Harbor Town in Memphis and

■ **FIGURE 11-1** Survey results regarding preferences for walking, United States, 2000. The question asked was worded as follows: "Please tell me which of the following statements describe you more: (a) If it were possible, I would like to walk more throughout the day either to get to specific places or for exercise or (b) I prefer to drive my car wherever I go?" More than half of respondents indicate a desire to walk more.

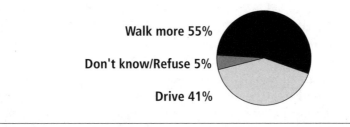

Walk more 55%

Don't know/Refuse 5%

Drive 41%

SOURCE: Belden Russonello, and Stewart, "American's Attitudes Toward Smart Growth," September, 2000. Belden Russonello & Stewart, 1320 19th Street, NW, Suite 700, Washington DC 20036. Available: http://www.brspoll.com/Reports/STPP%20report.pdf.

■ **FIGURE 11-2**   Americans' views on the best long-term solution to traffic congestion, United States, 2000. The question asked was worded as follows: "Which one of the following proposals is the best long-term solution to reducing traffic in your state: build new roads, improve public transportation, such as trains, buses and light rail, or develop communities where people do not have to drive long distances to work or shop?" Two-thirds of respondents favor either developing communities in ways that mitigate the need to drive, or improving public transportation.

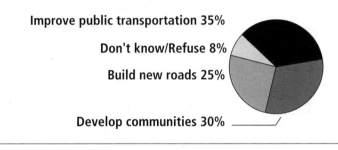

Improve public transportation 35%

Don't know/Refuse 8%

Build new roads 25%

Develop communities 30%

SOURCE: Belden Russonello, and Stewart, "American's Attitudes Toward Smart Growth," September, 2000. Belden Russonello & Stewart, 1320 19th Street, NW, Suite 700, Washington DC 20036. Available: http://www.brspoll.com/Reports/STPP%20report.pdf.

Carillon Point in Seattle—Smart Growth property values have surpassed those of nearby conventional developments, sometimes by very large margins. Some of the highest real estate values in the country are in traditional downtowns such as Manhattan, San Francisco, and Boston, also reflecting consumer demand for such neighborhoods.

A second argument against Smart Growth is that it is a form of coercive social engineering, an elitist effort to whack suburban homebuyers and force specific lifestyles on people. In fact, some proponents of Smart Growth do have explicit social goals—creating a sense of community, advancing social equity, maximizing the common good.[31] But Smart Growth developers emphasize that they seek to *increase* consumer choice, not to limit it. Existing zoning and financing practices constrain what can be built, so the menu for consumers is limited. Smart Growth represents a new entry on the menu in most markets, one that attracts willing buyers but does not force other people's hand.

Third, some scholars have argued that the best way to decrease driving, relieve congestion, and improve air quality is not through greater density, land use mix, and connectivity, or through building transit systems. Citing cost and practicality, they have advocated alternative approaches such as pricing schemes that transfer the social and environmental costs of driving to drivers[32] and improving automobile technology to reduce emissions.[33] These strategies, of course, may play an important role in addressing traffic and environmental problems, but they can easily coexist with Smart Growth initiatives.

Fourth, critics have pointed out that some of the best known New Urbanist developments, such as Seaside, were built on undeveloped land, far from destinations such as work and recreation. Such projects may offer charming, walkable neighborhoods, but their residents still need to travel long distances and rely heavily on automobiles. This pattern of development, while exemplifying Smart Growth in some ways, may contribute to sprawl. Indeed, more recent New Urbanist developments have focused on infill in cities rather than on "Greenfield" projects.

Finally, as poor and working class urban neighborhoods are rebuilt and revitalized according to Smart Growth principles, new arrivals may displace long-term residents. This process is known as gentrification.[34] It poses not only a social equity challenge, but also a public health challenge, as disruption and displacement of longstanding communities is not healthy for its residents. Policy approaches that promote mixed-income housing, to enable people from across the economic spectrum to live in walkable neighborhoods close to where they work, shop, and play, are an important part of Smart Growth efforts.

A PUBLIC HEALTH APPROACH TO SMART GROWTH

Smart Growth has primarily been the domain of architects, designers, and planners, and these fields offer a vast literature on the subject. But Smart Growth is also a public health strategy, and the paradigms of health sciences complement those that gave rise to Smart Growth. In particular, health care providers and public health professionals typically begin by assessing health needs—a clinical diagnosis by a physician or nurse, a community assessment by a public health professional. This assessment process is as precise and accurate as possible, relying on validated measurement tools. With a diagnosis in hand, interventions can be planned—treatments for individual patients, or community programs in the public health context. Importantly, the next step is evaluation; health professionals monitor their patients or communities to check on the success of their interventions, and change course if necessary. The entire process is grounded in empirical evidence. A familiar example is the PRECEDE/PROCEED model of health promotion. This model calls for systematic diagnostic steps at the outset—social diagnosis, epidemiologic diagnosis, behavioral and environmental diagnosis, educational and organizational diagnosis, and administrative and policy diagnosis. When these are completed, the implementation phase begins, and it is followed by process evaluation, impact evaluation, and outcome evaluation.[35]

What does this evidence-based approach have to offer the fields of architecture, design, and urban and regional planning? We offer three examples: the use of measurement indicators, empirical health research, and a technique known as Health Impact Assessment.

In an evidence-based process, we need to be able to measure important outcomes. If a community decides to adopt Smart Growth initiatives and hopes to improve health in the process, what should be measured? The community might measure "upstream" variables such as the availability of sidewalks, or health-related variables such as walking trips or air emissions, or health outcomes such as body weight or motor vehicle injury rates.

A very useful model for systematic measurement at the community level comes from the sustainability literature. Sustainability is defined as meeting "the needs of the present without compromising the ability of future generations to meet their own needs."[36] At the local level, many practices contribute to sustainability, such as reducing energy use, protecting land from development, minimizing waste generation, and supporting local agriculture. In recent years, many cities and communities have launched sustainability initiatives.[37] Many of these initiatives have identified indicators of sustainability, which are monitored over time.[38] The best indicators are based on good science, objectively measurable, relevant to outcomes that matter, reflective of community values, and "leading" rather than "lagging."[39] Examples of sustainability indicators include transit ridership, percentage of the population living within ten minutes of a park, incidence of asthma, and extent of recycling. Many of these indicators, of course, are relevant to healthy community design, and dovetail with Smart Growth goals.

In fact, public health professionals have started identifying indicators to use in evaluating the health of cities and communities. Often, these indicators are measures already made for other purposes. For example, in a study of over 300 cities or parts of cities in Japan, investigators identified several indices potentially related to health. The "environmental quality" index included indicators of nearby vegetation and the amount of sunlight reaching the house, the "housing" index included indicators of housing age and the width of streets, and the "urban clutter" index included indicators of roadway mileage, traffic volume, and access to rail and bus stations. All of these indicators were available from routinely collected data sources, and all three indices turned out to correlate with health.[40] In a study comparing the twenty ward units of metropolitan Shanghai, investigators identified indicators relating to population density, per capita floor space in buildings, proportion of total land area devoted to parks and gardens, and a variety of other demographic, economic, and social factors. They found that mortality rates were associated with larger per capita amounts of residential floor space, with more parks and gardens, with more health professionals per population, and with more retail employees per population.[41] And a study in London used a "Built Environment Site Survey Checklist" (BESSC), a twenty-seven-item survey that included housing style, the quality of space outside buildings, the number of trees and gardens, the presence of shared recreational space, and similar factors. Although not all of these indicators were available in existing databases (some had to be assessed by the researchers), they were found to be highly reliable.[42] Many of these examples focus on urban areas, but the core concept—that measures of the built environment are available and can be used to assess its effect on health—is equally applicable to suburban and rural locations. The public health approach, measuring and tracking variables that are relevant to health, is clearly applicable to the world of architects and planners.

Indicators imply the ability to measure both "exposures" such as neighborhood design and "outcomes" such as health and well-being. This ability is essential for both research and program assessment. In fact, both functions are central to public health.

Research about the effects of the built environment on health is crucial. Throughout this book we have identified gaps in our knowledge. If sidewalks are built, will people walk? What determinants of walking have the greatest impact? How do different ethnic groups respond to different aspects of the built environment? What is the optimal distribution and design of parks? What transportation strategies are best in terms of air quality, safety, and physical activity? How can public spaces best maximize convivial social interactions?

These are empirical questions, and they are best answered by solid data. The architecture and design literature is full of pronouncements about the best way to build, but the skeptical reader often asks, "Says who? What is the basis for this conclusion?" In the health sciences, evidence-based recommendations are increasingly expected. When a physician prescribes a medication, the patient expects that the medication has been shown to be effective and safe. A similar foundation for guidelines on the built environment is within reach, but it will require combining health research techniques with the expertise of architects and designers.[43] Health research agencies are beginning to define the research agendas that, in coming years, they will pursue.[44]

In applying public health analysis to the built environment, a method called Health Impact Assessment (HIA) has great promise. HIA is defined as "a combination of procedures, methods and tools by which a policy, program or project may be judged as to its potential effects on the health of a population, and the distribution of those effects within the population."[45] This approach emerged in Europe during the 1990s, promoted by the World Health Organization's European Regional Office. Like its first cousin, the Environmental Impact Assessment, HIA is both a process and a document.[46] It is a structured, multidisciplinary approach to assessing a project such as a highway, a transit station, or a shopping mall with respect to its impact on human health.

HIA is usually carried out in advance, as part of the planning process. It attempts to anticipate all important health impacts and to quantify them. For example, in assessing a proposed bypass road around a city, HIA might quantify vehicle emissions associated with the traffic, injuries to drivers and pedestrians, noise levels along the road route, and the indirect effects of economic development along the road and in the central city. These projections would be made for both the proposed road and alternative scenarios. With such data in hand, planners and members of the public could make an informed decision about the project. In fact, it is remarkable that health impact has so rarely been incorporated into infrastructure decisions. HIAs have now been performed for proposed roadways,[47] transit projects,[48] waste site expansions,[49] urban renewal plans,[50] housing policy,[51] and water privatization plans.[52] They have important advantages in explicitly incorporating health into design and planning decisions, and (in some cases) in forcing consideration of social equity.[53] However, critics charge that HIA has not yet lived up to the expectations—that it is "excessively subjective, subject to political drivers, and insufficiently rigorous."[54] Certainly, HIA needs to be further refined, and data sources and methods improved. However, the concept of methodical advance consideration of health impacts of infrastructure projects is highly promising. If sprawling communities had been subject to such evaluation, it is likely that the current balance of land use and transportation would be tipped further in favor of good health.

A Shared Vision: Land Use and Transportation for Public Health

How do we move forward? How do we identify the best ways to design and build our communities—the ways that are not only safe and healthy but also environmentally sustainable, aesthetically appealing, and commercially viable?

In this book, we have reviewed a large body of evidence about what features of architecture, design, and planning are most healthy. We still do not have all the evidence we need to guide architecture, design, and planning to maximize health. But we know a great deal. In situations such as this, where evidence is compelling if not complete, public health measures are commonly guided by the Precautionary Principle. As articulated in the Wingspread Statement of 1998, this principle holds that "when an activity raises threats of harm to human health or the environment, precautionary measures should be taken even if some cause and effect relationships are not fully established scientifically."[55] The Precautionary Principle is generally applied to health hazards such as chemical exposures,[56] but land use and transportation are just as clearly determinants of human health.

Architects, planners, designers, and transportation engineers need to understand that they are public health professionals—that land use and transportation are profoundly important "upstream" determinants of health. Similarly, those directly responsible for protecting and promoting public health—members of boards of health, public health officials, doctors and nurses—need to understand that their concerns extend to the built environment. And the two worlds need to come together.

Increasingly, this is happening. Consider the National Association of County and City Health Officials (NACCHO), the national association of local public health leaders. In early 2003, NACCHO devoted an issue of its newsletter to land use, transportation, and community design.[57] Readers were urged to go beyond traditional regulatory involvement in land use, and to engage the science and art of land planning. Examples were provided. The Ingham County (Michigan) Health Department had recently started a collaborative effort to participate in land use decisions, including active involvement in the Regional Growth Project. NACCHO has urged public health professionals to serve as catalysts and facilitators for community change; to provide the epidemiologic data needed to support public health recommendations about the built environment; to engage in advocacy and policy stewardship; to train and educate planners, traffic engineers, and other key professional groups; and to mobilize the community and interject the issue of health inequalities.[58]

To support such efforts, the leaders of tomorrow in public health, planning, architecture, and design need to be trained in each other's perspectives. The fields have had few formal links since the nineteenth century,[59] but as land use and transportation once again emerge as health issues, so does the need for collaborative training. Several universities have training programs in both public health and planning, including Columbia, Harvard, Rutgers, Tufts, and the Universities of Iowa, Cincinnati, Michigan, Minnesota, Washington, Illinois (at Chicago), North Carolina, and California (at Los Angeles and Berkeley). There is enormous potential for joint courses and degree programs to produce a generation of planners conversant with public health and a generation of public health professionals conversant with planning.

CONCLUSION

For many decades, American towns and cities have expanded from traditional cores out into surrounding countryside. Population has grown, but land area has grown faster, and we have become a predominantly suburban nation. Americans made this move in search of better lives, and in many ways they succeeded.

But we can now appreciate some unintended consequences of suburban sprawl. Dependence on the automobile for almost all travel has contributed to air pollution, threatening respiratory health, and increased the risk of injuries among drivers, passengers, and pedestrians. With less walking and bicycling, sedentary lifestyles contribute to epidemics of obesity, diabetes, and associated diseases. Sprawl can compromise water quantity and quality, which are essential for public health. And the effects of sprawl on mental health and on social capital may be profound. We routinely find ourselves in environments that are dispiriting and ugly—miles of strip malls, vast parking lots, neighborhoods with no way to walk and with no places to which to walk. Many of these health impacts are unequally distributed across the population; vulnerable groups include children, the elderly, the poor, and members of racial and ethnic minorities.

Designing and building healthy places is not a new concept; for centuries, those who care about health, across the professions, have turned their attention to the built environment. We are now rediscovering some of this old wisdom, and identifying principles for healthy placemaking for the new century. At its best, Smart Growth is like a medicine that treats a multitude of diseases—protecting respiratory health, improving cardiovascular health, preventing cancer, avoiding traumatic injuries and fatalities, controlling depression and anxiety, improving well-being. In the medical world, such an intervention would be miraculous. In the worlds of land use and transportation, it is a thrilling, and attainable, possibility.

NOTES

■ ══════════ ■

PREFACE

1. Kuczmarski RJ, Flegal KM, Campbell SM, Johnson CL. Increasing prevalence of overweight among US adults. The National Health and Nutrition Examination Surveys, 1960 to 1991. *Journal of the American Medical Association* 1994;272:205–11; Mokdad AH, Bowman BA, Ford ES, et al. The continuing epidemics of obesity and diabetes in the United States. *Journal of the American Medical Association* 2001;286:1195–1200.

2. Calle EE, Rodriguez C, Walker-Thurmond K, Thun MJ. Overweight, obesity, and mortality from cancer in a prospectively studied cohort of U.S. adults. *New England Journal of Medicine* 2003;348:1625–38; Must A, Spadano J, Coakley EH, Field AE, Colditz G, Dietz WH. The disease burden associated with overweight and obesity. *Journal of the American Medical Association* 1999;282:1523–29.

3. Hu FB, Manson JE, Stampfer MJ, Colditz G, et al. Diet, lifestyle, and the risk of type 2 diabetes mellitus in women. *New England Journal of Medicine* 2001;345(11):790–97.

4. Centers for Disease Control and Prevention, National Center for Chronic Disease Prevention and Health Promotion, Diabetes Public Health Resource. Prevalence of Diabetes. Available: www.cdc.gov/diabetes/statistics/prev/national/table8.htm.

5. Narayan KM, Boyle JP, Thompson TJ, Sorensen SW, Williamson DF. Lifetime risk for diabetes mellitus in the United States. *Journal of the American Medical Association* 2003;290(14):1884–90.

6. Mokdad AH, Marks JS, Stroup DF, Gerberding JL. Actual causes of death in the United States, 2000. *Journal of the American Medical Association* 2004;291:1238–45.

7. Centers for Disease Contol and Prevention, National Center for Health Statistics. Asthma Prevalence, Health Care Use and Mortality, 2000–2001. Available: www.cdc.gov/nchs/products/pubs/pubd/hestats/asthma/asthma.htm.

8. National Safety Council. *Report on Injuries in America, 2002.* October, 2003. Available: http://www.nsc.org/library/report_injury_usa.htm.

9. Olfson M, Marcus SC, Druss B, et al. National trends in the outpatient treatment of depression. *Journal of the American Medical Association* 2002;287(2):203–09.

10. Safer DJ, Zito JM, Fine EM. Increased methylphenidate usage for attention deficit disorder in the 1990s. *Pediatrics* 1996;98:1084–88; Zito JM, Safer DJ, dosReis S, Gardner JF, et al. Psychotropic practice patterns for youth: A 10-year perspective. *Archives of Pediatric and Adolescent Medicine* 2003;157:17–25; Greenhill LL, Halperin JM, Abikoff H. Stimulant medications. *Journal of the American Academy of Child and Adolescent Psychiatry* 1999;38:503–12.

11. Centers for Disease Control and Prevention. Mean physically or mentally unhealthy days. Health-related quality of life: Prevalence data. CDC, National Center for Chronic Disease Prevention and Health Promotion, 2003. Available: http://apps.nccd.cdc.gov/HRQOL/TrendV.asp.

12. National Center for Health Statistics. *Health, United States, 2003.* Hyattsville, MD: NCHS, 2003. Table 112. Gross domestic product, federal and state and local government expenditures, national health expenditures, and average annual percent change: United States, selected years 1960–2001. Available: http://www.cdc.gov/nchs/data/hus/tables/2003/03hus112.pdf (accessed on February 8, 2004).

13. National Center for Health Statistics. *Health, United States, 2003.* Hyattsville, MD: NCHS, 2003. Table 117. Expenditures for health care and prescribed medicine according to selected population characteristics: United States, selected years 1987–99. Available: http://www.cdc.gov/nchs/data/hus/tables/2003/03hus117.pdf.

14. Redefining Progress. Genuine Progress Indicator. Available: www.redefiningprogress.org/projects/gpi/ (accessed February 8, 2004).

15. United States Department of Agriculture, Natural Resources Conservation Service. National Resources Inventory. January, 2001. Available: http://www.nrcs.usda.gov/technical/land/pubs/97highlights.pdf.

16. Salins P. *New York City's Housing Gap Revisited.* Civic Report No. 25, February 2002. Manhattan Institute for Policy Studies. Available: http://www.manhattan-institute.org/html/cr_25.htm.

17. Bureau of Transportation Statistics. *National Transportation Statistics 2003.* Available: http://www.bts.gov/publications/national_transportation_statistics/2003/index.html.

18. Schrank D, Lomax T. *2003 Urban Mobility Study.* College Station, Texas: Texas Transportation Institute, 2003. Available: http://mobility.tamu.edu/ums/report/.

19. Surface Transportation Policy Project. *High Mileage Moms.* Washington: STPP, 1999. Available: http://www.transact.org/report.asp?id=182.

20. U.S. Department of Labor, Bureau of International Labor Affairs. *A Chartbook of International Labor Comparisons: United States, Europe, and Asia.* Washington: USDOL, May 2003. Chart 19. Annual hours worked per employed person, 1990 and 2001. Available: http://www.dol.gov/ILAB/media/reports/oiea/chartbook/chart19.htm.

21. U.S. Department of Energy, Energy Information Administration. Residential Energy Consumption Survey. November, 2002. Available: www.eia.doe.gov/emeu/recs/cookingtrends/cooking.html.

22. U.S. Department of Health and Human Services, Substance Abuse and Mental Health Services Administration, National Mental Health Information Center. *Major Depression in Children and Adolescents.* Document CA-0011, April 2003. www.mentalhealth.org/publications/allpubs/CA-0011/default.asp#2.

23. Gregg EW, Gerzoff RB, Caspersen CJ, Williamson DF, Narayan KM. Relationship of walking to mortality among U.S. adults with diabetes. *Archives of Internal Medicine* 2003;163912:1440–47.

24. Frank L, Engelke PO, Schmid TL. *Health and Community Design: The Impact of the Built Environment on Physical Activity.* Washington, DC: Island Press, 2003.

CHAPTER 1

1. Whyte WH Jr. Urban sprawl. *Fortune* January 1958. Reprinted in Whyte WH Jr., Ed. *The Exploding Metropolis.* New York: Doubleday, 1958, reprinted Berkeley: University of California Press, 1993, p 133.

2. Ibid. pp 134–35.

3. Kunstler J. *The Geography of Nowhere: The Rise and Decline of America's Man-Made Landscape.* New York: Simon & Schuster, 1994, p 10.

4. Gillham O. *The Limitless City: A Primer on the Urban Sprawl Debate.* Washington, DC: Island Press, 2002, p 8.

5. Cervero R, Kockelman K. Travel demand and the 3Ds: Density, diversity and design. *Transportation Research Part D* 1997;2(3):199–219.

6. Galster G, Hanson R, Wolman H, Coleman S, Freihage J. *Wrestling Sprawl to the Ground: Defining and Measuring an Elusive Concept.* Washington, DC: Fannie Mae Foundation, 2000. Available: http://www.fanniemaefoundation.org/programs/pdf/proc_fairgrowth_galster2.pdf (accessed November 30, 2003).

7. Lopez R, Hynes HP. Sprawl in the 1990s: Measurement, distribution, and trends. *Urban Affairs Review* 2003;38(3):325–55.

8. Ewing R, Pendall R, Chen D. *Measuring Sprawl and Its Impact.* Washington, DC: Smart Growth America, 2002. Available: http://www.smartgrowthamerica.com/sprawlindex/MeasuringSprawl.PDF.

9. Dunphy R, Fisher K. Transportation, congestion, and density: New insights. *Transportation Research Record* 1994;1552:89–96.

10. Frank L, Pivo G. Impacts of mixed use and density on utilization of three modes of travel: Single-occupant vehicle, transit, and walking. *Transportation Research Record* 1995;1466:44–52; Steiner R. Residential density and travel patterns: Review of the literature. *Transportation Research Record* 1994;1466:37–43.

11. Dunphy and Fisher, 1994, op. cit.; Frank and Pivo, 1994, op. cit.; Frank L, Stone B Jr, Bachman W. Linking land use with household vehicle emissions in the central Puget Sound: Methodological framework and findings. *Transportation Research Part D* 2000;5(3):173–96.

12. Southworth M, Owens P. The evolving metropolis: Studies of community, neighborhood, and street form at the urban edge. *Journal of the American Planning Association* 1993;59, 3:271–87.

13. Fulton W, Pendall R, Nguyen M, Harrison A. *Who Sprawls Most? How Growth Patterns Differ Across the U.S.* Washington, DC: Brookings Institution Center on Urban and Metropolitan Policy, 2001. Available: http://www.brookings.org/dybdocroot/es/urban/publications/fulton.pdf (accessed November 30, 2003).

14. Schrank D, Lomax T. 2003 Urban Mobility Study. College Station: Texas A&M University System, Texas Transportation Institute, 2003. Available: http://mobility.tamu.edu/ums/ (accessed November 30, 2003).

15. Ibid.

16. Lawton K. The urban structure and personal travel: An analysis of Portland, OR data and some national and international data. In: *E-Vision 2000: Key Issues That Will Shape Our Energy Future. Summary of Proceedings, Scenario Analysis, Expert Elicitation, and Submitted Papers.* CF-170/1-1-DOE. Santa Monica, CA: RAND, 2001, pp 231–32. Available: http://www.rand.org/scitech/stpi/Evision/Supplement/lawton.pdf (accessed November 30, 2003).

17. Frank and Pivo, 1994, op. cit.; Friedman B, Gordon S, Peers J. Effect of neo-traditional neighborhood design on travel characteristics. *Transportation Research Record* 1994;1466:63–70; Holtzclaw J. *Using Residential Patterns and Transit to Decrease Auto Dependence and Costs.* San Francisco: Natural Resources Defense Council, 1994; Cervero R, Kockelman K. Travel demand and the 3Ds: Density, diversity and design. *Transportation Research Part D* 1997;2(3):199–219; Cervero R, Gorham R. Commuting in transit versus automobile neighborhoods. *APA Journal* 1995;Spring 1995:210–25; Apogee Research, Inc. *The Effects of Urban Form on Travel and Emissions: A Review and Synthesis of the Literature.* Draft report prepared for the United States Environmental Protection Agency. HBIX Reference C611-005. Washington, DC, 1998; Ewing R, Cervero R. Travel and the built environment: A synthesis. *Transportation Research Record* 2001;1780:87–114.

18. Cervero R. Mixed land uses and commuting: Evidence from the American Housing Survey. *Transportation Research* A, 1996;30(5):361–77.

19. Holtzclaw, 1994, op. cit.

20. Cervero and Gorham, op. cit., 1995.

21. Moudon A, Hess P, Snyder M, Stanilov K. Effects of site design on pedestrian travel in mixed-use, medium-density environments. *Transportation Research Record* 1997;1578:48–55; Handy S. Regional versus local accessibility: Neo-traditional development and its implications for non-work travel. *Built Environment* 1992;18, 4:253–67; Handy S. Understanding the link between urban form and nonwork travel behavior. *Journal of Planning*

*Education and Research*1996;15:183–98; Fehrs and Peers Associates. *Metro-politan Transportation Commission Bay Area Trip Rate Survey Analysis.* Oakland, CA: Metropolitan Transportation Commission, 1992; Ewing R, Haliyur P, Page GW. Getting around a traditional city, a suburban planned unit development, and everything in between. *Transportation Research Record* 1994;1466:53–62.

22. Dunphy and Fisher, 1994, op. cit.

23. Frank and Pivo, 1994, op. cit.

24. Ewing and Cervero, 2001, op. cit.

25. Boarnet M, Sarmiento S. Can land use policy really affect travel behavior? A study of the link between non-work travel and land use characteristics. *Urban Studies* 1998;35(7):1155–69.

26. Crane R. *The Impacts of Urban Form on Travel: A Critical Review.* Cambridge, MA: Lincoln Institute of Land Policy Working Paper No. WP99RC1. 1999.

27. Krizek KJ, Waddell P. Analysis of lifestyle choices: Neighborhood type, travel patterns, and activity participation. *Transportation Research Record* 2002;1807:119–28.

28. Mokhtarian PL, Salomon I, Redmond LS. Understanding the demand for travel: It's not purely "derived." *Innovation: European Journal of Social Science* 2001;14(4):355–81.

29. Ibid; Krizek KJ. A pre-test/post-test strategy for researching neighborhood-scale urban form and travel behavior. *Transportation Research Record* 2000; 1722:48–55; Kitamura R, Mokhtarian PL, Laidet L. A micro-analysis of land use and travel in five neighborhoods in the San Francisco Bay area. *Transportation* 1997;24(2):125–58.

30. Levine J, Inam A, Werbel R, Torng G-W. Land use and transportation alternatives: Constraint or expansion of household choice? MTI Report 01-19. San Jose, CA: Mineta Transportation Institute, San Jose State University, June 2002. Available: http://www.transweb.sjsu.edu/publications/LandUse.pdf (accessed November 30, 2003).

31. Belden Russonello & Stewart. *Americans' Attitudes Toward Smart Growth.* September 2000. Belden Russonello & Stewart, 1320 19th Street, NW, Suite 700, Washington, DC 20036. Available: http://www.brspoll.com/Reports/STPP%20report.pdf (accessed November 30, 2003).

32. Moudon AV, Hess P. Suburban clusters: The nucleation of multifamily housing in suburban areas of the central Puget Sound. *Journal of the American Planning Association* 2000;66(3):243–64.

33. Jacobs J. *The Death and Life of Great American Cities.* New York: Random House, 1961.

34. Rapoport A. Pedestrian street use: Culture and perception. In: Moudon A, Ed. *Public Streets for Public Use.* New York: Van Nostrand Reinhold, 1987.

35. Frank, Stone, and Bachman, 2000, op. cit.; Holtzclaw J, Clear R, Dittmar H, Goldstein D, Haas P. Location efficiency: Neighborhood and

socioeconomic characteristics determine auto ownership and use—Studies in Chicago, Los Angeles and San Francisco. *Transportation Planning and Technology* 2002;25:1–27.

36. Pushkarev B, Zupan J. *Urban Rail in America: An Exploration of Criteria for Fixed-Guideway Transit.* UMTA-NY-06-0061-80-1 Final Report. 368p. 1980; Cervero and Kockelman, 1997, op. cit.; Kockelman KM. Travel behavior as function of accessibility, land use mixing, and land use balance: Evidence from San Francisco Bay Area. *Transportation Research Record* 1997;1607:116–25; Messenger T, Ewing R. Transit-oriented development in the sun belt. *Transportation Research Record* 1996;1552:145–53.

37. Frank and Pivo, 1994, op. cit.; Hess P, Moudon AV, Snyder M, Stanilov K. Site design and pedestrian travel. *Transportation Research Record* 1999;1674: 9–19.

38. Frank, Stone, and Bachman, 2000, op. cit.

CHAPTER 2

1. Jackson KT. *Crabgrass Frontier: The Suburbanization of the United States.* New York: Oxford University Press, 1985, p 19.

2. Ibid.

3. Ibid., p 13.

4. Ibid., p 28.

5. Ibid., p 29.

6. Muller PO. Transportation and urban form: Stages in the spatial evolution of the American metropolis. In: Hanson S, Ed. *The Geography of Urban Transportation*, Second Edition. New York: Guilford Press, 1995, pp 26–52.

7. Jackson, 1985, op. cit., p 50.

8. Jefferson, Thomas, in a letter to Benjamin Rush, 1800. In: Lipscomb AA, Bergh AE, Johnston RH, Eds. *The Writings of Thomas Jefferson.* Washington, DC: Thomas Jefferson Memorial Association of the United States, 1903–04. Vol. 10, p 173.

9. Jackson, 1985, op. cit., p 70.

10. Ibid., p 71.

11. Ibid., p 118.

12. Ibid., pp 130–32.

13. Ibid., p 135.

14. Ibid., p 163; McShane C. *Down the Automobile Path: The Automobile and the American City.* New York: Columbia University Press, 1994; Flink JJ. *The Automobile Age.* Cambridge, MA: MIT Press, 1998.

15. Jackson, 1985, op. cit., p 164.

16. Ibid., p 170; Kay JH. *Asphalt Nation: How the Automobile Took over America, and How We Can Take It Back.* Berkeley: University of California Press, 1997, pp 213–14.

17. Jackson, 1985, op. cit., p 175.

18. Kay, 1997, op. cit., p 196.

19. Relph E. *The Modern Urban Landscape*. Baltimore: Johns Hopkins University Press, 1987, pp 67–68.

20. Knack R. Return to Euclid. *Planning* 1996;62(11):4–8.

21. Haar CM, Kayden JS. Zoning at sixty: A time for anniversary reckonings. In: Haar CM, Kayden JS, Eds. *Zoning and the American Dream: Promises Still to Keep*. Chicago: Planners Press, 1989, pp ix–xi; Fischel W. Zoning and land use regulation. In: Boudewijn B, de Geest G, Eds. *Encyclopedia of Law and Economics, Volume II. Civil Law and Economics*. Cheltenham, UK: Edward Elgar, 2000, pp 403–23; Fischel W. Does the American way of zoning cause the suburbs of U.S. metropolitan areas to be too spread out? In: Altsuler A, Morrill W, Wolman H, Mitchell F, Eds. *Governance and Opportunity in Metropolitan Areas*. Washington, DC: National Academy Press, 1999, pp 151–91; Freilich RH. *From Sprawl to Smart Growth: Successful Legal, Planning, and Environmental Systems*. Chicago: American Bar Association, 1999.

22. Jackson, 1985, op. cit., pp 197–203; Kay, 1997, op. cit., p 200.

23. Jackson, 1985, op. cit., p 250.

24. Mumford L. *The Highway and the City*. New York: Mentor, 1964, p 244.

25. Jackson, 1985, op. cit., pp 269–70.

26. Leinberger C. Financing Progressive Development. *Capital Xchange*, May 2001. Washington and Boston: Brookings Institution Center on Urban and Metropolitan Policy and Harvard University Joint Center for Housing Studies. Available: http://www.brook.edu/es/urban/capitalxchange/leinberger.pdf (accessed November 16, 2003).

CHAPTER 3

1. Leavitt JW. *The Healthiest City: Milwaukee and the Politics of Health Reform*. Princeton, NJ: Princeton University Press, 1982, p 22.

2. Jefferson T, in a letter Benjamin Rush, 1800. In: Lipscomb AA, Bergh AE, Johnston RH, Eds. *The Writings of Thomas Jefferson*, Volume 10. Washington, DC: Thomas Jefferson Memorial Association of the United States, 1903–04, p 173.

3. Quoted in Glaab CN, Brown AT. *A History of Urban America*. New York: Macmillan, 1983, p 64.

4. Omran A. The epidemiologic transition: A theory of the epidemiology of population change. *Milbank Quarterly* 1971;49:509–38.

5. Rogers RG, Hackenberg R. Extending epidemiologic transition theory: A new stage. *Social Biology* 1987;34:234–43; Olshansky SJ, Ault B. The fourth stage of the epidemiologic transition: The age of delayed degenerative diseases. *Milbank Quarterly* 1986;64:355–91.

6. Quoted in Duffy J. *The Sanitarians: A History of American Public Health.* Urbana: University of Illinois Press, 1990, p 9.

7. Ibid., p 10.

8. Ibid., p 33.

9. Rosenberg C. *The Cholera Years: The United States in 1832, 1849, and 1866.* Chicago: University of Chicago Press, 1962, p 18.

10. Tarr JA. Urban pollution—Many long years ago. *American Heritage* XXII (October 1971):65–69, 106. Reprinted in altered form as: Tarr JA. The horse—Polluter of the city. In: Tarr JA. *The Search for the Ultimate Sink: Urban Pollution in Historical Perspective.* Akron: University of Akron Press, 1996, pp 323–34.

11. Larsen LH. Nineteenth-century street sanitation: A study of filth and frustration. *Wisconsin Magazine of History* LII (Spring 1969):239–47.

12. Duffy, 1990, op. cit., p 13.

13. Ibid., p 28.

14. Rosenberg C, 1962, op. cit., p 17.

15. Duffy, 1990, op. cit., p 71.

16. Quoted in Glaab and Brown, 1983, op. cit., p 76.

17. Ibid., p 77.

18. Quoted in Duffy, 1990, op. cit., p 69.

19. Tarr, 1971, op. cit., p 106.

20. Quoted in Brieger GH, *Medical America in the Nineteenth Century: Readings from the Literature.* Baltimore: Johns Hopkins University Press, 1972, p 268.

21. Duffy, 1990, op. cit., p 176; Tarr, 1971, op. cit., p 68.

22. Duffy, 1990, op. cit., p 30.

23. Ibid., p 16.

24. Quoted in Leavitt, 1982, op. cit., p 55.

25. Duffy, 1990, op. cit., p 13.

26. Ibid., p 29.

27. Ibid., p 73.

28. Ibid., p 88.

29. Blake JB. *Public Health in the Town of Boston, 1630–1822.* Cambridge, MA: Harvard University Press, 1959, at pp 156–57, as quoted in Duffy, 1990, op. cit., at p 47.

30. Melosi M. *The Sanitary City: Urban Infrastructure in America from Colonial Times to the Present.* Baltimore: Johns Hopkins University Press, 2000, p 74.

31. Ibid., p 87.

32. Duffy, 1990, op. cit., p 16.

33. Ibid., p 187.

34. Ibid., p 187.

35. Ibid., p 77.

36. Glaab and Brown, 1983, op. cit., p 77.

37. Smith S. *The City That Was*. New York: Allaben, 1911, quoted in Brieger GH, *Medical America in the Nineteenth Century: Readings from the Literature*. Baltimore: Johns Hopkins University Press, 1972, p 275.

38. Quoted in Leavitt, 1982, op. cit., p 30.

39. Smith, 1911, op. cit., quoted in Brieger, 1972, op. cit, at p 269.

40. Duffy, 1990, p 21.

41. Quoted in Glaab and Brown, 1983, op. cit., p 79.

42. Duffy, 1990, op. cit., pp 77–78.

43. Rosenberg C, 1962, op. cit., p 7.

44. Quoted in Rosenberg, 1962, op. cit., p 143.

45. Caldwell M. *The Last Crusade: The War on Consumption 1862–1954*. New York: Atheneum, 1988.

46. Quoted in Caldwell M, 1988, op. cit., p 34.

47. McCarthy MP. *Typhoid and the Politics of Public Health in Eighteenth Century Philadelphia*. Philadelphia: American Philosophical Society, 1987, p 7.

48. Quoted in Brimblecombe P, *The Big Smoke*. London: Routledge, 1988, p 48.

49. Quoted in Duffy, 1990, p 69.

50. Ibid., p 70.

51. Hurley A. Creating ecological wastelands: Oil pollution in New York City, 1870–1900. *Journal of Urban History* 1994;20:340–64.

52. Tarr J. Industrial waste disposal in the United States as a historical problem. *Ambix: The Journal of the Society for the History of Alchemy and Chemistry* 2002;49:4–20.

53. Duffy, 1990, op. cit., p 177.

54. Quoted in McCarthy, 1987, op. cit., p 6.

55. Kirkwood JP. A Special Report on the Pollution of River Waters, Annual Report Massachusetts State Board of Health—1876. Quoted in Tarr JA, Industrial wastes, water pollution, and public health, 1876–1962. Chap XIV in Tarr JA, *The Search for the Ultimate Sink: Urban Pollution in Historical Perspective*. Akron, OH: University of Akron Press, 1996, p 356.

56. Norris F. *The Pit: A Story of Chicago*. New York: Doubleday Page, 1903, pp 62–63.

57. Ibid., p 60.

58. Tarkington B. *The Turmoil* [1915]. Reprint edition Urbana: University of Illinois Press, 2003, pp 1–2.

59. Colburn T, et al. *Great Lakes, Great Legacy?* Washington, DC: The Conservation Foundation, 1990. Quoted in Markham A, *A Brief History of Pollution.* New York: St. Martin's Press, 1994, at p 62.

60. Warren C. *Brush with Death: A Social History of Lead Poisoning.* Baltimore: Johns Hopkins University Press, 2000; Markowitz G, Rosner D. *Deceit and Denial: The Deadly Politics of Industrial Pollution.* Berkeley: University of California Press, and New York: Milbank Memorial Fund, 2002.

61. Grosse SD, Matte TD, Schwartz J, Jackson RJ. Economic gains resulting from the reduction in children's exposure to lead in the United States. *Environmental Health Perspective* 2002;110(6):563–69.

62. Mohl RA. Poverty, pauperism and the social order in the preindustrial American city, 1780–1840. *Social Science Quarterly* 1972 (March):934–48; Nash GB. *The Urban Crucible: The Northern Seaports and the Origins of the American Revolution.* Cambridge, MA: Harvard University Press, 1986.

63. Quoted in Glaab and Brown, 1983, op. cit., p 16.

64. Quoted in Nash GB. The social evolution of pre-industrial American cities, 1700–1820. In: Mohl RA, Ed. *The Making of Urban America,* Second Edition. Wilmington, DE: Scholarly Resources, 1997, pp 15–36, at p 21.

65. Glaab and Brown, 1983, op. cit., p 16.

66. Harrington M. *The Other America: Poverty in the United States.* New York: Macmillan, 1962, p 143.

67. Wilson WJ. *The Truly Disadvantaged: The Inner City, the Underclass, and Public Policy.* Chicago: The University of Chicago Press, 1987.

68. Butts JA. Youth Crime Drop. The Urban Institute, December 2000. http://www.urban.org/UploadedPDF/youth-crime-drop.pdf (accessed November 20, 2003); Blumstein A, Wallman J, Eds. *The Crime Drop in America.* New York: Cambridge University Press, 2000.

69. Weaver RC. Major factors in urban planning. In: Duhl LJ, Ed. *The Urban Condition: People and Policy in the Metropolis.* New York: Basic Books, 1963, pp 97–112, at p 101.

70. Allman TD. The urban crisis leaves town. *Harper's Magazine,* December 1978, pp 41–56. Reprinted in Callow AB Jr, Ed. *American Urban History,* Third Edition. New York: Oxford University Press, 1982, pp 534–57.

71. Andrulis D, Shaw-Taylor Y, Ginsberg C, et al. *Urban Social Health: A Chartbook Profiling the Nation's One Hundred Largest Cities.* Washington, DC: The National Public Health and Hospital Institute, 1995.

72. National Advisory Commission on Civil Disorders [Kerner Commission]. *Report of the National Advisory Commission on Civil Disorders.* New York: Dutton, 1968, p 262.

73. Hawkins DR, Rosenbaum S. *Lives in the Balance: A National, State and County Profile of America's Medically Underserved.* Washington, DC: (March) 1992.

74. Greenberg M. American cities: Good and bad news about public health. *Bulletin of the New York Academy of Medicine* 1991;67:17–21; Andrulis DP. *The Urban Health Penalty: New Dimensions and Directions in Inner-City Health*

Care. American College of Physicians Position Paper No.1. Washington, DC, 1997. Available: http://www.acponline.org/hpp/pospaper/andrulis.htm (accessed November 18, 2003).

75. McCord C, Freeman H. Excess mortality in Harlem. *New England Journal of Medicine* 1990;322:173–79.

76. Andrulis DP, Goodman NJ, National Public Health and Hospital Institute. *The Social and Health Landscape of Urban and Suburban America*. Chicago: American Hospital Association Press, 1999, p 243.

77. Link B, Susser E, Stueve A, et al. Lifetime and five-year prevalence of homelessness in the United States. *American Journal of Public Health* 1994;84:1907–12.

78. Ards S, Mincy R. Neighborhood ecology. In: Besharov D, Ed. *When Drug Addicts Have Children*. Washington, DC: Child Welfare League of America, 1994, pp 33–49; Wallace R. Urban desertification, public health and public order: Planned shrinkage, violent death, substance abuse and AIDS in the Bronx. *Social Science Medicine* 1990;31:801–13; Wallace R. Social disintegration and the spread of AIDS-II. Meltdown of sociogeographic structure in urban minority neighborhoods. *Social Science Medicine* 1993;37(7):887–96.

79. For example: Norman JC, Ed. *Medicine in the Ghetto*. New York: Appleton-Century-Crofts, 1969; Ford AB. *Urban Health in America*. New York: Oxford University Press, 1976; Davis E, Millman M, Eds. *Health Care for the Urban Poor: Directions for Policy*. Lanham, MD: Rowman & Littlefield, 1983; Krasner MI, Ed. *Poverty and Health in New York City*. New York: United Hospital Fund of New York, 1989; Fitzpatrick K, LaGory M. *Unhealthy Places: The Ecology of Risk in the Urban Landscape*. New York: Routledge, 2000; Moller DW. *Dancing with Broken Bones: A Portrait of Death and Dying Among Inner-City Poor*. New York: Oxford University Press, 2003.

CHAPTER 4

1. Burns LD, McCormick JB, Borroni-Bird CE. Vehicle of change. *Scientific American* 2002;287(4):64–73.

2. Bullard, Robert. D. *Dumping in Dixie: Race, Class, and Environmental Quality*. Boulder, CO: Westview, 1990.

3. Shi JP, Khan AA, Harrison RM. Measurements of ultrafine particle concentration and size distribution in the urban atmosphere. *Science of the Total Environment* 1999;235:51–64.

4. Bachman W, Sarasua W, Hallmark S, Guensler R. Modeling regional mobile source emissions in a geographic information system framework. *Transportation Research Part C* 2000;8:205–29.

5. Bielaczyc P, Merkisz J. A study of gaseous emissions measured under ambient cold start and warm-up conditions. Fourth International Conference on Urban Transport and Environment for the 21st Century. Wessex Institute of Technology, UK, and the University of Aveiro, Portugal, 1998, pp 491–500.

6. Frank L, Stone B Jr, Bachman W. Linking land use with household vehicle emissions in the central Puget Sound: Methodological framework and findings. *Transportation Research Part D* 2000;5(3):173–96.

7. Brunekreef B, Holgate ST. Air pollution and health. *Lancet* 2002;360: 1233–42.

8. Roemer WH, van Wijnen JH. Daily mortality and air pollution along busy streets in Amsterdam, 1987–1998. *Epidemiology* 2001;12(6):649–53.

9. Fischer PH, Hoek G, van Reeuwijk H, Briggs DJ, Lebret E, van Wijnen JH, et al. Traffic-related differences in outdoor and indoor concentrations of particles and volatile organic compounds in Amsterdam. *Atmospheric Environment* 2000;34:3713–22.

10. Zhu Y, Hinds WC, Kim S, Shen S, Sioutas C. Study of ultrafine particles near a major highway with heavy-duty diesel traffic. *Atmospheric Environment* 2002;36:4323–35; Zhu Y, Hinds WC, Kim S, Sioutas C. Concentration and size distribution of ultrafine particles near a major highway. *Journal of the Air and Waste Management Association* 2002;52:1032–42.

11. Lebret E, Briggs D, van Reeuwijk H, Fischer P, Smallbone K, Harssema H, et al. Small area variations in ambient NO_2 concentrations in four European areas. *Atmospheric Environment* 2000;34:177–85.

12. Rijnders E, Janssen NAH, van Vliet PHN, Brunekreef B. Personal and outdoor nitrogen dioxide concentrations in relation to degree of urbanization and traffic density. *Environmental Health Perspectives* 2001;109(suppl 3): 411–17.

13. Frank L, Engelke P. Air quality and physical activity impacts of the built environment: Regional and micro scale considerations. *International Regional Science Review*, in press.

14. Frank et al., 2000, op. cit.

15. Crane R. Cars and drivers in the new suburbs: Linking access to travel in neotraditional planning. *Journal of the American Planning Association* 1996;62(1):51–63.

16. Bell M, Davis DL. Reassessment of the lethal London fog of 1952: Novel indicators of acute and chronic consequences of acute exposures to air pollution. *Environmental Health Perspectives* 2001;109(3):389–94.

17. Dockery DW, Pope CA, Xu X, Spenger JD, Ware JH, Fay ME, Ferris BG Jr, Speizer FE. An association between air pollution and mortality in six U.S. cities. *New England Journal of Medicine* 1993;329:1753–59.

18. Pope CA, Burnett RT, Thun MJ, Calle EE, Krewski D, Ito K, Thurston GD. Lung cancer, cardiopulmonary mortality, and long-term exposure to fine particulate air pollution. *Journal of the American Medical Association* 2002;287:1132–41.

19. Brunekreef and Holgate, 2002, op. cit.

20. Katsouyanni K, Pershagen G. Ambient air pollution exposure and cancer. *Cancer Causes & Control* 1997;8(3):284–91.

21. Samet J, Zeger S, Dominici F, Curriero F, Coursac I, Dockery D, Schwartz J, Zanobetti A. Morbidity and Mortality from Air Pollution in the United States. Final Report NMMAPS, Health Effects Institute, Boston, 1999. Available: http://www.healtheffects.org/Pubs/Samet2.pdf (accessed December 2, 2003); Samet JM, Dominici F, Curriero FC, Coursac I, Zeger SL. Fine particulate air pollution and mortality in 20 U.S. cities, 1987–1994. *New England Journal of Medicine* 2000;343:1742–49.

22. Shprentz DS, Bryner GC, Shprentz JS. *Breath-Taking: Premature Mortality Due to Particulate Air Pollution in 239 American Cities.* New York: Natural Resources Defense Council, 1996.

23. Brunekreef B. Air pollution and life expectancy: Is there a relation? *Occupational and Environmental Medicine* 1997;54(11):781–84.

24. Thurston GD, Ito K. Epidemiological studies of acute ozone exposures and mortality. *Journal of Exposure Analysis and Environmental Epidemiology* 2001;11:286–94.

25. Zanobetti A, Schwartz J, Samoli E, Gryparis A, Touloumi G, Atkinson R, et al. The temporal pattern of mortality responses to air pollution: A multicity assessment of mortality displacement. *Epidemiology* 2002;13(1):87–93; Dominici F, McDermott A, Zeger SL, Samet JM. Airborne particulate matter and mortality: Timescale effects in four US cities. *American Journal of Epidemiology* 2003;157(12):1055–65.

26. Laden F, Neas LM, Dockery DW, Schwartz J. Association of fine particulate matter from different sources with daily mortality in six U.S. cities. *Environmental Health Perspectives* 2000;108(10):941–47.

27. Hoek G, Brunekreef B, Goldbohm S, Fischer P, van den Brandt PA. Association between mortality and indicators of traffic-related air pollution in the Netherlands: A cohort study. *Lancet* 2002;360(9341):1203–09.

28. Roemer and van Wijnen, 2001, op. cit.

29. Pope CA 3rd. Epidemiology of fine particulate air pollution and human health: Biologic mechanisms and who's at risk? *Environmental Health Perspectives* 2000;108 suppl 4:713–23; Dockery D. Epidemiologic evidence of cardiovascular effects of particulate air pollution. *Environmental Health Perspectives* 2001;109 suppl 4:483–86; Donaldson K, Stone V, Seaton A, MacNee W. Ambient particle inhalation and the cardiovascular system: Potential mechanisms. *Environmental Health Perspectives* 2001;109 suppl 4:523–27.

30. Brunekreef and Holgate, 2002, op. cit; Peden DB. Air pollution in asthma: Effect of pollutants on airway inflammation. *Annals of Allergy, Asthma and Immunology* 2001;87:12–17.

31. Bergamaschi E, De Palma G, Mozzoni P, Vanni S, Vettori MV, Broeckaert F, et al. Polymorphism of quinone-metabolizing enzymes and susceptibility to ozone-induced acute effects. *American Journal of Respiratory and Critical Care Medicine* 2001;163(6):1426–31.

32. Ciccone G, Gruppo collaborativo SIDRIA. Caratteristiche del traffico nei pressi dell'abitazione e danni respiratori in età pediatrica: I risultati di

SIDRIA [Characteristics of traffic near residences and respiratory effects in children: Results from SIDRIA]. *Annali dell'Istituto Superiore di Sanita Sanità* 2000;36(3):305–09; Weiland SK, Mundt KA, Ruckmann A, Keil U. Self-reported wheezing and allergic rhinitis in children and traffic density on street of residence. *Annals of Epidemiology* 1994;4:243–47; Oosterlee A, Drijver M, Lebret E, et al. Chronic respiratory symptoms in children and adults living along streets with high traffic density. *Occupational and Environmental Medicine* 1996;53:241–47; Keil U, Weiland SK, Duhme H, Chambless L. The International Study of Asthma and Allergies in Childhood (ISAAC): Objectives and methods; results from German ISAAC centres concerning traffic density and wheezing and allergic rhinitis. *Toxicology Letters* 1996;86:99–103; Gehring U, Cyrys J, Sedlmeir G, Brunekreef B, Bellander T, et al. Traffic-related air pollution and respiratory health during the first two years of life. *European Respiratory Journal* 2002;19:690–98.

33. Korrick SA, Neas LM, Dockery DW, Gold DR, Allen GA, Hill LB, et al. Effects of ozone and other pollutants on the pulmonary function of adult hikers. *Environmental Health Perspectives* 1998;106(2):93–99.

34. Friedman MS, Powell KE, Hutwagner L, Graham LM, Teague WG. Impact of changes in transportation and commuting behaviors during the 1996 Summer Olympic Games in Atlanta on air quality and childhood asthma. *Journal of the American Medical Association* 2001;285(7):897–905.

35. Gauderman WJ, Gilliland GF, Vora H, Avol E, Stram D, McConnell R, et al. Association between air pollution and lung function growth in southern California children: Results from a second cohort. *American Journal of Respiratory and Critical Care Medicine* 2002;166(1):76–84; Gauderman WJ, McConnell R, Gilliland F, London S, Thomas D, Avol E, et al. Association between air pollution and lung function growth in southern California children. *American Journal of Respiratory and Critical Care Medicine* 2000; 162(4 Pt 1):1383–90.

36. Avol EL, Gauderman WJ, Tan SM, London SJ, Peters JM. Respiratory effects of relocating to areas of differing air pollution levels. *American Journal of Respiratory and Critical Care Medicine* 2001;164:2067–72.

37. Künzli N, Lurmann F, Segal M, Ngo L, Balmes J, Tager IB. Association between lifetime ambient ozone exposure and pulmonary function in college freshmen: Results of a pilot study. *Environmental Research* 1997;72:8–23.

38. McConnell R, Berhane K, Gilliland F, London SJ, Islam T, et al. Asthma in exercising children exposed to ozone: A cohort study. *Lancet* 2002;359: 386–91.

39. Pekkanen J, Peters A, Hoek G, Tiittanen P, Brunekreef B, de Hartog J, et al. Particulate air pollution and risk of ST-segment depression during repeated submaximal exercise tests among subjects with coronary heart disease: The Exposure and Risk Assessment for Fine and Ultrafine Particles in Ambient Air (ULTRA) Study. *Circulation* 2002;106:933–38.

40. Morris RD. Airborne particulates and hospital admissions for cardiovascular disease: A quantitative review of the evidence. *Environmental Health Perspectives* 2001;109 suppl 4:495–500.

41. IARC (International Agency for Research on Cancer). Diesel and Gasoline Engine Exhausts and Some Nitroarenes. *IARC Monographs on the Evaluation of Carcinogenic Risks to Humans, Volume 46.* Lyon: IARC, 1989.

42. IARC (International Agency for Research on Cancer). Re-evaluation of Some Organic Chemicals, Hydrazine and Hydrogen Peroxide. *IARC Monographs on the Evaluation of Carcinogenic Risks to Humans, Volume 71.* Lyon: IARC, 1999.

43. IARC (International Agency for Research on Cancer). Wood Dust and Formaldehyde. *IARC Monographs on the Evaluation of Carcinogenic Risks to Humans, Volume 62.* Lyon: IARC, 1995.

44. Cohen AJ. Outdoor air pollution and lung cancer. *Environmental Health Perspectives* 2000;108 suppl 4:743–50; Katsouyanni and Pershagen, 1997, op. cit.

45. Pope et al., 2002, op. cit.

46. Ritz B, Yu F, Fruin S, Chapa G, Shaw GM, Harris JA. Ambient air pollution and risk of birth defects in Southern California. *American Journal of Epidemiology* 2002;155:17–25.

CHAPTER 5

1. Macera CA, Jones DA, Yore MM, Ham SA, Kohl HW, Kimsey CD, Buchner D. Prevalence of physical activity, including lifestyle activities among adults—United States, 2000–2001. *Morbidity and Mortality Weekly Report* 2003;52(32):764–69.

2. Duke J, Huhman M, Heitzler C. Physical activity levels among children aged 9–13 years—United States, 2002. *Morbidity and Mortality Weekly Report* 2003;52(33):785–88.

3. Sallis JF, Owen N. *Physical Activity and Behavioral Medicine.* Thousand Oaks, CA: Sage Publications, 1999.

4. Frank LD, Engelke PE, Schmid TL. *Health and Community Design: The Impacts of the Built Environment on Physical Activity.* Washington, DC: Island Press, 2003.

5. Ainsworth BE, Haskell WL, Leon AS, et al. Compendium of physical activities: Classification of energy costs of human physical activities. *Medicine and Science in Sports and Exercise* 1993;25:71–80; Centers for Disease Control (CDC) and Prevention. *Physical Activity and Health: A Report of the Surgeon General.* Centers for Disease Control and Prevention, National Center for Chronic Disease Prevention and Health Promotion, 1996.

6. Pate RR, Pratt M, Blair SN, Haskell WL, Macera CA, Bouchard C, et al. Physical activity and public health: A recommendation from the Centers for Disease Control and Prevention and the American College of Sports Medicine. *Journal of the American Medical Association* 1995;273:402–07; CDC, 1996, op. cit.

7. Institute of Medicine, Food and Nutrition Board. *Dietary Reference Intakes for Energy, Carbohydrate, Fiber, Fat, Fatty Acids, Cholesterol, Protein, and Amino Acids (Macronutrients).* Washington, DC: National Academy Press, 2002.

8. Manson JE, Greenland P, LaCroix AZ, Stefanick ML, Mouton CP, Ober-man A, et al. Walking compared with vigorous exercise for the prevention of cardiovascular events in women. *New England Journal of Medicine* 2002;347(10):716–25.

9. Eyler AA, Baker E, Cromer L, King AC, Brownson RC, Donatelle RJ. Physical activity and minority women: A qualitative study. *Health Education and Behavior* 1998;25:640–52; King AC, Rejeski WJ, Buchner DM. Physical activity interventions targeting older adults: A critical review and recom-mendations. *American Journal of Preventive Medicine* 1998;15:316–33; Rans-dell LB, Wells CL. Physical activity in urban White, African-American, and Mexican-American women. *Medicine and Science in Sports and Exercise* 1998;30:1608–15; Taylor WC, Baranowski T, Young DR. Physical activity interventions in low-income, ethnic minority, and populations with disabili-ty. *American Journal of Preventive Medicine* 1998;15:334–43; King AC, Cas-tro C, Wilcox S, Eyler AA, Sallis JF, Brownson RC. Personal and environ-mental factors associated with physical inactivity among different racial-ethnic groups of US middle-aged and older aged adults. *Health Psy-chology* 2000;19:354–64; Booth MN, Owen A, Bauman A, Clavisi O, Leslie E. Social-cognitive and perceived environmental influences associated with physical activity in older Australians. *Preventive Medicine* 2000;31:15–22; Richter DL, Wilcox S, Greaney ML, Henderson KA, Ainsworth BE. Envi-ronmental, policy, and cultural factors related to physical activity in African American women. *Women & Health* 2002;36(2):91–109; Henderson KA, Ainsworth BE. A synthesis of perceptions about physical activity among older African American and American Indian women. *American Journal of Public Health* 2003;93(2):313–17; Crespo CJ, Smit E, Andersen RE, Carter-Pokras O, Ainsworth BE. Race/ethnicity, social class and their relation to physical inactivity during leisure time: Results from the Third National Health and Nutrition Examination Survey, 1988–1994. *American Journal of Preventive Medicine* 2000;18(1):46–53; Eyler AA, Brownson RC, Donatelle RJ, King AC, Brown D, Sallis JF. Physical activity social support and middle- and older-aged minority women: Results from a US survey. *Social Science & Medicine* 1999;49(6):781–89.

10. CDC, 1996, op. cit; National Institutes of Health Consensus Development Panel on Physical Activity and Cardiovascular Health. NIH Consensus Conference: Physical activity and cardiovascular health. *Journal of the American Medical Association* 1996;276:241–46; Wannamethee SG, Shaper AG, Walker M, Ebrahim S. Lifestyle and 15-year survival free of heart attack, stroke, and diabetes in middle-aged British men. *Archives of Internal Medicine* 1998;158(22):2433–40; Wannamethee SG, Shaper AG. Physical activity and the prevention of stroke. *Journal of Cardiovascular Risk* 1999;6(4):213–16; Pate et al., 1995, op. cit.

11. Lee IM, Paffenbarger RS Jr. Associations of light, moderate, and vigorous intensity physical activity with longevity. The Harvard Alumni Health Study. *American Journal of Epidemiology* 2000;151:293–99; Wannamethee SG, Shaper AG, Walker M. Changes in physical activity, mortality and incidence of coronary heart disease in older men. *Lancet* 1998;351:1603–08.

12. Wei M, Kampert JB, Barlow CE, Nichaman MZ, Gibbons LW, Paffen-barger RS, Blair SN. Relationship between low cardiorespiratory fitness and mortality in normal-weight, overweight, and obese men. *Journal of the American Medical Association* 1999;282:1547–53.

13. Sesso HD, Paffenbarger RS, Ha T, Lee IM. Physical activity and cardiovas-cular disease risk in middle-aged and older women. *American Journal of Epi-demiolology* 1999;150(4):408–16.

14. Wei et al., 1999, op. cit; Blair SN, Kampert JB, Kohl HW III, et al. Influ-ences of cardiorespiratory fitness and other precursors on cardiovascular disease and all-cause mortality in men and women. *Journal of the American Medical Association* 1996;276:205–10.

15. Kohl HW III, Gordon NF, Villegas JA, Blair SN. Cardiorespiratory fitness, glycemic status, and mortality risk in men. *Diabetes Care* 1992;15:184–92.

16. Kampert JB, Blair SN, Barlow CE, Kohl HW III. Physical activity, physical fitness, and all-cause and cancer mortality: A prospective study of men and women. *Annals of Epidemiology* 1996;6:452–57; Lee IM, Sesso HD, Paffen-barger RS Jr. Physical activity and risk of lung cancer. *International Journal of Epidemiology* 1999;28:620–25; Slattery ML, Edwards SL, Boucher KM, Anderson K, Caan BJ. Lifestyle and colon cancer: An assessment of factors associated with risk. *American Journal of Epidemiology* 1999;150:869–77; Thune I, Brenn T, Lund E, Gaard M. Physical activity and the risk of breast cancer. *New England Journal of Medicine* 1997;336(18):1269–75; Sesso HD, Paffenbarger RS Jr, Lee IM. Physical activity and breast cancer risk in the College Alumni Health Study (United States). *Cancer Causes & Control* 1998;9:433–39; Oliveria SA, Christos PJ. The epidemiology of physical activity and cancer. *Annals of the New York Academy of Sciences* 1997;833:79–90.

17. Yaffe K, Barnes D, Nevitt M, Lui L-Y, Covinsky K. A prospective study of physical activity and cognitive decline in elderly women: Women who walk. *Archives of Internal Medicine* 2001;161(14):1703–08.

18. Brosse AL, Sheets ES, Lett HS, Blumenthal JA. Exercise and the treatment of clinical depression in adults: Recent findings and future directions. *Sports Medicine* 2002;32(12):741–60; Dunn AL, Trivedi MH, O'Neal HA. Physical activity dose-response effects on outcomes of depression and anxiety. *Medi-cine & Science in Sports & Exercise.* 2001;33(6 Suppl):S587–97; Strawbridge WJ, Deleger S, Roberts RE, Kaplan GA. Physical activity reduces the risk of subsequent depression for older adults. *American Journal of Epidemiology* 2002;156(4):328–34.

19. Bonaiuti D, Shea B, Iovine R, Negrini S, Robinson V, Kemper HC, Wells G, Tugwell P, Cranney A. Exercise for preventing and treating osteoporosis in postmenopausal women (Cochrane Methodology Review). In: *The Cochrane Library*, Issue 4, 2003. Chichester, UK: John Wiley & Sons, Ltd.

20. Nestle M. *Food Politics: How the Food Industry Influences Nutrition and Health.* Berkeley: University of California Press, 2002; Schell ER. *The Hungry Gene: The Science of Fat and the Future of Thin.* New York: Atlantic Monthly Press, 2002; Critser G. *Fat Land: How Americans Became the Fattest People in*

the World. Boston: Houghton Mifflin, 2003; Brownell KD, Horgen KB. *Food Fight: The Inside Story of the Food Industry, America's Obesity Crisis, and What We Can Do About It.* New York: McGraw-Hill, 2003.

21. Prentice AM, Jebb SA. Obesity in Britain: Gluttony or sloth? *British Medical Journal* 1995;311:437–39.

22. Kuczmarski RJ, Flegal KM, Campbell SM, Johnson CL. Increasing prevalence of overweight among US adults. The National Health and Nutrition Examination Surveys, 1960 to 1991. *Journal of the American Medical Association* 1994;272:205–11.

23. Flegal KM, Carroll MD, Kuczmarksi RJ, Johnson CL. Overweight and obesity in the United States: Prevalence and trends, 1960–1994. *International Journal of Obesity Related Metabolic Disorders* 1998;22:39–47.

24. Mokdad AH, Serdula MK, Dietz WH, Bowman BA, Marks JM, Koplan JP. The spread of the obesity epidemic in the United States, 1991–1998. *Journal of the American Medical Association* 1999;282:1519–22; Mokdad AH, Bowman BA, Ford ES, et al. The continuing epidemics of obesity and diabetes in the United States. *Journal of the American Medical Association* 2001;286(10):1195–1200.

25. Mokdad AH, Ford ES, Bowman BA, Dietz WH, Vinicor F, Bales VS, Marks JS. Prevalence of obesity, diabetes, and obesity-related health risk factors, 2001. *Journal of the American Medical Association* 2003;289(1): 76–79.

26. Willett WC, Dietz WH, Colditz GA. Guidelines for healthy weight. *New England Journal of Medicine* 1999;341:427–34; Must A, Spadano J, Coakley EH, Field AE, Colditz G, Dietz WH. The disease burden associated with overweight and obesity. *Journal of the American Medical Association* 1999; 282:1523–29.

27. Stevens J, Plankey MW, Williamson DF, et al. The body mass index–mortality relationship in white and African American women. *Obesity Research* 1998;6:268–77; Calle EE, Thun MJ, Petrelli JM, Rodriguez C, Heath CW Jr. Body-mass index and mortality in a prospective cohort of U.S. adults. *New England Journal of Medicine* 1999;341:1097–1105.

28. Allison DB, Fontaine KR, Manson JE, Stevens J, VanItallie TB. Annual deaths attributable to obesity in the United States. *Journal of the American Medical Association* 1999;282:1530–38.

29. Chen Y, Dales R, Tang M, et al. Obesity may increase the incidence of asthma in women but not in men: Longitudinal observations from the Canadian National Population Health Surveys. *American Journal of Epidemiology* 2002;155:191–97.

30. Mokdad et al., 2003, op cit; Must et al., 1999, op cit.

31. Hu FB, Manson JE, Stampfer MJ, Colditz G, Liu S, Solomon CG, Willet WC. Diet lifestyle, and the risk of type 2 diabetes mellitus in women. *New England Journal of Medicine* 2001;345(11):790–97.

32. Mokdad et al., 2003, op cit.

33. Calle EE, Rodriguez C, Walker-Thurmond K, Thun MJ. Overweight, obesity, and mortality from cancer in a prospectively studied cohort of U.S. adults. *New England Journal of Medicine* 2003;348:1625–38.

34. Stunkard AJ, Faith MS, Allison KC. Depression and obesity. *Biological Psychiatry* 2003;54(3):330–37.

35. Frankston J. Health pros link sprawl with spread. Suburbs, obesity stir debate. *Atlanta Journal-Constitution*, 17 November 2003, p F1.

36. Saelens B, Sallis J, Frank L. Environmental correlates of walking and cycling: Findings from the transportation, urban design, and planning literatures. *Annals of Behavioral Medicine* 2003;25(2):80–91; Humpel N, Owen N, Leslie E. Environmental factors associated with adults' participation in physical activity: A review. *American Journal of Preventive Medicine* 2002;22(3):188–99; Trost SG, Owen N, Bauman AE, Sallis JF, Brown W. Correlates of adults' participation in physical activity: Review and update. *Med Sci Sports Med* 2002;34(12):1996–2001; Handy S, Boarnet M, Ewing R, Killingsworth R. How the built environment affects physical activity: Views from urban planning. *American Journal of Preventive Medicine* 2002;23(2S): 64–73; French SA, Story M, Jeffery RW. Environmental influences on eating and physical activity. *Ann Rev Public Health* 2001;22:309–35; Kahn EB, Ramsey LT, Brownson RC, Heath GW, Howze EH, Powell KE, et al. The effectiveness of interventions to increase physical activity: A systematic review. *American Journal of Preventive Medicine* 2002;22(4S):73–107; Sallis JF, Bauman A, Pratt M. Physical activity interventions: Environmental and policy interventions to promote physical activity. *American Journal of Preventive Medicine* 1998;15(4):379–97.

37. Frank et al., 2003, op. cit.

38. Pikora T, Giles-Corti B, Bull F, Jamrozik K, Donovan R. Developing a framework for assessment of the environmental determinants of walking and cycling. *Social Science & Medicine* 2003;56:1693–1703.

39. Cook J, Adams BB, Breukelman F, Mitchell C, Steiner B, Costello N, et al. Self-reported physical inactivity by degree of urbanization—United States, 1996. *Morbidity and Mortality Weekly Report* 1998;47(50):1097–1100; Wilcox S, Castro C, King AC, Housemann R, Brownson RC. Determinants of leisure time physical activity in rural compared with urban older and ethnically diverse women in the United States. *Journal of Epidemiology and Community Health* 2000;54:667–72.

40. Saelens BE, Sallis JF, Black JB, Chen D. Neighborhood-based differences in physical activity: An environment scale evaluation. *Am J Public Health* 2003;93(9):1552–58.

41. Ibid.

42. Frank et al., 2003, op. cit.

43. Ewing R, Schmid T, Killingsworth R, Zlot A, Raudenhush S. Relationship between urban sprawl and physical activity, obesity, and morbidity. *American Journal of Health Promotion* 2003;18(1):47–57.

44. Huston SL, Evenson KR, Bors P, Gizlice Z. Neighborhood environment, access to places for activity, and leisure-time physical activity in a diverse North Carolina population. *American Journal of Health Promotion* 2003;18(1):58–69.

45. Berrigan D, Troiano RP. The association between urban form and physical activity in U.S. adults. *American Journal of Preventive Medicine* 2002;23(2S):74–79.

46. Ross CL, Dunning AE. *Land Use Transportation Interaction: An Examination of the 1995 NPTS Data.* Atlanta: USDOT, Federal Highway Administration, 1997. Available: http://npts.ornl.gov/npts/1995/Doc/landuse3.pdf.

47. Frank and Pivo, 1995, op. cit.

48. Kockelman KM. Travel behavior as function of accessibility, land use mixing, and land use balance: Evidence from San Francisco Bay Area. *Transportation Research Record* 1997;1607:116–25.

49. Craig CL, Brownson RC, Cragg SE, Dunn AL. Exploring the effect of the environment on physical activity: A study examining walking to work. *American Journal of Preventive Medicine* 2002;23(2S):36–43.

50. Powell KE, Martin LM, Chowdhury PP. Places to walk: Convenience and regular physical activity. *American Journal of Public Health* 2003;93(9):1519–21.

51. Booth et al., 2000, op. cit; Huston et al., 2003, op. cit.

52. Troped PJ, Saunders RP, Pate RR, Reininger B, Ureda JR, Thompson SJ. Associations between self-reported and objective physical environmental factors and use of a community rail-trail. *Preventive Medicine* 2001;32:191–200.

53. Giles-Corti B, Donovan RJ. The relative influence of individual, social and physical environment determinants of physical activity. *Social Science & Medicine* 2002;54:1793–1812.

54. King et al., 2000, op. cit; Wilcox et al., 2000, op. cit.

55. Wilcox et al., 2000, op. cit; King et al., 2000, op. cit.

56. Ball K, Bauman A, Leslie E, Owen N. Perceived environmental and social influences on walking for exercise in Australian adults. *Preventive Medicine* 2001;33:434–40.

57. Pretty J, Griffin M, Sellens M, Pretty C. *Green Exercise: Complementary Roles of Nature, Exercise and Diet in Physical and Emotional Well-Being and Implications for Public Health Policy.* CES Occasional Paper 2003-1, University of Essex, March 2003. Available: http://www2.essex.ac.uk/ces/ResearchProgrammes/CESOccasionalPapers/GreenExercise.pdf; Bodin M, Hartig T. Does the outdoor environment matter for psychological restoration gained through running? *Psychology of Sport and Exercise* 2003;4:141–53.

58. Booth et al., 2000, op. cit.

59. King et al., 2000, op. cit.

60. Weinstein A, Feigley P, Pullen P, Mann L, Redman L. Neighborhood safety and the prevalence of physical inactivity—Selected states, 1996. *Morbidity and Mortality Weekly Report* 1999;48(07):143–46.

61. Booth et al., 2000, op. cit.

62. Wilcox et al., 2000, op. cit.

63. Sallis and Owen, 1999, op. cit.

64. Lewis BA, Marcus BH, Pate RR, Dunn AL. Psychosocial mediators of physical activity behavior among adults and children. *American Journal of Preventive Medicine* 2002;23(2S):26–35.

65. Task Force on Community Preventive Services. Recommendations to increase physical activity in communities. *American Journal of Preventive Medicine* 2002;22(4S):67–72.

66. Frank L, Pivo G. Impacts of mixed use and density on utilization of three modes of travel: Single occupant vehicle, transit and walking. *Transportation Research Record* 1995;1466:44–52

67. Untermann RK. Accommodating the pedestrian: Adapting towns and neighborhoods for walking and bicycling. In: *Personal Travel in the US, Volume II. A Report of Findings from 1983–1984 NPTS, Source Control Programs.* Washington, DC: US DOT, 1990.

68. Barber G. Aggregate characteristics of urban travel. In: Hanson S, Ed. *The Geography of Urban Transportation.* New York: The Guilford Press, 1986, pp 73–90.

69. Ewing et al., 2003, op. cit.

70. Southworth M. Walkable suburbs? An evaluation of neotraditional communities at the urban edge. *Journal of the American Planning Association* 1997; 63:28–44.

71. Krizek KJ. Pretest-posttest strategy for researching neighborhood-scale urban form and travel behavior. *Transportation Research Record* 2000;1722: 48–55.

CHAPTER 6

1. Roberts I. Why have child pedestrian death rates fallen? *British Medical Journal* 1993;306:1737–39.

2. National Highway Traffic Safety Administration (US), National Center for Statistics and Analysis. *Traffic safety facts 2001: A compilation of motor vehicle crash data from the Fatality Analysis Reporting System and the General Estimates System.* DOT HS 809 484. Washington, DC: NHTSA, 2002. Available: http://www-nrd.nhtsa.dot.gov/pdf/nrd-30/NCSA/TSFAnn/TSF2001.pdf (accessed December 4, 2003).

3. Centers for Disease Control and Prevention (CDC). Motor-vehicle safety: A 20th century public health achievement. *Morbidity and Mortality Weekly Report* 1999;48:369–74.

4. Halperin K. A comparative analysis of six methods for calculating travel fatality risk. *Risk: Health, Safety Environment* 1993;4:15–33. Available: http://www.piercelaw.edu/risk/vol4/winter/halperin.htm (accessed December 4, 2003).

5. National Safety Council. What Are the Odds of Dying? Available: http://www.nsc.org/lrs/statinfo/odds.htm (accessed December 4, 2003).

6. Peterson TD, Jolly BT, Runge JW, Hunt RC. Motor vehicle safety: Current concepts and challenges for emergency physicians. *Annals of Emergency Medicine* 1999;34:384–93.

7. Lourens PF, Vissers JA, Jessurum M. Annual mileage, driving violations, and accident involvement in relation to drivers' sex, age, and level of education. *Accident Analysis and Prevention* 1999;31:593–97.

8. Philip P, Ghorayeb I, Stoohs R, Menny JC, Dabadie P, Bioulac B, Guilleminault C. Determinants of sleepiness in automobile drivers. *Journal of Psychosomatic Research* 1996;41:279–88.

9. Philip P, Taillard J, Guilleminault C, Quera Salva MA, Bioulac B, Ohayon M. Long distance driving and self-induced sleep deprivation among automobile drivers. *Sleep* 1999;22:475–80.

10. Pack AM, Cucchiara A, Schwab CW, Rodgman E, Pack AI. Characteristics of accidents attributed to the driver having fallen asleep. *Sleep Research* 1994;23:141; Horne JA, Reyner LA. Sleep related vehicle accidents. *British Medical Journal* 1995;4:565–67.

11. Crawford JA. Extent and Effects of Handheld Cellular Telephone Use While Driving. Research Report SWUTC/01/167706-1. Texas Transportation Institute, February 2001. Available: http://swutc.tamu.edu/Reports/167706-1.pdf (accessed December 4, 2003).

12. Lissy KS, Cohen JT, Park MY, Graham JD. *Cellular Phone Use While Driving: Risks and Benefits.* Boston: Harvard Center for Risk Analysis, 2000.

13. Strayer DL, Johnston WA. Driven to distraction: Dual-task studies of simulated driving and conversing on a cellular phone. *Psychological Science* 2001;12(6). Available: http://www.psych.utah.edu/AppliedCognitionLab/PS-Reprint.pdf (accessed December 4, 2003); Strayer DL, Drews FA, Johnston WA. Cell phone–induced failures of visual attention during simulated driving. *Journal of Experimental Psychology: Applied* 2003;9(1):23–32.

14. Violanti JM. Cellular phones and traffic accidents. *Public Health* 1997;111(6):423–28; Violanti JM. Cellular phones and fatal traffic collisions. *Accident Analysis and Prevention* 1998;30(4):519–24; Redelmeier DA, Tibshirani RJ. Association between cellular-telephone calls and motor vehicle collisions. *New England Journal of Medicine* 1997;336(7):453–58.

15. Ossenbruggen PJ, Pendharkar J, Ivan J. Roadway safety in rural and small urbanized areas. *Accident Analysis and Prevention* 2001;33:485–98.

16. Troy P, Ed. *The Perils of Urban Consolidation.* Sydney: Federation, 1996.

17. Jenks M, Burton E, Williams K, Eds. *The Compact City: A Sustainable Urban Form?* London: E&FN Spon, 1996; Rydin Y. Environmental dimensions of residential development and the implications for local planning practice. *Journal of Environmental Planning Management* 1992;35:43–61.

18. Swift P, Painter D, Goldstein M. Residential street typology and injury accident frequency. Report by Swift Associates, Longmont CO, 1998. Available: http://www.fivepts.com/streetutah.htm (accessed December 4, 2003).

19. National Highway Traffic Safety Administration, 2002, op. cit.

20. Ibid.

21. Ibid.

22. Ewing R, Schieber RA, Zegeer CV. Urban sprawl as a risk factor in motor vehicle occupant and pedestrian fatalities. *American Journal of Public Health* 2003;93(9):1541–45.

23. Cubbin C, LeClerc FB, Smith GS. Socioeconomic status and the occurrence of fatal and nonfatal injury in the United States. *American Journal of Public Health* 2000;90:70–77.

24. Anonymous. Mall accused of racism in a wrongful death trial in Buffalo. *New York Times* 15 November 1999, p B4; Chen D. Remembering Cynthia Wiggins: A lesson in transportation and community revitalization. *Environmental Action* 1996;28(1/2):31–32

25. Cohen BA, Wiles R, Campbell C, Chen D, Kruse J, Corless J. *Mean Streets: Pedestrian Safety and Reform of the Nation's Transportation Law.* Washington, DC: Surface Transportation Policy Project and Environmental Working Group; 1997. Also available: http://www.ewg.org/pub/home/reports/meanstreets/mean.html (accessed December 4, 2003); McCann B, DeLille B. *Mean Streets 2000: Pedestrian Safety, Health and Federal Transportation Spending.* Washington, DC: Surface Transportation Policy Project; 2000.

26. Pucher J, Dijkstra L. Promoting safe walking and cycling to improve public health: Lessons from the Netherlands and Germany. *American Journal of Public Health* 2003;93:1509–16.

27. Hanzlick R, McGowan D, Havlak J, Bishop M, Bennett H, Rawlins R, et al. Pedestrian fatalities—Cobb, DeKalb, Fulton, and Gwinnett Counties, Georgia, 1994–98. *Morbidity and Mortality Weekly Report* 1999;48:601–05.

28. National Highway Traffic Safety Administration, 2002, op. cit.

29. Roberts, 1993, op. cit.

30. Hillman M, Adams J, Whitelegg J. *One False Move: A Study of Children's Independent Mobility.* London: Policy Studies Institute, 1991; Roberts, 1993, op. cit.

31. Dellinger AM, Staunton CE. Barriers to children walking and biking to school—United States, 1999. *Morbidity and Mortality Weekly Report* 2002;51(32):701–04.

32. Macpherson A, Roberts I, Pless IB. Children's exposure to traffic and pedestrian injuries. *American Journal of Public Health* 1998;88:1840–43.

33. Roberts I, Marshall R, Norton R. Child pedestrian mortality and traffic volume in New Zealand. *British Medical Journal* 1992;305:283.

34. Roberts I, Crombie I. Child pedestrian deaths: Sensitivity to traffic volume—evidence from the USA. *Journal of Epidemiology and Community Health* 1995;49(2):186–88.

35. Posner JC, Liao E, Winston FK, Cnaan A, Shaw KN, Durbin DR. Exposure to traffic among urban children injured as pedestrians. *Injury Prevention* 2002;8(3):231–35.

36. Retting RA, Ferguson SA, McCartt AT. A review of evidence-based traffic engineering measures designed to reduce pedestrian–motor vehicle crashes. *American Journal of Public Health* 2003;93:1456–63.

37. Pucher and Dijkstra, 2003, op. cit.

38. Ibid.

39. Shaw, Gordon R. Impact of residential street standards on neo-traditional neighborhood concepts. *Institute of Transportation Engineers Journal* 1994 (July):30–33; Sarkar S, Nederveen AAJ, Pols A. Renewed commitment to traffic calming for pedestrian safety. *Transportation Research Record* 1997;1578:11–19; Bunn F, Collier T, Frost C, Ker K, Roberts I, Wentz R. Area-wide traffic calming for preventing traffic related injuries. *Cochrane Database of Systematic Reviews* 2003;1:CD003110; Elvik R. Area-wide urban traffic calming schemes: A meta-analysis of safety effects. *Accident Analysis and Prevention* 2001;33(3):327–36.

40. Quinn C. DOT to look at risks, benefits of tree-lined sidewalks. *Atlanta Journal-Constitution*, 27 January 2003, p B2.

41. Koepsell T, McCloskey L, Wolf M, Moudon AV, Buchner D, Kraus J, Patterson M. Crosswalk markings and the risk of pedestrian-motor vehicle collisions in older pedestrians. *Journal of the American Medical Association* 2002;288(17):2136–43.

42. Retting et al., 2003, op. cit.

43. Pucher J, Dijkstra L. Making walking and cycling safer: Lessons from Europe. *Transportation Quarterly* 2000;54(3):25–51.

44. Ekman L. On the treatment of traffic safety analysis—a non-parametric approach applied on vulnerable road users. Bulletin 136. Lund, Sweden: Department of Technology and Society, Lund Institute of Technology, 1996.

45. Leden L. Pedestrian risk decreases with pedestrian flow. A case study based on data from signalized intersections in Hamilton, Ontario. *Accident Analysis and Prevention* 2002;34:457–64.

46. Jacobsen PL. Safety in numbers: More walkers and bicyclists, safer walking and bicycling. *Injury Prevention* 2003;9:205–09.

47. Stutts JC, Hunter W. Injuries to Pedestrians and Bicyclists: An Analysis Based on Hospital Emergency Department Data. U.S. Department of Transportation Publication No. FHWA-RD-99-078. 1999.

48. Pless IB, Verreault R, Arsenault L, Frappier J, Stulginskas J. The epidemiology of road accidents in childhood. *American Journal of Public Health* 1987; 77:358–60; Dougherty G, Pless IB, Wilkins R. Social class and the occurrence of traffic injuries and deaths in urban children. *Canadian Journal of Public Health* 1990;81:204–09; Roberts I, Marshall R, Norton R, Borman B. An area analysis of child injury morbidity in Auckland. *Journal of Pediatrics and Child Health* 1992;28:438–41; Preston B. Statistical analysis of child pedestrian accidents in Manchester and Salford. *Accident Analysis and Prevention* 1972;4:323–32; Kendrick D. Prevention of pedestrian accidents. *Archives of Diseases of Childhood* 1993;68:669–72; Rivara FP, Barber M.

Demographic analysis of child pedestrian injuries. *Pediatrics* 1985;76:375–81; Braddock M, Papidus G, Gregorio D, et al. Population, income and ecological correlates of child pedestrian injury. *Pediatrics* 1991;88:1242–44; Bagley C. The urban setting of juvenile pedestrian injuries: A study of behavioral ecology and social disadvantage. *Accident Analysis and Prevention* 1992;24:673–78.

49. Pless IB, Verreault R, Tenina S. A case-control study of pedestrian and bicyclist injuries in childhood. *American Journal of Public Health* 1989;79:995–98.

50. Durkin MS, Laraque D, Lubman I, Barlow B. Epidemiology and prevention of traffic injuries to urban children and adolescents. *Pediatrics* 1999;103(6):1273–74.

51. Malizia E, Exline S. *Consumer Preferences for Residential Development Alternatives.* Working Paper 2000–02, University of North Carolina Center for Urban and Regional Studies, February 2000. Available from UNC Center for Urban and Regional Studies, Campus Box 3410, UNC Chapel Hill, Chapel Hill, NC 27599-3410.

52. Myers D, Gearin E. Current preferences and future demand for denser residential environments. *Housing Policy Debate* 2001;12(4):633–59.

53. Lucy WH. Mortality risk associated with leaving home: Recognizing the relevance of the built environment. *American Journal of Public Health* 2003;93(9):1564–69.

54. Ibid., p 1568.

55. Ibid., p 1564.

CHAPTER 7

1. McKeown, T. *The Role of Medicine: Dream, Mirage, or Nemesis?* Princeton: Princeton University Press, 1979; Okun DA. From cholera to cancer to cryptosporidiosis. *Journal of Environmental Engineering* 1996;122(6):453–58; Melosi M. *Effluent America: Cities, Industry, Energy, and the Environment.* Pittsburgh: University of Pittsburgh Press, 2001.

2. United Nations Environment Programme, United Nations Children's Fund, and World Health Organization. *Children in the New Millennium: Environmental Impact on Health.* Geneva, 2002.

3. Barwick RS, Levy DA, Craun GF, Beach MJ, Calderon RL. Surveillance for waterborne-disease outbreaks—United States, 1997–1998. *Morbidity and Mortality Weekly Report* 2000;49(SS-4):1–35; Lee SH, Levy DA, Craun GF, Beach MJ, Calderon RL. Surveillance for waterborne-disease outbreaks—United States, 1999–2000. *Morbidity and Mortality Weekly Report* 2002;51(SS-8):1–28; Craun GF, Nwachuku N, Calderon RL, Craun MF. Outbreaks in drinking-water systems, 1991–1998. *Journal of Environmental Health* 2002;65(1):16–23.

4. Garthright WE, Archer DL, Kvenberg JE. Estimates of incidence and costs of intestinal infectious diseases in the United States. *Public Health Reports*

1988;103:107–15; Frost FJ, Craun GF, Calderon RL. Waterborne disease surveillance. *Journal of the American Water Works Association* 1996;88(9): 66–75; Levin RB, Epstein PR, Ford TE, Harrington W, Olson E, Reichard EG. U.S. drinking water challenges in the twenty-first century. *Environmental Health Perspectives* 2002;110(1):43–52; Frost FJ, Muller T, Craun GF, Fraser D, Thompson D, Notenboom R, Calderon RL. Serological analysis of a cryptosporidiosis epidemic. *International Journal of Epidemiology* 2000;29(2):376–79.

5. Garthright et al., 1988, op. cit.

6. Chute CG, Smith RP, Baron JA. Risk factors for endemic giardiasis. *American Journal of Public Health* 1987;77:585–87; Payment P, Richardson L, Siemiatycki J, Dewar R, Edwardes M, Franco E. A randomized trial to evaluate the risk of gastrointestinal disease due to consumption of drinking water meeting current microbiological standards. *American Journal of Public Health* 1991;81:703–08; Levin et al., 2002, op. cit.; Garthright et al., 1988, op. cit.

7. Parashar UD, Holman RC, Clarke MJ, Bresee JS, Glass RI. Hospitalizations associated with rotavirus diarrhea in the United States, 1993 through 1995: Surveillance based on the new ICD-9-CM rotavirus specific diagnostic code. *Journal of Infectious Diseases* 1998;177:7–13.

8. Kramer MH, Herwaldt BL, Craun GF, Calderon RL, Juranek DD. Surveillance for waterborne-disease outbreaks—United States, 1993–1994. *Morbidity and Mortality Weekly Report* 1996;45(1):1–33; MacKenzie W, Hoxie N, Proctor M, Gradus M, Blair K, Peterson D. A massive outbreak in Milwaukee of *Cryptosporidium* infection transmitted through public water supply. *New England Journal of Medicine* 1994;331:161–67.

9. Hoxie NJ, Davis JP, Vergeront JM, Nashold RD, Blair KA. Cryptosporidiosis-associated mortality following a massive waterborne outbreak in Milwaukee, Wisconsin. *American Journal of Public Health* 1997;87:2032–35.

10. Craun GF. Waterborne disease outbreaks in the United States of America: Causes and prevention. *World Health Statistics Quarterly* 1992;45:192–99; Rose JB, Epstein PR, Lipp EK, Sherman BH, Bernard SM, Patz JA. Climate variability and change in the United States: Potential impacts on water- and foodborne diseases caused by microbiologic agents. *Environ Health Perspectives* 2001;109(2):211–21.

11. Schwartz J, Levin R, Hodge K. Drinking water turbidity and pediatric hospital use for gastrointestinal illness in Philadelphia. *Epidemiology* 1997;8: 615–20; Schwartz J, Levin R, Goldstein R. Drinking water turbidity and gastrointestinal illness in the elderly of Philadelphia. *Journal of Epidemiology and Community Health* 2000;54:45–51; Goldstein ST, Juranek DD, Ravenholt O, et al. Cryptosporidiosis: An outbreak associated with drinking water despite state-of-the-art water treatment. *Annals of Internal Medicine* 1996;124:459–68.

12. Morris RD, Naumova EN, Levin R, Munasinghe RL. Temporal variation in drinking water turbidity and diagnosed gastroenteritis in Milwaukee. *American Journal of Public Health* 1996;86:237–39.

13. Cantor KP. Drinking water and cancer. *Cancer Causes Control* 1997;8(3): 292–308; Bove F, Shim Y, Zeitz P. Drinking water contaminants and adverse pregnancy outcomes: A review. *Environmental Health Perspectives* 2002;110(1):61–74; Environmental Working Group. *Consider the Source: Farm Runoff, Chlorination Byproducts, and Human Health.* Washington, DC: Environmental Working Group, 2002.

14. Levin et al., 2002, op. cit.

15. Snyder D. A new direction in water law: Frederick ordinance resembles western U.S. approach. *Washington Post*, 23 September 2002, p B1.

16. Shelton S. Water war now headed to federal courts. *Atlanta Journal-Constitution*, 2 September 2003, p 1.

17. Alley WM, Healy RW, LaBaugh JW, Reilly TE. Flow and storage in groundwater systems. *Science* 2002;296(5575):1985–90.

18. Solley WB, Pierce RR, Perlman HA. *Estimated Use of Water in the United States in 1995.* Reston, VA: US Geological Survey, 1998. Circular 1200.

19. Schreiber ME, Simo JA, Freiberg PG. Stratigraphic and geochemical controls on naturally occurring arsenic in groundwater, eastern Wisconsin, USA. *Hydrogeology Journal* 2000;8:161–76.

20. Soil Conservation Service. *Urban Hydrology for Small Watersheds.* United States Department of Agriculture Soil Conservation Service Technical Release 55, 2nd edition. 1986.

21. Brabec E, Schulte S, Richards PL. Impervious surfaces and water quality: A review of current literature and its implications for watershed planning. *Journal of Planning Literature* 2002;16:499–514.

22. Stephenson D. Comparison of the water balance for an undeveloped and a suburban catchment. *Hydrological Sciences Journal* 1994;39:295–307.

23. Bhaduri B, Harbor J, Engel B, Grove M. Assessing watershed-scale long-term hydrologic impacts of land-use change using a GIS-NPS model. *Environmental Management* 2000;26:643–58.

24. Klein R. Urbanization and stream quality assessment. *Water Resources Bulletin* 1979;15(4):948–63.

25. Brun SE, Band LE. Simulating runoff behavior in an urbanizing watershed. *Computers, Environment and Urban Systems* 2000;24:5–22.

26. Buttle JM, Xu F. Snowmelt runoff in suburban environments (Ontario, Canada). *Nordic Hydrology* 1988;19:19–40.

27. Arnold CL, Gibbons CJ. Impervious surface coverage: The emergence of a key environmental indicator. *Journal of the American Planning Association* 1996;62:243–58.

28. Zielinski J. The benefits of better site design in commercial development. In: Schueler TR, Holland HK, Eds. *The Practice of Watershed Protection.* Ellicott City, MD: Center for Watershed Protection, 2000, pp 25–34.

29. City of Olympia, Washington. Impervious Surface Reduction Study: Technical and Policy Analysis Final Report. City of Olympia Public Works Department, 1995.

30. Legg A, Bannerman R, Panuska J. *Variation in the Relation of Rainfall to Runoff from Residential Lawns in Madison, Wisconsin, July and August, 1995.* Madison, WI: US Geological Survey; 1996. Water-Resources Investigation Report 96-4194; Wignosta M, Burges S, Meena J. *Modeling and Monitoring to Predict Spatial and Temporal Hydrological Characteristics in Small Catchments.* Water Resources Series Technical Report 137. Seattle: University of Washington, Dept. of Civil Engineering, 1994.

31. Harbor J, Muthukrishnan S, Engel B, Jones D, Lim KJ. *A Comparison of the Long-Term Hydrological Impacts of Urban Renewal versus Urban Sprawl.* Presented at the National Conference on Tools for Urban Water Resource Management and Protection, Chicago, IL, 2000.

32. Liu AJ, Tong ST, Goodrich JA. Land use as a mitigation strategy for the water-quality impacts of global warming: A scenario analysis on two watersheds in the Ohio River Basin. *Environmental Engineering and Policy* 2000; 2:65–76.

33. Otto B, Ransel K, Todd J, Lovaas D, Stutzman H, Bailey J. *Paving Our Way to Water Shortages: How Sprawl Aggravates Drought.* Washington, DC: American Rivers, Natural Resources Defense Council, Smart Growth America, 2002, p 34.

34. Alley et al., 2002, op. cit.

35. Harbor J. Engineering geomorphology at the cutting edge of land disturbance: Erosion and sediment control on construction sites. *Geomorphology* 1999;31(1–4):247–63.

36. Bannerman RT, Owens DW, Dodds RB, Hornewer NJ. Sources of pollutants in Wisconsin stormwater. *Water Science and Technology* 1993;28(3–5): 241–59.

37. Gannon JJ, Busse MK. *E. coli* and *enterococci* levels in urban stormwater, river water, and chlorinated treatment plant effluent. *Water Research* 1989;23(9):1167–76.

38. Curriero FC, Patz JA, Rose JB, Lele SD. The association between extreme precipitation and waterborne disease outbreaks in the United States, 1948–1994. *American Journal of Public Health* 2001;91:1194–99.

39. LeChevallier MW, Norton WD. *Giardia* and *Cryptosporidium* in raw and finished water. *Journal of the American Water Works Association* 1995;87(9): 54–68.

40. MacKenzie W, Hoxie N, Proctor M, Gradus M, Blair K, Peterson D. A massive outbreak in Milwaukee of *Cryptosporidium* infection transmitted through public water supply. *New England Journal of Medicine* 1994;331:161–67.

41. Solley et al., 1998, op. cit.

42. Levin et al., 2002, op. cit.

43. U.S. Geological Survey. *The Quality of Our Nation's Waters: Nutrients and Pesticides.* U.S. Geological Survey Circular 1225, 1999, p 82.

44. Young KD, Thackston EL. Housing density and bacterial loading in urban streams. *Journal of Environmental Engineering* 1999;125:1177–80.

45. Schueler TR. Microbes and urban watersheds: Concentrations, sources, and pathways. In: Schueler TR, Holland HK, Eds. *The Practice of Watershed Protection.* Ellicott City, MD: Center for Watershed Protection, 2000, pp 68–78.

46. Levin et al., 2002, op. cit.; National Council on Public Works Improvements. *Rebuilding the Foundations: A Special Report on State and Local Public Works Financing and Management.* OTA-SET-447. Washington, DC: Office of Technology Assessment, 1990; American Society of Civil Engineers. ASCE's 2001 Report Card for America's Infrastructure. Washington, DC: Civil Engineering Research Foundation, 2001.

47. U.S. General Accounting Office. *Drinking Water Infrastructure: Information on Estimated Needs and Financial Assistance.* Testimony before the Subcommittee on Environment and Hazardous Materials, Committee on Energy and Commerce, House of Representatives. GAO-02-592T. Washington, DC: General Accounting Office, April 11, 2002.

48. Lerner DN. Identifying and quantifying urban recharge: A review. *Hydrogeology Journal* 2002;10:143–52.

49. Levin et al., 2002, op. cit.

50. Ellis JB, Yu W. Bacteriology of urban runoff: The combined sewer as a bacterial reactor and generator. In: *The Sewer as a Physical, Chemical and Biological Reactor,* Proceedings Specialized International Conference, Aalborg, Denmark, 1994, p 7; Marino RP, Gannon JJ. Survival of fecal coliforms and fecal streptococci in storm drain sediment. *Water Resources* 1991;25:1089–98.

51. Bannerman et al., 1993, op. cit.; Whipple W, Grigg S, Gizzard T, Randall CW, Shubinski RP, Tucker LS. *Stormwater Management in Urbanizing Areas.* Englewood Cliffs, NJ: Prentice-Hall, 1983.

52. Van Metre PC, Mahler BJ, Furlong ET. Urban sprawl leaves its PAH signature. *Environmental Science and Technology* 2000;34:4064–70.

53. Dierberg FE. Non–point source loadings of nutrients and dissolved organic carbon from an agricultural-suburban watershed in east central Florida. *Water Resources* 1991;25:363–74.

54. Callender E, Rice KC. The urban environmental gradient: Anthropogenic influences on the spatial and temporal distributions of lead and zinc in sediments. *Environmental Science and Technology* 2000;34:232–38.

55. U.S. Geological Survey, 1999, op. cit.

56. Whipple et al., 1983, op. cit.; Carpenter SR, Caraco NF, Correll DL, Howarth RW, Sharpley AN, Smith VH. Nonpoint pollution of surface water with phosphorus and nitrogen. *Ecological Applications* 1998;8(3):559–68.

57. Van Metre et al., 2000, op. cit.

58. Gaffield SJ, Goo RL, Richards LA, Jackson RJ. Public health effects of inadequately managed stormwater runoff. *American Journal of Public Health* 2003;93:1527–33; National Research Council. *Watershed Management for Potable Water Supply: Assessing the New York City Strategy.* Washington, DC: National Academy Press, 2000.

59. Zheng PQ, Baetz BW. GIS-based analysis of development options from a hydrology perspective. *Journal of Urban Planning and Development* 1999; 125:164–70; Greenberg M, Mayer H, Miller T, Hordon R, Knee D. Reestablishing public health and land use planning to protect public water supplies. *American Journal of Public Health* 2003;93:1522–26.

CHAPTER 8

1. Kunstler JH. Big and Blue in the USA. *Orion Online*, autumn 2003. Available: http://www.oriononline.org/pages/oo/curmudgeon/index_curmudgeon. html (accessed November 22, 2003).

2. Frías C. Brave commute. Reliever's drive to work is 90 miles. *Atlanta Journal-Constitution*, 26 July 2002, pp C1, C5.

3. DeForest RW, Veiller L, Eds. *The Tenement House Problem, I.* New York: New York State Tenement House Commission, 1903.

4. Calhoun JB. Population density and social pathology. *Scientific American* 1972;206:139–48; Christian JJ. The pathology of overpopulation. *Military Medicine* 1973;123:571–603; Ostfeld AM, D'Atri DA. Psychophysiological responses to the urban environment. *International Journal of Psychiatry in Medicine* 1975;6(1–2):15–28; Altman I. *The Environment and Social Behavior: Privacy, Personal Space, Territory, and Crowding.* Monterey, CA: Brooks-Cole, 1975; Baum A, Aiello JR, Calesnick LE. Crowding and personal control: Social density and the development of learned helplessness. *Journal of Personality and Social Psychology* 1978;36:1000–11; Baum A, Epstein J, Eds. *Human Response to Crowding.* Hillsdale, NJ: Lawrence Erlbaum, 1978; Evans GW. Behavioral and physiological consequences of crowding in humans; Aiello JR, Baum A, Gormley FP. Social determinants of residential crowding stress. *Personality and Social Psychology Bulletin* 1981;7:643–49; Aiello JR, Nicosia G, Thompson E. Physiological, social, and behavioral consequences of crowding on children and adolescents. *Child Development* 1979;50:195–202; Burger H, Kaiser HE. Crowding. *In Vivo* 1996;10(2): 249–53.

5. Jackson KT. *Crabgrass Frontier: The Suburbanization of the United States.* New York: Oxford University Press, 1985.

6. Kaplan R, Kaplan S, Ryan RL. *With People in Mind: Design and Management of Everyday Nature.* Washington, DC: Island Press, 1998; Frumkin H. Beyond toxicity: The greening of environmental health. *American Journal of Preventive Medicine* 2001;20:47–53.

7. Moore EO. A prison environment's effect on health care service demands. *Journal of Environmental Systems* 1981–82;11:17–34.

8. Ulrich RS. View through a window may influence recovery from surgery. *Science* 1984;224:420–21.

9. Diette GB, Lechtzin N, Haponik E, Devrotes A, Rubin HR. Distraction therapy with nature sights and sounds reduces pain during flexible bron-

choscopy: A complementary approach to routine analgesia. *Chest* 2003; 123(3):941–48.

10. Cowan RS. *More Work for Mother: The Ironies of Household Technology from the Open Hearth to the Microwave.* New York: Basic Books, 1983; Schor JB. *The Overworked American: The Unexpected Decline of Leisure.* New York: Basic Books, 1992.

11. Parsons R, Tassinary L, Ulrich R, Hebl M, Grossman-Alexander M. The view from the road: Implications for stress recovery and immunization. *Journal of Environmental Psychology* 1998;18:113–40.

12. Alexander C, Ishikawa S, Silverstein M, Jacobson M, Fiksdahl-King I, Angel S. *A Pattern Language: Towns, Buildings, Construction.* New York: Oxford University Press, 1977; Tuan Y-F. *Space and Place: The Perspective of Experience.* Minneapolis: University of Minnesota Press, 1977; Whyte WH. *The Social Life of Small Urban Spaces.* Washington, DC: The Conservation Foundation, 1980; Walter EV. *Placeways: A Theory of the Human Environment.* Chapel Hill: University of North Carolina Press, 1988; Gallagher W. *The Power of Place: How Our Surroundings Shape Our Thoughts, Emotions, and Actions.* New York: Poseidon Press, 1993; Kaplan et al., 1998, op. cit.

13. Hoffman H, Reygers W. Kreislaufuntersuchungen bei Kraftfahrzeug-fahrern unter variierten fahrbedingungen [Studies on the circulation of drivers under varying driving conditions]. *Zentralblatt fur Verkehrs-Medizin* 1960;3:131–51; Hoffman H. Medizinisch-Psychologische Untersuchungen Zum Fahren im Verkehrsfluss [Medical-psychological studies on driving in traffic]. *Zeitschrift fur Verkerhrswissenschaft* 1965;11:145–55.

14. Taggart P, Gibbons D, Somerville W. Some effects of motor-car driving on the normal and abnormal heart. *British Medical Journal* 1969;4:130–34.

15. Simonson E, Baker C, Burns N, Keiper C, Schmitt OH, Stackhouse S. Cardiovascular stress (electrocardiographic changes) produced by driving an automobile. *American Heart Journal* 1968;75(1):125–35.

16. Bellet S, Roman L, Kostis J. The effects of automobile driving on cate-cholamine and adrenocortical excretion. *American Journal of Cardiology* 1969;24:365–68.

17. Hoffman, 1965, op. cit.

18. Hoffman and Reygers, 1960, op. cit.

19. Simonson et al., 1968, op. cit.

20. Bellet et al., 1969, op. cit.

21. White S, Rotton J. Type of commute, behavioral aftereffects, and cardio-vascular activity. *Environment & Behavior* 1998;30:763–80.

22. Hennessy DA, Wiesenthal DL. The relationship between traffic conges-tion, driver stress, and direct versus indirect coping behaviours. *Ergonomics* 1997;40:348–61.

23. Platt FN. Heart rate measurements of drivers with the highway systems research car. *Industrial Medicine & Surgery* 1969;38(10):339–48; Burns NM, Baker CA, Simonson E, Keiper C. Electrocardiogram changes in prolonged

automobile driving. *Perceptual & Motor Skills* 1966;23(1):210; Tomasini M. [Current knowledge of cardiac changes in motor vehicle drivers]. [Italian] *Medicina del Lavoro* 1979;70(2):90–96.

24. Gulian E, Matthews G, Glendon AI, Davies DR, et al. Dimensions of driver stress. *Ergonomics* 1989;32(6):585–602; Gulian E, Glendon AI, Matthews G, Davies DR, Debney LM. The stress of driving: A diary study. *Work and Stress* 1990;4:7–16; Matthews G, Dorn L, Glendon AI. Personality correlates of driver stress. *Personality and Individual Differences* 1991;12:535–49; Dorn L, Matthews G. Two further studies of personality correlates of driver stress. *Personality and Individual Differences* 1992;13:949–51; Glendon AI, Dorn L, Matthews G, Gulian E, Davies DR, Debney LM. Reliability of the driving behavior inventory. *Ergonomics* 1993;36:719–22; Hartley L, el Hassani J. Stress, violations and accidents. *Applied Ergonomics* 1994;25:221–30.

25. Hartley et al., 1994, op. cit.

26. Karasek RA. Job demands, job decision latitude and mental strain: Implications for job redesign. *Administrative Science Quarterly* 1979;24:285–307.

27. Belkić K, Savić C, Theorell T, Rakić L, Ercegovac D, Djordjević M. Mechanisms of cardiac risk among professional drivers. *Scandinavian Journal of Work, Environment & Health* 1994;20(2):73–86.

28. Joint M. Road rage. In: *Aggressive Driving: Three Studies.* Washington: AAA Foundation for Traffic Safety, March 1997. Available: http://www.aaafoundation.org/pdf/agdr3study.pdf (accessed November 23, 2003).

29. Koslowsky M, Kluger AN, Reich M. *Commuting Stress: Causes, Effects, and Methods of Coping.* New York: Plenum Press, 1995; Koslowsky, M. Commuting and mental health. In: Friedman HS, Ed. *Encyclopedia of Mental Health*, Vol. 1. New York: Academic Press, 1998, pp 521–30.

30. Stokols D, Novaco R, Stokols J, Campbell J. Traffic congestion, type A behavior, and stress. *Journal of Applied Psychology* 1978;63:467–80; Novaco R, Stokols D, Campbell J, Stokols J. Transportation, stress, and community psychology. *American Journal of Community Psychology* 1979;7:361–80; Stokols D, Novaco RW. Transportation and well-being. In: Altman I, Wohlwill JF, Everett PB, Eds. *Transportation and Behavior.* New York: Plenum Press, 1981, pp 85–130.

31. Stokols et al., 1978, op. cit; Novaco et al., 1979, op. cit.

32. Novaco R, Stokols D, Milanesi L. Objective and subjective dimensions of travel impedance as determinants of commuting stress. *American Journal of Community Psychology* 1990;18:231–57.

33. Stokols and Novaco, 1981, op. cit.

34. Schaeffer M, Street S, Singer JE, Baum A. Effects of control on the stress reactions of commuters. *Journal of Applied Social Psychology* 1988;11:944–57.

35. Novaco et al., 1990, op. cit.

36. Koslowsky M. Commuting stress: Problems of definition and variable identification. *Applied Psychology: An International Review* 1997;46(2):153–73.

37. Novaco R, Kliewer W, Broquet A. Home environmental consequences of commute travel impedance. *American Journal of Community Psychology* 1991;18:881–909.

38. Ibid.

39. Costa G, Pickup L, DiMartino V. Commuting—A further stress factor for working people: Evidence from the European community. II. An empirical study. *International Archives of Occupational & Environmental Health* 1988b; 60:377–85; Martin J. Some aspects of absence in a light engineering factory. *Occupational Psychology* 1971;45:77–89; Taylor PJ, Pocock SJ. Commuter travel and sickness: Absence of London office workers. *Brit Journal of Preventive and Social Medicine* 1972;26:165–72.

40. Gaffuri E, Costa G. Applied aspects of chronoergohygiene. *Chronobiologia* 1986;13:39–51.

41. Seyforth JY, Bost WA. Teacher turnover and the quality of work-life in schools: An empirical study. *Journal of Research and Development in Education* 1986;20:1–6.

42. Nicholson N, Goodge PM. The influence of social, organization, and biographical factors on female absence. *Journal of Management Studies* 1976; 13:234–54; Popp PO, Belohlav JA. Absenteeism in low status environments. *Academy of Management Journal* 1982;25:677–83.

43. Novaco et al., 1990, op. cit.

44. Koslowsky M, Krausz M. On the relationship between commuting, stress symptoms and attitudinal measures: A LISREL application. *Journal of Applied Behavioral Science* 1993;29:485–92.

45. Kluger A. Commute variability and strain. *Journal of Organizational Behavior* 1998;19:147–65; Koslowsky et al., 1995, op. cit.

46. Kluger, 1998, op. cit.

47. Ibid.

48. Novaco et al., 1990, op. cit.

49. Karasek, 1979, op. cit.

50. Evans GW, Carrère S. Traffic congestion, perceived control, and psychophysiological stress among urban bus drivers. *Journal of Psychology* 1991;76:658–63; Belkić et al., 1994, op. cit.; Evans GW, Johansson G. Urban bus driving. *Journal of Occupational Health Psychology* 199;3:99–108.

51. Koslowsky, 1997, op. cit.

52. James L, Nahl D. *Road Rage and Aggressive Driving: Steering Clear of Highway Warfare.* Amherst, NY: Prometheus Books, 2000; McKay GE. *Road Rage: Commuter Combat in America. The Tragic Stories, the Many Causes, the Keys to Survival.* Herculaneum, MO: Silvertip Books, 2000; DrDriving.org.: http://www.drdriving.org/ (accessed November 23, 2003).

53. Häfner S, Kordy H, Kächele H. Psychosozialer versorgungsbedarf bei berufspendlern [Need for mental health care in commuters]. *Psychotherapie Psychosomatik Medizinische Psychologie* 2001;51(9–10):373–76.

54. Kluger, 1998, op. cit.

55. Stokols et al., 1978, op. cit.

56. Matthews et al., 1991, op. cit; Hennessy and Wiesenthal, 1997, op. cit.

57. Gulian et al., 1989, op. cit.

58. Lundberg U. Urban commuting: Crowdedness and catecholamine excretion. *Journal of Human Stress* 1976;2:26–32; Singer J, Lundberg U, Frankenhauser M. Stress on the train: A study of urban commuting. In: Baum A, Singer J, Valins S, Eds. *The Urban Environment* (Advances in Environmental Psychology, Vol 1). Hillsdale, NJ: Erlbaum, 1978, pp 41–56; Evans GW, Wener RE, Phillips D. The morning rush hour: Predictability and commuter stress. *Environment & Behavior* 2002;34: 521–30.

59. Taylor and Pocock, 1972, op. cit; Koslowsky and Krausz, 1993, op. cit.

60. LeCount ER, Rukstinat GJ. Sudden death from heart disease while motoring. *Journal of the American Medical Association* 1929;92:1347–48.

61. Aronow WS, Harris CN, Isbell MW, Rokaw MD, Imparato B. Effect of freeway travel on angina pectoris. *Annals of Internal Medicine* 1972;77:669–76.

62. Hedberg G, Jacobsson KA, Langendoen S, Nystrom L. Mortality in circulatory diseases, especially ischaemic heart disease, among Swedish professional drivers: A retrospective cohort study. *Journal of Human Ergology* 1991;20(1):1–5; Belkić et al., 1994, op. cit.

63. Krause N, Ragland DR, Greiner BA, Syme SL, Fisher JM. Psychosocial job factors associated with back and neck pain in public transit operators. *Scandinavian Journal of Work, Environment & Health* 1997;23(3):179–86; Magnusson ML, Pope MH, Wilder DG, Areskoug B. Are occupational drivers at an increased risk for developing musculoskeletal disorders? *Spine* 1996; 21(6):710–17; Bovenzi M, Zadini A. Self-reported low back symptoms in urban bus drivers exposed to whole body vibration. *Spine* 1992;17:1048–59; Backman AL. Health survey of professional drivers. *Scandinavian Journal of Work, Environment, and Health* 1983;9:36–41.

64. Kelsey JL. An epidemiological study of acute herniated lumbar intervertebral discs. *Rheumatolology and Rehabilitation* 1975;14:144–59; Kelsey JL, Hardy RJ. Driving of motor vehicles as a risk factor for acute herniated lumbar intervertebral disc. *American Journal of Epidemiology* 1975;102: 63–73.

65. Kelsey JL, Githens PB, O'Conner T, Weil U, Calogero JA, Holford TR, et al. Acute prolapsed lumbar intervertebral disc. An epidemiologic study with special reference to driving automobiles and cigarette smoking. *Spine* 1984; 9(6):608–13.

66. Pietri F, Leclerc A, Boitel L, Chastang JF, Morcet JF, Blondet M. Low-back pain in commercial travelers. *Scandinavian Journal of Work, Environment & Health* 1992;18(1):52–58.

67. Skov T, Borg V, Orhede E. Psychosocial and physical risk factors for musculoskeletal disorders of the neck, shoulders, and lower back in salespeople. *Occupational & Environmental Medicine* 1996;53(5):351–56.

68. Selzer ML, Vinokur A. Life events, subjective stress and traffic accidents. *American Journal of Psychiatry* 1974;131:903–06; Donovan DM, Marlatt GA, Salzberg PM. Drinking behaviour, personality factors and high risk driving: A review and theoretical formulation. *Journal of Studies in Alcohol* 1983;44:395–428; McMurray L. Emotional stress and driving performance: The effects of divorce. *Behavioral Research in Highway Safety* 1970;1: 100–14; Isherwood J, Adam KS, Hornblower AR. Life event stress, psychosocial factors, suicide attempt and auto-accident proclivity. *Journal of Psychosomatic Research* 1982;26:371–83.

69. Simon F, Corbett C. Road traffic offending, stress, age, and accident history among male and female drivers. *Ergonomics* 1996;39(5):757–80; Porter BE, Berry TD. A nationwide survey of self-reported red light running: Measuring prevalence, predictors, and perceived consequences. *Accident Analysis & Prevention* 2001;33(6):735–41.

70. Selzer and Vinokur, 1974, op. cit.; Hartley and el Hassani, 1994, op. cit.

71. Fong G, Frost D, Stansfeld S. Road rage: A psychiatric phenomenon? *Social Psychiatry & Psychiatric Epidemiology* 2001;36:277–86.

72. Deffenbacher JL, Oetting ER, Lynch RS. Development of a driver anger scale. *Psychological Reports* 1994;74:83–91.

73. Parry MH. *Aggression on the Road.* London: Tavistock, 1968.

74. Turner CW, Layton JF, Simons LS. Naturalistic studies of aggressive behavior: Aggressive stimuli, victim visibility, and horn honking. *Journal of Personality and Social Psychology* 1975;31:1098–1107.

75. Hauber AR. The social psychology of driving behaviour and the traffic environment: Research on aggressive behavior in traffic. *International Review of Applied Psychology* 1980;29:461–74.

76. Joint, 1995, op. cit.; Connell D, Joint M. Driver aggression. In: *Aggressive Driving: Three Studies.* Washington, DC: AAA Foundation for Traffic Safety, March 1997. Available: http://www.aaafoundation.org/pdf/agdr3study.pdf (accessed November 23, 2003).

77. National Highway Traffic Safety Administration. National Survey of Speeding and Other Unsafe Driving Actions. Volume II: Driver Attitudes and Behavior. Washington, DC: NHTSA, September 1998. DOT HS 808 749. Available: http://www.nhtsa.dot.gov/people/injury/aggressive/unsafe/ (accessed November 23, 2003).

78. Curbow B, Griffin J. Road rage or road benefit? Relationships with demographic, home and work variables. Presented at the 1999 American Psychological Association/National Institute of Occupational Safety and Health Conference, Baltimore.

79. Porter and Berry, 2001, op. cit.

80. Parry, 1968, op. cit.

81. Novaco R. Aggression on roadways. In: Baenninger R, Ed. *Targets of Violence and Aggression.* Amsterdam: Elsevier, 1991.

82. Deffenbacher, 1994, op. cit.

83. Parry, 1968, op. cit.; Donovan et al., 1983, op. cit.; Lawton R, Parker D, Stradling S, Manstead A. The role of affect in predicting social behaviors: The case of road traffic violations. *Journal of Applied Social Psychology* 1997;27:1258–76; Lowenstein LF. Research into cause and manifestations of aggression in car driving. *Police Journal* 1997;70:263–70.

84. Lawton et al., 1997, op. cit.

85. Martinez R. Statement before the Subcommittee on Surface Transportation, Committee on Transportation and Infrastructure, U.S. House of Representatives. July 17, 1997. Available: http://www.nhtsa.dot.gov/nhtsa/announce/testimony/aggres2.html (accessed November 23, 2003).

86. Spencer JR. Motor vehicles as weapons of offence. *Criminal Law Review* 1985;January:29–41.

87. Whitlock FA. *Death on the Road: A Study in Social Violence.* London: Tavistock Publications, 1971; Lajunen T, Parker D, Summala H. Does traffic congestion increase driver aggression? *Transportation Research Part F* 1999;2:225–36.

88. Connell and Joint, 1996, op. cit.; Novaco, 1991, op. cit.; Fong et al., 2001, op. cit.

89. Hines J. The stress of driving. *Occupational Health* 1986;38(10):320–22.

90. Novaco, 1991, op. cit.

91. Baxter JS, Macrae CN, Manstead ASR, Stradling SG, Parker D. Attributional biases and driver behavior. *Social Behavior* 1990;5:185–92; Connell and Joint, 1996, op. cit.

92. Hennessy and Wiesenthal, 1997, op. cit.

93. Shinar D. Aggressive driving: The contributions of the drivers and situation. *Transportation Research Part F* 1998;1:137–60.

94. Lajunen T, Parker D, Stradling SG. Dimensions of driver anger, aggressive and highway code violations and their mediation by safety orientation in UK drivers. *Transportation Research Part F* 1997;1:107–21.

95. Connell and Joint, 1996, op. cit.

96. James and Nahl, 2000, op. cit.

97. Lajunen et al., 1999, op. cit.

98. Surface Transportation Policy Project. *Aggressive Driving: Are You at Risk?* Washington, DC: STPP, 1999. Available: http://www.transact.org/report.asp?id=56 (accessed November 23, 2003).

99. Knowles E, Elliott J. *Oxford Dictionary of New Words.* New York: Oxford University Press, 1997.

100. Mizell L. Aggressive driving. In: *Aggressive Driving: Three Studies.* Washington, DC: AAA Foundation for Traffic Safety, March 1997. Available: http://www.aaafoundation.org/pdf/agdr3study.pdf (accessed November 23, 2003).

101. Ferguson A. Road rage: Aggressive driving is America's car sickness du jour. *Time.* January 12, 1998, pp 64-68.

102. Mizell, 1997, op. cit.

103. McKay, 2000, op. cit.

104. Montgomery B. Road rage: Needless deaths. *Atlanta Journal-Constitution,* 13 May 2000, p 1.

105. McKay, 2000, op. cit.

106. Mizell, 1997, op. cit.; Vest J, Cohen W, Tharp M, Mulrine A, Lord M, Koerner BI, et al. Road rage. Tailgating, giving the finger, outright violence—Americans grow more likely to take out their frustrations on other drivers. *U.S. News & World Report.* June 2, 1997, pp 24-28.

107. Vest et al., op cit.

108. Mizell, 1997, op. cit.

109. Harding RW, Morgan FH, Indermaur D, Ferrante AM, Blagg H. Road rage and the epidemiology of violence: Something old, something new. *Studies on Crime and Crime Prevention* 1998;7:221–28.

110. Marshall E, Thomas N. Traffic Calming: The Reality of "Road Rage." Briefing Note, Policing and Reducing Crime Unit, Development and Statistics Directorate, Home Office Research. London: Home Office, November 2000. Available: http://www.homeoffice.gov.uk/rds/prgpdfs/brf1200.pdf (accessed November 23, 2003).

111. Ibid.

112. Fong et al., 2001, op. cit.

113. Batten PJ, Penn DW, Bloom JD. A 36-year history of fatal road rage in Marion County, Oregon: 1963–1998. *Journal of Forensic Sciences* 2000;45:397–99.

114. Costa G, Pickup L, Di Martino V. Commuting—A further stress factor for working people: Evidence from the European community. I. A review. *International Archives of Occupational & Environmental Health* 1988;60(5): 371–76.

115. Murray CJL, Lopez A, Eds. *The Global Burden of Disease: A Comprehensive Assessment of Mortality and Disability from Diseases, Injuries and Risk Factors in 1990 and Projected to 2020.* Cambridge, MA: Harvard School of Public Health on behalf of the World Health Organization and the World Bank, 1996.

116. Weissman MM, Bland RC, Canino GJ, Faravelli C, Greenwald S, et al. Cross-national epidemiology of major depression and bipolar disorder. *Journal of the American Medical Association* 1996;276:293–99.

117. Surgeon General of the United States. *Mental Health: A Report of the Surgeon General.* Rockville, MD: US DHHS, Substance Abuse and Mental Health Services Administration, Center for Mental Health Services, National Institutes of Health, National Institute of Mental Health, 1999.

118. Simon GE, Goldberg DP, Von Korff M, Üstün TB. Understanding cross-national differences in depression prevalence. *Psychological Medicine* 2002; 32:585–94.

119. Cross-National Collaborative Group. The changing rate of major depression: Cross-national comparisons. *Journal of the American Medical Association* 1992;268:3098–3105.

120. Moore KA, Blumenthal JA. Exercise training as an alternative treatment for depression among older adults. *Alternative Therapies* 1998;4:48–56; Blumenthal JA, Babyak MA, Moore KA, Craighead WE, Herman S, Khatri P, Waugh R, Napolitano MA, Forman LM, Appelbaum M, Doraiswamy PM, Krishnan KR. Effects of exercise training on older patients with major depression. *Archives of Internal Medicine* 1999;159(19):2349–56; Babyak M, Blumenthal JA, Herman S, Khatri P, Doraiswamy M, Moore K, Craighead WE, Baldewicz TT, Krishnan KR. Exercise treatment for major depression: Maintenance of therapeutic benefit at 10 months. *Psychosomatic Medicine* 2000;62(5):633–38.

121. Murphy E. Social origins of depression in old age. *British Journal of Psychiatry* 1982;141:135–42; Champion L. The relationship between social vulnerability and the occurrence of severely threatening life events. *Psychological Medicine* 1990;20(1):157–61.

122. Kunstler JH. Home from nowhere. *The Atlantic Monthly* 1996; (September)278:43–66.

123. Lépine J-P. Epidemiology, burden, and disability in depression and anxiety. *Journal of Clinical Psychiatry* 2001;62(13):4–10; Kessler RC, Wittchen HU. Patterns and correlates of generalized anxiety disorder in community samples. *Journal of Clinical Psychiatry* 2002;63(8):4–10.

124. Surgeon General of the United States, 1999, op. cit.

125. Ibid.

CHAPTER 9

1. de Tocqueville A. *Democracy in America.* London: 1835, 1840. Reprinted by University of Chicago Press, 2000, p 114.

2. Sarason SB. *The Psychological Sense of Community: Prospects for a Community Psychology.* San Francisco: Jossey-Bass, 1974; McMillan DW, Chavis DM. Sense of community: A definition and theory. *American Journal of Community Psychology* 1986;14:6–23; Chavis DM, Pretty G. Sense of community: Advances in measurement and application. *Journal of Community Psychology* 1999;27:635–42.

3. McMillan and Chavis, 1986, op. cit., p 6.

4. Ibid.

5. Glynn T. Psychological sense of community: Measurement and application. *Human Relations* 1981;34(7):789–818; Cochrun S. Understanding and enhancing neighborhood sense of community. *Journal of Planning Literature* 1994;9:92–99.

6. Smith RA. Measuring neighborhood cohesion: A review and some suggestions. *Human Ecology* 1975;3(3):143–60.

7. Edwards B, Foley MW. Civil society and social capital: A primer. In: Edwards B, Foley MW, Diani M, Eds. *Beyond Tocqueville: Civil Society and the Social Capital Debate in Comparative Perspective.* Hanover, NH: Tufts University/University Press of New England, 2001, pp 1–14.

8. Ibid., p 6.

9. Carothers T. Think again: The concept of civil society is a recent invention. *Foreign Policy* 1999;Winter:18–29.

10. Jacobs J. *The Death and Life of Great American Cities.* New York: Random House, Modern Library Edition, 1993, p 73.

11. Putnam R. *Bowling Alone: The Collapse and Revival of American Community.* New York: Simon & Schuster, 2000, p 19.

12. Bourdieu P. The forms of capital. In: Richardson J., Ed. *Handbook of Theory and Research for the Sociology of Education.* New York: Greenwood Press, 1986, pp 241–58.

13. Coleman J. Social capital in the creation of human capital. *American Journal of Sociology* 1988;94:S95–S120; Coleman JS. *Foundations of Social Theory.* Cambridge, MA: Belknap Press, 1990.

14. Putnam, 2000, op. cit., p 19.

15. Newton K. Social capital and democracy. In: Edwards B, Foley MS, Diani M, Eds. *Beyond Tocqueville: Civil Society and the Social Capital Debate in Comparative Perspective.* Hanover, NH: Tufts University/University Press of New England, 2001, p 226.

16. Stolle D, Rochon T. Are all associations alike? Member diversity, associational type, and the creation of social capital. In: Edwards B, Foley MS, Diani M, Eds. *Beyond Tocqueville: Civil Society and the Social Capital Debate in Comparative Perspective.* Hanover, NH: Tufts University/University Press of New England, 2001, p 143.

17. Fukuyama F. *Trust: The Social Virtues and the Creation of Prosperity.* New York: Free Press, 1995.

18. Hawe P, Shiell A. Social capital and health promotion: A review. *Social Science and Medicine* 2000;51:871–85.

19. Putnam, 2000, op. cit., pp 22–23.

20. Ibid., pp 136–37.

21. Stolle and Rochon, 2001, op. cit.

22. Schulman MD, Anderson C. The dark side of the force: Economic restructuring and social capital in a company town. In: Edwards B, Foley MS, Diani M, Eds. *Beyond Tocqueville: Civil Society and the Social Capital Debate in Comparative Perspective.* Hanover, NH: Tufts University/University Press of New England, 2001, pp 112–24.

23. Carothers, 1999, op. cit.

24. Lochner K, Kawachi I, Kennedy BP. Social capital: A guide to its measurement. *Health & Place* 1999;5:259–70.

25. Hawe and Shiell, 2000, op. cit.

26. Kawachi I, Kennedy BP. Income inequality and health: Pathways and mechanisms. *Health Services Research* 1999;34(1 Pt 2):215–27.

27. Glynn, 1981, op. cit.

28. Poplin DE. *Communities: A Survey of Theories and Methods of Research.* New York: Macmillan, 1972, p 7.

29. Broadhead EW, Kaplan BH, James SA, et al. The epidemiologic evidence for a relationship between social support and health. *American Journal of Epidemiology* 1983;117:521–37; House JS, Landis KR, Umberson D. Social relationships and health. *Science* 1988;241:540–45; Berkman LF. The role of social relations in health promotion. *Psychosomatic Medicine* 1995;57:245–54; Seeman TE. Social ties and health: The benefits of social integration. *Annals of Epidemiology* 1996;6:442–51; Hawe and Shiell, 2000, op. cit.; Kawachi I. Social capital and community effects on population and individual health. *Annals of the NY Academy of Sciences* 2000;896:120–30.

30. Seeman TE, Crimmins E. Social environment effects on health and aging: Integrating epidemiologic and demographic approaches and perspectives. *Annals of the NY Academy of Sciences* 2001;954:88–117.

31. House J, Robbins C, Metzner H, et al. The association of social relationships and activities with mortality: Prospective evidence from the Tecumseh Community Health Study. *American Journal of Epidemiology* 1982;116:123–40.

32. Berkman LF, Syme SL. Social networks, host resistance, and mortality: A nine-year follow-up study of Alameda County residents. *American Journal of Epidemiology* 1979;109:186–204.

33. Schoenback V, Kaplan B, Fredman L, et al. Social ties and mortality in Evans County, Georgia. *American Journal of Epidemiology* 1985;123:577–91.

34. Hirdes JP, Forbes WF. The importance of social relationships, socioeconomic status and health practices with respect to mortality among healthy Ontario males. *Journal of Clinical Epidemiology* 1992;45:175–82; House et al., 1982, op. cit.

35. Kawachi I, Colditz GA, Ascherio A, Rimm EB, Giovannucci E, Stampfer MJ, et al. A prospective study of social networks in relation to total mortality and cardiovascular disease in men in the US. *Journal of Epidemiology and Community Health* 1996;50:245–51.

36. Kawachi I, Kennedy BP, Lochner K, Prothrow-Stith D. Social capital, income inequality, and mortality. *American Journal of Public Health* 1997;87: 1491–98.

37. Veenstra G. Social capital and health (plus wealth, income inequality and regional health governance). *Social Science and Medicine* 2002;54:849–68.

38. Kawachi I, Kennedy BP, Glass R. Social capital and self-rated health: A contextual analysis. *American Journal of Public Health* 1999;89(8):1187–93.

39. Veenstra G. Social capital, SES, and health: An individual-level analysis. *Social Science & Medicine* 2000;50:619–29.

40. Orth-Gomer K, Rosengren A, Wilhelmsen L. Lack of social support and incidence of coronary heart disease in middle-aged Swedish men. *Psychosomatic Medicine* 1993;55:37–43.

41. Blumenthal JA, Burg MM, Barefoot J, Williams RB, Haney T, Zimet G. Social support, type A behavior, and coronary artery disease. *Psychosomatic Medicine* 1987;49(4):331–40.

42. Case RB, Moss AJ, Case N, McDermott M, Eberly S. Living alone after myocardial infarction: Impact on prognosis. *Journal of the American Medical Association* 1992;267:520–24.

43. Brezinka V, Kittel F. Psychosocial factors of coronary heart disease in women: A review. *Social Science & Medicine* 1996;42(10):1351–65.

44. Vogt TM, Mullooly JP, Ernst D, Pope CR, Hollis JF. Social networks as predictors of ischemic heart disease, cancer, stroke and hypertension: Incidence, survival and mortality. *Journal of Clinical Epidemiology* 1992;45:659–66.

45. Reed D, McGee D, Yano K, Geinleib M. Social networks and coronary heart disease among Japanese men in Hawaii. *American Journal of Epidemiology* 1983;117:384–96.

46. Seeman TE, Syme SL. Social networks and coronary artery disease: A comparative analysis of network structural and support characteristics. *Psychosomatic Medicine* 1987;49:341–54.

47. Medalie JH, Goldbourt U. Angina pectoris among 10,000 men. II. Psychosocial and other risk factors as evidenced by a multivariate analysis of a five-year incidence study. *American Journal of Medicine* 1976;60:910–21.

48. Broadhead et al., 1983, op. cit; Biegel BE, McCardle I, Mendelson S. *Social Networks and Mental Health: An Annotated Bibliography.* Beverly Hills, CA: Sage, 1985; Johnson TP. Mental health, social relations, and social selection: A longitudinal analysis. *Journal of Health and Social Behavior* 1991;32: 408–23; Dean A, Kolody B, Wood P. Effects of social support from various sources on depression in elderly persons. *Journal of Health and Social Behavior* 1990;31:148–61; Krantz DS, McCeney MK. Effects of psychological and social factors on organic disease: A critical assessment of research on coronary heart disease. *Annual Review of Psychology* 2002;53: 341–69.

49. Veenstra G, 2002, op. cit.

50. Kawachi I, Berkman L. Social ties and mental health. *Journal of Urban Health* 2001;78:458–67.

51. Kennedy BP, Kawachi R, Glass R, Prothrow-Stith D. Income distribution, socioeconomic status, and self-rated health: A U.S. multi-level analysis. *British Medical Journal* 1998;317:917–21.

52. Weitzman ER, Kawachi I. Giving means receiving: The protective effect of social capital on binge drinking on college campuses. *American Journal of Public Health* 2000;90(12):1936–39.

53. Gold R, Kennedy B, Connell F, Kawachi I. Teen births, income inequality, and social capital: Developing an understanding of the causal pathway. *Health & Place* 2002;8:77–83.

54. Lindström M., Hanson B, Östergren P-O. Socioeconomic differences in leisure-time physical activity: The role of social participation and social capital in shaping health related behavior. *Social Science and Medicine* 2001;52:441–51.

55. Kawachi and Berkman, 2001, op. cit.; Kawachi, 2000, op. cit.

56. McEwen BS, Seeman T. Protective and damaging effects of mediators of stress: Elaborating and testing the concepts of allostasis and allostatic load. *Annals of the New York Academy of Sciences* 1999;896:30–47.

57. Lindström et al., 2001, op. cit.

58. Putnam, 2000, op. cit., p 209.

59. Quoted in Whyte WH. *The Organization Man.* New York: Simon & Schuster, 1956, p 287.

60. Quoted in ibid., p 284.

61. Quoted in ibid., p 285.

62. Gans H. *The Levittowners.* London: Penguin Press, 1967, pp 44–67.

63. Ibid., p 257.

64. Baxandall R, Ewen E. *Picture Windows: How the Suburbs Happened.* New York: Basic Books, 2000, pp 152–57.

65. Wilson G, Baldassare M. Overall "sense of community" in a suburban region: The effects of localism, privacy, and urbanization. *Environment and Behavior* 1996;28(1):28–29.

66. Mumford L. *The Culture of Cities.* New York: Harcourt, Brace, 1938, p 412.

67. Jackson KT. *Crabgrass Frontier: The Suburbanization of the United States.* Oxford, UK: Oxford University Press, 1985, p 272.

68. Ewing R. Is Los Angeles-style sprawl desirable? *Journal of the American Planning Association* 1997;63(1):107–26.

69. Donaldson S. *The Suburban Myth.* New York: Columbia University Press, 1969, quoted in Popenoe D. Urban sprawl: Some neglected sociological considerations. *Sociology & Social Research* 1979;63, p 257.

70. Popenoe D. Urban sprawl: Some neglected sociological considerations. *Sociology & Social Research* 1979;63:255–68.

71. Martin WT. The structuring of social relationships engendered by suburban residence. *American Sociology Review* 1956;21:446–53.

72. Scaff AH. The effect of commuting on participation in community organizations. *American Sociology Review* 1952;17:215–20.

73. Putnam, 2000, op. cit., p 213.

74. Oldenburg R. *The Great Good Place: Cafés, Coffee Shops, Community Centers, Beauty Parlors, General Stores, Bars, Hangouts and How They Get You Through*

the Day. New York: Paragon House, 1989; Oldenburg R. *Celebrating the Third Place: Inspiring Stories About the "Great Good Places" at the Heart of Our Communities.* New York: Marlowe & Company, 2000.

75. Thomas GS. *The United States of Suburbia: How the Suburbs Took Control of America and What They Plan to Do with It.* Amherst, NY: Prometheus Books, 1998, p 139.

76. Thomas, 1998, op. cit.; Oliver JE. *Democracy in Suburbia.* Princeton, NJ: Princeton University Press, 2001.

77. Oliver, 2001, op. cit.

78. Putnam, 2000, op. cit., p 214.

79. Burchell RW, Shad NA, Listokin D, Phillips H, Downs A, Seskins S, Davis JS, Moore T, Helton D, Gall M. *The Costs of Sprawl—Revisited.* Transportation Research Board; Transit Cooperative Research Program. Report 39. Washington, DC: National Academy Press, 1998.

80. Glynn, 1981, op. cit.

81. Baumgartner MP. *The Moral Order of a Suburb.* New York: Oxford University Press, 1989.

82. Nasar JL, Julian DA. The psychological sense of community in the neighborhood. *Journal of the American Planning Association* 1995;61:178–84.

83. Wilson and Baldassare, 1996, op. cit.

84. Skjaeveland O, Garling T. Effects of interactional space on neighboring. *Journal of Environmental Psychology* 1997;17:181–98.

85. Plas JM, Lewis SE. Environmental factors and sense of community in a planned town. *American Journal of Community Psychology* 1996;24(1):109–43.

86. Freeman L. The effects of sprawl on neighborhood social ties. *Journal of the American Planning Association* 2001;67:69–77.

87. Leyden K. Social capital and the built environment: The importance of walkable neighborhoods. *American Journal of Public Health* 2003;93: 1546–51.

88. Lund H. Pedestrian environments and sense of community. *Journal of Planning, Education and Research* 2002;21:301–12.

89. Nasar and Julian, 1995, op. cit.

90. Popenoe, 1979, op. cit., p 261.

91. Kaplan GA, Pamuk ER, Lynch JW, Cohen RD, Balfour JL. Inequality in income and mortality in the United States: Analysis of mortality and potential pathways. *British Medical Journal* 1996;312:999–1003.

92. Kahn HS, Patel AV, Jacobs EJ, Calle EE, Kennedy BP, Kawachi I. Pathways between area-level income inequality and increased mortality in U.S. men. *Annals of the NY Academy of Sciences* 1999;896:332–34.

93. Kennedy BP, Kawachi I, Prothrow-Stith D. Income distribution and mortality: Cross-sectional ecological study of the Robin Hood Index in the United States. *British Medical Journal* 1996;312:1004–07.

94. Ibid.

95. Ibid.

96. Wilkinson RG. *Unhealthy Societies: The Afflictions of Inequality.* London: Routledge, 1996; Kawachi I, Kennedy BP, Wilkinson RC, Eds. *Income Inequality and Health.* New York: New Press, 1999.

97. Kennedy et al., 1996, op. cit.

98. Brodish PH, Massing M, Tyroler HA. Income inequality and all-cause mortality in the 100 counties of North Carolina. *Southern Medical Journal* 2000;93(4):386–91.

99. Kaplan et al., 1996, op. cit.; Lynch JW, Kaplan GA, Pamuk ER, Cohen RD, Heck KE, Balfour JL, Yen IH. Income inequality and mortality in metropolitan areas of the United States. *American Journal of Public Health* 1998;88:1074–80; Daly MC, Duncan GJ, Kaplan GA, Lynch JW. Macro-to-micro links in the relation between income inequality and mortality. *Milbank Quarterly* 1998;76:315–39; Lochner K, Pamuk E, Makuc D, Kennedy BP, Kawachi I. State-level income inequality and individual mortality risk: A prospective, multilevel study. *American Journal of Public Health* 2001;91:385–91.

100. Wilkinson RG. Income distribution and life expectancy. *British Medical Journal* 1992;304:165–68; Stanistreet D, Scott-Samuel A, Bellis MA. Income inequality and mortality in England. *Journal of Public Health Medicine* 1999;21:205–07.

101. Rodgers GB. Income and inequality as determinants of mortality: An international cross-sectional analysis. *Population Studies* 1979;33:343–51; Wilkinson, 1992, op. cit.

102. Kennedy et al., 1998, op. cit.

103. Fiscella K, Franks P. Poverty or income inequality as predictor of mortality: Longitudinal cohort study. *BMJ* 1997;314(7096):1724–27.

104. Kennedy et al., 1996, op. cit.

105. Kawachi et al., 1997, op. cit., pp 1, 497.

106. Kahn et al., 1999, op. cit.

107. Gold et al., 2002, op cit., p 79.

108. Kawachi and Kennedy, 1999, op. cit.

109. Kaplan et al., 1997, op. cit.

110. Shively CA, Laber-Laird K, Anton RF. Behavior and physiology of social stress and depression in female Cynomolgus monkeys. *Biological Psychiatry* 1997;41:871–82.

111. Shively CA, Clarkson TB. Social status and coronary artery atherosclerosis in female monkeys. *Arteriosclerosis and Thrombosis* 1994;14:721–26.

112. Oliver, 2001, op. cit.; Jargowsky P. Sprawl, concentration of poverty, and urban inequality. In: Squires GD, Ed. *Urban Sprawl: Causes, Consequences, and Policy Responses.* Washington, DC: Urban Institute Press, 2002, pp 39–71.

CHAPTER 10

1. STPP (Surface Transportation Policy Project). *High Mileage Moms.* Washington, DC: STPP, May 1999. Available: http://www.transact.org (accessed December 5, 2003).

2. Novaco R, Kliewer W, Broquet A. Home environmental consequences of commute travel impedance. *American Journal of Community Psychology* 1991;18:881–909.

3. Baker L. The Wheel Deal: Sprawl: Soccer moms' public enemy No. 1. *Northern Californian Bohemian*, January 4–10, 2001. Available: http://www. metroactive.com/papers/sonoma/01.04.01/soccermoms-0101.html (accessed December 5, 2003).

4. Etzel RA, Balk SJ, Eds. *Pediatric Environmental Health*, 2nd Edition. Elk Grove Village, IL: American Academy of Pediatrics Committee on Environmental Health, 2003.

5. Künzli N, Lurmann F, Segal M, Ngo L, Balmes J, Tager IB. Association between lifetime ambient ozone exposure and pulmonary function in college freshmen—results of a pilot study. *Environmental Research* 1997;72(1):8–23.

6. McConnell R, Berhane K, Gilliland F, London SJ, Islam T, Gauderman WJ, Avol E, Margolis HG, Peters JM. Asthma in exercising children exposed to ozone: A cohort study. *Lancet* 2002;359(9304):386–91.

7. McConnell R, Berhand K, Gilliland F, Molitor J, et al. Prospective study of air pollution and bronchitic symptoms in children with asthma. *American Review of Respiratory and Critical Care Medicine* 2003;168:790–97.

8. Norris G, Young Pong SN, Koenig JQ, Larson TV, Sheppard L, Stout JW. An association between fine particles and asthma emergency department visits for children in Seattle. *Environmental Health Perspectives* 1999;107(6):489–93.

9. Lin S, Munsie JP, Hwang S-A, Fitzgerald E, Cayo MR. Childhood asthma hospitalization and residential exposure to state route traffic. *Environmental Research Section A* 2002;88:73–81.

10. van Vliet P, Knape M, de Hartog J, Janssen N, Harssema H, Brunekreef B. Motor vehicle exhaust and chronic respiratory symptoms in children living near freeways. *Environmental Research* 1997;74(2):122–32.

11. Gauderman WJ, McConnell R, Gilliland F, London S, Thomas D, Avol E, et al. Association between air pollution and lung function growth in southern California children. *American Review of Respiratory and Critical Care Medicine* 2000;162(4 Pt 1):1383–90.

12. Chen L, Yang W, Jennison BL, Goodrich A, Omaye ST. Air pollution and birth weight in northern Nevada, 1991–1999. *Inhalation Toxicology* 2002;14(2):141–57.

13. Woodruff TJ, Grillo J, Schoendorf KC. The relationship between selected causes of postneonatal infant mortality and particulate air pollution in the United States. *Environmental Health Perspectives* 1997;105(6):608–12.

14. Strauss RS, Pollack HA. Epidemic increase in childhood overweight, 1986–1998. *Journal of the American Medical Association* 2001;286:2845–48; Ogden CL, Flegal KM, Carroll MD, Johnson CL. Prevalence and trends in overweight among US children and adolescents, 1999–2000. *Journal of the American Medical Association* 2002;288(14):1728–32.

15. Ogden, 2002, op. cit.

16. Dellinger AM, Staunton CE. Barriers to children walking and biking to school—United States, 1999. *Morbidity and Mortality Weekly Report* 2002; 51(32):701–04.

17. Ibid.

18. Bricker SK, Kanny D, PhD, Mellinger-Birdsong A, Powell KE, Shisler JL. School transportation modes—Georgia 2000. *Morbidity and Mortality Weekly Report* 2002;51:704–05.

19. Strauss RS, Rodzilsky D, Burack G, Colin M. Psychosocial correlates of physical activity in healthy children. *Archives of Pediatrics and Adolescent Medicine* 2001;155(8):897–902.

20. Dietz WH. Health consequences of obesity in youth: Childhood predictors of adult disease. *Pediatrics* 1998;101(3 Pt 2):518–25.

21. Fagot-Campagna A, Pettitt DJ, Engelgau MM, et al. Type 2 diabetes among North American children and adolescents: An epidemiologic review and a public health perspective. *Journal of Pediatrics* 2000;136: 664–72.

22. Dietz, 1998, op. cit.

23. Serdula MK, Ivery D, Coates RJ, Freedman DS, Williamson DF, Byers T. Do obese children become obese adults? A review of the literature. *Preventive Medicine* 1993;22:167–77; Dietz, 1998, op. cit.; Wright CM, Parker L, Lamont D, Craft AW. Implications of childhood obesity for adult health: Findings from thousand families cohort study. *British Medical Journal* 2001;323:1280–84.

24. National Highway Traffic Safety Administration. Traffic Safety Facts 2001: A Compilation of Motor Vehicle Crash Data from the Fatality Analysis Reporting System and the General Estimates System. DOT HS 809 484. Washington, DC: USDOT, NHTSA, December 2002. Available: http://www-nrd.nhtsa.dot.gov/pdf/nrd-30/NCSA/TSFAnn/TSF2001.pdf (accessed December 5, 2003).

25. Malek M, Guyer B, Lescohier I. The epidemiology and prevention of child pedestrian injuries. *Accident Analysis and Prevention* 1990;22:301–13; Roberts I, Norton R, Jackson R, Dunn R, Hassall I. Effect of environmental factors on risk of injury of child pedestrians by motor vehicles: A case-control study. *British Medical Journal* 1995;310:91–94; Schieber RA, Thompson NJ. Developmental risk factors for childhood pedestrian injuries. *Injury Prevention* 1996;2(3):228–36; Rivara FP. Pediatric injury control in 1999: Where do we go from here? *Pediatrics* 1999;103(4 Pt 2): 883–88; Wazana A, Rynard VL, Raina P, Krueger P, Chambers LW. Are child pedestrians at increased risk of injury on one-way compared to

two-way streets? *Canadian Journal of Public Health* 2000;91(3):201–06; DiMaggio C, Durkin M. Child pedestrian injury in an urban setting: Descriptive epidemiology. *Academic Emergency Medicine* 2002;9(1):54–62.

26. Kraus JF, Hooten EG, Brown KA, Peek-Asa C, Heye C, McArthur DL. Child pedestrian and bicyclist injuries: Results of community surveillance and a case-control study. *Injury Prevention* 1996;2:212–18.

27. Lightstone AS, Dhillon PK, Peek-Asa C, Kraus JF. A geographic analysis of motor vehicle collisions with child pedestrians in Long Beach, California: Comparing intersection and midblock incident locations. *Injury Prevention* 2001;7(2):155–60.

28. Rivara FP, Barber M. Demographic analysis of childhood pedestrian injuries. *Pediatrics* 1985;76:375–81.

29. Rao R, Hawkins M, Guyer B. Children's exposure to traffic and risk of pedestrian injury in an urban setting. *Bulletin of the NY Academy of Medicine* 1997;74:65–80.

30. Posner JC, Liao E, Winston FK, Cnaan A, Shaw KN, Durbin DR. Exposure to traffic among urban children injured as pedestrians. *Injury Prevention* 2002;8:231–35.

31. Roberts I, Ashton T, Dunn R, Lee-Joe T. Preventing child pedestrian injury: Pedestrian education or traffic calming? *Australian Journal of Public Health* 1994;18(2):209–12.

32. Quoted in: Hart R. *Children's Experience of Place.* New York: Irvington, 1979, p 373.

33. Moore, Robin. *Childhood's Domain: Place and Play in Child Development.* London: Croom Helm, 1986.

34. Hart, 1979, op. cit.; Matthews MH. *Making Sense of Place: Children's Understanding of Large-Scale Environments.* Savage, MD: Barnes & Noble, 1992; Gaster S. Rethinking the children's home-range concept. *Architecture et Comportement* 1995;11:35–42.

35. van Vliet W. Exploring the fourth environment: An examination of the home range of city and suburban teenagers. *Environment and Behavior* 1983;15:567–88.

36. David TG, Weinstein CS. The built environment and children's development. In: Weinstein CS, David TG, Eds. *Spaces for Children: The Built Environment and Child Development.* York: Plenum, 1987, pp 3–20.

37. Proshansky HM, Fabian AK. The development of place identity in the child. In: Weinstein CS, David TG, Eds. *Spaces for Children: The Built Environment and Child Development.* York: Plenum, 1987, pp 21–40.

38. Siegel AW, Kirasic KC, Kail RV Jr. Stalking the elusive cognitive map: The development of children's representations of geographic space. In: Altman I, Wohlwill JF, Eds. *Children and the Environment. Human Behavior and Environment,* Volume 3. New York: Plenum, 1978, pp 223–58; Spencer C, Woolley H. Children and the city: A summary of recent environmental psychology research. *Child: Care, Health and Development* 2000;26(3):181–98.

39. Wallace PA, Firestone IJ. Modes of exploration and environmental learning by preschool children. *Environmental Design Research Association* 1979;10;284–89; David and Weinstein, 1987, op. cit.; Matthews, 1992, op. cit.

40. Goodenough E. Secret spaces of childhood: Introduction. *Michigan Quarterly Review* 2000;39(2):179–93.

41. Moore R, Young D. Childhood outdoors: Toward a social ecology of the landscape. In: Altman I, Wohlwill JF, Eds. *Children and the Environment. Human Behavior and Environment,* Volume 3. New York: Plenum, 1978, pp 83–130.

42. Bronfenbrenner U. *The Ecology of Human Development: Experiments by Nature and Design.* Cambridge, MA: Harvard University Press, 1979, p 213.

43. Spencer and Woolley, 2000, op. cit.

44. Gaster S. Urban children's access to their neighborhood: Changes over three generations. *Environment and Behavior* 1991;23(1):70–85.

45. Blakely KS. Parents' conception of social dangers to children in the urban environment. *Children's Environments* 1994;11:16–25.

46. Hart, 1979, op. cit.; Matthews, 1992, op. cit.

47. Anderson J, Tindall M. The concept of home range: New data for the study of territorial behavior. In: Mitchell WJ, Ed. *Environmental Design: Research and Practice.* Los Angeles: Environmental Design Research Association, 1972. Cited in van Vliet W. Exploring the fourth environment: An examination of the home range of city and suburban teenagers. *Environment and Behavior* 1983;15:567–88; van Vliet W, 1983, op. cit.

48. Childress H. *Landscapes of Betrayal, Landscapes of Joy: Curtisville in the Lives of Its Teenagers.* Albany: State University of New York Press, 2000.

49. Ibid., p 14.

50. Ibid., p 18.

51. Langdon P. Can design make community? *Responsive Community* 1997;7(2):25–37.

52. Morrow V. Children's experiences of "community": Implications of social capital discourses. In: Swann C, Morgan A, Eds. *Social Capital for Health: Insights from Qualitative Research.* London: National Health Service, Health Development Agency, 2002, pp 9–28. Available: http://www.hda-online. org.uk/downloads/pdfs/social_capital_complete_jul02.pdf (accessed December 5, 2003); Earls F, Carlson M. The social ecology of child health and well-being. *Annual Review of Public Health* 2001;22:143–66.

53. Parcel TL, Menaghan EG. Family social capital and children's behavior problems. *Social Psychology Quarterly* 1993;56:120–35.

54. Teachmann J, Paasch K, Carver K. Social capital and dropping out of school early. *Journal of Marriage Family* 1996;58:773–83; Smith MH, Beaulieu LJ, Israel GD. Effects of human capital and social capital on dropping out of high school in the South. *Journal of Research in Rural Education*

1992;8(1):75–87; Furstenburg FF, Hughes ME. Social capital and successful development among at-risk youth. *Journal of Marriage Family* 1995;57:580–92.

55. Furstenburg, 1995, op. cit.

56. Runyan D, Hunter WM, Socolar RR, Amaya-Jackson L, English D, et al. Children who prosper in unfavorable environments: The relationship to social capital. *Pediatrics* 1998;101:12–19.

57. Brooks-Gunn J, Duncan G, Klebanov P, Sealand N. Do neighborhoods influence child and adolescent development? *American Journal of Sociology* 1993;99:353–95.

58. Hetzel L, Smith A. The 65 Years and Over Population: 2000. Census 2000 Brief C2KB/01-10. Washington, DC: U.S. Bureau of the Census, October 2001.

59. Knickman JR, Snell EK. The 2030 problem: Caring for aging baby boomers. *Health Services Research* 2002;37(4):849–84.

60. Wachs M. The role of transportation in the social integration of the aged. In: Committee on an Aging Society, Institute of Medicine. *America's Aging: The Social and Built Environment in an Older Society.* Washington, DC: National Academy Press, 1988.

61. Coughlin J, Lacombe A. Ten myths about transportation for the elderly. *Transportation Quarterly* 1997;51(1):91–100.

62. Mazzeo R, Cavanagh P, Evans W. American College of Sports Medicine Position Stand: Exercise and physical activity for older adults. *Medicine & Science Sports & Exercise* 1998;30:992–1008.

63. Batty GD. Physical activity and coronary heart disease in older adults. A systematic review of epidemiological studies. *European Journal of Public Health* 2002;12(3):171–76.

64. Camacho TC, Roberts RE, Lazarus NB, Kaplan GA, Cohen RD. Physical activity and depression: Evidence from the Alameda County Study. *American Journal of Epidemiology* 1991;134:220–30; O'Connor PJ, Aenchenbacher LE, Dishman RK. Physical activity and depression in the elderly. *Journal of Aging and Physical Activity* 1993;1:34–58; Mobily KE, Rubenstein LM, Lemke JH, O'Hara MW, Wallace RB. Walking and depression in a cohort of older adults: The Iowa 65+ Rural Health Study. *Journal of Aging and Physical Activity* 1996;4:119–35.

65. Todd JA, Robinson RJ. Osteoporosis and exercise. *Postgraduate Medical Journal* 2003;79(932):320–23; Berard A, Bravo G, Gauthier P. Meta-analysis of the effectiveness of physical activity for the prevention of bone loss in postmenopausal women. *Osteoporosis International* 1997;7:331–37; Wallace BA, Cumming RG. Systematic review of randomized trials of the effect of exercise on bone mass in pre- and postmenopausal women. *Calcified Tissue International* 2000;67:10–18.

66. Gillespie LD, Gillespie WJ, Cumming R, Lamb SE, Rowe BH. Interventions to reduce the incidence of falling in the elderly. *Cochrane Database of Systemic Reviews* 1999;(1).

67. Geffken D, Cushman M, Burke G, et al. Association between physical activity and markers of inflammation in a healthy elderly population. *American Journal of Epidemiology* 2001;153:242–50.

68. Seeman TE, Lusignolo TM, Albert M, Berkman L. Social relationships, social support, and patterns of cognitive aging in healthy, high-functioning older adults: MacArthur studies of successful aging. *Health Psychology* 2001; 20(4):243–55; Seeman TE, Crimmins E. Social environment effects on health and aging: Integrating epidemiologic and demographic approaches and perspectives. *Annals of the New York Academy of Sciences* 2001;954:88–117.

69. Fabrigoule C, Letenneur L, Dartigues J, Zarrouk M, Commenges D, Barberger-Gateau P. Social and leisure activities and risk of dementia: A prospective longitudinal study. *Journal of the American Geriatric Society* 1995;43:485–90; Bassuk SS, Glass TA, Berkman LF. Social disengagement and incident cognitive decline in community-dwelling elderly persons. *Annals of Internal Medicine* 1999;131:165–73; Fratiglioni L, Wang H, Ericsson K, Maytan M, Winblad B. The influence of social network on the occurrence of dementia: A community-based longitudinal study. *Lancet* 2000;355:1315–19; Wang HX, Karp A, Winblad B, Fratiglioni L. Late-life engagement in social and leisure activities is associated with a decreased risk of dementia: A longitudinal study from the Kungsholmen project. *American Journal of Epidemiology* 2002;155(12):1081–87.

70. Mendes de Leon CF, Glass TA, Beckett LA, Seeman TE, Evans DA, Berkman LF. Social networks and disability transitions across eight intervals of yearly data in the New Haven EPESE. *Journal of Gerontology Series B—Psychological Sciences & Social Sciences* 1999;54(3):S162–72.

71. Golant SM. Deciding where to live: The emerging residential settlement patterns of retired Americans. *Generations* 2002;26:66–73.

72. Jackson KT. Gentleman's agreement: Discrimination in metropolitan America. In: Katz B, Ed. *Reflections on Regionalism.* Washington, DC: Brookings Institution Press, 2000, pp 185–217.

73. Quoted in Schill MH, Wachter SM. The spatial bias of federal housing law and policy: Concentrated poverty in urban America. *University of Pennsylvania Law Review* 1995;143(5):1285–1342.

74. Powell J. Sprawl, fragmentation, and the persistence of racial inequality: Limiting civil rights by fragmenting space. In: Squires GD, Ed. *Urban Sprawl: Causes, Consequences & Policy Responses.* Washington, DC: Urban Institute Press, 2002, pp 73–117.

75. Jackson, KT. *Crabgrass Frontier: The Suburbanization of the United States.* New York: Oxford University Press, 2000, op. cit., pp 197–203.

76. Ibid., p 206.

77. Kain JF. Housing segregation, Negro employment, and metropolitan decentralization. *Quarterly Journal of Economics* 1968;82(2):175–97.

78. Jargowsky PA. Sprawl, concentration of poverty, and urban inequality. In: Squires GD, Ed. *Urban Sprawl: Causes, Consequences & Policy Responses.* Washington, DC: Urban Institute Press, 2002, pp 39–71.

79. Bullard RD, Johnson GS. *Just Transportation: Dismantling Race & Class Barriers to Mobility.* Gabriola Island, BC, and Stony Creek, CT: New Society Publishers, 1997; Bullard RD, Johnson GS, Torres AO. *Sprawl City: Race, Politics, and Planning in Atlanta.* Washington, DC: Island Press, 2000.

80. Wilson, WJ. *The Truly Disadvantaged: The Inner City, the Underclass and Public Policy.* Chicago: University of Chicago Press, 1987; Wilson, WJ. *When Work Disappears: The World of the New Urban Poor.* New York: Knopf, 1996.

81. McCord C, Freeman HP. Excess mortality in Harlem. *New England Journal of Medicine* 1990;322:173–77.

82. Friedman LN, Williams MT, Singh TP, Frieden TR. Tuberculosis, AIDS and death among substance abusers on welfare in New York City. *New England Journal of Medicine* 1996;334(13):828–33.

83. Singer M. A dose of drugs, a touch of violence, a case of AIDS: Conceptualizing the SAVA syndemic. *Free Inquiry* 1996;24(2):99–110.

84. Jargowsky, 2002, op. cit.

85. Andrulis DP. The urban health penalty: New dimensions and directions in inner-city health care. American College of Physicians Position Paper No.1. Washington, DC, 1997. Available: http://www.acponline.org/hpp/pospaper/andrulis.htm (accessed December 5, 2003).

86. Perlin SA, Sexton K, Wong DW. An examination of race and poverty for populations living near industrial sources of air pollution. *Journal of Exposure Analysis and Environmental Epidemiology* 1999;9(1):29–48.

87. Wernette DR, Nieves LA. Breathing polluted air: Minorities are disproportionately exposed. *EPA Journal* 1992;18:16–17.

88. Persky VW, Slezak J, Contreras A, Becker L, Hernandez E, Ramakrishnan V, Piorkowski J. Relationships of race and socioeconomic status with prevalence, severity, and symptoms of asthma in Chicago school children. *Annals of Allergy, Asthma and Immunology* 1998;81(3):266–71.

89. National Heart, Lung, and Blood Institute Working Group. Respiratory diseases disproportionately affect minorities. *Chest* 1995;108:1380–92; Mannino DM, Homa DM, Akinbami LJ, Moorman JE, Gwynn C, Redd SC. Surveillance for asthma—United States, 1980–1999. *Morbidity and Mortality Weekly Report* 2002;51(SS-1):1–13.

90. Rodriguez MA, Winkleby MA, Ahn D, Sundquist J, Kraemer HC. Identification of population subgroups of children and adolescents with high asthma prevalence: Findings from the Third National Health and Nutrition Examination Survey. *Archives of Pediatrics & Adolescent Medicine* 2002; 156(3):269–75.

91. Metzger R, Delgado JL, Herrell R. Environmental health and Hispanic children. *Environmental Health Perspectives* 1995;103 Suppl 6:539–50.

92. Chabra A, Chavez GF, Adams EJ, Taylor D. Characteristics of children having multiple Medicaid-paid asthma hospitalizations. *Maternal and Child Health Journal* 1998;2(4):223–29.

93. Litonjua AA, Carey VJ, Weiss ST, Gold DR. Race, socioeconomic factors, and area of residence are associated with asthma prevalence. *Pediatric Pulmonology* 1999;28(6):394–401.

94. Hanzlick R, McGowan D, Havlak J, Bishop M, Bennett H, Rawlins R, et al. Pedestrian fatalities—Cobb, DeKalb, Fulton, and Gwinnett Counties, Georgia, 1994–98. *Morbidity and Mortality Weekly Report* 1999;48:601–05.

95. Marosi R. Pedestrian deaths reveal O.C.'s car culture clash; Safety: Latinos, 28% of Orange County's population, are victims in 40% of walking injuries, 43% of deaths. *Los Angeles Times*, November 28, 1999, p 1.

96. Moreno S, Sipress A. Fatalities higher for Latino pedestrians; Area's Hispanic immigrants apt to walk but unaccustomed to urban traffic. *Washington Post*, August 27, 1999, p A01.

97. Austin City Connection. Who is at risk for pedestrian injuries? 2001. Available: http://www.ci.austin.tx.us/trafficsafety/pedwho.htm (accessed December 5, 2003).

98. Barlow JM, Bentzen BL, Tabor LS, et al. Accessible Pedestrian Signals: Synthesis and Guide to Best Practice. A report to the National Cooperative Highway Research Program, Transportation Research Board, National Research Council, May 2003. Available: http://www.walkinginfo.org/aps/home.cfm (accessed December 5, 2003).

99. ITE (Institute of Transportation Engineers) Technical Committee 5A-5. Design and Safety of Pedestrian Facilities. Washington, DC: ITE, 1998; AASHTO (American Association of State Highway and Transportation Officials). *A Policy on Geometric Design of Highways and Streets*, 4th Edition. Publication GDHS-4. Washington, DC: AASHTO, 2001.

CHAPTER 11

1. U.S. Bureau of the Census. Population Projections of the Total Resident Population by Quarter: Middle Series, April 1, 1999 to January 1, 2101. Table NP-T2. Available: http://www.census.gov/population/projections/nation/summary/np-t2.txt.

2. Szczygiel B, Hewitt R. Nineteenth-century medical landscapes: John H. Rauch, Frederick Law Olmsted, and the search for salubrity. *Bulletin of the History of Medicine* 2000;74:708–34.

3. Ashton J. The origins of healthy cities. In: Ashton J, Ed. *Healthy Cities*. Buckingham, UK: Open University Press, 1992, at pp 1–12.

4. McKeown T. *The Role of Medicine: Dream, Mirage or Nemesis?* Princeton, NJ: Princeton University Press, 1979.

5. Duhl L, Ed. *The Urban Condition*. New York: Basic Books, 1963.

6. Hancock T, Duhl L. *Healthy Cities: Promoting Health in the Urban Context*. Healthy Cities Paper #1. Copenhagen: WHO Europe, 1986.

7. Ibid.

8. Belfast Declaration for Healthy Cities. The Power of Local Action. Adopted 22 October 2003. http://www.healthycitiesbelfast2003.com/Belfast/BelfastDeclarationFinalUK.pdf.

9. Norris T, Pittman M. The Healthy Communities movement and the Coalition for Healthier Cities and Communities. *Public Health Reports* 2000;115:118–24.

10. Leccese M, McCormick K, Eds. *Charter of the New Urbanism.* New York: McGraw-Hill, 2000.

11. Maantay J. Zoning, equity and public health. *American Journal of Public Health* 2001;91:1033–41.

12. Haar CM, Kayden JS. *Zoning and the American Dream: Promises Still to Keep.* Chicago: American Planning Association, 1989.

13. Haar CM, Kayden JS. Zoning at sixty: A time for anniversary reckonings. In: Haar CM, Kayden JS. *Zoning and the American Dream: Promises Still to Keep.* Chicago: American Planning Association, 1989, pp ix–xi.

14. Local Government Commission. *Smart Growth Zoning Codes: A Resource Guide.* Sacramento: Local Government Commission, n.d.

15. Orfield M. *Metropolitics: A Regional Agenda for Community and Stability.* Washington, DC: Brookings Institution Press, 1997; Bollier D. *How Smart Growth Can Stop Sprawl: A Fledgling Citizen Movement Expands.* Washington, DC: Essential Books, 1998, pp 33–35.

16. Knaap GJ, Hopkins LD. The inventory approach to urban growth boundaries. *Journal of the American Planning Association* 2001;67:314–26; Weitz J. From quiet revolution to smart growth: State growth management programs, 1960 to 1999. *Journal of Planning Literature* 1999;14:268–338; Carruthers JI. The impact of state growth management programmes: A comparative analysis. *Urban Studies* 2002;39:1959–82.

17. Bollier, 1998, op. cit.; Katz B. Smart Growth: The future of the American metropolis? Centre for Analysis of Social Exclusion, London School of Economics. CASE paper 58, July 2002. Available: http://sticerd.lse.ac.uk/dps/case/cp/casepaper58.pdf.

18. Leinberger CB. Financing progressive development. A Capital Xchange journal article prepared for The Brookings Institution, Center on Urban and Metropolitan Policy, and Harvard University, Joint Center for Housing Studies. May 2001.

19. Katz, 2002, op. cit., p 24.

20. Boarnet M, Haughwout AF. *Do Highways Matter? Evidence and Policy Implications of Highway's Influence on Metropolitan Development.* Discussion Paper. Brookings Institution, Center on Urban and Metropolitan Policy, Washington, DC, 2000.

21. Surface Transportation Policy Project. *Stay the Course: How to Make TEA-21 Even Better.* Washington, DC: STPP, 2003. Available: http://www.transact.org/report.asp?id=203.

22. Gyourko J, Voith R. Does the U.S. Tax Treatment of Housing Promote Suburbanization and Central City Decline? Working Paper 97-13. Federal Reserve Bank of Philadelphia. 1997. Available: http://www.phil.frb.org/files/wps/1997/wp97-13.pdf; Katz, 2002, op. cit.

23. Litt JS, Burke TA. Uncovering the historic environmental hazards of urban brownfields. *Journal of Urban Health* 2002;79(4):464–81; Greenberg M. Reversing urban decay: Brownfield redevelopment and environmental health. *Environmental Health Perspectives* 2003;111(2):A74–A75.

24. Greenberg M. Should housing be built on former brownfield sites? *American Journal of Public Health* 2002;92(5):703–05.

25. Ahluwahlia G. Public attitudes toward growth. *Housing Economics* 1999; 37:7–12.

26. Malizia EE, Exline S. Consumer preferences for residential development alternatives. Working Paper 2000–02. University of North Carolina at Chapel Hill, Center for Urban and Regional Studies, 2000; Myers D, Gearin E. Current preferences and future demand for denser residential environments. *Housing Policy Debate* 2001;12:633–59.

27. Myers and Gearin, 2001, op. cit.

28. Ibid.

29. Belden Russonello & Stewart. *Americans' Attitudes Toward Smart Growth.* September 2000. Belden Russonello & Stewart, 1320 19th Street, NW, Suite 700, Washington, DC 20036. Available: http://www.brspoll.com/Reports/STPP%20report.pdf.

30. Myers and Gearin, 2001, op. cit.

31. Talen E. The social goals of New Urbanism. *Housing Policy Debate* 2002;13:165–88.

32. Giuliano G. The weakening transportation–land use connection. *Access* 1995;6:3–11.

33. Bae C-HC. Air quality and travel behavior. *Journal of the American Planning Association* 1993;59(1):65–74.

34. Kennedy M, Leonard P. Dealing with Neighborhood Change: A Primer on Gentrification and Policy Choices. Washington: Brookings Institution Center on Urban and Metropolitan Policy and PolicyLink, April 2001. Available: http://www.brookings.edu/dybdocroot/es/urban/gentrification/gentrification.pdf.

35. Green L, Kreuter M. *Health Promotion Planning,* Second Edition. Mountain View, CA: Mayfield Publishing, 1991; Donovan RJ. Steps in planning and developing health communication campaigns: A comment on CDC's framework for health communication. *Public Health Reports* 1995;110(2): 215–18.

36. World Commission on Environment and Development. *Our Common Future.* New York: Oxford University Press, 1987.

37. Portney KE. *Taking Sustainable Cities Seriously.* Cambridge: MIT Press, 2003.

38. Moldan B, Billharz S, Matravers S. *Sustainability Indicators: A Report on the Project on Indicators of Sustainable Development.* New York: Wiley, 1998.

39. Hart M. *Guide to Sustainable Community Indicators,* Second Edition. North Andover, MA: Sustainable Measures, 1999.

40. Takano T, Nakamura K. An analysis of health levels and various indicators of urban environments for Healthy Cities projects. *Journal of Epidemiology and Community Health* 2001;55:263–70.

41. Takano T, Fu J, Nakamura K, Uji K, Fukuda Y, Watanabe M, Nakajima H. Age-adjusted mortality and its association to variations in urban conditions in Shanghai. *Health Policy* 2002;61:239–53.

42. Weich S, Burton E, Blanchard M, Prince M, Sproston K, Erens B. Measuring the built environment: Validity of a site survey instrument for use in urban settings. *Health & Place* 2001;283–92.

43. Frumkin H. Healthy places: Exploring the evidence. *American Journal of Public Health* 2003;93(9):1451–55.

44. Dannenberg AL, Jackson RJ, Frumkin H, Schieber RA, Pratt M, Kochtitzky C, Tilson HH. The impact of community design and land use choices on public health: A scientific research agenda. *American Journal of Public Health* 2003;93(9):1500–08.

45. European Centre for Health Policy. *Gothenburg Consensus Paper: Health Impact Assessment: Main Concepts and Suggested Approach.* Brussels: WHO Regional Office for Europe, 1999. Available: http://www.who.dk/document/PAE/Gothenburgpaper.pdf.

46. Banken R. From concept to practice: Including the social determinants of health in environmental assessments. *Canadian Journal of Public Health. Revue Canadienne de Sante Publique* 1999;90 Suppl 1:S27–30; Alenius K. Consideration of health aspects in environmental impact assessments for roads. Stockholm: National Institute of Public Health, 2001. Available: http://www.airimpacts.org/documents/local/consider.pdf.

47. Fehr R. Environmental health impact assessment: Evaluation of a ten-step model. *Epidemiology* 1999;10(5):618–25.

48. Kjellstrom T, van Kerkhoff L, Bammer G, McMichael T. Comparative assessment of transport risks—how it can contribute to health impact assessment of transport policies. *Bulletin of the World Health Organization* 2003;81(6):451–57; Dora C, Racioppi F. Including health in transport policy agendas: The role of health impact assessment analyses and procedures in the European experience. *Bulletin of the World Health Organization* 2003;81(6):399–403.

49. Fehr R, 1999, op. cit.

50. Cave B, Curtis S. Developing a practical guide to assess the potential health impact of urban regeneration schemes. *Promotion & Education* 2001;8(1):12–16.

51. Douglas MJ, Conway L, Gorman D, Gavin S, Hanlon P. Developing principles for health impact assessment. *Journal of Public Health Medicine* 2001;

23(2):148–54; den Broeder L, Penris M, Put GV. Soft data, hard effects. Strategies for effective policy on health impact assessment—an example from the Netherlands. *Bulletin of the World Health Organization* 2003; 81(6):404–07.

52. Fehr R, Mekel O, Lacombe M, Wolf U. Towards health impact assessment of drinking-water privatization—the example of waterborne carcinogens in North Rhine-Westphalia (Germany). *Bulletin of the World Health Organization* 2003;81(6):408–14.

53. Gorman D, Douglas MJ, Conway L, Noble P, Hanlon P. Transport policy and health inequalities: A health impact assessment of Edinburgh's transport policy. *Public Health* 2003;117(1):15–24.

54. Parry J, Stevens A. Prospective health impact assessment: Pitfalls, problems, and possible ways forward. *British Medical Journal* 2001;323:1177–82.

55. Wingspread Statement on the Precautionary Principle. January, 1998. Available: http://www.gdrc.org/u-gov/precaution-3.html.

56. Raffensberger C, Tickner J, Jackson W. *Protecting Public Health and the Environment: Implementing the Precautionary Principle.* Washington, DC: Island Press, 1999.

57. *NACCHO Exchange* 2003;2(1):1–28.

58. NACCHO. *The Role for Local Public Health Agencies in Land Use Planning and Community Design.* Washington, DC: NACCHO, n.d.

59. Greenberg M, Popper F, West B, Krueckeberg D. Linking city planning and public health in the United States. *Journal of Planning Literature* 1994;8(3):235–39.

BIBLIOGRAPHY

■ ══════════ ■

Adler NE, Marmot M, McEwen B, Stewart J, Eds. Socioeconomic status and health in industrial nations: Social, psychological and biological pathways. *Annals of the New York Academy of Sciences* Vol 896. New York: NYAS, 1999.

Adler NE, Ostrove JM. Socioeconomic status and health: What we know and what we don't. *Annals of the New York Academy of Sciences* 1999;896:3–15.

Agran PF, Winn DG, Anderson CL, et al. The role of the physical and traffic environment in child pedestrian injuries. *Pediatrics* 1996;98:1096–1103.

Ahluwahlia G. Public attitudes toward growth. *Housing Economics* 1999;37:7–12.

Aicher J. *Designing Healthy Cities: Prescriptions, Principles and Practice*. Malabar, FL: Krieger Publishing Company, 1998.

Aiello JR, Baum A, Gormley FP. Social determinants of residential crowding stress. *Personality and Social Psychology Bulletin* 1981;7:643–49.

Aiello JR, Nicosia G, Thompson E. Physiological, social, and behavioral consequences of crowding on children and adolescents. *Child Development* 1979;50:195–202.

Ainsworth BE, Haskell WL, Leon AS, et al. Compendium of physical activities: Classification of energy costs of human physical activities. *Medicine and Science in Sports and Exercise* 1993;25:71–80.

Alenius K. Consideration of health aspects in environmental impact assessments for roads. Stockholm: National Institute of Public Health, 2001. Available: http://www.airimpacts.org/documents/local/consider.pdf.

Alexander C, Ishikawa S, Silverstein M, Jacobson M, Fiksdahl-King I, Angel S. *A Pattern Language: Towns, Buildings, Construction*. New York: Oxford University Press, 1977.

Alley WM, Healy RW, LaBaugh JW, Reilly TE. Flow and storage in groundwater systems. *Science* 2002;296(5575):1985–90.

Allison DB, Fontaine KR, Manson JE, Stevens J, VanItallie TB. Annual deaths attributable to obesity in the United States. *JAMA*. 1999;282:1530–38.

Allman TD. The urban crisis leaves town. *Harper's Magazine*, December 1978, pp 41–56. Reprinted in Callow AB Jr, Ed. *American Urban History*, Third Edition. New York: Oxford University Press, 1982, pp 534–57.

Altman I. *The Environment and Social Behavior: Privacy, Personal Space, Territory, and Crowding*. Monterey, CA: Brooks-Cole, 1975.

Altsuler A, Morrill W, Wolman H, Mitchell F, Eds. *Governance and Opportunity in Metropolitan Areas*. Washington, DC: National Academy Press, 1999.

American Association of State Highway and Transportation Officials (AASHTO). *A Policy on Geometric Design of Highways and Streets*, 4th Edition. Publication GDHS-4. Washington, DC: AASHTO, 2001.

American Society of Civil Engineers. *ASCE's 2001 Report Card for America's*

Infrastructure. Washington, DC: Civil Engineering Research Foundation, 2001.

Anderson J, Tindall M. The concept of home range: New data for the study of territorial behavior. In: Mitchell WJ, Ed. *Environmental Design: Research and Practice*. Los Angeles: Environmental Design Research Association, 1972. Cited in van Vliet W. Exploring the fourth environment: An examination of the home range of city and suburban teenagers. *Environment and Behavior* 1983;15: 567–88.

Andrulis D, Shaw-Taylor Y, Ginsberg C, et al. *Urban Social Health: A Chartbook Profiling the Nation's One Hundred Largest Cities*. Washington, DC: The National Public Health and Hospital Institute, 1995.

Andrulis DP. The urban health penalty: New dimensions and directions in inner-city health care. American College of Physicians Position Paper No.1. Washington, DC, 1997. Available: http://www.acponline.org/hpp/pospaper/andrulis.htm.

Andrulis DP, Goodman NJ, National Public Health and Hospital Institute. *The Social and Health Landscape of Urban and Suburban America*. Chicago: American Hospital Association Press, 1999.

Anonymous. *Building Livable Communities: Sustaining Prosperity, Improving Quality of Life, Building a Sense of Community*. A Report from the Clinton-Gore Administration. Washington, DC: Livable Communities, 2000.

Anonymous. *Getting to Smart Growth: 100 Policies for Implementation*. Washington, DC: Smart Growth Network and International City/County Management Association, 2002.

Anonymous. Mall accused of racism in a wrongful death trial in Buffalo. *New York Times* 1999 Nov 15; B4.

Apogee Research, Inc. *The Effects of Urban Form on Travel and Emissions: A Review and Synthesis of the Literature*. Draft report prepared for the United States Environmental Protection Agency. HBIX Reference C611-005. Washington, DC, 1998.

Ards S, Mincy R. Neighborhood ecology. In: Besharov D, Ed. *When Drug Addicts Have Children*. Washington, DC: Child Welfare League of America, 1994, pp 33–49.

Arnold CL, Gibbons CJ. Impervious surface coverage: The emergence of a key environmental indicator. *Journal of the American Planning Association* 1996;62:243–58.

Aronow WS, Harris CN, Isbell MW, Rokaw MD, Imparato B. Effect of freeway travel on angina pectoris. *Annals of Internal Medicine* 1972;77: 669–76.

Ashton J, Ed. *Healthy Cities*. Buckingham, UK: Open University Press, 1992.

Ashton JR. Healthy cities and healthy settings. *Promotion et Education* 2002; Suppl 1:12–14.

Austin City Connection. Who is at risk for pedestrian injuries? 2001. Available: http://www.ci.austin.tx.us/trafficsafety/pedwho.htm.

Avol EL, Gauderman WJ, Tan SM, London SJ, Peters JM. Respiratory effects of relocating to areas of differing air pollution levels. *American Journal of Respiratory and Critical Care Medicine* 2001;164:2067–72.

Avramopoulos D, Asvall JE. Athens Declaration for Healthy Cities. *Journal of Public Health Medicine* 1998;20(4): 372–74.

Babyak M, Blumenthal JA, Herman S, Khatri P, Doraiswamy M, Moore K, Craighead WE, Baldewicz TT, Krishnan KR. Exercise treatment for major depression: Maintenance of therapeutic benefit at 10 months. *Psychosomatic Medicine* 2000;62(5): 633–38.

Bachman W, Sarasua W, Hallmark S, Guensler R. Modeling regional mobile source emissions in a geographic information system framework. *Transportation Research Part C* 2000;8:205–29.

Backman AL. Health survey of professional drivers. *Scandinavian Journal of Work, Environment and Health* 1983;9:36–41.

Bae C-HC. Air quality and travel behavior. *Journal of the American Planning Association* 1993;59(1):65–74.

Bagley C. The urban setting of juvenile pedestrian injuries: A study of behavioral ecology and social disadvantage. *Accident Analysis and Prevention* 1992; 24:673–78.

Baker L. The wheel deal: Sprawl: Soccer moms' public enemy No. 1. *Northern Californian Bohemian*, January 4–10, 2001. Available: http://www.metroactive.com/papers/sonoma/01.04.01/soccermoms-0101.html.

Ball K, Bauman A, Leslie E, Owen N. Perceived environmental and social influences on walking for exercise in Australian adults. *Preventive Medicine* 2001;33:434–40.

Banken R. From concept to practice: Including the social determinants of health in environmental assessments. *Canadian Journal of Public Health/ Revue Canadienne de Sante Publique* 1999;90 Suppl 1:S27–30.

Bannerman RT, Owens DW, Dodds RB, Hornewer NJ. Sources of pollutants in Wisconsin stormwater. *Water Science and Technology* 1993;28(3–5): 241–59.

Barber G. Aggregate characteristics of urban travel. In: Hanson S, Ed. *The Geography of Urban Transportation.* New York: The Guilford Press, 1986, pp 73–90.

Barlow JM, Bentzen BL, Tabor LS, et al. Accessible Pedestrian Signals: Synthesis and Guide to Best Practice. A report to the National Cooperative Highway Research Program, Transportation Research Board, National Research Council. May 2003. Available: http://www.walkinginfo.org/aps/home.cfm.

Barwick RS, Levy DA, Craun GF, Beach MJ, Calderon RL. Surveillance for waterborne-disease outbreaks— United States, 1997–1998. *Morbidity and Mortality Weekly Report* 2000; 49(SS-4):1–35.

Bassuk SS, Glass TA, Berkman LF. Social disengagement and incident cognitive decline in community-dwelling elderly persons. *Annals of Internal Medicine* 1999;131:165–73.

Batten PJ, Penn DW, Bloom JD. A 36-year history of fatal road rage in Marion County, Oregon: 1963–1998. *Journal of Forensic Sciences* 2000;45:397–99.

Batty GD. Physical activity and coronary heart disease in older adults. A systematic review of epidemiological studies. *European Journal of Public Health* 2002;12(3):171–76.

Baum A, Aiello JR, Calesnick LE. Crowding and personal control: Social density and the development of learned helplessness. *Journal of Personality and Social Psychology* 1978;36:1000–11.

Baum A, Epstein J, Eds. *Human Response to Crowding.* Hillsdale, NJ: Lawrence Erlbaum, 1978.

Baum F. Social capital, economic capital and power: Further issues for a public health agenda. *Journal of Epidemiology and Community Health* 2000;54: 409–10.

Baum F. Social capital: Is it good for your health? Issues for a public health agenda. *Journal of Epidemiology and Community Health* 1999;53:195–96.

Baumgartner MP. *The Moral Order of a Suburb.* New York: Oxford University Press, 1989.

Baxandall R, Ewen E. *Picture Windows: How the Suburbs Happened.* New York: Basic Books, 2000.

Baxter JS, Macrae CN, Manstead ASR, Stradling SG, Parker D. Attributional biases and driver behavior. *Social Behavior* 1990;5:185–92.

Belden Russonello & Stewart. *Americans' Attitudes Toward Smart Growth.* September 2000. Belden Russonello & Stewart, 1320 19th Street, NW, Suite 700, Washington, DC 20036. Available: http://www.brspoll.com/Reports/STPP%20report.pdf.

Belfast Declaration for Healthy Cities. The Power of Local Action. Adopted 22 October 2003. Available: http://www.healthycitiesbelfast2003.com/Belfast/BelfastDeclarationFinalUK.pdf.

Belkić K, Savić C, Theorell T, Rakić L, Ercegovac D, Djordjević M.

Mechanisms of cardiac risk among professional drivers. *Scandinavian Journal of Work, Environment and Health* 1994;20(2):73–86.

Bell M, Davis DL. Reassessment of the lethal London fog of 1952: Novel indicators of acute and chronic consequences of acute exposures to air pollution. *Environmental Health Perspectives* 2001;109(3):389–94.

Bellet S, Roman L, Kostis J. The effects of automobile driving on catecholamine and adrenocortical excretion. *American Journal of Cardiology* 1969;24: 365–68.

Berard A, Bravo G, Gauthier P. Meta-analysis of the effectiveness of physical activity for the prevention of bone loss in postmenopausal women. *Osteoporosis International* 1997;7:331–37.

Bergamaschi E, De Palma G, Mozzoni P, Vanni S, Vettori MV, Broeckaert F, et al. Polymorphism of quinone-metabolizing enzymes and susceptibility to ozone-induced acute effects. *American Journal of Respiratory and Critical Care Medicine* 2001;163(6):1426–31.

Berkman LF. The role of social relations in health promotion. *Psychosomatic Medicine* 1995;57:245–54.

Berkman LF, Syme SL. Social networks, host resistance, and mortality: A nine-year follow-up study of Alameda County residents. *American Journal of Epidemiology* 1979;109:186–204.

Berrigan D, Troiano RP. The association between urban form and physical activity in U.S. adults. *American Journal of Preventive Medicine* 2002;23(2S): 74–79.

Besharov D, Ed. *When Drug Addicts Have Children*. Washington, DC: Child Welfare League of America, 1994.

Better Together: Report of the Saguaro Seminar on Civic Engagement in America, John F. Kennedy School of Government, Harvard University. Cambridge, MA: 2000. http://www. bettertogether.org/report.php3.

Bhaduri B, Harbor J, Engel B, Grove M. Assessing watershed-scale long-term hydrologic impacts of land-use change using a GIS-NPS model.

Environmental Management 2000;26: 643–58.

Biegel BE, McCardle I, Mendelson S. *Social Networks and Mental Health: An Annotated Bibliography*. Beverly Hills, CA: Sage, 1985.

Bielaczyc P, Merkisz J. A study of gaseous emissions measured under ambient cold start and warm-up conditions. Fourth International Conference on Urban Transport and Environment for the 21st Century. Wessex Institute of Technology, UK, and the University of Aveiro, Portugal, 1998, pp 491–500.

Blair S, Kohl H, Paffenbarger R, Clark D, Cooper K, Gibbons L. Physical fitness and all-cause mortality: A prospective study of healthy men and women. *JAMA* 1989;273:1093–98.

Blair SN, Kampert JB, Kohl HW III, Barlow CE, Macera CA, Paffenbarger RS Jr, Gibbons LW. Influences of cardiorespiratory fitness and other precursors on cardiovascular disease and all-cause mortality in men and women. *JAMA* 1996;276:205–10.

Blakely KS. Parents' conception of social dangers to children in the urban environment. *Children's Environments* 1994;11:16–25.

Blumenthal JA, Babyak MA, Moore KA, Craighead WE, Herman S, Khatri P, Waugh R, Napolitano MA, Forman LM, Appelbaum M, Doraiswamy PM, Krishnan KR. Effects of exercise training on older patients with major depression. *Archives of Internal Medicine* 1999;159(19):2349–56.

Blumenthal JA, Burg MM, Barefoot J, Williams RB, Haney T, Zimet G. Social support, type A behavior, and coronary artery disease. *Psychosomatic Medicine* 1987;49(4):331–40.

Blumstein A, Wallman J, Eds. *The Crime Drop in America*. New York: Cambridge University Press, 2000.

Boarnet M, Haughwout AF. *Do Highways Matter? Evidence and Policy Implications of Highways' Influence on Metropolitan Development*. Discussion Paper. Brookings Institution, Center on Urban and Metropolitan Policy. Washington, DC, 2000.

Boarnet M, Sarmiento S. Can land use policy really affect travel behavior? A study of the link between non-work travel and land use characteristics. *Urban Studies* 1998;35(7):1155–69.

Bodin M, Hartig T. Does the outdoor environment matter for psychological restoration gained through running? *Psychology of Sport and Exercise* 2003;4: 141–53.

Bollier D. *How Smart Growth Can Stop Sprawl: A Fledgling Citizen Movement Expands.* Washington, DC: Essential Books, 1998.

Bonaiuti D, Shea B, Iovine R, Negrini S, Robinson V, Kemper HC, Wells G, Tugwell P, Cranney A. Exercise for preventing and treating osteoporosis in postmenopausal women (Cochrane Methodology Review). In: *The Cochrane Library*, Issue 4, 2003. Chichester, UK: John Wiley & Sons, Ltd.

Boorman GA. Drinking water disinfection byproducts: Review and approach to toxicity evaluation. *Environmental Health Perspectives* 1999;10(Suppl 1): 207–17.

Booth MN, Owen A, Bauman A, Clavisi O, Leslie E. Social-cognitive and perceived environmental influences associated with physical activity in older Australians. *Preventive Medicine* 2000; 31:15–22.

Bothwell S, Gindroz R, Lang R. Restoring community through traditional neighborhood design: A case study of Diggs Town public housing. *Housing Policy Debate* 1998;9(1):89–114.

Boudewijn B, de Geest G, Eds. *Encyclopedia of Law and Economics, Volume II. Civil Law and Economics.* Cheltenham, UK: Edward Elgar, 2000.

Bourdieu P. The forms of capital. In: Richardson J., Ed. *Handbook of Theory and Research for the Sociology of Education.* New York: Greenwood Press, 1986, pp 241–58.

Bove F, Shim Y, Zeitz P. Drinking water contaminants and adverse pregnancy outcomes: A review. *Environmental Health Perspectives* 2002;110(suppl 1): 61–74.

Bovenzi M, Zadini A. Self-reported low back symptoms in urban bus drivers exposed to whole body vibration. *Spine* 1992;17:1048–59.

Brabec E, Schulte S, Richards PL. Impervious surfaces and water quality: A review of current literature and its implications for watershed planning. *Journal of Planning Literature* 2002;16: 499–514.

Braddock M, Papidus G, Gregorio D, et al. Population, income and ecological correlates of child pedestrian injury. *Pediatrics* 1991;88:1242–47.

Brehm J, Rahn W. Individual-level evidence for the causes and consequences of social capital. *American Journal of Political Science* 1997;41(3):999–1023.

Brezinka V, Kittel F. Psychosocial factors of coronary heart disease in women: A review. *Social Science and Medicine* 1996;42(10):1351–65.

Bricker SK, Kanny D, PhD, Mellinger-Birdsong A, Powell KE, Shisler JL. School transportation modes— Georgia, 2000. *Morbidity and Mortality Weekly Report* 2002;51:704–05.

Brieger GH. *Medical America in the Nineteenth Century: Readings from the Literature.* Baltimore: Johns Hopkins University Press, 1972.

Briggs, XN de S. Social capital and the cities: Advice to change agents. *National Civic Review* 1997;86:111–17.

Brimblecombe P. *The Big Smoke.* London: Routeldge, 1988, p 48.

Broadhead EW, Kaplan BH, James SA, et al. The epidemiologic evidence for a relationship between social support and health. *American Journal of Epidemiology* 1983;117:521–37.

Brodish PH, Massing M, Tyroler HA. Income inequality and all-cause mortality in the 100 counties of North Carolina. *Southern Medical Journal* 2000;93(4):386–91.

Brooks-Gunn J, Duncan G, Klebanov P, Sealand N. Do neighborhoods influence child and adolescent development? *American Journal of Sociology* 1993;99:353–95.

Brosse AL, Sheets ES, Lett HS, Blumenthal JA. Exercise and the treatment of clinical depression in adults: Recent findings and future directions. *Sports Medicine* 2002;32(12):741–60.

Brownell KD, Horgen KB. *Food Fight: The Inside Story of the Food Industry, America's Obesity Crisis, and What We Can Do About It.* New York: McGraw-Hill, 2003.

Brun SE, Band LE. Simulating runoff behavior in an urbanizing watershed. *Computers, Environment and Urban Systems* 2000;24:5–22.

Brunekreef B, Holgate ST. Air pollution and health. *Lancet* 2002;360:1233–42.

Brunekreef B. Air pollution and life expectancy: Is there a relation? *Occupational and Environmental Medicine* 1997;54(11):781–84.

Bullard RD, Johnson GS, Torres AO. *Sprawl City: Race, Politics, and Planning in Atlanta.* Washington, DC: Island Press, 2000.

Bullard RD, Johnson GS. *Just Transportation: Dismantling Race and Class Barriers to Mobility.* Gabriola Island, BC, and Stony Creek, CT: New Society Publishers, 1997.

Bullard, Robert. D. 1990. *Dumping in Dixie: Race, Class, and Environmental Quality.* Boulder, CO: Westview.

Bunn F, Collier T, Frost C, Ker K, Roberts I, Wentz R. Area-wide traffic calming for preventing traffic related injuries. *Cochrane Database of Systematic Reviews* 2003;1:CD003110.

Burchell RW, Shad NA, Listokin D, Phillips H, Downs A, Seskins S, Davis JS, Moore T, Helton D, Gall M. *The Costs of Sprawl-Revisited.* Transportation Research Board; Transit Cooperative Research Program, Report 39. Washington, DC: National Academy Press, 1998.

Bureau of Transportation Statistics. National Transportation Statistics 2003. 2003. Available: http://www.bts.gov/publications/national_transportation_statistics/2003/index.html.

Burger H, Kaiser HE. Crowding. *In Vivo* 1996;10(2):249–53.

Burns LD, McCormick JB, Borroni-Bird CE. Vehicle of change. *Scientific American* 2002;287(4):64–73.

Burns NM, Baker CA, Simonson E, Keiper C. Electrocardiogram changes in prolonged automobile driving. *Perceptual and Motor Skills* 1966;23(1):210.

Buttle JM, Xu F. Snowmelt runoff in suburban environments (Ontario, Canada). *Nordic Hydrology* 1988;19:19–40.

Butts JA. Youth Crime Drop. The Urban Institute, December 2000. http://www.urban.org/crime/module/butts/youth-crime-drop.html.

Caldwell M. *The Last Crusade: The War on Consumption 1862–1954.* New York: Atheneum, 1988.

Calhoun JB. Population density and social pathology. *Scientific American* 1972; 206:139–48.

Calle EE, Rodriguez C, Walker-Thurmond K, Thun MJ. Overweight, obesity, and mortality from cancer in a prospectively studied cohort of U.S. adults. *New England Journal of Medicine* 2003;348:1625–38.

Calle EE, Thun MJ, Petrelli JM, Rodriguez C, Heath CW Jr. Body-mass index and mortality in a prospective cohort of U.S. adults. *New England Journal of Medicine* 1999;341:1097–1105.

Callender E, Rice KC. The urban environmental gradient: Anthropogenic influences on the spatial and temporal distributions of lead and zinc in sediments. *Environmental Science and Technology* 2000;34:232–38.

Calthrope P. *The Next American Metropolis: Ecology, Community, and the American Dream.* Princeton, NJ: Princeton Architectural Press, 1993.

Camacho TC, Roberts RE, Lazarus NB, Kaplan GA, Cohen RD. Physical activity and depression: Evidence from the Alameda County Study. *American Journal of Epidemiology* 1991;134:220–30.

Cantor KP. Drinking water and cancer. *Cancer Causes and Control* 1997;8(3): 292–308.

Carothers T. Think again: The concept of civil society is a recent invention. *Foreign Policy* 1999(winter):18–29.

Carpenter SR, Caraco NF, Correll DL, Howarth RW, Sharpley AN, Smith VH. Nonpoint pollution of surface water with phosphorus and nitrogen.

Ecological Applications 1998;8(3): 559–68.

Carruthers JI. The impact of state growth management programmes: A comparative analysis. *Urban Studies* 2002; 39:1959–82.

Case RB, Moss AJ, Case N, McDermott M, Eberly S. Living alone after myocardial infarction: Impact on prognosis. *JAMA* 1992;267: 520–24.

Catell V. Poor people, poor places, and poor health: The mediating role of social networks and social capital. *Social Science and Medicine* 2001;52: 1501–16.

Cave B, Curtis S. Developing a practical guide to assess the potential health impact of urban regeneration schemes. *Promotion et Education* 2001; 8(1):12–16.

Centers for Disease Control and Prevention (CDC). *Chronic Diseases and Their Risk Factors: The Nation's Leading Causes of Death.* Atlanta: Centers for Disease Control and Prevention, 1999a.

———. Coronary heart disease attributable to sedentary lifestyle—selected states, 1988. *Morbidity and Mortality Weekly Report* 1990;39: 541–44.

———. Mean physically or mentally unhealthy days. Health-related quality of life: Prevalence data. CDC, National Center for Chronic Disease Prevention and Health Promotion, 2003. Available: http://apps.nccd. cdc.gov/HRQOL/TrendV.asp.

———. Motor-vehicle safety: A 20th century public health achievement. *Morbidity and Mortality Weekly Report* 1999;48:369–74.

———. *Physical Activity and Health: A Report of the Surgeon General.* Centers for Disease Control and Prevention, National Center for Chronic Disease Prevention and Health Promotion, 1996.

———. National Center for Chronic Disease Prevention and Health Promotion, Diabetes Public Health Resource. Prevalence of Diabetes. Available: www.cdc.gov/diabetes/ statistics/prev/national/table8.htm.

———. National Center for Health Statistics. Asthma Prevalence, Health Care Use and Mortality, 2000–2001. Available: www.cdc.gov/nchs/products/ pubs/pubd/hestats/asthma/asthma.htm.

———. National Center for Health Statistics. Health, United States, 2003. Hyattsville, MD: NCHS, 2003. Table 112. Gross domestic product, federal and state and local government expenditures, national health expenditures, and average annual percent change: United States, selected years 1960–2001. Available http://www. cdc.gov/nchs/data/hus/tables/2003/ 03hus112.pdf (accessed on 8 Feb 2004).

———. National Center for Health Statistics. *Health, United States, 2003.* Hyattsville, MD: NCHS, 2003. Table 117. Expenditures for health care and prescribed medicine according to selected population characteristics: United States, selected years 1987–99. Available: http://www.cdc.gov/nchs/ data/hus/tables/2003/03hus117.pdf.

Cervero R. *The Transit Metropolis: A Global Inquiry.* Washington, DC: Island Press, 1998.

Cervero R. Land-use mixing and suburban mobility. *Transportation Quarterly* 1988;42(3):429–46.

Cervero R. Mixed land uses and commuting: Evidence from the American Housing Survey. *Transportation Research Part A* 1996;30(5):361–77.

Cervero R, Gorham R. Commuting in transit versus automobile neighborhoods. *Journal of the American Planning Association* 1995;61:210–25.

Cervero R, Kockelman K. Travel demand and the 3Ds: Density, diversity and design. *Transportation Research Part D* 1997;2(3):199–219.

Chabra A, Chavez GF, Adams EJ, Taylor D. Characteristics of children having multiple Medicaid-paid asthma hospitalizations. *Maternal Child and Health Journal* 1998;2(4):223–29.

Champion L. The relationship between social vulnerability and the occurrence of severely threatening life events. *Psychological Medicine* 1990; 20(1):157–61.

Chan CC, Ozkaynak H, Spengler JD, Sheldon L. Driver exposure to volatile organic compounds, CO, ozone, and NO$_2$ under different driving conditions. *Environmental Science and Technology* 1991;25:964–72.

Chan CC, Spengler JD, Ozkaynak H, Lefkopoulou M. Commuter exposures to VOCs in Boston, Massachusetts. *Journal of the Air and Waste Management Association* 1991;41:1594–1600.

Chavis DM, Pretty G. Sense of community: Advances in measurement and application. *Journal of Community Psychology* 1999;27:635–42.

Chen D. Remembering Cynthia Wiggins: A lesson in transportation and community revitalization. *Environmental Action* 1996;28(1/2):31–32.

Chen L, Yang W, Jennison BL, Goodrich A, Omaye ST. Air pollution and birth weight in northern Nevada, 1991–1999. *Inhalation Toxicology* 2002;14(2):141–57.

Chen Y, Dales R, Tang M, et al. Obesity may increase the incidence of asthma in women but not in men: Longitudinal observations from the Canadian National Population Health Surveys. *American Journal of Epidemiology* 2002;155:191–97.

Childress H. *Landscapes of Betrayal, Landscapes of Joy: Curtisville in the Lives of Its Teenagers*. Albany: State University of New York Press, 2000.

Christian JJ. The pathology of overpopulation. *Military Medicine* 1973;123:571–603.

Churchman A. Disentangling the concept of density. *Journal of Planning Literature* 1999;13:389–411.

Chute CG, Smith RP, Baron JA. Risk factors for endemic giardiasis. *American Journal of Public Health* 1987;77:585–87.

Ciccone G, Gruppo collaborativo SIDRIA. Caratteristiche del traffico nei pressi dell'abitazione e danni respiratori in età pediatrica: I risultati di SIDRIA [Characteristics of traffic near residences and respiratory effects in children: Results from SIDRIA]. *Annali dell'Istituto Superiore di Sanitàà* 2000;36(3):305–09.

City of Olympia, Washington. Impervious surface reduction study: Technical and policy analysis final report. City of Olympia Public Works Department, 1995.

Cochrun S. Understanding and enhancing neighborhood sense of community. *Journal of Planning Literature* 1994;9:92–99.

Cohen AJ. Outdoor air pollution and lung cancer. *Environmental Health Perspectives* 2000;108(Suppl 4):743–50.

Cohen BA, Wiles R, Campbell C, Chen D, Kruse J, Corless J. *Mean streets: Pedestrian safety and reform of the nation's transportation law*. Washington, DC: Surface Transportation Policy Project and Environmental Working Group, 1997. Also available: http://www.ewg.org/pub/home/reports/meanstreets/mean.html [cited July 30, 2002].

Colburn T, et al. *Great Lakes, Great Legacy?* Washington, DC: The Conservation Foundation, 1990. Quoted in Markham A. *A Brief History of Pollution*. New York: St. Martin's Press, 1994, at p 62.

Coleman J. Social capital in the creation of human capital. *American Journal of Sociology* 1988;94:S95–S120.

Connell D, Joint M. Driver aggression. In: *Aggressive Driving: Three Studies*. Washington, DC: AAA Foundation for Traffic Safety, March 1997. Available: http://www.aaafoundation.org/pdf/agdr3study.pdf (accessed June 23, 2002).

Cook J, Adams BB, Breukelman F, Mitchell C, Steiner B, Costello N, et al. Self-reported physical inactivity by degree of urbanization—United States, 1996. *Morbidity and Mortality Weekly Report* 1998;47(50):1097–1100.

Costa G, Pickup L, Di Martino V. Commuting—a further stress factor for working people: Evidence from the European Community. I. A review. *International Archives of Occupational and Environmental Health* 1988a;60(5):371–76.

Costa G, Pickup L, DiMartino V. Commuting—a further stress factor for working people: Evidence from the

European community. II. An empirical study. *International Archives of Occupational and Environmental Health* 1988b;60:377–85.

Coughlin J, Lacombe A. Ten myths about transportation for the elderly. *Transportation Quarterly* 1997;51(1): 91–100.

Cowan RS. *More Work for Mother: The Ironies of Household Technology from the Open Hearth to the Microwave.* New York: Basic Books, 1983.

Craig CL, Brownson RC, Cragg SE, Dunn AL. Exploring the effect of the environment on physical activity: A study examining walking to work. *American Journal of Preventive Medicine* 2002;23(2S):36–43.

Crane R. Cars and drivers in the new suburbs: Linking access to travel in neo-traditional planning. *Journal of the American Planning Association* 1996; 62(1):51–63.

Crane R. *The Impacts of Urban Form on Travel: A Critical Review.* Cambridge, MA: Lincoln Institute of Land Policy Working Paper No. WP99RC1, 1999.

Craun GF, Nwachuku N, Calderon RL, Craun MF. Outbreaks in drinking-water systems, 1991–1998. *Journal of Environmental Health* 2002;65(1): 16–23.

Craun GF. Waterborne disease outbreaks in the United States of America: Causes and prevention. *World Health Statistics Quarterly* 1992;45: 192–99.

Crawford JA. Extent and effects of hand-held cellular telephone use while driving. Research Report SWUTC/ 01/167706-1. Texas Transportation Institute, February 2001. Available: http://swutc.tamu.edu/Reports/ 167706-1.pdf.

Crespo CJ, Smit E, Andersen RE, Carter-Pokras O, Ainsworth BE. Race/ethnicity, social class and their relation to physical inactivity during leisure time: Results from the Third National Health and Nutrition Examination Survey, 1988–1994. *American Journal of Preventive Medicine* 2000;18(1): 46–53.

Critser G. *Fat Land: How Americans Became the Fattest People in the World.* Boston: Houghton Mifflin, 2003.

Cross-National Collaborative Group. The changing rate of major depression: Cross-national comparisons. *JAMA* 1992;268:3098–3105.

Cubbin C, LeClerc FB, Smith GS. Socioeconomic status and the occurrence of fatal and nonfatal injury in the United States. *American Journal of Public Health* 2000;90:70–77.

Curbow B, Griffin J. Road rage or road benefit? Relationships with demographic, home and work variables. Presented at the 1999 American Psychological Association/National Institute of Occupational Safety and Health Conference, Baltimore.

Curriero FC, Patz JA, Rose JB, Lele SD. The association between extreme precipitation and waterborne disease outbreaks in the United States, 1948–1994. *American Journal of Public Health* 2001;91:1194–99.

Curtice L, Springett J, Kennedy A. Evaluation in urban settings: The challenge of Healthy Cities. *WHO Regional Publications. European Series* 2001;92: 309–34.

Daly MC, Duncan GJ, Kaplan GA, Lynch JW. Macro-to-micro links in the relation between income inequality and mortality. *Milbank Quarterly* 1998;76:315–39.

Dannenberg AL, Jackson RJ, Frumkin H, Schieber RA, Pratt M, Kochtitzky C, Tilson HH. The impact of community design and land use choices on public health: A scientific research agenda. *American Journal of Public Health* 2003;93(9):1500–08.

David TG, Weinstein CS. The built environment and children's development. In: Weinstein CS, David TG, Eds. *Spaces for Children: The Built Environment and Child Development.* York: Plenum, 1987, pp 3–20.

Davis E, Millman M, Eds. Health Care for the Urban Poor: Directions for Policy. Lamham, Maryland:Davis E, Millman M, Eds. *Health Care for the Urban Poor: Directions for Policy.*

Lanham, MD: Rowman & Littlefield, 1983.

Dean A, Kolody B, Wood P. Effects of social support from various sources on depression in elderly persons. *Journal of Health and Social Behavior* 1990;31:148–61.

Deffenbacher JL, Oetting ER, Lynch RS. Development of a driver anger scale. *Psychological Reports* 1994;74: 83–91.

DeForest RW, Veiller L, Eds. *The Tenement House Problem, I.* New York: New York State Tenement House Commission, 1903.

Dellinger AM, Staunton CE. Barriers to children walking and biking to school—United States, 1999. *Morbidity and Mortality Weekly Report* 2002; 51(32):701–04.

den Broeder L, Penris M, Put GV. Soft data, hard effects. Strategies for effective policy on health impact assessment—an example from the Netherlands. *Bulletin of the World Health Organization* 2003;81(6):404–07.

Department of Agriculture, Natural Resources Conservation Service. National Resources Inventory. January, 2001. Available: http://www.nrcs.usda.gov/technical/land/pubs/97highlights.pdf.

Department of Energy, Energy Information Administration. Residential Energy Consumption Survey. November, 2002. Available: www.eia.doe.gov/emeu/recs/cookingtrends/cooking.html.

Department of Labor, Bureau of International Labor Affairs. *A Chartbook of International Labor Comparisons: United States, Europe, and Asia.* Washington: USDOL, May 2003. Chart 19. Annual hours worked per employed person, 1990 and 2001. Available: http://www.dol.gov/ILAB/media/reports/oiea/chartbook/chart19.htm.

Dierberg FE. Non-point source loadings of nutrients and dissolved organic carbon from an agricultural-suburban watershed in east central Florida. *Water Resources* 1991;25:363–74.

Diette GB, Lechtzin N, Haponik E, Devrotes A, Rubin HR. Distraction therapy with nature sights and sounds reduces pain during flexible bronchoscopy: A complementary approach to routine analgesia. *Chest* 2003; 123(3):941–48.

Dietz WH. Health consequences of obesity in youth: Childhood predictors of adult disease. *Pediatrics* 1998;101 (3 Pt 2):518–25.

DiLiberti JH. The relationship between social stratification and all-cause mortality among children in the United States, 1968–1992. *Pediatrics* 2000; 105:105–06.

DiMaggio C, Durkin M. Child pedestrian injury in an urban setting: Descriptive epidemiology. *Academic Emergency Medicine* 2002;9(1):54–62.

Dockery D. Epidemiologic evidence of cardiovascular effects of particulate air pollution. *Environmental Health Perspectives* 2001;109(suppl 4): 483–86.

Dockery DW, Pope CA, Xu X, Spenger JD, Ware JH, Fay ME, Ferris BG Jr, Speizer FE. An association between air pollution and mortality in six U.S. cities. *New England Journal of Medicine* 1993;329:1753–59.

Dominici F, McDermott A, Zeger SL, Samet JM. Airborne particulate matter and mortality: Timescale effects in four US cities. *American Journal of Epidemiology* 2003;157(12):1055–65.

Donaldson K, Stone V, Seaton A, MacNee W. Ambient particle inhalation and the cardiovascular system: Potential mechanisms. *Environmental Health Perspectives* 2001;109(suppl 4): 523–27.

Donovan DM, Marlatt GA, Salzberg PM. Drinking behaviour, personality factors and high risk driving: A review and theoretical formulation. *Journal of Studies in Alcohol* 1983;44:395–428.

Donovan RJ. Steps in planning and developing health communication campaigns: A comment on CDC's framework for health communication. *Public Health Reports* 1995;110(2): 215–18.

Dora C, Racioppi F. Including health in transport policy agendas: The role of health impact assessment analyses and procedures in the European experience. *Bulletin of the World Health Organization* 2003;81(6):399–403.

Dorn L, Matthews G. Two further studies of personality correlates of driver stress. *Personality and Individual Differences* 1992;13:949–51.

Dougherty G, Pless IB, Wilkins R. Social class and the occurrence of traffic injuries and deaths in urban children. *Canadian Journal of Public Health* 1990; 81:204–09.

Douglas MJ, Conway L, Gorman D, Gavin S, Hanlon P. Developing principles for health impact assessment. *Journal of Public Health Medicine* 2001;23(2): 148–54.

Duany A, Plater-Zyberk E, Speck J. *Suburban Nation: The Rise of Sprawl and the Decline of the American Dream.* New York: North Point Press, 2000.

Duffy BL, Nelson AF. Exposure to emissions of 1,3-butadiene and benzene in the cabins of moving vehicles and buses in Sydney, Australia. *Atmospheric Environment* 1997;31:3877–85.

Duffy J. *The Sanitarians: A History of American Public Health.* Urbana: University of Illinois Press, 1990.

Duhl LJ, Ed. *The Urban Condition: People and Policy in the Metropolis.* New York: Basic Books, 1963.

Duke J, Huhman M, Heitzler C. Physical activity levels among children aged 9–13 years—United States, 2002. *Morbidity and Mortality Weekly Report* 2003;52(33):785–88.

Dunn A, Andersen R, Jakicic J. Lifestyle physical activity interventions: History, short- and long-term effects, and recommendations. *American Journal of Preventive Medicine* 1998;15, 4: 398–412.

Dunn AL, Trivedi MH, O'Neal HA. Physical activity dose-response effects on outcomes of depression and anxiety. *Medicine and Science in Sports and Exercise* 2001;33(6 Suppl):S587–97.

Dunphy R, Fisher K. Transportation, congestion, and density: New insights.

Transportation Research Record 1994;1552:89–96.

Durbin DR. Preventing motor vehicle injuries. *Current Opinion in Pediatrics* 1999;11(6):583–87.

Durkin MS, Laraque D, Lubman I, Barlow B. Epidemiology and prevention of traffic injuries to urban children and adolescents. *Pediatrics* 1999; 103(6):1273–74.

Earls F, Carlson M. The social ecology of child health and well-being. *Annual Review of Public Health* 2001;22: 143–66.

Edwards B, Foley MW, Diani M, Eds. *Beyond Tocqueville: Civil Society and the Social Capital Debate in Comparative Perspective.* Hanover, NH: Tufts University/University Press of New England, 2001.

Edwards B, Foley MW. Civil society and social capital: A primer. In: Edwards B, Foley MW, Diani M, Eds. *Beyond Tocqueville: Civil Society and the Social Capital Debate in Comparative Perspective.* Hanover, NH: Tufts University/University Press of New England, 2001, pp 1–14.

Ekman L. On the treatment of traffic safety analysis—a non-parametric approach applied on vulnerable road users. Bulletin 136. Lund, Sweden: Department of Technology and Society, Lund Institute of Technology, 1996.

Ellis JB, Yu W. Bacteriology of urban runoff: The combined sewer as a bacterial reactor and generator. In: The Sewer as a Physical, Chemical and Biological Reactor, Proceedings Specialized International Conference, Aalborg, Denmark, 1994, 7p.

Ellison GT. Income inequality, social trust, and self-reported health status in high-income countries. *Annals of the New York Academy of Sciences* 1999; 896:325–28.

Elvik R. Area-wide urban traffic calming schemes: A meta-analysis of safety effects. *Accident Analysis and Prevention* 2001;33(3):327–36.

Environmental Protection Agency (EPA). *Urbanization and Streams: Studies of Hydrologic Impacts.* Washington, DC:

US Environmental Protection Agency, 1997. Report EPA-841-R-97-009.

Environmental Working Group (EWG). *Consider the Source: Farm Runoff, Chlorination Byproducts, and Human Health.* Washington, DC: Environmental Working Group, 2002.

Etzel RA, Balk SJ, Eds. *Pediatric Environmental Health,* 2nd Edition. Elk Grove Village, IL: American Academy of Pediatrics Committee on Environmental Health, 2003.

European Centre for Health Policy. *Gothenburg Consensus Paper: Health Impact Assessment: Main Concepts and Suggested Approach.* Brussels: WHO Regional Office for Europe, 1999. Available: http://www.who.dk/document/PAE/Gothenburgpaper.pdf.

Evans GW. Behavioral and physiological consequences of crowding in humans. *Journal of Applied Social Psychology* 1979;9:27–46.

Evans GW, Carrère S. Traffic congestion, perceived control, and psychophysiological stress among urban bus drivers. *Journal of Psychology* 1991;76;658–63.

Evans GW, Johansson G. Urban bus driving. *Journal of Occupational Health Psychology* 1998;3:99–108.

Evans GW, Wener RE, Phillips D. The morning rush hour: Predictability and commuter stress. *Environment and Behavior* 2002;34:521–30.

Ewing R. Characteristics, causes and effects of sprawl: A literature review. *Environmental and Urban Issues* 1994; 21:1–15.

Ewing R. Is Los Angeles–style sprawl desirable? *Journal of the American Planning Association* 1997;63(1):107–26.

Ewing R, Cervero R. Travel and the built environment: A synthesis. *Transportation Research Record* 2001;1780: 87–114.

Ewing R, Haliyur P, Page GW. Getting around a traditional city, a suburban planned unit development, and everything in between. *Transportation Research Record* 1994;1466:53–62.

Ewing R, Hodder R. *Best Development Practices: A Primer for Smart Growth.* Washington, DC: Smart Growth Network and International City/County Management Association, 1998.

Ewing R, Pendall R, Chen D. *Measuring Sprawl and Its Impact.* Washington, DC: Smart Growth America, 2002. Available: http://www.smartgrowthamerica.com/sprawlindex/MeasuringSprawl.PDF.

Ewing R, Schieber RA, Zegeer CV. Urban sprawl as a risk factor in motor vehicle occupant and pedestrian fatalities. *American Journal of Public Health* 2003;93(9):1541–45.

Ewing R, Schmid T, Killingsworth R, Zlot A, Raudenbush S. Relationship between urban sprawl and physical activity, obesity, and morbidity. *American Journal of Health Promotion* 2003;18(1):47–57.

Eyler AA, Baker E, Cromer L, King AC, Brownson RC, Donatelle RJ. Physical activity and minority women: A qualitative study. *Health Education and Behavior* 1998;25:640–52.

Eyler AA, Brownson RC, Donatelle RJ, King AC, Brown D, Sallis JF. Physical activity social support and middle- and older-aged minority women: Results from a US survey. *Social Science and Medicine* 1999;49(6):781–89.

Fabrigoule C, Letenneur L, Dartigues J, Zarrouk M, Commenges D, Barberger-Gateau P. Social and leisure activities and risk of dementia: A prospective longitudinal study. *Journal of the American Geriatric Society* 1995;43:485–90.

Fagot-Campagna A, Pettitt DJ, Engelgau MM, et al. Type 2 diabetes among North American children and adolescents: An epidemiologic review and a public health perspective. *Journal of Pediatrics* 2000;136:664–72.

Farouki O, Nixon W. The effect of the width of suburban roads on the mean free speed of cars. *Traffic Engineering and Control* 1976;17(2):508–09.

Federal Highway Administration. *Our Nation's Travel: 1995 NPTS Early Results Report.* Washington, DC: U.S. Department of Transportation, 1997.

Fedoruk MJ, Kerger BD. Measurement of volatile organic compounds inside automobiles. *Journal of Exposure Analysis and Environmental Epidemiology* 2003;13:31–41.

Fehr R. Environmental health impact assessment: Evaluation of a ten-step model. *Epidemiology* 1999;10(5): 618–25.

Fehr R, Mekel O, Lacombe M, Wolf U. Towards health impact assessment of drinking-water privatization—the example of waterborne carcinogens in North Rhine-Westphalia (Germany). *Bulletin of the World Health Organization* 2003;81(6):408–14.

Fehrs and Peers Associates. *Metropolitan Transportation Commission Bay Area Trip Rate Survey Analysis.* Oakland, CA: Metropolitan Transportation Commission, 1992.

Ferguson A. Road rage: Aggressive driving is America's car sickness du jour. *Time*, January 12, 1998: 64–68

Fiscella K, Franks P. Individual income, income inequality, health, and mortality: What are the relationships? *Health Services Research* 2000;35 (1 Pt 2):307–18.

Fiscella K, Franks P. Poverty or income inequality as predictor of mortality: Longitudinal cohort study. *British Medical Journal* 1997;314(7096): 1724–27.

Fischel W. Does the American way of zoning cause the suburbs of U.S. metropolitan areas to be too spread out? In: Altsuler A, Morrill W, Wolman H, Mitchell F, Eds. *Governance and Opportunity in Metropolitan Areas.* Washington, DC: National Academy Press, 1999, pp 151–91.

Fischel W. Zoning and land use regulation. In: Boudewijn B, de Geest G, Eds. *Encyclopedia of Law and Economics, Volume II. Civil Law and Economics.* Cheltenham, UK: Edward Elgar, 2000, pp 403–23.

Fischer PH, Hoek G, van Reeuwijk H, Briggs DJ, Lebret E, van Wijnen JH, et al. Traffic-related differences in outdoor and indoor concentrations of particles and volatile organic compounds in Amsterdam. *Atmospheric Environment* 2000;34:3713–22.

Fitz DR, Winer AM, Colome S, et al. Characterizing the Range of Children's Pollutant Exposure During School Bus commutes. Final Report to the California Air Resources Board, Contract No. 00-322. Department of Environmental Health Sciences, UCLA School of Public Health, and College of Engineering, UC Riverside. October 2003. Available: ftp://ftp.arb.ca.gov/carbis/ research/schoolbus/report.pdf.

Fitzpatrick K, LaGory M. *Unhealthy Places: The Ecology of Risk in the Urban Landscape.* New York: Routledge, 2000.

Flegal KM, Carroll MD, Kuczmarksi RJ, Johnson CL. Overweight and obesity in the United States: Prevalence and trends, 1960–1994. *International Journal of Obesity and Related Metabolic Disorders* 1998;22:39–47.

Flink JJ. *The Automobile Age.* Cambridge, MA: MIT Press, 1998.

Foley M, Edwards B, Diani M. Social capital reconsidered. In: Edwards B, Foley MS, Diani M, Eds. *Beyond Tocqueville: Civil Society and the Social Capital Debate in Comparative Perspective.* Hanover, NH: Tufts University/University Press of New England, 2001, pp 266–80.

Fong G, Frost D, Stansfeld S. Road rage: A psychiatric phenomenon? *Social Psychiatry and Psychiatric Epidemiology* 2001;36:277–86.

Ford AB. *Urban Health in America.* New York: Oxford University Press, 1976.

Foster-Bey J. Sprawl, smart growth and economic opportunity. The Urban Institute, Metropolitan Housing and Communities Policy Center. June 2002.

Francis K. The burden of physical inactivity and cardiovascular heart disease. *Comprehensive Therapy* 1997;24(2): 87–92.

Frank L, Engelke P. Air quality and physical activity impacts of the built environment: Regional and micro scale considerations. *International Regional Science Review*, in press.

Frank L, Engelke P, Schmid T. *Health and Community Design: How Urban Form*

Impacts Physical Activity. Washington, DC: Island Press, 2003.

Frank L, Pivo G. Impacts of mixed use and density on utilization of three modes of travel: Single-occupant vehicle, transit, and walking. *Transportation Research Record* 1995;1466:44–52.

Frank L, Stone B Jr, Bachman W. Linking land use with household vehicle emissions in the central Puget Sound: Methodological framework and findings. *Transportation Research Part D* 2000;5(3):173–96.

Frank LD. Transportation, air quality, and thinking big: Pollution control requires a holistic approach. *Transportation Research News* 2001;213: 35–37.

Frankston J. Health pros link sprawl with spread. Suburbs, obesity stir debate. *Atlanta Journal-Constitution*, November 17, 2003, p F1.

Fratiglioni L, Wang H, Ericsson K, Maytan M, Winblad B. The influence of social network on the occurrence of dementia: A community-based longitudinal study. *Lancet* 2000;355: 1315–19.

Freeman L. The effects of sprawl on neighborhood social ties. *Journal of the American Planning Association* 2001;67:69–77.

Freilich RH. *From Sprawl to Smart Growth: Successful Legal, Planning, and Environmental Systems.* Chicago: American Bar Association, 1999.

French SA, Story M, Jeffery RW. Environmental influences on eating and physical activity. *Annual Review of Public Health* 2001;22:309–35.

Frías C. Brave commute. Reliever's drive to work is 90 miles. *Atlanta Journal-Constitution*, July 26, 2002, pp C1, C5.

Friedman B, Gordon S, Peers J. Effect of neo-traditional neighborhood design on travel characteristics. *Transportation Research Record* 1994; 1466:63–70.

Friedman B, Gordon SP, Peers JB. Effect of neotraditional neighborhood design on travel characteristics. *Transportation Research Record* 1994;1466: 63–70.

Friedman HS, Ed. *Encyclopedia of Mental Health*, Vol. 1. New York: Academic Press, 1998.

Friedman LN, Williams MT, Singh TP, Frieden TR. Tuberculosis, AIDS and death among substance abusers on welfare in New York City. *New England Journal of Medicine* 1996;334(13): 828–33.

Friedman MS, Powell KE, Hutwagner L, Graham LM, Teague WG. Impact of changes in transportation and commuting behaviors during the 1996 Summer Olympic Games in Atlanta on air quality and childhood asthma. *JAMA* 2001;285(7):897–905.

Frumkin H. Beyond toxicity: The greening of environmental health. *American Journal of Preventive Medicine* 2001; 20:47–53.

Frumkin H. Healthy places: Exploring the evidence. *American Journal of Public Health* 2003;93(9):1451–55.

Frumkin H. Urban sprawl and public health. *Public Health Reports* 2002; 117(3):201–17.

Fukuyama F. *Trust: The Social Virtues and the Creation of Prosperity.* New York: Free Press, 1995.

Fulton W, Pendall R, Nguyen M, Harrison A. *Who Sprawls Most? How Growth Patterns Differ Across the U.S.* Washington, DC: Brookings Institution Center on Urban and Metropolitan Policy, 2001. Available: http://www. brookings.org/dybdocroot/es/urban/ publications/fulton.pdf.

Furstenburg FF, Hughes ME. Social capital and successful development among at-risk youth. *Journal of Marriage and Family* 1995;57:580–92.

Gaffield SJ, Goo RL, Richards LA, Jackson RJ. Public health effects of inadequately managed stormwater runoff. *American Journal of Public Health* 2003;93:1527–33.

Gaffuri E, Costa G. Applied aspects of chronoergohygiene. *Chronobiologia* 1986;13:39–51.

Gallagher W. *The Power of Place: How Our Surroundings Shape Our Thoughts, Emotions, and Actions.* New York: Poseidon Press, 1993.

Galster G, Hanson R, Wolman H, Coleman S, Freihage J. *Wrestling Sprawl to the Ground: Defining and Measuring an Elusive Concept.* Washington, DC: Fannie Mae Foundation, 2000. Available: http://www.fanniemaefoundation. org/programs/pdf/proc_fairgrowth_ galster2.pdf.

Gans H. *The Levittowners.* London: Penguin Press, 1967.

GAO (U.S. General Accounting Office). *Drinking Water Infrastructure: Information on Estimated Needs and Financial Assistance.* Testimony before the Subcommittee on Environment and Hazardous Materials, Committee on Energy and Commerce, House of Representatives. GAO-02-592T. Washington, DC: General Accounting Office, April 11, 2002.

Garbarino J, Sherman D. High-risk neighborhoods and high-risk families: The human ecology of child maltreatment. *Child Development* 1980;51:188–89.

Garthright WE, Archer DL, Kvenberg JE. Estimates of incidence and costs of intestinal infectious diseases in the United States. *Public Health Reports* 1988;103:107–15.

Gaster S. Rethinking the children's home-range concept. *Architecture et Comportement* 1995;11:35–42.

Gaster S. Urban children's access to their neighborhood: Changes over three generations. *Environment and Behavior* 1991;23(1):70–85.

Gauderman WJ, Gilliland GF, Vora H, Avol E, Stram D, McConnell R, et al. Association between air pollution and lung function growth in southern California children: Results from a second cohort. *American Journal of Respiratory and Critical Care Medicine* 2002;166(1):76–84.

Gauderman WJ, McConnell R, Gilliland F, London S, Thomas D, Avol E, et al. Association between air pollution and lung function growth in southern California children. *American Journal of Respiratory and Critical Care Medicine* 2000;162(4 Pt 1):1383–90.

Geffken D, Cushman M, Burke G, et al. Association between physical activity and markers of inflammation in a healthy elderly population. *American Journal of Epidemiology* 2001;153: 242–50.

Gehring U, Cyrys J, Sedlmeir G, Brunekreef B, Bellander T, et al. Traffic-related air pollution and respiratory health during the first two years of life. *European Respiratory Journal* 2002;19:690–98.

Giese JL, Davis GA, Sykes RD. The relationship between residential street design and pedestrian safety. ITE Annual Meeting Compendium, 1997(January):1097–1104. Available from ITE as document CD 2/AHA97K97.

Giles-Corti B, Donovan RJ. The relative influence of individual, social and physical environment determinants of physical activity. *Social Science and Medicine* 2002;54:1793–1812.

Gillespie LD, Gillespie WJ, Robertson MC, Lamb SE, Cumming RG, Rowe BH. Interventions for preventing falls in elderly people (Cochrane Methodology Review). In: *The Cochrane Library,* Issue 4, 2003. Chichester, UK: John Wiley & Sons, Ltd.

Gillham O. *The Limitless City: A Primer on the Urban Sprawl Debate.* Washington, DC: Island Press, 2002.

Giuliano G. The weakening transportation–land use connection. *Access* 1995; 6:3–11.

Giuliano G. Travel, location, and race/ ethnicity. *Transportation Research Part A* 2003;37(4):351–72.

Glaab CN, Brown AT. *A History of Urban America.* New York: Macmillan, 1983, p 64.

Glanz K, Lewis FM, Rimer BK. *Health Behavior and Health Education,* Second Edition. San Francisco: Jossey-Bass Publishers, 1997.

Glendon AI, Dorn L, Matthews G, Gulian E, Davies DR, Debney LM. Reliability of the Driving Behavior Inventory. *Ergonomics* 1993;36:719–26.

Glynn T. Psychological sense of community: Measurement and application. *Human Relations* 1981;34,7:789–818.

Golant SM. Deciding where to live: The emerging residential settlement patterns of retired Americans. *Generations* 2002;26:66–73.

Gold R, Kennedy B, Connell F, Kawachi I. Teen births, income inequality, and social capital: Developing an understanding of the causal pathway. *Health and Place* 2002;8:77–83.

Goldstein G. Healthy cities: Overview of a WHO international program. *Reviews on Environmental Health* 2000;15(1–2): 207–14.

Goldstein ST, Juranek DD, Ravenholt O, et al. Cryptosporidiosis: An outbreak associated with drinking water despite state-of-the-art water treatment. *Annals of Internal Medicine* 1996;124: 459–68.

Goodenough E. Secret spaces of childhood: Introduction. *Michigan Quarterly Review* 2000;39(2):179–93.

Gorman D, Douglas MJ, Conway L, Noble P, Hanlon P. Transport policy and health inequalities: A health impact assessment of Edinburgh's transport policy. *Public Health* 2003; 117(1):15–24.

Green L, Kreuter M. *Health Promotion Planning*, Second Edition. Mountain View, CA: Mayfield Publishing, 1991.

Greenberg M. American cities: Good and bad news about public health. *Bulletin of the New York Academy of Medicine* 1991;67:17–21.

Greenberg M. Reversing urban decay: Brownfield redevelopment and environmental health. *Environmental Health Perspectives* 2003;111(2): A74–A75.

Greenberg M. Should housing be built on former brownfield sites? *American Journal of Public Health* 2002;92(5): 703–05.

Greenberg M, Mayer H, Miller T, Hordon R, Knee D. Reestablishing public health and land use planning to protect public water supplies. *American Journal of Public Health* 2003;93: 1522–26.

Greenberg M, Popper F, West B, Krueckeberg D. Linking city planning and public health in the United States.

Journal of Planning Literature 1994; 8(3):235–39.

Greene DL, Schafer A. *Reducing Greenhouse Gas Emissions From U.S. Transportation*. Philadelphia: Pew Center on Global Climate Change, May 2003. Available: http://www.pewclimate.org/projects/ustransp.cfm.

Greenhill LL, Halperin JM, Abikoff H. Stimulant medications. *Journal of the American Academy of Child and Adolescent Psychiatry* 1999;38:503–12

Greenwald M, Boarnet MG. The built environment as a determinant of walking behavior: Analyzing nonwork pedestrian travel in Portland, Oregon. *Transportation Research Record* 2002;1780:33–42.

Gregg EW, Gerzoff RB, Caspersen CJ, Williamson DF, Narayan KM. Relationship of walking to mortality among US adults with diabetes. *Archives of Internal Medicine* 2003;163912):1440-47.

Grosse SD, Matte TD, Schwartz J, Jackson RJ. Economic gains resulting from the reduction in children's exposure to lead in the United States. *Environmental Health Perspectives* 2002;110(6): 563–69.

Gulian E, Glendon AI, Matthews G, Davies DR, Debney LM. The stress of driving: A diary study. *Work and Stress* 1990;4:7–16.

Gulian E, Matthews G, Glendon AI, Davies DR, et al. Dimensions of driver stress. *Ergonomics* 1989;32(6):585–602.

Gyourko J, Voith R. Does the U.S. Tax Treatment of Housing Promote Suburbanization and Central City Decline? Working Paper 97-13. Federal Reserve Bank of Philadelphia, 1997. Available: http://www.phil.frb.org/files/wps/1997/wp97-13.pdf.

Haar CM, Kayden JS, Eds. *Zoning and the American Dream: Promises Still to Keep*. Chicago: Planners Press, 1989.

Haar CM, Kayden JS. Zoning at sixty: A time for anniversary reckonings. In: Haar CM, Kayden JS, Eds. *Zoning and the American Dream: Promises Still to Keep*. Chicago: Planners Press, 1989, pp ix–xi.

Haeuber R. Sprawl tales: Maryland's Smart Growth Initiative and the evolution of growth management. *Urban Ecosystems* 1999;3:131–47.

Häfner S, Kordy H, Kächele H. Psychosozialer Versorgungsbedarf bei Berufspendlern [Need for mental health care in commuters]. *Psychotherapie Psychosomatik Medizinische Psychologie* 2001;51(9–10):373–76.

Hahn R, Teutsch S, Rothenberg R, Marks J. Excess deaths from nine chronic diseases in the United States, 1986. *JAMA* 1990;264(20): 2654–59.

Haines A, McMichael AJ, Epstein PR. Environment and health: 2. Global climate change and health. *Canadian Medical Association Journal* 2000; 163(6):729–34.

Halperin K. A comparative analysis of six methods for calculating travel fatality risk. *Risk: Health, Safety and Environment* 1993;4:15–33. Available: http://www.piercelaw.edu/risk/vol4/winter/halperin.htm.

Hancock T. Healthy communities must also be sustainable communities. *Public Health Reports* 2000;115(2–3): 151–56.

Hancock T. Indicators of environmental health in the urban setting. *Canadian Journal of Public Health. Revue Canadienne de Sante Publique* 2002;93(Suppl 1):S45–51.

Hancock T. The evolution, impact and significance of the healthy cities/healthy communities movement. *Journal of Public Health Policy* 1993;14(1):5–18.

Hancock T, Duhl L. *Healthy Cities: Promoting Health in the Urban Context.* Healthy Cities Paper #1. Copenhagen: WHO Europe, 1986.

Handy S. Regional versus local accessibility: Neo-traditional development and its implications for non-work travel. *Built Environment* 1992;18, 4:253–67.

Handy S. Understanding the link between urban form and nonwork travel behavior. *Journal of Planning Education and Research* 1996;15:183–98.

Handy S, Boarnet M, Ewing R, Killingsworth R. How the built environment affects physical activity: Views from urban planning. *American Journal of Preventive Medicine* 2002; 23(2S):64–73.

Hanzlick R, McGowan D, Havlak J, Bishop M, Bennett H, Rawlins R, et al. Pedestrian fatalities—Cobb, DeKalb, Fulton, and Gwinnett Counties, Georgia, 1994–98. *Morbidity and Mortality Weekly Report* 1999;48:601–05.

Harbor J. Engineering geomorphology at the cutting edge of land disturbance: Erosion and sediment control on construction sites. *Geomorphology* 1999;31(1–4):247–63.

Harbor J, Muthukrishnan S, Engel B, Jones D, Lim KJ. A comparison of the long-term hydrological impacts of urban renewal versus urban sprawl. Conference Proceedings, National Conference on Tools for Urban Water Resource Management and Protection, USEPA, Chicago, IL, 2000.

Harding RW, Morgan FH, Indermaur D, Ferrante AM, Blagg H. Road rage and the epidemiology of violence: Something old, something new. *Studies on Crime and Crime Prevention* 1998;7:221–28.

Harrington M. *The Other America: Poverty in the United States.* New York: Macmillan, 1962.

Hart M. *Guide to Sustainable Community Indicators,* Second Edition. North Andover, MA: Sustainable Measures, 1999.

Hart R. *Children's Experience of Place.* New York: Irvington, 1979.

Hartley L, el Hassani J. Stress, violations and accidents. *Applied Ergonomics* 1994;25:221–30.

Hauber AR. The social psychology of driving behaviour and the traffic environment: Research on aggressive behavior in traffic. *International Review of Applied Psychology* 1980;29:461–74.

Hawe P, Shiell A. Social capital and health promotion: A review. *Social Science and Medicine* 2000;51:871–85.

Hawkins DR, Rosenbaum S. *Lives in the Balance: A National, State and County*

Profile of America's Medically Underserved. Washington, DC: National Association of Community Health Centers (March) 1992.

Hedberg G, Jacobsson KA, Langendoen S, Nystrom L. Mortality in circulatory diseases, especially ischaemic heart disease, among Swedish professional drivers: A retrospective cohort study. *Journal of Human Ergology* 1991; 20(1):1–5.

Henderson KA, Ainsworth BE. A synthesis of perceptions about physical activity among older African American and American Indian women. *American Journal of Public Health* 2003;93(2): 313–17.

Hennessy DA, Wiesenthal DL. The relationship between traffic congestion, driver stress, and direct versus indirect coping behaviours. *Ergonomics* 1997;40:348–61.

Herms BF. Pedestrian crosswalk study: Accidents in painted and unpainted crosswalks. *Highway Research Record* 1972;406:1–13.

Hess P, Moudon AV, Snyder M, Stanilov K. Site design and pedestrian travel. *Transportation Research Record* 1999; 1674:9–19.

Hetzel L, Smith A. The 65 Years and Over Population: 2000. Census 2000 Brief C2KB/01-10. Washington, DC: U.S. Bureau of the Census, October 2001.

Hillman M, Adams J, Whitelegg J. *One False Move: A Study of Children's Independent Mobility.* London: Policy Studies Institute, 1991.

Hines J. The stress of driving. *Occupational Health* 1986;38(10):320–22.

Hirdes JP, Forbes WF. The importance of social relationships, socioeconomic status and health practices with respect to mortality among healthy Ontario males. *Journal of Clinical Epidemiology* 1992;45:175–82.

Hoek G, Brunekreef B, Goldbohm S, Fischer P, van den Brandt PA. Association between mortality and indicators of traffic-related air pollution in the Netherlands: A cohort study. *Lancet* 2002;360(9341): 1203–09.

Hoffman H. Medizinisch-Psychologische Untersuchungen Zum Fahren im Verkehrsfluss [Medical-psychological studies on driving in traffic]. *Zeitschrift fur Verkerswissenschaft* 1965;11:145–55.

Hoffman H, Reygers W. Kreislaufuntersuchungen bei Kraftfahrzeugfahrern unter variierten fahrbedingungen [Studies on the circulation of drivers under varying driving conditions]. *Zentralblatt fur Verkehrs-Medizin* 1960;3:131–51.

Holtzclaw J. *Using Residential Patterns and Transit to Decrease Auto Dependence and Costs.* San Francisco: Natural Resources Defense Council, 1994.

Holtzclaw J, Clear R, Dittmar H, Goldstein D, Haas P. Location efficiency: Neighborhood and socio-economic characteristics determine auto ownership and use—Studies in Chicago, Los Angeles and San Francisco. *Transportation Planning and Technology* 2002;25:1–27.

Horne C. Reconnecting: A study of social capital in Metropolitan Atlanta: Findings; from the social capital bench mark survey. Atlanta: Community Foundation for Greater Atalanta, June 2001. Available: http://www. atlcf.org/Webdata/Documents/33/ social%20capital.pdf.

Horne JA, Reyner LA. Sleep related vehicle accidents. *British Medical Journal* 1995;4:565–67.

House J, Robbins C, Metzner H, et al. The association of social relationships and activities with mortality: Prospective evidence from the Tecumseh Community Health Study. *American Journal of Epidemiology* 1982;116:123–40.

House JS, Landis KR, Umberson D. Social relationships and health. *Science* 1988; 241:540–45.

Hoxie NJ, Davis JP, Vergeront JM, Nashold RD, Blair KA. Cryptosporidiosis-associated mortality following a massive waterborne outbreak in Milwaukee, Wisconsin. *American Journal of Public Health* 1997;87: 2032–35.

Hu FB, Manson JE, Stampfer MJ, Colditz G, et al. Diet, lifestyle, and the risk of type 2 diabetes mellitus in women. *New England Journal of Medicine* 2001;345(11):790-7.

Humpel N, Owen N, Leslie E. Environmental factors associated with adults' participation in physical activity: A review. *American Journal of Preventive Medicine* 2002;22(3):188–99.

Humphries S. Who's afraid of the big, bad firm: The impact of economic scale on political participation. *American Journal of Political Science* 2001;45: 678–99.

Hupkes G. The law of constant travel time and trip rates. *Futures* 1982;14(1): 38–46.

Hurley A. Creating ecological wastelands: Oil pollution in New York City, 1870–1900. *Journal of Urban History* 1994;20:340–64.

Huston SL, Evenson KR, Bors P, Gizlice Z. Neighborhood environment, access to places for activity, and leisure-time physical activity in a diverse North Carolina population. *American Journal of Health Promotion* 2003;18(1):58–69.

IARC (International Agency for Research on Cancer). Diesel and Gasoline Engine Exhausts and Some Nitroarenes. *IARC Monographs on the Evaluation of Carcinogenic Risks to Humans, Volume 46.* Lyon: IARC, 1989.

IARC (International Agency for Research on Cancer). Re-evaluation of Some Organic Chemicals, Hydrazine and Hydrogen Peroxide. *IARC Monographs on the Evaluation of Carcinogenic Risks to Humans, Volume 71.* Lyon: IARC, 1999.

IARC (International Agency for Research on Cancer). Wood Dust and Formaldehyde. *IARC Monographs on the Evaluation of Carcinogenic Risks to Humans, Volume 62.* Lyon: IARC, 1995.

Institute of Medicine, Food and Nutrition Board. *Dietary Reference Intakes for Energy, Carbohydrate, Fiber, Fat, Fatty Acids, Cholesterol, Protein, and Amino Acids (Macronutrients).* Washington, DC: National Academy Press, 2002.

Institute of Transportation Engineers (ITE) Technical Committee 5A-5. Design and Safety of Pedestrian Facilities. Washington: ITE, 1998.

Intergovernmental Panel on Climate Change (IPCC). *Climate Change 2001* (4 Volumes). Geneva: IPCC, 2001. Available: http://www.ipcc.ch/pub/reports.htm.

International City/County Management Association, Anderson G. *Why Smart Growth: A Primer.* Washington, DC: Smart Growth Network and International City/County Management Association, 1998.

Iowa Department of Transportation. Road Rage. N.D. Available: http://www.dot.state.ia.us/roadrage.htm.

Isherwood J, Adam KS, Hornblower AR. Life event stress, psychosocial factors, suicide attempt and auto-accident proclivity. *Journal of Psychosomatic Research* 1982;26:371–83.

Jackman RW, Miller RA. Social capital and politics. *Annual Review of Political Science* 1998;1:47–73.

Jackson KT. *Crabgrass Frontier: The Suburbanization of the United States.* New York: Oxford University Press, 1985.

Jackson KT. Gentleman's agreement: Discrimination in metropolitan America. In: Katz B, Ed. *Reflections on Regionalism.* Washington, DC: Brookings Institution Press, 2000, pp 185–217.

Jacobs J. *The Death and Life of Great American Cities.* New York: Random House, 1961.

Jacobsen PL. Safety in numbers: More walkers and bicyclists, safer walking and bicycling. *Injury Prevention* 2003; 9:205–09.

James L, Nahl D. *Road Rage and Aggressive Driving: Steering Clear of Highway Warfare.* Amherst, NY: Prometheus Books, 2000.

James SA, Schulz AJ, van Olphen J. Social capital, poverty, and community health: An exploration of linkages. In: Saegert S, Thompson JP, Warren MR, Eds. *Social Capital and Poor Communities.* New York: Russell Sage Foundation, 2001, pp 165–88.

Jargowsky P. Sprawl, concentration of poverty, and urban inequality. In: Squires GD, Ed. *Urban Sprawl: Causes, Consequences, and Policy Responses.* Washington, DC: Urban Institute Press, 2002, pp 39–71.

Jefferson, Thomas, in a letter to Benjamin Rush, 1800. In: Lipscomb AA, Bergh AE, Johnston RH, Eds. *The Writings of Thomas Jefferson,* Volume 10. Washington, DC: Thomas Jefferson Memorial Association of the United States, 1903–04, p 173.

Jenks M, Burton E, Williams K, Eds. *The Compact City: A Sustainable Urban Form?* London, E&FN Spon, 1996.

Jenks M, Williams K, Burton E. A sustainable future through the compact city? Urban intensification in the United Kingdom. *Environments by Design* 1996;1:5–20.

Jo WK, Choi SJ. Vehicle occupant's exposure to aromatic volatile organic compounds while commuting in an urban-suburban route in Korea. *Journal of the Air and Waste Management Association* 1996;46:749–54.

Jo WK, Park KH. Concentrations of volatile organic compounds in the passenger side and the back seat of automobiles. *Journal of Exposure Analysis and Environmental Epidemiology* 1999;9(3):217–27.

Johnson TP. Mental health, social relations, and social selection: A longitudinal analysis. *Journal of Health and Social Behavior* 1991;32:408–23.

Joint M. Road rage. In: *Aggressive Driving: Three Studies.* Washington, DC: AAA Foundation for Traffic Safety, March 1997. Available: http://www.aaafoundation.org/pdf/agdr3study.pdf (accessed June 23, 2002).

Joly MF, Foggin PM, Pless IB. Les déterminants socio-écologiques du risqué d'accident du juene piéton. *Revue d'Epidiemolgie et de Santé Publique* 1991;39:345–51.

Judge K, Mulligan JA, Benzeval M. The relationship between income inequality and population health. *Social Science and Medicine* 1998; 47(7):983–85.

Kahn EB, Heath GW, Powell KE, Stone EJ, Brownson RJ. Increasing physical activity: A report on recommendations of the Task Force on Community Preventive Services. *Morbidity and Mortality Weekly Report* 2001;50:1–14.

Kahn EB, Ramsey LT, Brownson RC, Heath GW, Howze EH, Powell KE, et al. The effectiveness of interventions to increase physical activity: A systematic review. *American Journal of Preventive Medicine* 2002;22(4S): 73–107.

Kahn HS, Patel AV, Jacobs EJ, Calle EE, Kennedy BP, Kawachi I. Pathways between area-level income inequality and increased mortality in U.S. men. *Annals of the New York Academy of Sciences* 1999;896:332–34.

Kain JF. Housing segregation, Negro employment, and metropolitan decentralization. *Quarterly Journal of Economics* 1868;82(2):175–97.

Kampert JB, Blair SN, Barlow CE, Kohl HW III. Physical activity, physical fitness, and all-cause and cancer mortality: A prospective study of men and women. *Annals of Epidemiology* 1996; 6:452–57.

Kaplan G, Salonen J, Cohen R, Brand R, Syme S, Puska P. Social connections and mortality from all causes and from cardiovascular disease: Prospective evidence from eastern Finland. *American Journal of Epidemiology* 1998;128:370–80.

Kaplan GA, Pamuk ER, Lynch JW, Cohen RD, Balfour JL. Inequality in income and morality in the United States: Analysis of mortality and potential pathways. *British Medical Journal* 1996;312:999–1003.

Kaplan R, Kaplan S, Ryan RL. *With People in Mind: Design and Management of Everyday Nature.* Washington, DC: Island Press, 1998.

Kaplan S, Kaplan R, Eds. *Humanscape: Environments for People.* Ann Arbor, MI: Ulrich's Books, 1982.

Karasek RA. Job demands, job decision latitude and mental strain: Implications for job redesign. *Administrative Sciences Quarterly* 1979;24:285–307.

Katsouyanni K, Pershagen G. Ambient air pollution exposure and cancer. *Cancer Causes and Control* 1997;8(3):284–91.

Katz B. Smart Growth: The future of the American metropolis? Centre for Analysis of Social Exclusion, London School of Economics. CASE paper 58, July 2002. Available: http://sticerd.lse.ac.uk/dps/case/cp/casepaper58.pdf.

Kawachi I. Social capital and community effects on population and individual health. *Annals of the New York Academy of Sciences* 2000;896:120–30.

Kawachi I, Berkman L. Social ties and mental health. *Journal of Urban Health* 2001;78:458–67.

Kawachi I, Colditz GA, Ascherio A, Rimm EB, Giovannucci E, Stampfer MJ, et al. A prospective study of social networks in relation to total morality and cardiovascular disease in men in the US. *Journal of Epidemiology and Community Health* 1996;50:245–51.

Kawachi I, Kennedy BP. Health and social cohesion: Why care about income inequality? *British Medical Journal* 1997;314:1037–40.

Kawachi I, Kennedy BP. Income inequality and health: Pathways and mechanisms. *Health Services Research* 1999; 34(1 Pt 2):215–27.

Kawachi I, Kennedy BP, Glass R. Social capital and self-rated health: A contextual analysis. *American Journal of Public Health* 1999;89(8):1187–93.

Kawachi I, Kennedy BP, Lochner K, Prothrow-Stith D. Social capital, income inequality, and mortality. *American Journal of Public Health* 1997;87:1491–98.

Kawachi I, Kennedy BP, Wilkinson RC, Eds. *Income Inequality and Health.* New York: New Press, 1999.

Kay D. What do New Yorkers think about growth and development? Ithaca, NY: Cornell Local Government Program, 2001. Available: http://www.cardi.cornell.edu/cd_toolbox_2/tools/ny_growth_survey.cfm.

Kay JH. *Asphalt Nation: How the Automobile Took Over America and How We Can Take It Back.* Berkeley: University of California Press, 1997.

Keil U, Weiland SK, Duhme H, Chambless L. The International Study of Asthma and Allergies in Childhood (ISAAC): Objectives and methods; results from German ISAAC centres concerning traffic density and wheezing and allergic rhinitis. *Toxicology Letters* 1996;86:99–103.

Kelbaugh D. *Common Place: Toward Neighborhood and Regional Design.* Seattle: University of Washington Press, 1997.

Kelbaugh D. Three paradigms: New Urbanism, Everyday Urbanism, Post Urbanism—An Excerpt from the Essential Common Place. *Bulletin of Science, Technology and Society* 2000; 20:285–89.

Kelsey JL. An epidemiological study of acute herniated lumbar intervertebral discs. *Rheumatology and Rehabilitation* 1975;14:144–59.

Kelsey JL, Githens PB, O'Conner T, Weil U, Calogero JA, Holford TR, White AA 3rd, Walter SD, Ostfeld AM, Southwick WO. Acute prolapsed lumbar intervertebral disc. An epidemiologic study with special reference to driving automobiles and cigarette smoking. *Spine* 1984;9(6):608–13.

Kelsey JL, Hardy RJ. Driving of motor vehicles as a risk factor for acute herniated lumbar intervertebral disc. *American Journal of Epidemiology* 1975; 102:63–73.

Kendrick D. Prevention of pedestrian accidents. *Archives of Disease in Childhood* 1993;68:669–72.

Kennedy BP, Kawachi I, Glass R, Prothrow-Stith D. Income distribution, socioeconomic status, and self-rated health: A U.S. multi-level analysis. *British Medical Journal* 1998;317:917–21.

Kennedy BP, Kawachi I, Prothrow-Stith D. Income distribution and mortality: Cross sectional ecological study of the Robin Hood index in the United States. *British Medical Journal* 1996; 312:1004–07.

Kennedy B, Kawachi I, Prothrow-Stith D, Lochner K, Gupta V. Social capital, income inequality, and firearm violent crime. *Social Science and Medicine* 1998;47:7–17.

Kenzer M. Healthy Cities: A guide to the literature. *Public Health Reports* 2000;115(2–3):279–89.

Kennedy M, Leonard P. *Dealing with Neighborhood Change: A Primer on Gentrification and Policy Choices.* Washington: Brookings Institution Center on Urban and Metropolitan Policy and PolicyLink, April 2001. Available: http://www.brookings. edu/dybdocroot/es/urban/ gentrification.pdf.

Kessler RC, Wittchen HU. Patterns and correlates of generalized anxiety disorder in community samples. *Journal of Clinical Psychiatry* 2002; 63(suppl 8):4–10.

King AC, Castro C, Wilcox S, Eyler AA, Sallis JF, Brownson RC. Personal and environmental factors associated with physical inactivity among different racial-ethnic groups of US middle-aged and older aged adults. *Health Psychology* 2000;19:354–64.

King AC, Rejeski WJ, Buchner DM. Physical activity interventions targeting older adults: A critical review and recommendations. *American Journal of Preventive Medicine* 1998;15: 316–33.

Kirtland KA, Porter DE, Addy CL, et al. Environmental measures of physical activity supports: Perception versus reality. *American Journal of Preventive Medicine* 2003;24:323–31.

Kitamura R, Mokhtarian PL, Laidet L. A micro-analysis of land use and travel in five neighborhoods in the San Francisco Bay area. *Transportation* 1997;24(2):125–58.

Kjellstrom T, van Kerkhoff L, Bammer G, McMichael T. Comparative assessment of transport risks—how it can contribute to health impact assessment of transport policies. *Bulletin of the World Health Organization* 2003; 81(6):451–57.

Klein, R. *Urbanization and Stream Quality Assessment.* Water Resources Bulletin 1979;15(4): 948–63.

Kluger A. Commute variability and strain. *Journal of Organizational Behavior* 1998;19:147–65.

Knaap GJ, Hopkins LD. The inventory approach to urban growth boundaries. *Journal of the American Planning Association* 2001;67:314–26.

Knack R. Return to Euclid. *Planning* 1996;62(11):4–8.

Knickman JR, Snell EK. The 2030 problem: Caring for aging baby boomers. *Health Services Research* 2002;37(4): 849–84.

Kockelman KM. Travel behavior as function of accessibility, land use mixing, and land use balance: Evidence from San Francisco Bay Area. *Transportation Research Record* 1997;1607:116–25.

Koepsell T, McCloskey L, Wolf M, Moudon AV, Buchner D, Kraus J, Patterson M. Crosswalk markings and the risk of pedestrian–motor vehicle collisions in older pedestrians. *JAMA* 2002;288(17):2136–43.

Kohl HW III, Gordon NF, Villegas JA, Blair SN. Cardiorespiratory fitness, glycemic status, and mortality risk in men. *Diabetes Care* 1992;15: 184–92.

Korrick SA, Neas LM, Dockery DW, Gold DR, Allen GA, Hill LB, et al. Effects of ozone and other pollutants on the pulmonary function of adult hikers. *Environmental Health Perspectives* 1998;106(2):93–99.

Koslowsky M. Commuting stress: Problems of definition and variable identification. *Applied Psychology: An International Review* 1997;46(2):153–73.

Koslowsky M. Commuting and mental health. In: Friedman HS, Ed. *Encyclopedia of Mental Health,* Vol. 1. New York: Academic Press, 1998, pp 521–30.

Koslowsky M, Kluger AN, Reich M. *Commuting Stress: Causes, Effects, and Methods of Coping.* New York: Plenum Press, 1995.

Koslowsky M, Krausz M. On the relationship between commuting, stress symptoms and attitudinal measures: A LISREL application. *Journal of Applied Behavioral Science* 1993;29:485–92.

Kramer MH, Herwaldt BL, Craun GF, Calderon RL, Juranek DD. Surveillance for waterborne-disease outbreaks—United States, 1993–1994. *Morbidity and Mortality Weekly Report* 1996;45(SS-1):1–33.

Krantz DS, McCeney MK. Effects of psychological and social factors on organic disease: A critical assessment of research on coronary heart disease. *Annual Review of Psychology* 2002;53: 341–69.

Krasner MI, Ed. *Poverty and Health in New York City.* New York: United Hospital Fund of New York, 1989.

Kraus JF, Hooten EG, Brown KA, Peek-Asa C, Heye C, McArthur DL. Child pedestrian and bicyclist injuries: Results of community surveillance and a case-control study. *Injury Prevention* 1996;2:212–18.

Krause N, Ragland DR, Greiner BA, Syme SL, Fisher JM. Psychosocial job factors associated with back and neck pain in public transit operators. *Scandinavian Journal of Work, Environment and Health* 1997;23(3):179–86.

Krishna A, Shrader D. Social Capital Assessment Tool. Prepared for the Conference on Social Capital and Poverty Reduction, The World Bank, Washington, DC, June 22–24, 1999. Available: http://wbln0018.worldbank. org/external/lac/lac.nsf/ 51105678feaadaea852567d6006c1de4/ d2d929b5fff4b555852567ee000414ad/.

Krizek K. Pretest-posttest strategy for researching neighborhood-scale, urban form and travel behavior. *Transportation Research Record* 2000;1722:48–55.

Krizek KJ, Waddell P. Analysis of lifestyle choices: Neighborhood type, travel patterns, and activity participation. *Transportation Research Record* 2002;1807:119–28.

Kuczmarski RJ, Flegal KM, Campbell SM, Johnson CL. Increasing prevalence of overweight among US adults: The National Health and Nutrition Examination Surveys, 1960 to 1991. *JAMA* 1994;272:205–11.

Kujala U, Kaprio J, Sarna S, Koskenvuo M. Relationship of leisure-time physical activity and mortality: The Finnish twin cohort. *JAMA* 1998;279(6): 440–44.

Kunitz SJ. Accounts of social capital: The mixed health effects of personal communities and voluntary groups. In: Leon D, Walt G, Eds. *Poverty Inequality and Health: An International Perspective.* Oxford: Oxford University Press, 2001, pp 159–74.

Kunstler JH. *The Geography of Nowhere: The Rise and Decline of America's Man-Made Landscape.* New York: Simon & Schuster, 1993.

Kunstler JH. Big and blue in the USA. *Orion Online*, autumn 2003. Available: http://www.oriononline.org/pages/ oo/curmudgeon/index_curmudgeon. html.

Kunstler JH. Home from nowhere. *The Atlantic Monthly* 1996(September); 278:43–66.

Künzli N, Lurmann F, Segal M, Ngo L, Balmes J, Tager IB. Association between lifetime ambient ozone exposure and pulmonary function in college freshmen—results of a pilot study. *Environmental Research* 1997; 72(1):8–23.

Laden F, Neas LM, Dockery DW, Schwartz J. Association of fine particulate matter from different sources with daily mortality in six U.S. cities. *Environmental Health Perspectives* 2000;108(10):941–47.

Laflamme L, Diderichsen F. Social differences in traffic injury risks in childhood and youth—a literature review and a research agenda. *Injury Prevention* 2000;6:293–98.

Lajunen T, Parker D, Stradling SG. Dimensions of driver anger, aggressive and highway code violations and their mediation by safety orientation in UK drivers. *Transportation Research Part F* 1997;1:107–21.

Lajunen T, Parker D, Summala H. Does traffic congestion increase driver aggression? *Transportation Research Part F* 1999;2:225–36.

Langdon P. Can design make community? *Responsive Community* 1997;7(2): 25–37.

Larsen LH. Nineteenth-century street sanitation: A study of filth and frustration. *Wisconsin Magazine of History* LII (Spring 1969):239–47.

Lawryk NJ, Lioy PJ, Weisel CP. Exposure to volatile organic compounds in the passenger compartment of automobiles during periods of normal and malfunctioning operation. *Journal of Exposure Analysis and Environmental Epidemiology* 1995;5(4):511–31.

Lawton K. The urban structure and personal travel: An analysis of Portland, OR data and some national and international data. In: *E-Vision 2000: Key Issues That Will Shape Our Energy Future. Summary of Proceedings, Scenario Analysis, Expert Elicitation, and Submitted Papers.* CF-170/1-1-DOE. Santa Monica CA: RAND, 2001. Available: http://www.rand.org/scitech/stpi/Evision/Supplement/lawton.pdf.

Lawton R, Parker D, Stradling S, Manstead A. The role of affect in predicting social behaviors: The case of road traffic violations. *Journal of Applied Social Psychology* 1997;27:1258–76.

Leavitt JW. *The Healthiest City: Milwaukee and the Politics of Health Reform.* Princeton, NJ: Princeton University Press, 1982, p 22.

Lebret E, Briggs D, van Reeuwijk H, Fischer P, Smallbone K, Harssema H, et al. Small area variations in ambient NO_2 concentrations in four European areas. *Atmospheric Environment* 2000;34:177–85.

Leccese M, McCormick K, Eds. *Charter of the New Urbanism.* New York: McGraw-Hill, 2000.

LeChevallier MW, Norton WD. *Giardia* and *Cryptosporidium* in raw and finished water. *Journal of the American Water Works Association* 1995;87(9):54–68.

LeCount ER, Rukstinat GJ. Sudden death from heart disease while motoring. *JAMA* 1929;92:1347–48.

Leden L. Pedestrian risk decreases with pedestrian flow. A case study based on data from signalized intersections in Hamilton, Ontario. *Accident Analysis and Prevention* 2002;34:457–64.

Lee IM, Paffenbarger RS Jr. Associations of light, moderate, and vigorous intensity physical activity with longevity: The Harvard Alumni Health Study. *American Journal of Epidemiology* 2000;151:293–99.

Lee IM, Sesso HD, Paffenbarger RS Jr. Physical activity and risk of lung cancer. *International Journal of Epidemiology* 1999;28:620–25.

Lee SH, Levy DA, Craun GF, Beach MJ, Calderon RL. Surveillance for waterborne-disease outbreaks—United States, 1999–2000. *Morbidity and Mortality Weekly Report* 2002;51(SS-8):1–28.

Legg A, Bannerman R, Panuska J. *Variation in the Relation of Rainfall to Runoff from Residential Lawns in Madison, Wisconsin, July and August, 1995.* Madison, WI: US Geological Survey, 1996. Water-Resources Investigation Report 96-4194.

Leinberger C. Financing progressive development. *Capital Xchange*, May 2001. Washington and Boston: Brookings Institution Center on Urban and Metropolitan Policy and Harvard University Joint Center for Housing Studies. Available: http://www.brook.edu/es/urban/capitalxchange/leinberger.pdf.

Leon A, Connett J, Jacobs D, Rauramaa R. Leisure-time physical activity levels and risk of coronary heart disease and death in the multiple risk factor intervention trial. *JAMA* 1987;258:2388–95.

Lépine J-P. Epidemiology, burden, and disability in depression and anxiety. *Journal of Clinical Psychiatry* 2001;62(suppl 13):4–10.

Lerner DN. Identifying and quantifying urban recharge: A review. *Hydrogeology Journal* 2002;10:143–52.

Levin RB, Epstein PR, Ford TE, Harrington W, Olson E, Reichard EG. US drinking water challenges in the twenty-first century. *Environmental Health Perspectives* 2002;110(suppl 1):43–52.

Levine J, Inam A, Werbel R, Torng G-W. Land use and transportation alternatives: Constraint or expansion of household choice? MTI Report 01-19. San Jose, CA: Mineta Transportation Institute, San Jose State University, June 2002. Available: http://www.transweb.sjsu.edu/publications/LandUse.pdf.

Lewis BA, Marcus BH, Pate RR, Dunn AL. Psychosocial mediators of physical activity behavior among adults and children. *American Journal of Preventive Medicine* 2002;23(2S):26–35.

Leyden K. Social capital and the built environment: The importance of walkable neighborhoods. *American Journal of Public Health* 2003;93:1546–51.

Lightstone AS, Dhillon PK, Peek-Asa C, Kraus JF. A geographic analysis of motor vehicle collisions with child pedestrians in Long Beach, California: Comparing intersection and mid-block incident locations. *Injury Prevention* 2001;7(2):155–60.

Lin S, Munsie JP, Hwang S-A, Fitzgerald E, Cayo MR. Childhood asthma hospitalization and residential exposure to state route traffic. *Environmental Research Section A* 2002;88:73–81.

Lindström M., Hanson B, Östergren P-O. Socioeconomic differences in leisure-time physical activity: The role of social participation and social capital in shaping health related behavior. *Social Science and Medicine* 2001;52: 441–51.

Link B, Susser E, Stueve A, et al. Lifetime and five-year prevalence of homelessness in the United States. *American Journal of Public Health* 1994; 4:1907–12.

Lipscomb AA, Bergh AE, Johnston RH, Eds. *The Writings of Thomas Jefferson.* Washington, DC: Thomas Jefferson Memorial Association of the United States, 1903–04.

Lissy KS, Cohen JT, Park MY, Graham JD. *Cellular Phone Use While Driving: Risks and Benefits.* Boston: Harvard Center for Risk Analysis, 2000.

Litonjua AA, Carey VJ, Weiss ST, Gold DR. Race, socioeconomic factors, and area of residence are associated with asthma prevalence. *Pediatric Pulmonology* 1999;28(6):394–401.

Litt JS, Burke TA. Uncovering the historic environmental hazards of urban brownfields. *Journal of Urban Health* 2002;79(4):464–81.

Liu AJ, Tong ST, Goodrich JA. Land use as a mitigation strategy for the water-quality impacts of global warming: A scenario analysis on two watersheds in the Ohio River Basin. *Environmental Engineering and Policy* 2000; 2:65–76.

Livable Communities. *Building Livable Communities: Sustaining Prosperity, Improving Quality of Life, Building a Sense of Community.* A Report from the Clinton-Gore Administration. Washington, DC: Livable Communities, June 2002.

Local Government Commission. *Smart Growth Zoning Codes: A Resource Guide.* Sacramento, CA: Local Government Commission, n.d.

Lochner K, Kawachi I, Kennedy BP. Social capital: A guide to its measurement. *Health and Place* 1999;5:259–70.

Lochner K, Pamuk E, Makuc D, Kennedy BP, Kawachi I. State-level income inequality and individual mortality risk: A prospective, multilevel study. *American Journal of Public Health* 2001;91:385–91.

Lomas J. Social capital and health: Implementation for public health and epidemiology. *Social Science and Medicine* 1998;47:1181–88.

Lopez R, Hynes HP. Sprawl in the 1990s: Measurement, distribution, and trends. *Urban Affairs Review* 2003; 38(3):325–55.

Lourens PF, Vissers JA, Jessurum M. Annual mileage, driving violations, and accident involvement in relation to drivers' sex, age, and level of education. *Accident Analysis and Prevention* 1999;31:593–97.

Lowenstein LF. Research into cause and manifestations of aggression in car driving. *Police Journal* 1997;70:263–70.

Lucy WH. Mortality risk associated with leaving home: Recognizing the relevance of the built environment. *American Journal of Public Health* 2003;93(9):1564–69.

Lund H. Pedestrian environments and sense of community. *Journal of Planning Education and Research* 2002;21: 301–12.

Lundberg U. Urban commuting: Crowdedness and catecholamine excretion. *Journal of Human Stress* 1976;2:26–32.

Lynch J. Social capital—Is it a good investment strategy for public health? *Journal of Epidemiology and Community Health* 2000;54:404–08.

Lynch JW, Kaplan GA, Pamuk ER, Cohen RD, Heck KE, Balfour JL, Yen IH. Income inequality and mortality in metropolitan areas of the United States. *American Journal of Public Health* 1998;88:1074–80.

Lynch JW, Smith GD, Kaplan GA, House JS. Income inequality and mortality: Importance to health of individual income, psychosocial environment, or material conditions. *British Medical Journal* 2000;320:1200–04.

Maantay J. Zoning, equity and public health. *American Journal of Public Health* 2001;91:1033–41.

Macera CA, Jones DA, Yore MM, Ham SA, Kohl HW, Kimsey CD, Buchner D. Prevalence of physical activity, including lifestyle activities among adults—United States, 2000–2001. *Morbidity and Mortality Weekly Report* 2003;52(32):764–69.

Macinko J, Starfield B. The utility of social capital in research on health determinants. *Milbank Quarterly* 2001; 79:387–427.

MacKenzie W, Hoxie N, Proctor M, Gradus M, Blair K, Peterson D. A massive outbreak in Milwaukee of *Cryptosporidium* infection transmitted through public water supply. *New England Journal of Medicine* 1994;331: 161–67.

MacPherson A, Roberts I, Pless IB. Children's exposure to traffic and pedestrian injuries. *American Journal of Public Health* 1998;88:1840–43.

Magnusson ML, Pope MH, Wilder DG, Areskoug B. Are occupational drivers at an increased risk for developing musculoskeletal disorders? *Spine* 1996;21(6):710–17.

Malek M, Guyer B, Lescohier I. The epidemiology and prevention of child pedestrian injuries. *Accident Analysis and Prevention* 1990;22: 301–13.

Malizia E, Exline S. *Consumer Preferences for Residential Development Alternatives.* Working Paper 2000-02, University of North Carolina Center for Urban and Regional Studies, February, 2000. Available from UNC Center for Urban and Regional Studies, Campus Box 3410, UNC Chapel Hill, Chapel Hill, NC 27599-3410.

Maloney W, Smith G, Stoker G. Social capital and the city. In: Edwards B, Foley MS, Diani M, Eds. *Beyond Tocqueville: Civil Society and the Social Capital Debate in Comparative Perspective.* Hanover, NH: Tufts University/University Press of New England, 2001.

Mannino DM, Homa DM, Akinbami LJ, Moorman JE, Gwynn C, Redd SC. Surveillance for asthma—United States,1980–1999. *Morbidity and Mortality Weekly Report* 2002; 51(SS-1):1–13.

Manson JE, Greenland P, LaCroix AZ, Stefanick ML, Mouton CP, Oberman A, et al. Walking compared with vigorous exercise for the prevention of cardiovascular events in women. *New England Journal of Medicine* 2002; 347(10):716–25.

Marcus CC, Francis C. *People Places: Design Guidelines for Urban Open Space.* New York: Wiley, 1998.

Marino RP, Gannon JJ. Survival of fecal coliforms and fecal streptococci in storm drain sediment. *Water Resources* 1991;25:1089–98.

Markowitz G, Rosner D. *Deceit and Denial: The Deadly Politics of Industrial Pollution.* Berkeley: University of California Press and New York: Milbank Memorial Fund, 2002.

Marmot M, Feeney A. General explanations for social inequalities in health.

IARC Scientific Publications (Lyon) 1997;138:207–28.

Marmot M, Wilkinson RG. *Social Determinants of Health.* Oxford: Oxford University Press, 1999.

Marosi R. Pedestrian deaths reveal O.C.'s car culture clash. Safety: Latinos, 28% of Orange County's population, are victims in 40% of walking injuries, 43% of deaths. *Los Angeles Times,* November 28, 1999, p 1.

Marshall E, Thomas N. Traffic calming: The reality of "road rage." Briefing Note, Policing and Reducing Crime Unit, Development and Statistics Directorate, Home Office Research. London: Home Office, November, 2000. Available: http://www.homeoffice.gov.uk/rds/prgpdfs/brf1200.pdf (accessed June 23, 2002).

Martin J. Some aspects of absence in a light engineering factory. *Occupational Psychology* 1971;45:77–89.

Martin WT. The structuring of social relationships engendered by suburban residence. *American Sociological Review* 1956;21:446–53.

Martinez R. Statement Before the Subcommittee on Surface Transportation, Committee on Transportation and Infrastructure, U.S. House of Representatives. July 17, 1997. Available: http://www.nhtsa.dot.gov/nhtsa/announce/testimony/aggres2.html (accessed July 21, 2002).

Matthews G, Dorn L, Glendon AI. Personality correlates of driver stress. *Personality and Individual Differences* 1991;12:535–49.

Matthews MH. *Making Sense of Place: Children's Understanding of Large-Scale Environments.* Savage, MD: Barnes and Noble, 1992.

Mazzeo R, Cavanagh P, Evans W. American College of Sports Medicine Position Stand: Exercise and physical activity for older adults. *Medicine and Science in Sports and Exercise* 1998;30:992–1008.

McCann B, DeLille B. *Mean Streets 2000: Pedestrian Safety, Health and Federal Transportation Spending.* Washington, DC: Surface Transportation Policy Project, 2000.

McCarthy MP. *Typhoid and the Politics of Public Health in Eighteenth Century Philadelphia.* Philadelphia: American Philosophical Society, 1987, p 7.

McConnell R, Berhane K, Gilliland F, Molitor J, et al. Prospective study of air pollution and bronchitic symptoms in children with asthma. *American Review of Respiratory and Critical Care Medicine* 2003;168:790–97.

McConnell R, Berhane K, Gilliland F, London SJ, Islam T, Gauderman WJ, Avol E, Margolis HG, Peters JM. Asthma in exercising children exposed to ozone: A cohort study. *Lancet* 2002;359(9304):386–91.

McCord C, Freeman HP. Excess mortality in Harlem. *New England Journal of Medicine* 1990;322:173–79.

McEwen BS, Seeman T. Protective and damaging effects of mediators of stress: Elaborating and testing the concepts of allostasis and allostatic load. *Annals of the New York Academy of Sciences* 1999;896:30–47.

McGinnis JM, Foege W. Actual causes of death in the U.S. *JAMA* 1993;270(18):2207–12.

McKay GE. *Road Rage: Commuter Combat in America. The Tragic Stories, the Many Causes, the Keys to Survival.* Herculaneum, MO: Silvertip Books, 2000.

McKeown T. *The Role of Medicine: Dream, Mirage, or Nemesis?* Princeton, NJ: Princeton University Press, 1979.

McMichael AJ. Health consequences of global climate change. *Journal of the Royal Society of Medicine* 2001;94(3):111–14.

McMillan DW, Chavis DM. Sense of community: A definition and theory. *American Journal of Community Psychology* 1986;14:6–23.

McMurray L. Emotional stress and driving performance: The effects of divorce. *Behavioral Research in Highway Safety* 1970;1:100–114.

McShane C. *Down the Automobile Path: The Automobile and the American City.* New York: Columbia University Press, 1994.

Medalie JH, Goldbourt U. Angina pectoris among 10,000 men. II. Psychosocial and other risk factors as evidenced by a multivariate analysis of a five-year incidence study. *American Journal of Medicine* 1976;60:910–21.

Melosi M. *The Sanitary City: Urban Infrastructure in America from Colonial Times to the Present.* Baltimore: Johns Hopkins University Press, 2000, p 74.

Melosi M. *Effluent America: Cities, Industry, Energy, and the Environment.* Pittsburgh, PA: University of Pittsburgh Press, 2001.

Mendes de Leon CF, Glass TA, Beckett LA, Seeman TE, Evans DA, Berkman LF. Social networks and disability transitions across eight intervals of yearly data in the New Haven EPESE. *Journal of Gerontology Series B-Psychological Sciences and Social Sciences* 1999;54(3):S162–72.

Messenger T, Ewing R. Transit-oriented development in the sun belt. *Transportation Research Record* 1996;1552: 145–53.

Metropolitan Area Research Corporation. The Pattern of Social Separation and Sprawl. Minneapolis, Minnesota. 2003 Available: http://www.metroresearch.org.

Metzger R, Delgado JL, Herrell R. Environmental health and Hispanic children. *Environmental Health Perspectives* 1995;103 Suppl 6:539–50.

Mizell L. Aggressive driving. In: *Aggressive Driving: Three Studies.* Washington, DC: AAA Foundation for Traffic Safety, March 1997. Available: http://www.aaafoundation.org/pdf/agdr3study.pdf (accessed June 23, 2002).

Mobily KE, Rubenstein LM, Lemke JH, O'Hara MW, Wallace RB. Walking and depression in a cohort of older adults: The Iowa 65+ Rural Health Study. *Journal of Aging and Physical Activity* 1996;4:119–35.

Mohl RA. Poverty, pauperism and the social order in the preindustrial American city, 1780–1840. *Social Science Quarterly* March 1972:934–48.

Mokdad AH, Bowman BA, Ford ES, Vinicor F, Marks JS, Koplan JP. The continuing epidemics of obesity and diabetes in the United States. *JAMA* 2001;286:1195–1200.

Mokdad AH, Ford ES, Bowman BA, Dietz WH, Vinicor F, Bales VS, Marks JS. Prevalence of obesity, diabetes, and obesity-related health risk factors, 2001. *JAMA* 2003;289(1):76–79.

Mokdad AH, Ford ES, Bowman BA, Nelson DE, Engelgau MM, Vinicor F, et al. Diabetes trends in the U.S.: 1990–1998. *Diabetes Care* 2000;23: 1278–83.

Mokdad AH, Marks JS, Stroup DF, Gerberding JL. Actual causes of death in the United States, 2000. *JAMA* 2004; 291:1238–45.

Mokdad AH, Serdula MK, Dietz WH, Bowman BA, Marks JM, Koplan JP. The spread of the obesity epidemic in the United States, 1991–1998. *JAMA* 1999;282:1519–22.

Mokhtarian PL, Salomon I, Redmond LS. Understanding the demand for travel: It's not purely 'derived.' *Innovation: European Journal of Social Science* 2001; 14(4):355–81.

Moldan B, Billharz S, Matravers S. *Sustainability Indicators: A Report on the Project on Indicators of Sustainable Development.* New York: Wiley, 1998.

Moller DW. *Dancing with Broken Bones: A Portrait of Death and Dying Among Inner-City Poor.* New York: Oxford University Press, 2003.

Montgomery B. Road rage: Needless deaths. *Atlanta Journal-Constitution,* May 13, 2000, p 1.

Moore EO. A prison environment's effect on health care service demands. *Journal of Environmental Systems* 1981–2;11:17–34.

Moore KA, Blumenthal JA. Exercise training as an alternative treatment for depression among older adults. *Alternative Therapies* 1998;4:48–56.

Moore R, Young D. Childhood outdoors: Toward a social ecology of the landscape. In: Altman I, Wohlwill JF, Eds.

Children and the Environment. Human Behavior and Environment, Volume 3. New York: Plenum Press, 1978, pp 83–130.

Moreno S, Sipress A. Fatalities higher for Latino pedestrians; Area's Hispanic immigrants apt to walk but unaccustomed to urban traffic. *Washington Post*, August 27, 1999, p A01.

Morris RD. Airborne particulates and hospital admissions for cardiovascular disease: A quantitative review of the evidence. *Environmental Health Perspectives* 2001;109(suppl 4): 495–500.

Morris RD, Naumova EN, Levin R, Munasinghe RL. Temporal variation in drinking water turbidity and diagnosed gastroenteritis in Milwaukee. *American Journal of Public Health* 1996;86:237–39.

Morrow V. Children's experiences of "community": Implications of social capital discourses. In: Swann C, Morgan A, Eds. *Social Capital for Health: Insights from Qualitative Research*. London: National Health Service, Health Development Agency, 2002, pp 9–28. Available: http://www.hdaonline. org.uk/downloads/pdfs/ social_capital_complete_jul02.pdf.

Morrow V. Conceptualizing social capital in relation to the well-being of children and young people: A critical review. *Sociological Review* 1999;47: 744–65.

Moudon A, Hess P, Snyder M, Stanilov K. Effects of site design on pedestrian travel in mixed-use, medium-density environments. *Transportation Research Record* 1997;1578:48–55.

Moudon AV, Hess P. Suburban clusters: The nucleation of multifamily housing in suburban areas of the central Puget Sound. *Journal of the American Planning Association* 2000;66(3):243–64.

Mueller BA, Rivara FP, Shyh-Mine L, Weiss NS. Environmental factors and the risk of childhood pedestrian-motor vehicle collision occurrence. *American Journal of Epidemiology* 1990; 132:550–60.

Muller PO. Transportation and urban form: Stages in the spatial evolution of the American metropolis. In: Hanson S, Ed., *The Geography of Urban Transportation*, Second Edition. New York: Guilford Press, 1995.

Mumford L. *The Culture of Cities*. New York: Harcourt, Brace, 1938.

Mumford L. *The Highway and the City*. New York: Mentor, 1964.

Murphy E. Social origins of depression in old age. *British Journal of Psychiatry* 1982;141:135–42.

Murray CJL, Lopez A, Eds. *The Global Burden of Disease: A Comprehensive Assessment of Mortality and Disability from Diseases, Injuries and Risk Factors in 1990 and Projected to 2020*. Cambridge, MA: Harvard School of Public Health on behalf of the World Health Organization and the World Bank, 1996.

Must A, Spadano J, Coakley EH, Field AE, Colditz G, Dietz WH. The disease burden associated with overweight and obesity. *JAMA* 1999;282: 1523–29.

Myers D, Gearin E. Current preferences and future demand for denser residential environments. *Housing Policy Debate* 2001;12(4):633–59.

Narayan KM, Boyle JP. Thompson TJ. Sorensen SW. Williamson DF. Lifetime risk for diabetes mellitus in the United States. *JAMA* 2003; 290(14):1884-90.

Nasar JL, Julian DA. The psychological sense of community in the neighborhood. *Journal of the American Planning Association* 1995;61:178–84.

Nash GB. The social evolution of preindustrial American cities, 1700–1820. In: Mohl RA, Ed. *The Making of Urban America*, Second Edition. Wilmington, DE: Scholarly Resources, 1997.

Nash GB. *The Urban Crucible: The Northern Seaports and the Origins of the American Revolution*. Cambridge, MA: Harvard University Press, 1986.

National Advisory Commission on Civil Disorders [Kerner Copmmission]. *Report of the National Advisory*

Commission on Civil Disorders. New York: Dutton, 1968, p 262.

National Association of City and County Health Officials (NACCHO). *The Role for Local Public Health Agencies in Land Use Planning and Community Design.* Washington, DC: NACCHO, n.d.

National Council on Public Works Improvements. *Rebuilding the Foundations: A Special Report on State and Local Public Works Financing and Management.* OTA-SET-447. Washington, DC: Office of Technology Assessment, 1990.

National Heart, Lung, and Blood Institute Working Group. Respiratory diseases disproportionately affect minorities. *Chest* 1995;108:1380–92.

National Highway Traffic Safety Administration (NHTSA), National Center for Statistics and Analysis. *Traffic Safety Facts 2000: A Compilation of Motor Vehicle Crash Data from the Fatality Analysis Reporting System and the General Estimates System.* Washington, DC: NHTSA, December 2001, DOT HS 809 337.

National Highway Traffic Safety Administration (NHTSA). *National Survey of Speeding and Other Unsafe Driving Actions. Volume II: Driver Attitudes and Behavior.* Washington, DC: NHTSA, September 1998, DOT HS 808 749. Available: http://www.nhtsa.dot. gov/people/injury/aggressive/unsafe/.

National Highway Traffic Safety Administration (NHTSA). *Traffic Safety Facts 2001: A Compilation of Motor Vehicle Crash Data from the Fatality Analysis Reporting System and the General Estimates System.* Washington: USDOT, NHTSA, December 2002, DOT HS 809 484. Available: http://www-nrd. nhtsa.dot.gov/pdf/nrd-30/NCSA/ TSFAnn/TSF2001.pdf.

National Institutes of Health Consensus Development Panel on Physical Activity and Cardiovascular Health. NIH Consensus Conference: Physical activity and cardiovascular health. *JAMA* 1996;276:241–46.

National Research Council (NRC). *Watershed Management for Potable Water Supply: Assessing the New York City Strategy.* Washington, DC: National Academy Press, 2000.

National Safety Council. *Report on Injuries in America, 2002.* October, 2003. Available: http://www.nsc. org/library/report_injury_usa.htm.

National Safety Council (NSC). What Are the Odds of Dying? Available: http://www.nsc.org/lrs/statinfo/odds. htm (accessed August 14, 2003).

Navarro V. A critique of social capital. *International Journal of Health Services* 2002;32:423–32.

Nelson AC, Duncan JB. *Growth Management Principles and Practices.* Chicago: American Planning Association, 1995.

Nestle M. *Food Politics: How the Food Industry Influences Nutrition and Health.* Berkeley: University of California Press, 2002.

Newton K. Social capital and democracy. In: Edwards B, Foley MS, Diani M, Eds. *Beyond Tocqueville: Civil Society and the Social Capital Debate in Comparative Perspective.* Hanover, NH: Tufts University/University Press of New England, 2001.

Nicholson N, Goodge PM. The influence of social, organization, and biographical factors on female absence. *Journal of Management Studies* 1976;13: 234–54.

Norman JC, Ed. *Medicine in the Ghetto.* New York: Appleton-Century-Crofts, 1969.

Norris F. *The Pit: A Story of Chicago.* New York: Doubleday, Page, 1903.

Norris G, Young Pong SN, Koenig JQ, Larson TV, Sheppard L, Stout JW. An association between fine particles and asthma emergency department visits for children in Seattle. *Environmental Health Perspectives* 1999;107(6):489–93.

Norris T, Pittman M. The Healthy Communities movement and the Coalition for Healthier Cities and Communities. *Public Health Reports* 2000;115: 118–24.

Novaco R. Aggression on roadways. In: Baenninger R, Ed. *Targets of Violence and Aggression.* Amsterdam: Elsevier, 1991.

Novaco R, Kliewer W, Broquet A. Home environmental consequences of commute travel impedance. *American Journal of Community Psychology* 1991; 18:881–909.

Novaco R, Stokols D, Campbell J, Stoklols J. Transportation, stress, and community psychology. *American Journal of Community Psychology* 1979;7:361–80.

Novaco R, Stokols D, Milanesi L. Objective and subjective dimensions of travel impedance as determinants of commuting stress. *American Journal of Community Psychology* 1990;18:231–57.

O'Connor PJ, Aenchenbacher LE, Dishman RK. Physical activity and depression in the elderly. *Journal of Aging Physical Activity* 1993;1:34–58.

Ogden CL, Flegal KM, Carroll MD, Johnson CL. Prevalence and trends in overweight among US children and adolescents, 1999–2000. *JAMA* 2002; 288(14):1728–32.

Okun DA. From cholera to cancer to cryptosporidiosis. *Journal of Environmental Engineering* 1996;122(6):453–58.

Oldenburg R. *Celebrating the Third Place: Inspiring Stories About the "Great Good Places" at the Heart of Our Communities.* New York: Marlowe & Company, 2000.

Oldenburg R. *The Great Good Place: Cafés, Coffee Shops, Community Centers, Beauty Parlors, General Stores, Bars, Hangouts and How They Get You Through the Day.* New York: Paragon House, 1989.

Olfson M, Marcus SC, Druss B, et al. National trends in the outpatient treatment of depression. *JAMA* 2002;287(2):203-9.

Oliver JE. *Democracy in Suburbia.* Princeton, NJ: Princeton University Press, 2001.

Oliver JE. The effects of metropolitan economic segregation on local civic participation. *American Journal of Political Science* 1999;43:186–212.

Oliveria SA, Christos PJ. The epidemiology of physical activity and cancer. *Annals of the New York Academy of Sciences* 1997;833:79–90.

Olshansky SJ, Ault B. The fourth stage of the Epidemiologic Transition: The age of delayed degenerative diseases. *Milbank Quarterly* 1986;64:355–91.

Omran A. The Epidemiologic Transition: A theory of the epidemiology of population change. *Milbank Quarterly* 1971;49:509–38.

Oosterlee A, Drijver M, Lebret E, et al. Chronic respiratory symptoms in children and adults living along streets with high traffic density. *Occupational and Environmental Medicine* 1996;53:241–47.

Orfield M. *Metropolitics: A Regional Agenda for Community and Stability.* Washington, DC: Brookings Institution Press, 1997.

Organization for Economic Cooperation and Development (OECD). *Safety of Vulnerable Road Users.* DSTI/DOT/RTR/RS7(98)1/FINAL. Paris: OECD, Directorate for Science, Technology, and Industry, Scientific Expert Group and the Safety of Vulnerable Road Users, 1998.

Orth-Gomer K, Rosengren A, Wilhelmsen L. Lack of social support and incidence of coronary heart disease in middle-aged Swedish men. *Psychosomatic Medicine* 1993;55:37–43.

Ossenbruggen PJ, Pendharkar J, Ivan J. Roadway safety in rural and small urbanized areas. *Accident Analysis and Prevention* 2001;33:485–98.

Ostfeld AM, D'Atri DA. Psychophysiological responses to the urban environment. *International Journal of Psychiatry in Medicine* 1975;6(1–2): 15–28.

Otto B, Ransel K, Todd J, Lovaas D, Stutzman H, Bailey J. *Paving Our Way to Water Shortages: How Sprawl Aggravates Drought.* Washington, DC: American Rivers, Natural Resources Defense Council, Smart Growth America, 2002, p 34.

Owen N, Bauman A. The descriptive epidemiology of a sedentary lifestyle in adult Australians. *International Journal of Epidemiology* 1992;21(2):305–10.

Pack AM, Cucchiara A, Schwab CW, Rodgman E, Pack AI. Characteristics of accidents attributed to the driver having fallen asleep. *Sleep Research* 1994; 23:141.

Paffenbarger R, Lee I-M. Physical activity and fitness for health and longevity. *Research Quarterly for Exercise and Sport* 1996;67(suppl 3):11–28.

Pappano L. *The Connection Gap: Why Americans Feel So Alone.* New Brunswick: Rutgers University Press, 2001.

Parashar UD, Holman RC, Clarke MJ, Bresee JS, Glass RI. Hospitalizations associated with rotavirus diarrhea in the United States, 1993 through 1995: surveillance based on the new ICD-9-CM rotavirus specific diagnostic code. *Journal of Infectious Diseases* 1998;177:7–13.

Parcel TL, Menaghan EG. Family social capital and children's behavior problems. *Social Psychology Quarterly* 1993;56:120–35.

Park H, Lee B, Ha E-H, Lee J-T, Kim H, Hong Y-C. Association of air pollution with school absenteeism due to illness. *Archives of Pediatrics and Adolescent Medicine* 2002;156:1235–39.

Park JH, Spengler JD, Yoon DD, Dumyahn T, Lee K, Ozkaynak H. Measurement of air exchange rate of stationary vehicle and estimation of in-vehicle exposure. *Journal of Exposure Analysis and Environmental Epidemiology* 1998;8:(1):65–78.

Parry J, Stevens A. Prospective health impact assessment: pitfalls, problems, and possible ways forward. *British Medical Journal* 2001;323:1177–82.

Parry MH. *Aggression on the Road.* London: Tavistock: 1968.

Parsons R, Tassinary L, Ulrich R, Hebl M, Grossman-Alexander M. The view from the road: Implications for stress recovery and immunization. *Journal of Environmental Psychology* 1998; 18:113–40.

Pate RR, Pratt M, Blair SN, Haskell WL, Macera CA, Bouchard C, et al. Physical activity and public health: A recommendation from the Centers for Disease Control and Prevention and the American College of Sports Medicine. *JAMA* 1995;273:402–07.

Payment P, Richardson L, Siemiatycki J, Dewar R, Edwardes M, Franco E. A randomized trial to evaluate the risk of gastrointestinal disease due to consumption of drinking water meeting current microbiological standards. *American Journal of Public Health.* 1991;81:703–08.

Peden DB. Air pollution in asthma: Effect of pollutants on airway inflammation. *Annals of Allergy, Asthma, and Immunology* 2001;87:12–17.

Pekkanen J, Peters A, Hoek G, Tiittanen P, Brunekreef B, de Hartog J, et al. Particulate air pollution and risk of ST-segment depression during repeated submaximal exercise tests among subjects with coronary heart disease: The Exposure and Risk Assessment for Fine and Ultrafine Particles in Ambient Air (ULTRA) Study. *Circulation* 2002;106:933–38.

Perlin SA, Sexton K, Wong DW. An examination of race and poverty for populations living near industrial sources of air pollution. *Journal of Exposure Analysis and Environmental Epidemiology* 1999;9(1):29–48.

Persky VW, Slezak J, Contreras A, Becker L, Hernandez E, Ramakrishnan V, Piorkowski J. Relationships of race and socioeconomic status with prevalence, severity, and symptoms of asthma in Chicago school children. *Annals of Allergy, Asthma, and Immunology* 1998;81(3):266–71.

Peterson TD, Jolly BT, Runge JW, Hunt RC. Motor vehicle safety: current concepts and challenges for emergency physicians. *Annals of Emergency Medicine* 1999;34:384–93.

Philip P, Ghorayeb I, Stoohs R, Menny JC, Dabadie P, Bioulac B, Guilleminault C. Determinants of sleepiness in automobile drivers. *Journal of Psychosomatic Research* 1996;41:279–88.

Philip P, Taillard J, Guilleminault C, Quera Salva MA, Bioulac B, Ohayon M. Long distance driving and self-induced sleep deprivation among automobile drivers. *Sleep* 1999; 22:475–80.

Pickering T. Cardiovascular pathways: Socioeconomic status and stress effects on hypertension and cardiovascular function. *Annals of the New York Academy of Sciences* 1999;896:262–77.

Pietri F. Leclerc A. Boitel L. Chastang JF. Morcet JF, Blondet M. Low-back pain in commercial travelers. *Scandinavian Journal of Work, Environment and Health* 1992;18(1):52–58.

Pikora T, Giles-Corti B, Bull F, Jamrozik K, Donovan R. Developing a framework for assessment of the environmental determinants of walking and cycling. *Social Science and Medicine* 2003;56:1693–1703.

Plas JM, Lewis SE. Environmental factors and sense of community in a planned town. *American Journal of Community Psychology* 1996;24(1):109–43.

Platt FN. Heart rate measurements of drivers with the highway systems research car. *Industrial Medicine and Surgery* 1969;38(10):339–48.

Pless IB, Peckham CS, Power C. Predicting traffic injuries in childhood: A cohort analysis. *Journal of Pediatrics* 1989;15:932–38.

Pless IB, Verreault R, Arsenault L, Frappier J, Stulginskas J. The epidemiology of road accidents in childhood. *American Journal of Public Health* 1987; 77:358–60.

Pless IB, Verreault R, Tenina S. A case-control study of pedestrian and bicyclist injuries in childhood. *American Journal of Public Health* 1989;79: 995–98.

Pope CA 3rd. Epidemiology of fine particulate air pollution and human health: Biologic mechanisms and who's at risk? *Environmental Health Perspectives* 2000;108 suppl 4:713–23.

Pope CA, Burnett RT, Thun MJ, Calle EE, Krewski D, Ito K, Thurston GD. Lung cancer, cardiopulmonary mortality, and long-term exposure to fine particulate air pollution. *JAMA* 2002;287:1132–41.

Popenoe D. Urban sprawl: Some neglected sociological considerations. *Sociology and Social Research* 1979;63(2):255–68.

Poplin DE. Communities: *A Survey of Theories and Methods of Research.* New York: MacMillan, 1972.

Popp PO, Belohlav JA. Absenteeism in low status environments. *Academy of Management Journal* 1982;25:677–83.

Porter BE, Berry TD. A nationwide survey of self-reported red light running: measuring prevalence, predictors, and perceived consequences. *Accident Analysis and Prevention* 2001;33(6): 735–41.

Porter DR. *Making Smart Growth Work.* Washington: Urban Land Institute, 2002.

Portes A. Social capital: Its origins and applications in modern sociology. *Annual Review of Sociology* 1998;22: 1–24.

Portney KE. *Taking Sustainable Cities Seriously.* Cambridge: MIT Press, 2003.

Portney KE, Berry JM. Mobilizing minority communities: Social capital and participation in urban neighborhoods. *American Behavioral Scientist* 1997; 40:632–44.

Posner JC, Liao E, Winston FK, Cnaan A, Shaw KN, Durbin DR. Exposure to traffic among urban children injured as pedestrians. *Injury Prevention* 2002; 8(3):231–35.

Powell J. Sprawl, fragmentation, and the persistence of racial inequality: Limiting civil rights by fragmenting space. In: Squires GD, Ed. *Urban Sprawl: Causes, Consequences and Policy Responses.* Washington: Urban Institute Press, 2002, pp 73–117.

Powell J. Addressing regional dilemmas for minority communities. In: Squires GD, Ed. *Urban Sprawl: Causes, Consequences and Policy Responses.* Washington: Urban Institute Press, 2002, pp 218–46.

Powell KE, Martin LM, Chowdhury PP. Places to walk: Convenience and regular physical activity. *American Journal of Public Health* 2003;93(9):1519–21.

Prentice AM, Jebb SA. Obesity in Britain: Gluttony or sloth? *British Medical Journal* 1995;311:437–39.

Preston B. Statistical analysis of child pedestrian accidents in Manchester and Salford. *Accident Analysis and Prevention* 1972;4:323–32.

Pretty J, Griffin M, Sellens M, Pretty C. *Green Exercise: Complementary Roles of Nature, Exercise and Diet in Physical and Emotional Well-Bing and Implications for Public Health Policy.* CES Occasional Paper 2003-1, University of Essex, March 2003. Available: http://www2.essex.ac.uk/ces/Research Programmes/CESOccasionalPapers/GreenExercise.pdf.

Proshansky HM, Fabian AK. The development of place identity in the child. In: Weinstein CS, David TG, Eds. *Spaces for Children: The Built Environment and Child Development.* York: Plenum, 1987, pp 21–40.

Pucher J, Dijkstra L. Making walking and cycling safer: Lessons from Europe. *Transportation Quarterly* 2000;54(3): 25–51.

Pucher J, Dijkstra L. Promoting safe walking and cycling to improve public health: Lessons from the Netherlands and Germany. *American Journal of Public Health* 2003;93:1509–16.

Pushkarev B, Zupan J. *Urban Rail in America: An Exploration of Criteria for Fixed-Guideway Transit.* UMTA-NY-06-0061-80-1 Final Report. p 368. 1980.

Putnam R. *Bowling Alone: The Collapse and Revival of American Community.* New York: Simon & Schuster, 2000.

Quinn C. DOT to look at risks, benefits of tree-lined sidewalks. *Atlanta Journal-Constitution,* January 27 2003, p B2.

Raffensberger C, Tickner J, Jackson W. *Protecting Public Health and the Environment: Implementing the Precautionary Principle.* Washington, DC: Island Press, 1999.

Ransdell LB, Wells CL. Physical activity in urban White, African-American, and Mexican-American women. *Medicine and Science in Sports and Exercise* 1998; 30:1608–15.

Rao R, Hawkins M, Guyer B. Children's exposure to traffic and risk of pedestrian injury in an urban setting. *Bulletin of the New York Academy of Medicine* 1997;74:65–80.

Rapoport A. Pedestrian street use: Culture and perception. In: Anne Moudon, Ed. *Public Streets for Public Use.* New York: Van Nostrand Reinhold, 1987.

Redefining Progress. Genuine Progress Indicator. Available: www.redefiningprogress.org/projects/gpi/ (accessed February 8, 2004).

Redelmeier DA, Tibshirani RJ. Association between cellular-telephone calls and motor vehicle collisions. *New England Journal of Medicine* 1997;336(7): 453–58.

Reed D, McGee D, Yano K, Geinleib M. Social networks and coronary heart disease among Japanese men in Hawaii. *American Journal of Epidemiology* 1983;117:384–96.

Relph E. *The Modern Urban Landscape.* Baltimore: Johns Hopkins University Press, 1987.

Retting RA, Ferguson SA, McCartt AT. A review of evidence-based traffic engineering measures designed to reduce pedestrian-motor vehicle crashes. *American Journal of Public Health* 2003;93:1456–63.

Richter DL, Wilcox S, Greaney ML, Henderson KA, Ainsworth BE. Environmental, policy, and cultural factors related to physical activity in African American women. *Women and Health* 2002;36(2):91–109.

Rijnders E, Janssen NAH, van Vliet PHN, Brunekreef B. Personal and outdoor nitrogen dioxide concentrations in relation to degree of urbanization and traffic density. *Environmental Health Perspectives* 2001;109(suppl 3): 411–17.

Ritz B, Yu F, Fruin S, Chapa G, Shaw GM, Harris JA. Ambient air pollution and risk of birth defects in Southern California. *American Journal of Epidemiology* 2002;155:17–25.

Rivara FP. Pediatric injury control in 1999: Where do we go from here? *Pediatrics* 1999;103(4 Pt 2):883–88.

Rivara FP, Barber M. Demographic analysis of child pedestrian injuries. *Pediatrics* 1985;76:375–81.

Roberts I. Why have child pedestrian death rates fallen? *British Medical Journal* 1993;306:1737–39.

Roberts I, Ashton T, Dunn R, Lee-Joe T. Preventing child pedestrian injury: Pedestrian education or traffic calming? *Australian Journal of Public Health* 1994;18(2):209–12.

Roberts I, Crombie I. Child pedestrian deaths: Sensitivity to traffic volume— evidence from the USA. *Journal of Epidemiology and Community Health* 1995;49(2):186–88.

Roberts I, Marshall R, Lee-Joe T. The urban traffic environment and the risk of child pedestrian injury: A case-crossover approach. *Epidemiology* 1995;6(2):169–71.

Roberts I, Marshall R, Norton R, Borman B. An area analysis of child injury morbidity in Auckland. *Journal of Pediatrics and Child Health* 1992; 28:438–41.

Roberts I, Marshall R, Norton R. Child pedestrian mortality and traffic volume in New Zealand. *British Medical Journal* 1992;305:283.

Roberts I, Norton R, Jackson R, Dunn R, Hassall I. Effect of environmental factors on risk of injury of child pedestrians by motor vehicles: A case-control study. *British Medical Journal* 1995;310:91–94.

Rodgers GB. Income and inequality as determinants of mortality: An international cross-sectional analysis. *Population Studies* 1979;33:343–51.

Rodriguez MA, Winkleby MA, Ahn D, Sundquist J, Kraemer HC. Identification of population subgroups of children and adolescents with high asthma prevalence: Findings from the Third National Health and Nutrition Examination Survey. *Archives of Pediatrics and Adolescent Medicine* 2002; 156(3):269–75.

Roemer WH, van Wijnen JH. Daily mortality and air pollution along busy streets in Amsterdam, 1987–1998. *Epidemiology* 2001;12(6):649–53.

Rogers RG, Hackenberg R. Extending Epidemiologic Transition Theory: A new stage. *Social Biology* 1987;34: 234–43.

Roorda-Knape MC, Janssen NAH, de Hartog J, Van Vliet PHN, Harssema H, Brunekreef B. Traffic-related air pollution in city districts near motorways. *The Science of the Total Environment* 1999;235:339–41.

Rose JB, Epstein PR, Lipp EK, Sherman BH, Bernard SM, Patz JA. Climate variability and change in the United States: Potential impacts on water- and foodborne diseases caused by microbiologic agents. *Environmental Health Perspectives* 2001;109(suppl 2):211–21.

Rosenberg C. *The Cholera Years: The United States in 1832, 1849, and 1866.* Chicago: University of Chicago Press, 1962, p 18.

Ross CE. Walking, exercising, and smoking: Does neighborhood matter? *Social Science and Medicine* 2000;51: 265–74.

Ross CL, Dunning AE. *Land Use Transportation Interaction: An Examination of the 1995 NPTS Data.* Atlanta: USDOT, Federal Highway Administration, 1997. Available: http://npts.ornl.gov/npts/1995/Doc/landuse3.pdf.

Ross NA, Wolfson MC, Dunn JR, Berthelot JM, Kaplan GA, Lynch JW. Relation between income inequality and mortality in Canada and in the United States: Cross sectional assessment using census data and vital statistics. *British Medical Journal* 2000; 320(7239):898–902.

Runyan D, Hunter WM, Socolar RR, Amaya-Jackson L, English D, et al. Children who prosper in unfavorable environments: The relationship to social capital. *Pediatrics* 1998;101: 12–19.

Rydin Y. Environmental dimensions of residential development and the implications for local planning practice. *Journal of Environmental Planning and Management* 1992;35: 43–61.

Saegert S, Thompson JP, Warren MR, Eds. *Social Capital and Poor Communities.* New York: Russell Sage Foundation, 2001.

Saelens B, Sallis J, Frank L. Environmental correlates of walking and cycling: Findings from the transportation, urban design, and planning literatures. *Annals of Behavioral Medicine* 2003;25(2):80–91.

Safer DJ, Zito JM, Fine EM. Increased methylphenidate usage for attention deficit disorder in the 1990s. *Pediatrics* 1996;98:1084–88.

Saguaro Seminar. Better Together: Report of the Saguaro Seminar on Civic Engagement in America, John F. Kennedy School of Government, Harvard University (Cambridge, MA: 2000). Available at http://www. bettertogether.org/report.php3.

Salins P. New York City's Housing Gap Revisited. Civic Report No. 25, February 2002. Manhattan Institute for Policy Studies. Available: http:// www.manhattan-institute.org/html/ cr_25.htm.

Sallis JF, Bauman A, Pratt M. Physical activity interventions: Environmental and policy interventions to promote physical activity. *American Journal of Preventive Medicine* 1998;15(4): 379–97.

Sallis JF, Owen N. *Physical Activity and Behavioral Medicine.* Thousand Oaks CA: Sage Publications, 1999.

Samet J, Zeger S, Dominici F, Curriero F, Coursac I, Dockery D, Schwartz J, Zanobetti A. Morbidity and Mortality from Air Pollution in the United States. Final Report NMMAPS, Health Effects Institute, Boston, 1999. Available: http://www. healtheffects.org/Pubs/Samet2.pdf.

Samet JM, Dominici F, Curriero FC, Coursac I, Zeger SL. Fine particulate air pollution and mortality in 20 U.S. cities, 1987–1994. *New England Journal of Medicine* 2000;343:1742–49.

Sampson RJ, Raudenbush SW, Earls F. Neighborhoods and violent crime: A multilevel study of collective efficacy. *Science* 1997;277:918–24.

Sarason SB. *The Psychological Sense of Community: Prospects for a Community Psychology.* San Francisco: Jossey-Bass, 1974.

Sarkar S, Nederveen AAJ, Pols A. Renewed commitment to traffic calming for pedestrian safety. *Transportation Research Record* 1997;1578:11–19.

Scaff AH. The effect of commuting on participation in community organizations. *American Sociological Review* 1952;17:215–20.

Schaeffer M, Street S, Singer JE, Baum A. Effects of control on the stress reactions of commuters. *Journal of Applied Social Psychology* 1988;11:944–57.

Schell ER. *The Hungry Gene: The Science of Fat and the Future of Thin.* New York: Atlantic Monthly Press, 2002.

Schieber RA, Thompson NJ. Developmental risk factors for childhood pedestrian injuries. *Injury Prevention* 1996;2(3):228–36.

Schill MH, Wachter SM. The spatial bias of Federal housing law and policy: Concentrated poverty in urban America. *University of Pennsylvania Law Review* 1995;143(5):1285–1342.

Schlosser E. *Fast Food Nation: The Dark Side of the All-American Meal.* Boston: Houghton Mifflin, 2001.

Schoenback V, Kaplan B, Fredman L, et al. Social ties and mortality in Evans County, Georgia. *American Journal of Epidemiology* 1985;123:577–91.

Schor JB. *The Overworked American: The Unexpected Decline of Leisure.* New York: Basic Books, 1992.

Schrank D, Lomax T. 2003 Urban Mobility Study. College Station, TX: Texas A&M University System, Texas Transportation Institute, 2003. Available: http://mobility.tamu.edu/ums/.

Schreiber ME, Simo JA, Freiberg PG. Stratigraphic and geochemical controls on naturally occurring arsenic in groundwater, eastern Wisconsin, USA. *Hydrogeology Journal* 2000; 8:161–76.

Schueler TR. Microbes and urban watersheds: Concentrations, sources, and pathways. In: Schueler TR, Holland HK, Eds. *The Practice of Watershed*

Protection. Ellicott City MD: Center for Watershed Protection; 2000: 68–78.

Schueler TR, Holland HK, Eds. *The Practice of Watershed Protection.* Ellicott City, Md: Center for Watershed Protection, 2003.

Schulman MD, Anderson C. The dark side of the force: Economic restructuring and social capital in a company town. In: Edwards B, Foley MS, Diani M, Eds. *Beyond Tocqueville: Civil Society and the Social Capital Debate in Comparative Perspective.* Hanover NH: Tufts University/University Press of New England, 2001, pp 112–24.

Schwartz J, Levin R, Goldstein R. Drinking water turbidity and gastrointestinal illness in the elderly of Philadelphia. *Journal of Epidemiology and Community Health* 2000;54:45–51.

Schwartz J, Levin R, Hodge K. Drinking water turbidity and pediatric hospital use for gastrointestinal illness in Philadelphia. *Epidemiology* 1997;8: 615–20.

Seeman TE. Social ties and health: The benefits of social integration. *Annals of Epidemiology* 1996;6:442–51.

Seeman TE. Health promoting effects of friends and family on health outcomes in older adults. *American Journal of Health Promotion* 2000;14: 362–70.

Seeman TE, Crimmins E. Social environment effects on health and aging: Integrating epidemiologic and demographic approaches and perspectives. *Annals of the New York Academy of Sciences* 2001;954:88–117

Seeman TE, Lusignolo TM, Albert M, Berkman L. Social relationships, social support, and patterns of cognitive aging in healthy, high-functioning older adults: MacArthur studies of successful aging. *Health Psychology* 2001;20(4):243–55.

Seeman TE, Syme SL. Social networks and coronary artery disease: A comparative analysis of network structural and support characteristics. *Psychosomatic Medicine* 1987;49:341–54.

Selzer ML, Vinokur A. Life events, subjective stress and traffic accidents. *American Journal of Psychiatry* 1974;131: 903–06.

Serdula MK, Ivery D, Coates RJ, Freedman DS, Williamson DF, Byers T. Do obese children become obese adults? A review of the literature. *Preventive Medicine* 1993;22: 167–77.

Sesso HD, Paffenbarger RS, Ha T, Lee IM. Physical activity and cardiovascular disease risk in middle-aged and older women. *American Journal of Epidemiology* 1999;150:408–16.

Sesso HD, Paffenbarger RS Jr, Lee IM. Physical activity and breast cancer risk in the College Alumni Health Study (United States). *Cancer Causes Control* 1998;9:433–39.

Seyforth JY, Bost WA. Teacher turnover and the quality of worklife in schools: An empirical study. *Journal of Research and Development in Education* 1986; 20:1–6.

Shaper AG, Wannamethee SG. Walker M. Body weight: Implications for the prevention of coronary heart disease, stroke, and diabetes mellitus in a cohort study of middle aged men. *British Medical Journal* 1997;314: 1311–17.

Shaw, Gordon R. Impact of residential street standards on neo-traditional neighborhood concepts. *Institute of Transportation Engineers Journal* 1994 (July):30–33.

Shelton S. Water war now headed to federal courts. *Atlanta Journal-Constitution,* September 2, 2003, p 1.

Shi JP, Khan AA, Harrison RM. Measurements of ultrafine particle concentration and size distribution in the urban atmosphere. *The Science of the Total Environment* 1999;235:51–64.

Shi L, Starfield B, Kennedy B, Kawachi I. Income inequality, primary care, and health indicators. *Journal of Family Practice* 1999;48:275–84.

Shinar D. Aggressive driving: the contributions of the drivers and situation. *Transportation Research Part F* 1998;1: 137–60.

Shively CA, Clarkson TB. Social status and coronary artery atherosclerosis in female monkeys. *Arteriosclerosis and Thrombosis* 1994;14:721–26.

Shively CA, Laber-Laird K, Anton RF. Behavior and physiology of social stress and depression in female cynomolgus monkeys. *Biological Psychiatry* 1997;41:871–82.

Shprentz DS, Bryner GC, Shprentz JS. *Breath-Taking: Premature Mortality Due to Particulate Air Pollution in 239 American Cities.* New York: Natural Resources Defense Council, 1996.

Shriver K. Influence of environmental design on pedestrian travel behavior in four Austin neighborhoods. *Transportation Research Record* 1997;1578: 64–75.

Siegel AW, Kirasic KC, Kail RV Jr. Stalking the elusive cognitive map: The development of children's representations of geographic space. In: Altman I, Wohlwill JF, Eds. *Children and the Environment.* Human Behavior and Environment, Volume 3. New York, Plenum Press, 1978, pp 223–58.

Simon F, Corbett C. Road traffic offending, stress, age, and accident history among male and female drivers. *Ergonomics* 1996;39(5):757–80.

Simon GE, Goldberg DP, Von Korff M, Üstün TB. Understanding crossnational differences in depression prevalence. *Psychological Medicine* 2002;32:585–94.

Simonson E, Baker C, Burns N, Keiper C, Schmitt OH, Stackhouse S. Cardiovascular stress (electrocardiographic changes) produced by driving an automobile. *American Heart Journal* 1968;75(1):125–35.

Singer J, Lundberg U, Frankenhauser M. Stress on the train: A study of urban commuting. In: Baum A, Singer J, Valins S, Eds. *The Urban Environment* (Advances in Environmental Psychology, Vol 1). Hillsdale, NJ: Erlbaum, 1978, pp 41–56.

Singer M. A dose of drugs, a touch of violence, a case of AIDS: Conceptualizing the SAVA syndemic. *Free Inquiry* 1996;24(2):99–110.

Singh N, Clemets K, Fiatarone M. A randomized controlled trial of progressive resistance training in depressed elders. *Journal of Gerontology* 1997; 52A:M27–M35.

Skjaeveland O, Garling T. Effects of interactional space on neighboring. *Journal of Environmental Psychology* 1997;17:181–98.

Skov T, Borg V, Orhede E. Psychosocial and physical risk factors for musculoskeletal disorders of the neck, shoulders, and lower back in salespeople. *Occupational and Environmental Medicine* 1996;53(5):351–56.

Slattery ML, Edwards SL, Boucher KM, Anderson K, Caan BJ. Lifestyle and colon cancer: An assessment of factors associated with risk. *American Journal of Epidemiology* 1999;150:869–77.

Smith MH, Beaulieu LJ, Israel GD. Effects of human capital and social capital on dropping out of high school in the South. *Journal of Research in Rural Education* 1992;8(1):75–87.

Smith RA. Measuring neighborhood cohesion: A review and some suggestions. *Human Ecology* 1975;3(3):143–60.

Snow RW. *1999 National Highway Safety Survey. Monitoring American's Attitudes, Opinions, and Behaviors.* Mississippi State University, Social Science Research Center. January, 2000. Available at www.ssrc.msstate. edu/publications/srrs2000-1.pdf. Accessed July 18, 2002.

Snow RW. *2001 National Highway Safety Survey. Monitoring American's Attitudes, Opinions, and Behaviors.* Mississippi State University, Social Science Research Center. January, 2002. Available at http://www.ssrc.msstate. edu/publications/2001National HighwaySafetySurvey.pdf. Accessed July 18, 2002.

Snyder D. A new direction in water law: Frederick ordinance resembles western U.S. approach. *Washington Post,* September 23, 2002, B1.

Soil Conservation Service, 1986. Urban Hydrology for Small Watersheds. United States Department of Agriculture Soil Conservation Service Technical Release 55, 2nd edition.

Solley WB, Pierce RR, Perlman HA. *Estimated Use of Water in the United States in 1995*. Reston, Va: US Geological Survey; 1998. Circular 1200.

Solomon GM, Campbell TR, Feuer GR, Masters J, Samkian A, Paul KA. *No Breathing in the Aisles: Diesel Exhaust Inside School Buses*. New York and Los Angeles: Natural Resources Defense Council and Coalition for Clean Air, February 2001. Available: http://www.nrdc.org/air/transportation/schoolbus/sbusinx.asp.

Southworth M. Walkable suburbs? An evaluation of neotraditional communities at the urban edge. *Journal of the American Planning Association* 1997; 63:28–44.

Southworth M, Owens P. The evolving metropolis: Studies of community, neighborhood, and street form at the urban edge. *Journal of the American Planning Association* 1993;59, 3: 271–87.

Spencer C, Woolley H. Children and the city: A summary of recent environmental psychology research. *Child: Care, Health and Development* 2000; 26(3):181–98.

Spencer JR. Motor vehicles as weapons of offence. *Criminal Law Review* 1985; January: 29–41.

Squires GD, Ed. *Urban Sprawl: Causes, Consequences and Policy Responses*. Washington: Urban Institute Press, 2002.

Stanistreet D, Scott-Samuel A, Bellis MA. Income inequality and mortality in England. *Journal of Public Health Medicine* 1999;21:205–07.

Steiner R. Residential density and travel patterns: Review of the literature. *Transportation Research Record* 1994; 1466:37–43.

Stephenson D. Comparison of the water balance for an undeveloped and a suburban catchment. *Hydrological Sciences Journal* 1994;39:295–307.

Stevens J, Plankey MW, Williamson DF, et al. The body mass index-mortality relationship in white and African American women. *Obesity Research* 1998;6:268–77.

Stevenson MR, Jamrozik KD, Spittle J. A case-control study of traffic risk factors and child pedestrian injury. *International Journal of Epidemiology* 1995;24:957–64.

Stevenson MR, Sleet DA. Which prevention strategies for child pedestrian injuries? A review of the literature. *International Quarterly of Community Health Education* 1997;16:207–17.

Stokols D, Novaco RW. Transportation and well-being. In: Altman I, Wohlwill JF, Everett PB, Eds. *Transportation and Behavior*. New York: Plenum Press, 1981, pp 85–130.

Stokols D, Novaco R, Stokols J, Campbell J. Traffic congestion, type A behavior, and stress. *Journal of Applied Psychology* 1978;63:467–80.

Stolle D, Rochon T. Are all associations alike? Member diversity, associational type, and the creation of social capital. In: Edwards B, Foley MS, Diani M, Eds. *Beyond Tocqueville: Civil Society and the Social Capital Debate in Comparative Perspective*. Hanover NH: Tufts University/University Press of New England, 2001, pp 143–56.

Strauss RS, Pollack HA. Epidemic increase in childhood overweight, 1986–1998. *JAMA* 2001;286:2845–48.

Strauss RS, Rodzilsky D, Burack G, Colin M. Psychosocial correlates of physical activity in healthy children. *Archives of Pediatrics and Adolescent Medicine* 2001;155(8):897–902.

Strawbridge WJ, Deleger S, Roberts RE, Kaplan GA. Physical activity reduces the risk of subsequent depression for older adults. *American Journal of Epidemiology* 2002;156(4):328–34.

Strayer DL, Drews FA, Johnston WA. Cell phone-induced failures of visual attention during simulated driving. *Journal of Experimental Psychology: Applied* 2003;9(1):23–32.

Strayer DL, Johnston WA. Driven to distraction: Dual-task studies of simulated driving and conversing on a cellular phone. *Psychological Science* 2001;12(6): Available: http://www.Psych.Utah.Edu/Appliedcognitionlab/PS-Reprint.Pdf.

Stunkard AJ, Faith MS, Allison KC. Depression and obesity. *Biological Psychiatry* 2003;54(3):330–37.

Substance Abuse and Mental Health Services Administration, National Mental Health Information Center. Major Depression in Children and Adolescents. Document CA-0011, April 2003. www.mentalhealth.org/publications/allpubs/CA-0011/default.asp#2.

Surface Transportation Policy Project. *High Mileage Moms.* Washington: STPP, May, 1999. Available: http://www.transact.org/report.asp?id=182.

Surface Transportation Policy Project (STPP). *Aggressive Driving: Are You at Risk?* Washington: STPP, 1999. Available: http://www.transact.org/Reports/aggressivedriving99/ (accessed July 23, 2002).

Surgeon General of the United States. *Mental Health: A Report of the Surgeon General.* Rockville, MD: US DHHS, Substance Abuse and Mental Health Services Administration, Center for Mental Health Services, National Institutes of Health, National Institute of Mental Health, 1999.

Swann C, Morgan A, Eds. *Social Capital for Health: Insights from Qualitative Research.* London: Health Development Agency, July, 2002. Available: http://www.hda-online.org.uk/downloads/pdfs/social_capital_complete_jul02.pdf.

Swift P, Painter D, Goldstein M. Residential street typology and injury accident frequency. Report by Swift Associates, Longmont CO, 1998. Available: http://members.aol.com/Phswi/Swift-street.html.

Szczygiel B, Hewitt R. Nineteenth-century medical landscapes: John H. Rauch, Frederick Law Olmsted, and the search for salubrity. *Bulletin of the History of Medicine* 2000;74: 708–34.

Taggart P, Gibbons D, Somerville W. Some effects of motor-car driving on the normal and abnormal heart. *British Medical Journal* 1969;4:130–34.

Takano T, Fu J, Nakamura K, Uji K, Fukuda Y, Watanabe M, Nakajima H. Age-adjusted mortality and its association to variations in urban conditions in Shanghai. *Health Policy* 2002;61:239–53.

Takano T, Nakamura K. An analysis of health levels and various indicators of urban environments for Healthy Cities projects. *Journal of Epidemiology and Community Health* 2001;55(4): 263–70.

Talen E. The social goals of New Urbanism. *Housing Policy Debate* 2002;13: 165–88.

Tapia Granados JA. Reducing automobile traffic: An urgent policy for health promotion. *Pan American Journal of Public Health.* 1998;3(4):227–41.

Tarkington B. *The Turmoil* [1915]. Reprint edition Urbana, University of Illinois Press, 2003.

Tarr J. Industrial waste disposal in the United States as a historical problem. *Ambix: The Journal of the Society for the History of Alchemy and Chemistry* 2002;49:4–20

Tarr JA. Industrial wastes, water pollution, and public health, 1876–1962. Chap XIV in Tarr JA. *The Search for the Ultimate Sink: Urban Pollution in Historical Perspective.* Akron: University of Akron Press, 1996, p 356.

Tarr JA. The horse-polluter of the city. In: Tarr JA. *The Search for the Ultimate Sink: Urban Pollution in Historical Perspective.* Akron: University of Akron Press, 1996, pp 323–34.

Tarr JA. Urban pollution—Many long years ago. *American Heritage* XXII (October 1971) 65–69, 106.

Task Force on Community Preventive Services. Increasing physical activity. *Morbidity and Mortality Weekly Report* 2001;50(RR18):1–16.

Task Force on Community Preventive Services. Recommendations to increase physical activity in communities. *American Journal of Preventive Medicine* 2002;22(4S):67–72.

Taylor PJ, Pocock SJ. Commuter travel and sickness: Absence of London office workers. *British Journal of Preventive and Social Medicine* 1972;26: 165–72.

Taylor SE, Seeman TE. Psychosocial resources and the SES-health relationship. *Annals of the New York Academy of Sciences* 1999;896:210–25.

Taylor WC, Baranowski T, Young DR. Physical activity interventions in low-income, ethnic minority, and populations with disability. *American Journal of Preventive Medicine* 1998;15:334–43.

Teachmann J, Paasch K, Carver K. Social capital and dropping out of school early. *Journal of Marriage and the Family* 1996;58:773–83.

Texas Transportation Institute. 2001 Urban Mobility Study. http://mobility.tamu.edu/ums/.

Thomas GS. *The United States of Suburbia: How the Suburbs Took Control of America and What They Plan to Do with It.* Amherst, NY: Prometheus Books, 1998.

Thune I, Brenn T,Lund E, Gaard M. Physical activity and the risk of breast cancer. *New England Journal of Medicine* 1997; 336(18):1269–75.

Thurston GD, Ito K. Epidemiological studies of acute ozone exposures and mortality. *Journal of Exposure Analysis and Environmental Epidemiology* 2001; 11:286–94.

Tocqueville, Alexis de. *Democracy in America.* London: 1835, 1840. Reprinted by University of Chicago Press, 2000.

Todd JA, Robinson RJ. Osteoporosis and exercise. *Postgraduate Medical Journal* 2003;79(932):320–23.

Tomasini M. [Current knowledge of cardiac changes in motor vehicle drivers]. [Italian] *Medicina del Lavoro* 1979;70(2):90–96.

Troped PJ, Saunders RP, Pate RR, Reininger B, Ureda JR, Thompson SJ. Associations between self-reported and objective physical environmental factors and use of a community rail-trail. *Preventive Medicine* 2001; 32:191–200.

Trost SG, Owen N, Bauman AE, Sallis JF, Brown W. Correlates of adults' participation in physical activity: Review and update. *Medicine and Science in Sports and Exercise* 2002;34(12): 1996–2001.

Troy P, Ed. *The Perils of Urban Consolidation.* Sydney: Federation, 1996.

Tuan Y-F. *Space and Place: The Perspective of Experience.* Minneapolis: University of Minnesota Press, 1977.

Turner CW, Layton JF, Simons LS. Naturalistic studies of aggressive behavior: Aggressive stimuli, victim visibility, and horn honking. *Journal of Personality and Social Psychology* 1975;31: 1098–1107.

Ulrich RS. View through a window may influence recovery from surgery. *Science* 1984;224:420–21.

Unger J. Sedentary lifestyle as a risk factor for self-reported poor physical and mental health. *American Journal of Health Promotion* 1995;10(1):15–17.

United Nations Environment Programme (UNEP), United Nations Children's Fund (UNICEF), and World Health Organization (WHO). Children in the New Millennium: Environmental Impact on Health. Geneva: 2002.

United States Environmental Protection Agency (EPA). Inventory of U.S. Greenhouse Gas Emissions and Sinks: 1990-2001. USEPA #430-R-03-004. Washington: Office of Atmospheric Programs, U.S. Environmental Protection Agency, April 2003.

United States Geological Survey (USGS). *The Quality of Our Nation's Waters: Nutrients and Pesticides.* U.S. Geological Survey Circular 1225, 1999, p 82.

University of Washington, College of Forest Resources. Center for Urban Horticulture. The Calming Effect of Green: Roadside Landscape and Driver Stress. Fact Sheet 8. http://www.cfr.washington.edu/research.envmind/Roadside/Rsd-Stress-FS8.pdf.

Untermann RK. Accommodating the pedestrian: Adapting towns and neighborhoods for walking and bicycling. In: *Personal Travel in the US, Volume II. A Report of Findings from 1983–1984 NPTS, Source Control Programs.* Washington DC: US DOT, 1990.

Van Metre PC, Mahler BJ, Furlong ET. Urban sprawl leaves its PAH signature. *Environmental Science and Technology* 2000;34:4064–70.

van Vliet P, Knape M, de Hartog J, Janssen N, Harssema H, Brunekreef B. Motor vehicle exhaust and chronic respiratory symptoms in children living near freeways. *Environmental Research* 1997;74(2):122–32.

van Vliet W. Exploring the fourth environment: An examination of the home range of city and suburban teenagers. *Environment and Behavior* 1983;15: 567–88.

Veenstra G. Social capital and health (plus wealth, income inequality and regional health governance). *Social Science and Medicine* 2002;54:849–68.

Veenstra G. Social capital, SES and health: An individual-level analysis. *Social Science and Medicine* 2000;50: 619–29.

Vest J, Cohen W, Tharp M, Mulrine A, Lord M, Koerner BI, Murray B, Kaye SD. Road rage. Tailgating, giving the finger, outright violence—Americans grow more likely to take out their frustrations on other drivers. *U.S. News and World Report*, June 2, 1997.

Vimpani G. Child development and the civil society-does social capital matter? *Developmental and Behavioral Pediatrics* 2000;21:44–47.

Vimpani G. The role of social cohesiveness in promoting optimum child development. Youth Suicide Prevention Bulletin No. 5, Australian Institute of Family Studies, 2001, pp 20–24. Available: http://www.aifs.org.au/ysp/pubs/bull5gv.pdf.

Violanti JM. Cellular phones and fatal traffic collisions. *Accident Analysis and Prevention* 1998;30(4):519–24.

Violanti JM. Cellular phones and traffic accidents. *Public Health.* 1997;111(6): 423–28.

Vogt TM, Mullooly JP, Ernst D, Pope CR, Hollis JF. Social networks as predictors of ischemic heart disease, cancer, stroke and hypertension: Incidence, survival and mortality. *Journal of Clinical Epidemiology* 1992;45:659–66.

Vuchic VR. *Transportation for Livable Cities.* New Brunswick NJ: Rutgers University Center for Urban Policy Research, CUPR Press, 1999.

Wachs M. The role of transportation in the social integration of the aged. In: Committee on an Aging Society, Institute of Medicine. *America's Aging: The Social and Built Environment in an Older Society.* Washington: National Academy Press, 1988.

Wallace BA, Cumming RG. Systematic review of randomized trials of the effect of exercise on bone mass in pre- and postmenopausal women. *Calcified Tissue International* 2000;67:10–18.

Wallace PA, Firestone IJ. Modes of exploration and environmental learning by preschool children. *EDRA: Environmental Design Research Association.* 1979;10;284–89.

Wallace R. Social disintegration and the spread of AIDS-II. Meltdown of sociogeographic structure in urban minority neighborhoods. *Social Science and Medicine* 1993;37(7):887–96.

Wallace R. Urban desertification, public health and public order: planned shrinkage, violent death, substance abuse and AIDS in the Bronx. *Social Science and Medicine* 1990;31: 801–13.

Walter EV. *Placeways: A Theory of the Human Environment.* Chapel Hill: University of North Carolina Press, 1988.

Wang HX, Karp A, Winblad B, Fratiglioni L. Late-life engagement in social and leisure activities is associated with a decreased risk of dementia: A longitudinal study from the Kungsholmen project. *American Journal of Epidemiology* 2002;155(12):1081–87.

Wannamethee SG, Shaper AG. Physical activity and the prevention of stroke. *Journal of Cardiovascular Risk* 1999; 6:213–16.

Wannamethee SG, Shaper AG, Walker M. Changes in physical activity, mortality and incidence of coronary heart disease in older men. *Lancet* 1998;351: 1603–08.

Wannamethee SG, Shaper AG, Walker M, Ebrahim S. Lifestyle and 15-year survival free of heart attack, stroke, and diabetes in middle-aged British men. *Archives of Internal Medicine* 1998; 158:2433–40.

Wargo J, Brown D, Cullen M, Addiss S, Alderman N. *Children's Exposure to Diesel Exhaust on School Buses.* North Haven, CT: Environment and Human Health, 2002. Available: http://www.ehhi.org/pubs/children_diesel.html.

Warren C. *Brush with Death: A Social History of Lead Poisoning.* Baltimore: Johns Hopkins University Press, 2000.

Wazana A, Kreuger P, Raina P, et al. A review of risk factors for child pedestrian injuries: Are they modifiable? *Injury Prevention* 1997;3:295–304.

Wazana A, Rynard VL, Raina P, Krueger P, Chambers LW. Are child pedestrians at increased risk of injury on one-way compared to two-way streets? *Canadian Journal of Public Health* 2000; 91(3):201–06.

Weaver RC. Major factors in urban planning. In: *The Urban Condition: People and Policy in the Metropolis,* Leonard J. Duhl, Ed. New York: Basic Books, 1963. pp 97–112.

Wei M, Kampert JB, Barlow CE, Nichaman MZ, Gibbons LW, Paffenbarger RS, et al. Relationship between low cardiorespiratory fitness and mortality in normal-weight, overweight, and obese men. *JAMA* 1999;282:1547–53.

Weich S, Burton E, Blanchard M, Prince M, Sproston K, Erens B. Measuring the built environment: Validity of a site survey instrument for use in urban settings. *Health and Place* 2001; 283–92.

Weiland SK, Mundt KA, Ruckmann A, Keil U. Self-reported wheezing and allergic rhinitis in children and traffic density on street of residence. *Annals of Epidemiology* 1994;4:243–47.

Weinstein A, Feigley P, Pullen P, Mann L, Redman L. Neighborhood safety and the prevalence of physical activity— Selected states, 1996. *Morbidity and Mortality Weekly Report* 1999;48: 143–46.

Weisel CP, Lawryk NJ, Lioy PJ. Exposure to emissions from gasoline within automobile cabins. *Journal of Exposure Analysis and Environmental Epidemiology,* 1992;2:79–96.

Weissman MM, Bland RC, Canino GJ, Faravelli C, Greenwald S, et al. Cross-national epidemiology of major depression and bipolar disorder. *JAMA* 1996;276:293–99.

Weitz J. From quiet revolution to smart growth: State growth management programs, 1960 to 1999. *Journal of Planning Literature* 1999;14: 268–33.

Weitz J, Moore T. Development inside urban growth boundaries Oregon's empirical evidence of contiguous urban form. *Journal of the American Planning Association* 1998;64(4): 424–41.

Weitzman ER, Kawachi I. Giving means receiving: The protective effect of social capital on binge drinking on college campuses. *American Journal of Public Health* 2000;90(12):1936–39.

Wernette DR, Nieves LA. Breathing polluted air: Minorities are disproportionately exposed. *EPA Journal* 1992; 18:16–17.

Whipple W, Grigg S, Gizzard T, Randall CW, Shubinski RP, Tucker LS. *Stormwater Management in Urbanizing Areas.* Englewood Cliffs, NJ: Prentice-Hall; 1983.

White S, Rotton J. Type of commute, behavioral aftereffects, and cardiovascular activity. *Environment and Behavior* 1998;30:763–80.

Whitlock FA. *Death on the Road: A Study in Social Violence.* London: Tavistock Publications, 1971.

Whyte WH. *The Organization Man.* New York: Simon & Schuster, 1956.

Whyte WH. *The Social Life of Small Urban Spaces.* Washington: The Conservation Foundation, 1980.

Wignosta M, Burges S, Meena J. *Modeling and Monitoring to Predict Spatial and Temporal Hydrological Characteristics in Small Catchments.* Seattle: University of Washington, Dept of Civil Engineering; 1994. Water Resources Series Technical Report 137.

Wilcox S, Castro C, King AC, Housemann R, Brownson RC. Determinants of leisure time physical activity in rural compared with urban older and ethnically diverse women in the

United States. *Journal of Epidemiology and Community Health* 2000;54: 667–72.

Wilkinson RG. Comment: Income, inequality, and social cohesion. *American Journal of Public Health* 1997;87: 1504–06.

Wilkinson RG. *Unhealthy Societies: The Afflictions of Inequality.* London: Routledge, 1996.

Wilkinson RG. Commentary: Income inequality summarises the health burden of individual relative deprivation. *British Medical Journal* 1997;314: 1727–28.

Wilkinson RG. Income distribution and life expectancy. *British Medical Journal* 1992;304:165–68.

Willett WC, Dietz WH, Colditz GA. Guidelines for healthy weight. *New England Journal of Medicine* 1999; 341:427–34.

Wilson G, Baldassare M. Overall "sense of community" in a suburban region: The effects of localism, privacy, and urbanization. *Environment and Behavior* 1996;28(1):27–43.

Wilson WJ. *The Truly Disadvantaged: The Inner-City, the Underclass and Public Policy.* Chicago: University of Chicago Press, 1987.

Wilson WJ. *When Work Disappears: The World of the New Urban Poor.* New York: Knopf, 1996.

Wingspread Statement on the Precautionary Principle. January, 1998. Available: http://www.gdrc.org/u-gov/precaution-3.html.

Winter I. Towards a theorised understanding of family life and social capital. Working paper NO.21, Australian Institute of Family Studies, April 2000, 18p, ISBN 0 642 39472 5, ISSN 1440-4761. Available: http://www.aifs.gov.au/institute/pubs/WP21.pdf.

Wolfson M, Kaplan G, Lynch J, Ross N, Backlund E. Relation between income inequality and mortality: Empirical demonstration. *British Medical Journal* 1999;319:953–55.

Woodruff TJ, Grillo J, Schoendorf KC. The relationship between selected causes of postneonatal infant mortality and particulate air pollution in the United States. *Environmental Health Perspectives* 1997;105(6):608–12.

Woolcock M. Social capital and economic development: Toward a theoretical synthesis and policy framework. *Theory and Society* 1998;27:151–208.

World Bank. Social Capital and Urban Development. Poverty Net. http://www.worldbank.org/poverty/scapital/topic/urban1.htm.

World Commission on Environment and Development. *Our Common Future.* New York: Oxford University Press, 1987.

Wright CM, Parker L, Lamont D, Craft AW. Implications of childhood obesity for adult health: Findings from thousand families cohort study. *British Medical Journal* 2001;323:1280–84.

Yaffe K, Barnes D, Nevitt M, Lui L-Y, Covinsky K. A prospective study of physical activity and cognitive decline in elderly women: Women who walk. *Archives of Internal Medicine* 2001;161(14):1703–08.

Young KD, Thackston EL. Housing density and bacterial loading in urban streams. *Journal of Environmental Engineering* 1999;125:1177–80.

Zanobetti A, Schwartz J, Samoli E, Gryparis A, Touloumi G, Atkinson R, et al. The temporal pattern of mortality responses to air pollution: A multicity assessment of mortality displacement. *Epidemiology* 2002;13(1):87–93.

Zegeer CV, Stewart JR, Huang H, Lagerwey P. Safety effects of marked versus unmarked crosswalks at uncontrolled locations: Analysis of pedestrian crashes in 30 cities (with discussion and closure). *Transportation Research Record* 2001;1773:56–68.

Zein SR, Geddes E, Hemsing S, Johnson M. Safety benefits of traffic calming. *Transportation Research Record* 1997; 1578:3–10.

Zheng PQ, Baetz BW. GIS-based analysis of development options from a hydrology perspective. *Journal of Urban Planning and Development* 1999; 125:164–70.

Zhu Y, Hinds WC, Kim S, Shen S, Sioutas C. Study of ultrafine particles near a major highway with heavy-duty diesel traffic. *Atmospheric Environment* 2002; 36:4323–35.

Zhu Y, Hinds WC, Kim S, Sioutas C. Concentration and size distribution of ultrafine particles near a major highway. *Journal of the Air and Waste Management Association* 2002;52: 1032–42.

Zielinski J. The benefits of better site design in commercial development. In: Schueler TR, Holland HK, eds. *The Practice of Watershed Protection.* Ellicott City, Md: Center for Watershed Protection; 2000:25–34.

Zito JM, Safer, DJ, dosReis S, Gardner JF, et al. Psychotropic practice patterns for youth: A 10-year perspective. *Archives of Pediatric Adolescent Medicine* 2003;157:17–25.

INDEX

■ ══════ ■